To Carolyn & Jack

With regards

Wayne Seigal

June 2015

GOD'S
Facebook

Creating a Friendship of Civilizations in a Terror-ridden World

NAJMUS SAQUIB, PH.D.

TO

GOD

Thy will
  Is ever unfolding
    In my life
      In myriad ways

CONTENTS

PREFACE

This book was thirteen years in the making.

In the fall of 1999, I had a vision of assembling under the cover of a single book all that men and women have uttered about God during the past five thousand years. I hoped that it would help us overcome our prejudices, most of which were born out of unfamiliarity.

That same year, I finished reading Samuel Huntington's 1996 classic, *The Clash of Civilizations and the Remaking of World Order*. The realist in me was terrified by the prospects Huntington portrayed. But the poet in me rebelled and wandered into the wondrous world of imagination, for I believed what Albert Einstein once said: "Imagination is more important than knowledge."

I hypothesized that God, a universal force present in the consciousness of all humans, can become the unifying force for our world if we can deepen and widen our understanding of God.

I imagined a *Friendship of Civilizations*, which can be nurtured by connecting the dots of all religions that found expression in the words of the men and women of all centuries and all continents. However, I didn't want to write a scholarly tome with lengthy interpretations of the "words" of historical men and women; rather, I planned to capture their "true voices" by quoting them directly and create a "living history" by arranging the quotes chronologically.

My ambitious project progressed slowly over the next two years, as I pored over thousands of pages of scriptures as well as ancient and modern literature. To my great satisfaction, a fascinating story of the fundamental unity in human thought patterns on God started to emerge in my mind. Different religious scriptures lost their individual isolation, and I came to realize that the multifarious human words on God, written over a period of five thousand years, carry not merely information, but a transcendent harmony that unites all of humanity.

Then, suddenly, came the terrorist attacks on September 11, 2001, instantaneously changing the whole world. God and religion took center stage in human interactions, after a nearly hundred-year lull in the face of unprecedented advancements in science and technology during the twentieth century. We had come to believe, at the end of the millennium, that religious fundamentalism and religious wars were things of the past. However, the tragedies of September 11 grotesquely challenged that belief. The human "voice of violence" submerged God's "voice of compassion" and thrust the entirety of humanity into an endless debate about the "the good, the bad, and the ugly" sides of different religions. It alerted us to a grim reality: the potent danger of closing our minds to religions and cultures not our own.

This book tells a story of God, who transcends all religions and cultures and binds all humanity in a luminous unity of truth through the words and ideas of God and humans.

It is my earnest hope that this book will help open billions and billions of windows in our minds, for peaceful coexistence through a deeper interreligious understanding.

I also hope that every page of this book will give you something worthwhile to enjoy and ponder.

El Dorado Hills, California

December, 2012

READERS'S GUIDE

WHO IS THIS BOOK FOR?

☑ Anyone who is interested in discovering the transcendent harmony among all religions

☑ Anyone who is interested in a spiritual journey through the minds of God, man, and woman

☑ Anyone who is interested in world peace and interfaith dialogues

☑ A professor who is interested in building the next generation of interfaith leaders

☑ A community leader who is committed to nurturing mutual respect among followers of different religions

WHAT ARE THE BENEFITS FOR READERS?

☑ Instant access, in a single volume, to all significant thoughts on God

☑ Mind-boggling perspectives on God in Chapter 8 (God is Dead), Chapter 9 (God is Back), Chapter 10 (God of Nobel Laureates) and Chapter 11 (God of Children and Teenagers)

☑ Eye-opening comparison of all major religions

☑ Fascinating juxtaposition of socio-political background and human thoughts on God

☑ Inspiring new ideas for creating a *Friendship of Civilizations* in Chapter 14 (God of the Future)

HOW IS THIS BOOK ORGANIZED?

Each chapter consists of the following sections:

• "STATUS UPDATE" provides a summary of God's status in the corresponding historical period covered in the chapter;

• "NOTES FROM HISTORY" highlights the key socio-political events during the historical period so that a reader can connect a quote with its historical background;

• "HOLY WALL" presents God's spoken words from scriptures that were revealed during the historical period;

• "WALL OF MORTALS" presents humans' words on God, uttered during the historical period; and

• "CHAPTER DIGEST" presents a summary of the postings on the "Holy Wall" and the "Wall of Mortals".

In addition, the "COFFEE BREAK" interspersed throughout the book provides interesting information, insights, and tidbits.

All quotes are arranged in chronological order, according to the birth year of the quoted person.

HOW TO READ THIS BOOK?

It is not expected that a reader will plow through this book page by page in a sequential manner. Rather, this book is designed to be read randomly—a page, a few quotes or a chapter at a time—to allow for contemplation and maximum enjoyment of different human perspectives on God.

If you are interested in my motivation for writing this book, then do not skip the Preface. If you were to read only one complete chapter, then I would recommend the first, which tells a fascinating and inspiring story of the evolution of interfaith dialogues. If you enjoy poetry, then read "God's Song of Myself" in Chapter 2; in this collage poem, you will find almost all human conceptions of God through the ages. Those of you who are inspired enough to make a change in the world must read the last chapter, which contains new ideas for creating a *Friendship of Civilizations*.

Five thousand years of evolution of human thought on God is subdivided into thematic chapters and historical periods so that a reader can choose on the basis of chapter title or time frame. You must read the "Status Update" at the beginning of each chapter to fuel your curiosity about the milestone events of the corresponding historical period. If you are interested in the socio-political background of human thoughts on God, then you must read the "Notes From History." If you are interested in a summary of the evolution of human thought on God in a specific historical period, then read "Chapter Digest" at the end of the corresponding chapter.

The quotes in the book are arranged in chronological order according to the birth year of the quoted person to preserve the historical continuum in the book. To break the monotony of reading quote after quote, I have interspersed, throughout the book, numerous "Coffee Break" notes to heighten your appreciation and enjoyment of the preceding or following quotes; you can, if you wish, simply flip through the book and pick any of these breaks for your reading pleasure. In addition, I have included several one- to two-page sections on a few fascinating topics to demonstrate how God has influenced our lives and thoughts in myriad ways; this unique feature is found in no other published book.

HOW TO USE IT AS A TEXTBOOK?

This book can be used as a textbook for a full-semester introductory college course on general religion or comparative religion. There are fourteen chapters in this book; one chapter can be covered each week in a 14-week semester course. Students can be asked to synthesize the quotes of a particular historical period covered in a chapter and relate those quotes with the socio-political events and circumstances presented in the "Notes from History" section. They can be asked to identify and analyze the thought patterns of people living in different geographies and following different religions. Assignments can also be given to explore various themes across the timelines of history; example themes are – (i) Evolution of God in the minds of early to modern scientists; (ii) God as seen by mystics of different religions; (iii) Religion and violence; (iv) Atheism and violence; (v) God and woman; and (vi) God in modern society. Source materials for these topics are available in the "Coffee Breaks" and one- to two-page special sections in the book. Students can also be asked to write term papers on special topics by utilizing the materials provided in the book and the relevant source materials listed in the bibliography.

CHAPTER SUMMARY

CHAPTER 1 – *God, Man, and Facebook* begins with the story of a momentous event that took place in Chicago, USA, on September 11, 1893. This chapter takes the reader through an intellectual journey by raising several significant questions about God, and ends with a note of laughter about the whole notion of defining God in words.

CHAPTER 2 – *God's Song of Myself* starts with the story of Goddess from the caves of Germany, and then goes on to chronicle many other stories, including the story of the still-unending search for the *God Particle* by the best scientists of our days. This chapter contains excerpts of a fascinating dialogue on "the truth and the divine" between two Nobel Laureates—one a poet and the other a physicist—for readers to decide who was right. The chapter ends with a brand new idea: a collage poem entitled "God's Song of Myself" and composed by juxtaposing quotes from scriptures and humans to describe a transcendent identity of God. This poem captures the essence of God through 5,000 years of written words.

CHAPTER 3 – *God is Born (250,000 BC to 2000 BC)* traces the birth of God through the first written expressions on God in ancient Egypt. It answers questions such as, "What did the humans of antiquity think about God, kings, and the afterlife, and how similar are those thoughts to the current thinking in modern religions?"

CHAPTER 4 – *God Gives Us Religions (2000 BC to 1000 BC)* starts with the story of scriptures of the earliest known organized religion, Hinduism, then travels through the scriptures of other pre-Christian religions to capture their central messages. The chapter reveals surprising similarities among the messages within the holy scriptures of Hinduism, Judaism, Zoroastrianism, and the monotheistic philosophy of Pharaoh Aten.

CHAPTER 5 – *God of Prophets, Philosophers, and Poets (1000 BC to 1 AD)* weaves a fascinating tapestry of colorful thoughts from prophets, philosophers, and poets when early human civilizations were simultaneously emerging in Greece, India, China, Rome, and the Middle East. The human struggle with the choice between "reason" and "belief" that began in that historical period is evident in the selected quotes.

CHAPTER 6 – *God Speaks (1 AD to 1000 AD)* is primarily concerned with two major religions—Christianity and Islam—which appear to be at odds with each other today. It shows that there is great similarity between the central messages of these two religions, and that Muslims are commanded by God to believe in Jesus as a prophet. A comparison of the ten commandments of Christianity and Islam provides additional insights into the common ground between the world's two largest religions.

CHAPTER 7 – *God of Believers, Unbelievers, and Mystics (1000 AD to 1700 AD)* captures the varieties of human expressions, from atheism to pantheism, amidst revolutionary changes in science, art, and society throughout the world. Diverse opinions about God culminate in the war between science and religion that reaches its peak when Galileo is forced to recant his scientific theories that are at odds with the Christian church. The words of the mystics in this chapter provide deep insights into human spirituality.

CHAPTER TIMELINE

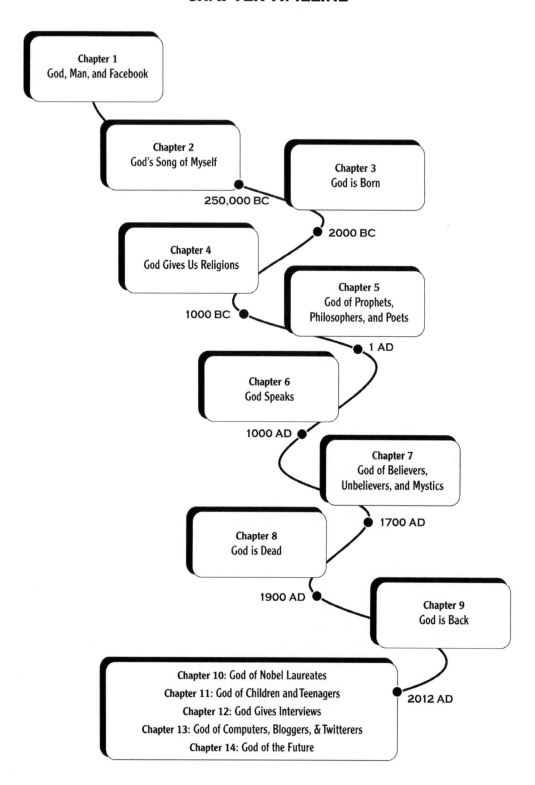

Chapter 1
God, Man, and Facebook

Chapter 2
God's Song of Myself

250,000 BC

Chapter 3
God is Born

2000 BC

Chapter 4
God Gives Us Religions

Chapter 5
God of Prophets,
Philosophers, and Poets

1000 BC

1 AD

Chapter 6
God Speaks

1000 AD

Chapter 7
God of Believers,
Unbelievers, and Mystics

Chapter 8
God is Dead

1700 AD

1900 AD

Chapter 9
God is Back

Chapter 10: God of Nobel Laureates
Chapter 11: God of Children and Teenagers
Chapter 12: God Gives Interviews
Chapter 13: God of Computers, Bloggers, & Twitterers
Chapter 14: God of the Future

2012 AD

CHAPTER 8 – *God is Dead (1700 AD to 1900 AD)* is a colorful journey into human minds, where men and women are busy rediscovering their self-worth and morality without reassurances and dictates from Heaven. We find that God is almost banished from human intellectual life in the West, while Eastern thinkers are wrapped in mysticism. The chapter contains excerpts from the *Woman's Bible*, written by mere mortals to denounce the patriarchal interpretations of the *Holy Bible*.

CHAPTER 9 – *God is Back (1900 AD to 2012 AD)* documents the glorious return of God, shining as a bright ray of hope over the ruins of two global wars, numerous genocides, and multiple regional conflicts that caused the loss of more than 160 million human lives in the twentieth century. We make the surprising discovery that belligerence is not the monopoly of a single religion, through a comparison of scriptures from the three major faiths. This chapter ends with a discussion on interfaith dialogues, which have been gaining momentum as intellectuals realize that *God Divide* must be a bridge among nations and cultures.

CHAPTER 10 – *God of Nobel Laureates* attempts to answer popular curiosity about the beliefs of the best human minds in science, art, and politics. The difference of opinions among these Nobel laureates on the topic of God is indicative of the humanness of these "earthly gods."

CHAPTER 11 – *God of Children and Teenagers* is a fascinating chapter that takes us into our childhood, and makes us sometimes cry and sometime laugh at the utter simplicity and genuineness of children's expressions about God. This chapter ends with a discussion of *Harry Potter and God*.

CHAPTER 12 – *God Gives Interviews* puts God face to face with humans and provides answers to some intriguing questions from a colorful group of interviewers: a Black girl, a Muslim poet, an American journalist, and a free-thinking citizen of New Zealand.

CHAPTER 13 – *God of Computers, Bloggers, and Twitterers* takes us into the new world of computers, where free spirits roam in their own glory and show unusual courage in ridiculing God. God also shows infinite tolerance by not sending a massive bolt of lightning to shut down the global network of computers. As a result, fake gods proliferate in the blogosphere, write e-mails to teens, and establish the Church of Google with its own ten commandments, all within a very few years of the Internet revolution.

CHAPTER 14 – *God of the Future* takes a closer look at our differences and similarities, and argues for a "God of Love" as the God of the future. We are encouraged to think about whether humanity can chart a new course for the future by accepting the proposed new paradigm of peaceful coexistence.

ACKNOWLEDGMENTS

First and foremost, I want to express my debt to those whose words are quoted in this book, capturing the fascinating tapestry of human–God interactions. Next, I want to thank my wife, Fahima, for her support and enormous patience during the past thirteen years of my research for this book. I also want to thank my two daughters, Samhita and Samara, for allowing me to work on this book during the weekends and holidays. Truly, a book of this magnitude has only been possible through the enormous sacrifices of my family.

I also want to thank a few other key people in my life for nurturing my inquisitiveness and for imbuing me with a free-thinking spirit: my father, Oheedun Noor, who introduced me to the worlds of Western and Eastern philosophy and had taught me how to think clearly; my mother, Ali Rawshana, who encouraged me in all my efforts; my paternal grandfather, Ibrahim Ali, a scholar of Islamic and Persian literature, who spent countless hours with me studying Rumi, Hafiz, Khayyam, and other mystic poets; and my maternal grandfather, Abdur Rahman, a seeker of knowledge, who introduced me to the world of knowledge and curiosity.

I am also indebted to my friend Dr. Abdul Quyyum Khan for reviewing the manuscript and providing invaluable suggestions that immensely improved this book. I want to thank Dania Sheldon for her outstanding editing work and valuable suggestions. My special thanks go to Christy Probst for her superb design and layout work for the book. Her creativity and patience with the changes were of immense value. I want to acknowledge, with love, my eldest daughter, Samhita Saquib, for her proofreading of the final version of the book.

Last, but not least, I want to express my indebtedness to the translators of ancient texts and scriptures, whose works have been quoted here as examples of human–God interactions. I have provided references to their work in the Bibliography at the end of this book. However, for a few of the quotations, I was unable to find the translators' names, despite my sincere effort. I extend my apology to those translators. I also promise that if such information is made available to me, I will add the references in the following editions of this book.

I could not have managed this book without the support of you all.

DISCLAIMER

The quotes cited in this book reflect only a view (or views) expressed by the cited person. These quotes do not reflect the final view or position of the cited person on any topic. In the case of fiction writers, quotes are sometimes uttered by a fictional character in a book and may or may not reflect writer's personal views.

Different religions have different names for the Creator. In this book, "God" is used as a generic term to indicate the Creator and Supreme Being who is the main object of worship in all religions. Therefore, readers can substitute the word "God" with their preferred name for the Supreme Being as used in a particular religion.

It is a tradition among Muslims to add "Peace be upon him" after uttering the name of the Prophet Muhammad. In this book, "Peace be upon him" is used only after the first occurrence of the Prophet's name, to avoid repetition. Muslim readers are requested to add the phrase every time they read the Prophet's name in this book.

Atheism is not a religion in the traditional sense. In this book, liberty is taken to use a broader definition of the word "religion" to mean a set of strong beliefs. Atheism, therefore, is treated in this book as a religion in this sense. Such a treatment is not unique to this book because in 2005, the United States 7th Circuit Court of Appeals ruled that Wisconsin prison officials had violated an inmate's rights by not treating his atheism as a religion. The court ruled: "Atheism is [the inmate's] religion, and the group that he wanted to start was religious in nature even though it expressly rejects a belief in a supreme being."

God and religion are complex topics to write about, especially in light of innumerable interpretations and opinions. The author has made every effort to avoid any misrepresentation of any faith and apologizes to believers and non-believers alike if any part of the book offends them. The author's key purpose is to foster an honest *Friendship of Civilizations* through informed consent.

1

God, Man, and Facebook

"I dreamed
That stone by stone I reared a sacred fane,
A temple; neither Pagod, Mosque, nor Church,
But loftier, simpler, always open-doored
To every breath from Heaven; and Truth and Peace
And Love and Justice came and dwelt therein."
— LORD ALFRED TENNYSON (1809–1892), AKBAR'S DREAM

STATUS UPDATE (ETERNITY TO NOW)

❖ Men and women seek a Universal God.

❖ The first global interfaith dialogue takes place in Chicago, USA. A *Cyclonic Monk* from India and a *Yankee Mohammedan* from the USA draw attention.

❖ God's fans exceed six billion.

❖ A human invents Facebook, which reaches more than one billion fans in fewer than eight years.

❖ God's fans forget God's universal message of compassion; so, God decides to open a Facebook account to bring everyone to the same page.

NOTES FROM HISTORY
(TIMELINE: ETERNITY TO NOW)

MAN GOES GLOBAL

Thousands of years ago, men and women emerged on the vast, lonely theater of time and space on the planet Earth. They knew not the meaning of their destinies, nor were they able to make sense of the furies of the thunderous storms, the devastating floods, and the angry fire. They noted with awe and wonder that a large fireball appeared every day, from a specific direction; they named the fireball "Sun" and the direction "East." Then they named the opposite direction "West." Thus, they divided the world into the East and the West, and then into the North and the South.

Then came a time when men and women began to feel the mysterious presence of something sublime that baffled them with the joy of elevated thoughts, as they wondered endlessly about the rising and setting of the sun, gazed with bewilderment at countless stars in the night sky, and pondered the tossing and turning of ocean waves. They did not have to wait long for that mystery to become manifest as God came down from the heavens and met men and women in the deep, dark shadows of their consciousness. Soon thereafter, men and women started worshipping God because doing so gave meaning to their existence and made living valuable and tolerable. That was the beginning of the relationship between Man and God, representing Man's aspiration to rise in dignity through tireless striving towards perfection.

Then many thousands of years passed; men and women migrated from one place to another in every possible direction, from the East to the West and from the South to the North, in search of food and shelter. Those were the baby steps towards a phenomenon that later humans would name "globalization."

The worshipping of God remained constant among humans, wherever they went, although variations in geography, climate, and human experiences in different parts of the world gave rise to different methods of worship, which they named "religion." God was pleased with the dedication of the worshippers and decided to expand the definition of "religion" to include additional guidance on how to live worthily and morally. He chose a few wise men to transmit his messages to the common men and women. Those wise men were later called "prophets" and God's messages were called "scriptures."

For thousands of years, men and women taught their religions to others and preached messages of selfless love, as well as self-preserving retribution. At the same time, they fought many wars over the differences among the religions, and killed millions of their own species.

More "globalization" happened and more theories of human religiosity and its impacts surfaced. Some predicted that humankind was inevitably progressing towards a *Clash of Civilizations"* in the twenty-first century—as if that hadn't already taken place through all the wars, local and global, of the past centuries. Some hypothesized that future conflicts would be along cultural and religious lines. Some opposed this prediction, arguing that men and women hold multiple identities (religious, national, cultural, ethnic, philosophical, linguistic, political, etc.), and that classifying individuals according to a single religious identity is an expression of intellectual confusion that ignores the inherent diversity within each civilization. Some others thought that if there were an imminent global clash, it would be a *"Clash of Ignorance."*

Amidst all these theorizations and disputations, one fact remained constant: most acts of compassion and terror were conducted in the name of God, who did not like the horrors of war and internecine strife. So God, in his infinite wisdom, chose few wise men and women to preach the need for peace among religions. These wise men and women began local and global meetings among worshippers of God of all religions, and they called these meetings "interfaith dialogues."

In the meantime, the theater of time and space, which had initially been vast and lonely, became smaller and less lonely thanks to unprecedented human progress in science and technology. Men and women seemed to have found the meaning of their blind destinies and also to have comprehended the mysteries of natural forces. It appeared that the Universe could have no existence independent of Man because the moral and scientific conception of it must be that of the moral and scientific Man. Thus the relationship between God and Man continued through a perpetual process of reconciliation until the end of nineteenth century. At the dawn of twentieth century, it took a tumultuous turn when God was almost banished from public life in the West, while remaining front and center in the East.

Then came the *Internet* and *Facebook*, connecting the East and the West, and the North and the South, in a complex web of networked computers. Men and women went fully global and coined the term "social networking", ushering in an era of unprecedented level of dialogue among humans from all corners of the world. This development seemed to reverse the journey that had begun millions of years ago when early men and women had dispersed in all directions in search of shelter and food, and made the entire geography of the earth their own. Now, the *Internet* and *Facebook* had created an opportunity for modern men and women from all corners of the world to embark on a different journey that would bring them together in search of shelter and food for their spiritual souls.

As the *Internet* and *Facebook* proliferated, the Almighty God, who was present with men and women in all their endeavors through the ages, came down from the heavens and announced his sublime presence in the vast virtual theater of *Facebook*. Thus, men, women, God, and *Facebook* became entangled in a complex and interdependent relationship that surpassed all imagination.

Then, God gave this author the idea to document this relationship in *God's Facebook*, to deepen and widen human understanding of God and foster a *Friendship of Civilizations* that will counter the terrifying prospect of a *"Clash of Civilizations."*

The rest is merely history.

THE CYCLONIC MONK

On September 11, 1893, exactly one hundred and eight years before the September 11, 2001 terrorist attack in New York, a unique event took place in Chicago, USA. A select audience of 7,000 enlightened people, from the East and the West and from the North and the South, gathered in the lecture hall of the Art Institute of Chicago on 111 South Michigan Avenue. For the first time in human history, people of ten world religions from all over the world gathered at the first World Parliament of Religions to discuss their faiths, with the hope of discovering common ground for cooperation and peaceful co-existence.

A man, 5 feet 9 inches tall and 30 years old, stood at the podium, with an orange turban wrapped around his head. He was from Bengal, India, a country where Muslim Emperor Akbar the Great (1542–1605) had once acted on a dream to unite all religions, and had held the world's first interfaith summit among Christians, Hindus, Muslims, Jains, and Sikhs. The man from Akbar's country, standing at the podium of the first World Parliament of Religions, had an olive complexion and his eyes were large, with prominent, heavy lids. There was an aura of kingliness in his stature as he stood and glanced with anticipation at the audience. He bowed and said: *"Sisters and Brothers of America."* Instantly, the magic of his rich and deep voice and the sincerity of his utterance transformed the audience's mood to an overwhelming feeling of togetherness, as if *"We are all a part of God's great big family."* The audience responded with a standing ovation that lasted for more than two minutes.

When silence was restored, the young man from India continued his brief lecture, which focused on religious tolerance. He cited two immensely meaningful quotations. The first was a Sanskrit hymn:

> "As the different streams
>
> Having their sources in different places
>
> All mingle their water in the sea,
>
> So O Lord, the different paths which men take,
>
> Through different tendencies,
>
> Various though they appear
>
> Crooked or straight,
>
> All lead to Thee."

The second was a verse from the Bhagavad Gita ("Song of God"), an ancient Hindu scripture:

> "Whosoever comes to Me, through whatsoever form, I reach him;
>
> All men are struggling through paths that in the end lead to Me."

 The young man was Swami Vivekananda (1863–1902), who introduced the *Vedanta* philosophy and yoga to America and Europe and became the messenger of Indian wisdom to the Western world. The US press dubbed him *"The Cyclonic Hindu Monk of India"* for his oratory. *The New York Herald* wrote: "Vivekananda is undoubtedly the greatest figure in the Parliament of Religions."

Vivekananda studied at the Scottish Church College in Calcutta, India, and obtained his Bachelor degree at Calcutta University. Later, he became a disciple of Bengali sage Ramakrishna Paramahansa (1836–1886), who was regarded by many Hindus as an *Avatar* ("Incarnation of God"). In 1897, Vivekananda founded in India the Ramakrishna Mission, a large philanthropic organization that still exists.

Vivekananda died young, at just 39. But, he left a lasting legacy of philanthropy and spiritual philosophy. Before his death, he wrote to a Western follower: "It may be that I shall find it good to get outside my body, to cast it off like a worn out garment. But I shall not cease to work. I shall inspire men everywhere until the whole world shall know that it is one with God."

Vivekananda was a man of unique personality. His biographer, French Nobel Laureate and writer Romain Rolland, wrote: "Equilibrium and synthesis are the keynotes of Vivekananda's personality. In him is harmonized all the various energies, like faith and reason, science and religion, East and West, which are at variance and conflict with each other everywhere, but in Vivekananda's personality they became perfectly harmonized."

Vivekananda ended his 1893 speech at the World Parliament of Religions with these words: "I fervently hope that the bell that tolled this morning in honor of this convention may be the death-knell of all fanaticism, of all persecutions with the sword or with the pen, and of all uncharitable feelings between persons wending their way to the same goal."

Unfortunately, Swami Vivekananda's hope didn't materialize. Fanaticism, an ancient social disease that has killed millions, continued with new fervor in the name of both religion and irreligion, causing untold human misery in the following centuries.

THE YANKEE MOHAMMEDAN

Nine days after Swami Vivekananda's speech on September 11, 1893 at the World Parliament of Religions in Chicago, an attractive and dignified man stood at the podium on the windy and rain-swept Wednesday morning of September 20, 1893. He was to speak on behalf of Islam and was, in fact, the only Muslim speaker at the World Parliament of Religions. The man was not an Arab, nor was he from any other populous Muslim country. He was wearing an impeccable Western suit and a red fez cap. He had large brown eyes and his radiant face displayed finely chiseled features that indicated a calm and deliberate mind. He was an American, born in New York, and was the first known white American convert to Islam. His name was Mohammed Alexander Russell Webb (1846–1916). In 1887, US President Grover Cleveland appointed Webb, then an assistant editor of the *Missouri Republican* in St. Louis, to be the US Consul to the Philippines, a Spanish colony at that time.

 Webb embraced the faith of Islam in 1888, resigned from his diplomatic post in 1892, and returned to America to start an Islamic mission. He established the first Muslim house of worship in America in Manhattan, New York in 1893, predating the earliest mosques of Ross, North Dakota, and Cedar Rapids, Iowa, by more than three decades. From that house of worship, the people of Manhattan heard the Muslim call to prayer for the first time on December 10, 1893. The following day, the *New York Times* reported: "For the first time in New York's history, cosmopolitan as the city is, the melodious call of the Muezzin, celebrated by every traveler in Mohammedan countries, was heard yesterday morning." At the World Parliament of Religions, the US press dubbed Webb *"The Yankee Mohammedan."*

Unlike Swami Vivekananda, Webb didn't utter sparkling ripples of words at the World Parliament of Religions. Rather, he spoke in a slow and steady tone; yet his speech was very forceful because it was apparent that he was moved by his convictions. In his speech on Islam at the World Parliament of Religions in 1893, Webb quoted two verses from the Quran. The first was from the tenth chapter:

"If the Lord had pleased
All who are on the earth would have believed together;
And wilt thou force men to be believers?"

— (QURAN, 10:99)

The second verse was from the second chapter:

"Let there be no compulsion in religion
Now is the right way made distinct from error;
Whoever, therefore, denieth Taghoot [literally, error]
And believeth in God,
Hath taken to hold on a strong handle that hath no flaw.
And god is He who heareth, knoweth."

— (QURAN, 2:256)

These two statements from the Quran epitomize the Islamic view of religious pluralism and religious tolerance, which, among other things, attracted Webb, a free-spirited American, to embrace Islam.

Mohammed Webb was not an ordinary man. His biographer, Umar Abd-Allah (Wymann-Landgraf), an American Muslim convert who received his doctorate from the University of Chicago, wrote: "His [Webb's] adoption of Islam in late-nineteenth-century America was utterly out of the ordinary, but the manner in which he pursued it was not. Webb embraced Islam in the spirit of classical American individual initiative in religion. Moreover, Webb regarded his conversion as a perfectly natural alternative for himself and any other American who chose it. Webb founded his life and his vision for Islam in America on the same broad spiritual ethos through which he himself initially made his journey to the faith."

Webb remained true to his American self and spirit, and never adopted the *"Arab dress"*, as was commonly done by Muslim converts. Thus, the title of *"The Yankee Mohammedan"* was a befitting one for him.

Unfortunately, Mohammed Webb's hope of a tolerant Islam to be practiced throughout the world didn't materialize, even after more than a century of spirited discussions begun at the first World Parliament of Religions in Chicago, where the East met the West and proclaimed to all quarters of the globe that there is God in every religion.

THE LORD'S PRAYER

Swami Vivekananda and Mohammed Webb belonged to a very small group of non-Christians attending the first World Parliament of Religions of 1893, which was organized and attended primarily by Christians in a country whose inhabitants were predominantly Christians. In fact, the English-speaking Christian representatives delivered 152 (78%) of the 194 papers in the Parliament.

The inaugural ceremony on September 11, 1893, began with "an act of common worship to Almighty God", and Psalm 100 of the Hebrew *Bible*, as paraphrased by the British hymn writer Isaac Watts (1674–1748), was sung first:

> "Praise God, from whom all blessings flow;
>
> Praise him, all creatures here below;
>
> Praise him above, ye heavenly host;
>
> Praise Father, Son, and Holy Ghost."

Afterwards, Cardinal Gibbons led the attendees in saying the *Lord's Prayer* from *Bible*. The "Amen" at the end of the *Lord's Prayer* was followed by a reverent silence, which was then broken by the President of the World's Congress, Charles Carroll Bonney (1831–1903), a lawyer and judge from Chicago, with his welcome address. Bonney opened his lecture with these words:

> "Worshippers of God and lovers of man—let us rejoice that we have lived to see this glorious day; let us give thanks to the Eternal God, whose mercy endureth forever, that we are permitted to take part in the solemn and majestic event of a World's Congress of Religions."

A total of ten religions were represented in the Parliament: Buddhism, Christianity, Confucianism, Hinduism, Islam, Jainism, Judaism, Shintoism, Taoism, and Zoroastrianism. The seventeen-day program included a wide range of topics presented by a great variety of speakers. On September 27, 1893, the Parliament was officially closed with the *Lord's Prayer*, led by Emil G. Hirsch, a rabbi from Chicago.

EXCLUSIVISM, INCLUSIVISM, AND PLURALISM

People of all major world religions came to the Parliament because of the American promise of cosmopolitanism exemplified in the ten official objectives of the Parliament. There was a clear attempt to create a true brotherhood of religions by enlightening each other through a sincere exploration and discovery of common ground. There was no agenda, implicit or explicit, to prove the superiority of one religion over another; rather, the Parliament—in an overwhelmingly Christian country—was posited, by design, against the exclusivist claim that Christianity is the only true divine religion and that Jesus Christ is the only way to salvation and to God.

The Archbishop of Canterbury virulently opposed the Parliament from an exclusivist position, and wrote a strong rebuke to the organizers, refusing their invitation: "The difficulties which I myself feel are not questions of distance and convenience, but rest on the fact that the Christian religion is the one religion. I do not understand how that religion can be regarded as a member of a Parliament of Religions without assuming the equality of the other intended members and the parity of their position and claims."

The European Roman Catholic hierarchy also opposed the Parliament, along with American evangelical leaders such as D. L. Moody, who camped outside the convention hall and prayed for the souls of the delegates.

In contrast, Charles Bonney's vision of the World Parliament of Religions was predicated on his belief in *pluralism*, which promotes peaceful coexistence of religions without any religion claiming superiority over others. His remarks in the welcome address were clairvoyant and inspiring:

> "As the finite can never fully comprehend the infinite, nor perfectly express its own view of the divine, it necessarily follows that individual opinions of the divine nature and attributes will differ. But, properly understood, these varieties of view are not causes of discord and strife, but rather incentives to deeper interest and examination. Necessarily God reveals himself differently to a child than to a man; to a philosopher than to one who cannot read. Each must see God with the eyes of his own soul. Each must behold him through the colored glasses of his own nature. Each one must receive him according to his own capacity of reception. The fraternal union of the religions of the world will come when each seeks truly to know how God has revealed himself in the other, and remembers the inexorable law that with what judgment it judges it shall itself be judged."

However, this attitude was not necessarily shared by all speakers and attendees. Many, including Reverend John Henry Barrows, the event chairman appointed by Bonney, viewed the Parliament as an unprecedented opportunity to present the Christian case persuasively to the admiration and consent of other religious leaders. His position was that of religious inclusivism, wherein one partially accepts the validity of truth in other religions but maintains the superiority of one's own religion, with the possibility of incorporating or subordinating the other religions into one's own. Barrows thought Christianity as the culmination of human religious progress and concluded: "The Parliament has shown that Christianity is still the great quickener of humanity, that it is now educating those who do not accept its doctrines, that there is no teacher to be compared with Christ, and no Saviour excepting Christ ... The non-Christian world may give us valuable criticism and confirm scriptural truths and make excellent suggestion as to Christian improvement, but it has nothing to add to the Christian creed."

Barrows's *inclusivism* was surpassed by the zealotry and rhetoric of those who staked out a position of religious *exclusivism*, wherein one denies the validity of the truth claims of all other religions. Professor William C. Wilkinson dismissed Barrows's compromise position of religious *inclusivism* and declared this in his speech at the Parliament: "Of any ethnic religion, therefore, can it be said that it is a true religion, only not perfect? Christianity says, No." Wilkinson further proclaimed: "Men need to be saved from false religion; they are in no way of being saved by false religion. Such, at least, is the teaching of Christianity. The attitude, therefore, of Christianity towards religions other than itself is an attitude of universal, absolute, eternal, unappeasable hostility."

Fortunately, Wilkinson's view was only a minority view among the delegates and the participants of the first World Parliament of Religions. The dominant voice was one of tolerance and mutual respect. Charles Bonney's declaration in the welcome address rang true throughout the seventeen-day conference: "This day a new fraternity is born into the world of human progress, to aid in the upholding of the kingdom of God in the hearts of men."

DOES GOD BELONG TO ANY RELIGION?

The *Cyclonic Monk*, Swami Vivekananda, representing Hinduism at the Parliament, drove his pluralist views home with calls for a universal religion, without claiming the superiority or admitting the inferiority of his own religion. Instead, he proposed a genuine togetherness of all religions, in which "each must assimilate the others and yet preserve its individuality and grow according to its law of growth."

In a similar vein, the *Yankee Mohammedan*, Mohammed Webb, representing Islam at the Parliament, highlighted the pluralist view of Islam in terms of other religions, with the hope of dispelling the false perceptions of his religion's apparent militancy towards others.

Despite all the conflicts and contradictions, the first World Parliament of Religions in 1893 stood out as a true brotherhood of religions and made a lasting positive contribution towards the growth of religious thinking in the next centuries. The Parliament was indeed a giant leap towards the *Friendship of Civilizations*. The men and women present at the Parliament learned that there are many ways to be religious and that no religion has a monopoly on God.

Unfortunately, throughout human history, many men and women have chosen to deny this eternal truth and have claimed a monopoly on God to promote their personal agendas in the name of God, causing enormous pain and suffering to their fellow humans. For example, Adolf Hitler, a Christian, wrote in his autobiography *Mein Kampf*: "I am convinced that I am acting as the agent of our Creator. By fighting off the Jews, I am doing the Lord's work." Hitler was responsible for the deaths of over six million Jews. Osama bin Laden, a Muslim, proclaimed that hostility towards the West and its citizenry is a duty to God. Bin Laden was responsible for the September 11, 2001 terrorist attack, which killed more than 3,000 civilians in a single day. Nathuram Godse, the Hindu activist who assassinated Mahatma Gandhi, claimed that he acted alone to save the Hindus because he considered "my first duty [is] to serve Hindudom and Hindus." Yigal Amir, the fanatic Jew who assassinated Israeli prime minister Yitzhak Rabin, was quoted as saying that he had "acted alone and on orders from God."

The problem lies in the exclusivist thinking of different religious groups, which defies the scriptural logic of all religions. The *Cyclonic Monk*, Swami Vivekananda, cited the Hindu holy book, *Gita*, to tell us that all paths lead to God. Therefore, obviously, God is not a Hindu. The *Yankee Mohammedan*, Mohammed Webb, cited verses from the Muslim holy book, the Quran, as proof that it is God who created the diversity of faiths in this world. Therefore, God is not a God only of Muslims, but a God of all human beings. More than a century later, Bishop Desmond Tutu sharply criticized in his 2011 book, *God Is Not A Christian*, those Christians who believe that they received an exclusivist mandate from the Bible. He provided ample biblical evidence to prove that Christianity does not have an exclusive and proprietary claim on God, and that God is, indeed, not a Christian.

Truly, God is too big to fit into one religion.

GOD'S SUBJECTS

In 1893, when the first Parliament of World Religions was held in Chicago, the population of the world stood at about 1.5 billion, with a similar number of fans of God. Currently, God has a huge following that numbers more than six billions humans, as shown in the Table below.

GOD'S SUBJECTS		
RELIGIOUS GROUP	WORLDWIDE POPULATION	NUMBER OF COUNTRIES
CHRISTIANS	2.26 Billion (33%)	239
MUSLIMS	1.52 Billion (22%)	213
HINDUS	935 Million (14%)	127
AGNOSTICS/ATHEISTS	840 Million (12%)	239
FOLK/TRADITIONAL BELIEVERS	750 Million (11%)	220
BUDDHISTS	465 Million (7%)	141
SIKHS	25 Million (0.4%)	53
JEWS	15 Million (0.2%)	138
BAHA'IS	7 Million (0.1%)	222
JAINS	6 Million (0.1%)	19
SHINTOISTS	3 Million (0.04%)	8
ZOROASTRIAN	182,000 (0.003%)	25
TOTAL WORLD POPULATION	*6.83 Billion*	*239*

Source: Summarized from Britannica Book of the Year, 2010, Encyclopedia Britannica, 2011

GOD CHANGETH OVER TIME

As the number of people inhabiting the planet Earth changed over time, so did God. From time immemorial, God has been roaming wide and far with all his might, geographically from the river banks of the Nile to the megalopolises on the shores of the Atlantic, and down the centuries from the Sumerian abacus to the Cray XT5 supercomputer, which can perform 1.759 quadrillion floating point operations in one second. If the XT5 were to process a digital image of God from the brain scans of all humans living on earth, we would find out that God today is not the same as God who existed at the beginning of human consciousness. This finding would be consistent with the evolution of *Homo sapiens*—we are not what we were when we began our journey on the planet Earth. Similarly, our God (or rather, our understanding of God) has also changed through a perpetual process of reconciliation, as we changed with the progression of time.

EVOLUTION OF GOD

God changeth over time through a perpetual process of reconciliation between the sacred and the mundane.

13

DOES GOD MATTER?

Why do we need to understand God? Does God matter? Does religion matter? Is interfaith dialogue important? American sociology professors Paul Froese and Christopher Bader offered an answer to one of these questions in an article published in the *Harvard Divinity Bulletin*, concluding that "God matters and lies at the heart of philosophical, ethical, and political differences in the world." Hans Küng, a Swiss professor of ecumenical theology and a prolific author, underscored the importance of interfaith dialogues by proclaiming, "There will be no peace among the nations without peace among the religions. There will be no peace among the religions without dialogue among the religions."

Political scientists Monica Toft, Daniel Philpott, and Timothy Shah went even farther, declaring the twenty-first century to be God's century. In a 2011 book entitled *God's Century*, they argued that God and religion have been on the rise in the socio-political arena all over the world since the 1970s, and will wield significant influence in setting the political agendas of this century.

The resurgence of religion and God can be attributed to the failures of socialism and secularism to fulfill the hopes, expectations, and inherent spiritual needs of modern men and women. Ironically, the very forces expected to "kill" God, such as industrialization, democratization, modernization, and globalization (recall *Time* magazine's 1966 cover, "Is God Dead?") had actually given a new life to God, as modern men and women again found themselves, like their earliest ancestors, lost in a "spiritually lonely" world where they knew not the meaning of their destinies in the face of rapid and complex changes. The Internet and Facebook nurtured this resurgence by connecting religiously minded people all over the world for common causes—political, social, moral, and theological. God and religion, like any other powerful forces, can be used for both peacemaking and violence. For their specific interpretations to prevail, the terrorists and bigots bank on the ignorance of the masses regarding holy scriptures and sacred history. The peacemakers, therefore, need to nurture and promote a culture of respectful education and engagement among people of all religious backgrounds, such that misinformation and disinformation cannot seize the imaginations of the uninformed.

Therefore, God surely matters for world peace.

But is that all? Doesn't God matter for human souls too? Hasn't God played a role in bestowing mental peace upon humans for as long as they have existed on the face of the earth? It is often said that "Man created God out of fear." But history points in a different direction. God, or the human conception of God, may have changed over time, but one thing that remained constant is that God is a supernatural being to be revered and worshipped. It was not all fear, as many would like to believe. Truly, the relationship between God and humans is similar to that between a kind, protecting parent and a child. God can get angry at times, but that anger is temporary and paternal. As such, God needs to be feared as a parent needs to be feared. However, the permanent attitude of God towards humans is one of compassion, forgiveness, and love. Karen Armstrong, in her book *The Case for God*, remarked that "Religion's task, closely allied to that of art, was to help us to live creatively, peacefully, and even joyously with realities for which there were no easy explanations and problems that we could not solve: morality, pain, grief, despair, and outrage at the injustice and cruelty of life." The same statement could also be made about God.

Therefore, God matters also for the health of the human soul.

REVIVAL OF INTERFAITH DIALOGUES

A long silence fell on global interfaith dialogues after the first World Parliament of Religions in 1893. Indeed, not until a hundred years later, in 1993, was the second World Parliament of Religions held, again in Chicago. The event was attended by 8,000 people belonging to different religious faiths. Bangladesh-born American spiritual master Chinmoy Kumar Ghose (1931–2007), known worldwide as Sri Chinmoy, led the opening meditation. Unlike Swami Vivekananda in 1893, Sri Chinmoy did not speak. But he later explained that during his silent meditation he had prayed for the oneness of all religions. During his 43 years of living in the USA, from 1964 to 2007, Sri Chinmoy propagated what Swami Vivekananda had started in the West: the practice of yoga combined with spiritual philosophy. The essence of Sri Chinmoy's belief is summarized in these words: "I was born into the Hindu religion, but now my only religion is to love God and to be of service to God. Love of God embraces all religions: Christianity, Hinduism, Judaism, Islam and others." This echoes the same sentiments expressed by numerous speakers at the 1893 World Parliament of Religions.

During the lull in interfaith dialogues between the first and second World Parliament of Religions, another set of revolutionary changes were taking place in Chicago, in the field of tall buildings design, which would make possible the construction of the Twin Towers of the World Trade Center. Fazlur Rahman Khan (1929–1982), a Bangladeshi-American Muslim engineer working in Chicago, introduced the idea of the "tube" structural system in the 1960s. He was the chief structural designer of the Sears Tower (now Willis Tower) in Chicago, the tallest building in the world from 1973 to 1998. Khan's tube structural system was used in the construction of the Twin Towers, the Petronas Tower of Malaysia, and the current tallest building in the world, the Burj Khalifa of Dubai.

The irony of fate was that the Twin Towers, made possible by the brilliant invention of a Muslim engineer in the 1960s, were destroyed in the name of God by a group of Muslim religious fundamentalists from the Middle East on September 11, 2001. This act of terror killed 2,606 people. Among the dead, excluding the terrorists, were Christians, Muslims, Hindus, Jews, Buddhists, Atheists, Agnostics, and citizens from more than ninety countries. The ages of those who died in the attack ranged from 3 to 82.

The tragedy of September 11 reawakened the humanity to the grim dangers of religious fanaticism and the need for dialogue among religious adherents. It also gave a strong impetus to the revival of global interfaith dialogues that had begun in Chicago in 1893. Since 2004, the World Parliament of Religions takes place every five years, and many other interfaith initiatives occur elsewhere throughout the world.

In March, 2011, US President Barack Obama launched the *President's Interfaith and Community Service Campus Challenge*, an initiative that promotes co-operation between believers and non-believers. Taking a pluralist position, the President stated: "I know that as we go forward it is going to take all of us, Christian and Jew, Hindu and Muslim, believer and non-believer, to meet the challenges of the twenty-first century." The inclusion of non-believers in interfaith dialogues is a key step towards fostering a *Friendship of Civilizations*, because atheists and agnostics account for about 12% of the world's population.

The tragedy of September 11 has turned into an inspiration, and there have been more interfaith initiatives in the world since that tragedy than ever before. It appears that the *Cyclonic Monk*'s last wish may have come true: "I shall inspire men everywhere until the whole world shall know that it is one with God."

THE CHICAGO CONNECTION

In 1893, Chicago gave birth to the first modern global interfaith dialogues by hosting the first World Parliament of Religions. In the 1960s, Chicago gave birth to a series of tall buildings, two of which, through their violent destruction on September 11, 2001, gave a strong impetus to the revival of interfaith dialogues. In 2002, Eboo Patel, an Indian Muslim from Chicago and a Rhodes scholar with a doctorate in the sociology of religion from Oxford University, founded the Interfaith Youth Core (IFYC), which has the potential to revolutionize the landscape of interfaith cooperation in the world in the twenty-first century.

Headquartered in Chicago, the IFYC supports religious pluralism and hopes to diffuse the faith line to stop the *Clash of Civilizations*. It argues: "The faith line does not divide people of divergent faith traditions, or religious people from secular people. Instead, this line divides religious totalitarians from religious pluralists." Eboo Patel, the founder of IFYC and an advisor to President Obama (who also hails from Chicago), took his inspiration from what Charles Bonney, a Chicago judge and the President of the 1893 World Parliament of Religions, declared in his concluding address: "Henceforth the religions of the world will make war not on each other, but on the giant evils that afflict mankind."

IFYC is building an interfaith youth movement, using service to fellow humans as a bridge. The *New York Times* commented in January, 2011: "Until Mr. Patel came along, the interfaith movement in the United States was largely the province of elders and clergy members hosting dialogues and, yes, book clubs—and drafting documents that had little impact at the grass roots."

IFYC has now gone global, spanning five continents and over 200 college and university campuses. It is building bridges towards a *Friendship of Civilizations*, not a clash.

FACEBOOK GOES GLOBAL

Amidst the turmoil and wars after September 11, 2001, a momentous event that would in a few years change the course of human history was taking place in a tiny corner of a small dormitory room at Harvard University in Boston, Massachusetts. A sophomore student by the name of Mark Zuckerberg (1984–) was diligently writing a computer code that would allow his fellow students to use his website to vote for the "hottest" (i.e., best-looking) person from a selection of student photos. He named his website *Facemash.com*.

He had no idea that his work would have impacts far beyond his wildest imagination. His website gained immediate popularity and brought Harvard's computer servers down. The university authority shut down his website, and Zuckerberg apologized for his unauthorized use of student photos.

Nonetheless, impressed by the popularity of his website, Zuckerberg expanded upon his ideas. In February, 2004, he launched "Facebook" from his dormitory room. In fewer than five years, *Facebook* profoundly changed the world by jump-starting the era of online social networking, a new way of connecting with people across the globe without the travails of journeying thousands of miles. On Facebook, users can post their ideas, share their thoughts, pictures, and videos, and communicate with others—whether they are neighbors or unknown people on the other side of the globe—instantly and at no cost.

Zuckerberg's Facebook spurred a revolution that touched the entire world and now has a fanatical following that rivals any of today's major religions. As of October 2012, *Facebook* had more than one billion active users, and it continues to grow.

POPE BLESSES FACEBOOK

The power of communication through Facebook was soon realized by the Vatican. In 2009, the Vatican launched a Facebook application, *Pope2You*, which allowed the faithful to "meet" the Pope on Facebook, hear his words, see photos, and receive his messages in the form of "virtual cards." The purpose was to build a network around the Pope. However, users didn't receive an email saying the Pope had added him/her as a friend, nor could the user "poke" the Pope or write on his wall. The following year, in March 2010, the Vatican launched its first Facebook page to celebrate the Pope's forthcoming visit to England in September 2010. This event-themed *Facebook* page remains open, with about 10,000–15,000 fans checking in from time to time.

The eighty-three-year-old pontiff doesn't have a personal Facebook account, but he endorsed the use of social networking in a January 2011 address entitled "Truth, Proclamation and Authenticity of Life in the Digital Age." This allowed many devout Christians to start using Facebook without feeling any Catholic guilt. The Pope encouraged social networkers to be open and honest in their communications, and warned: "It is important always to remember that virtual contact cannot and must not take the place of direct human contact with people at every level of our lives."

GRAND MUFTI BLESSES FACEBOOK

In 2010, there was widespread protest in the Muslim world against *Facebook*, in response to the page "Everybody Draw Mohammed Day", which carried sacrilegious, anti-Muslim content. Pakistan and Bangladesh temporarily blocked access to *Facebook*. India requested *Facebook* authorities to disallow access to the page. Numerous Muslim clerics called for an outright ban of Facebook among Muslims. But young Muslims didn't heed these calls. As an alternative to Facebook, some Muslim entrepreneurs started *MillatFacebook*, a Muslim-oriented social networking website, in 2010. However, the user experience was so abysmal that *MillatFacebook* was not able to attract even five percent of the 6.5 million Facebook users in Pakistan. A few investors are now working on the launch of a new Muslim Facebook, called *Salamworld*, scheduled for release in 2012. The investors hope to gain 50 million users by 2015.

In the Muslim world, there is ongoing debate about the use of *Facebook*, or any other social networking site, because of the lack of control over the content uploaded by users. In an interview in 2012, Sheikh Ali Gomaa (1952–), the Grand Mufti (highest official of Islamic law) of Egypt, rejected calls for a ban on social networking. As one of the world's most respected Islamic jurists, Sheikh Gomaa called for caution and understanding in guiding young Muslims to confront both the dangers and the benefits of the *Internet* and social networking. "If you close one form of communication," he said, "people will find a way around it." The Grand Mufti himself has a Twitter account and uses the *Internet* to communicate with followers.

JESUS TOPS FACEBOOK RANKING

Today, the biggest star on *Facebook* is not Eminem, Rihanna, Justin Bieber, Lady Gaga, or President Obama. The biggest star is Jesus. In September 2011, ABC News, citing *AllFacebook*.com, a website that keeps track of Facebook traffic, reported that a Facebook page called "Jesus Daily" ranked as the most engaging page in terms of number of posts, number of comments, number of likes, and number of responses. With only 11 million fans, *Jesus Daily* had about 6 million interactions. In contrast, the *Justin Bieber* page, which has about 40 million fans, had only 690,000 interactions over the same period. The second and third most engaging pages are also religion related: during the same period, the *Dios Es Bueno* (God is Good) page had 2.9 million interactions and *The Bible* page had 1.8 million. The *I'm a Muslim & I'm Proud* Facebook page ranked thirteenth, with 568,000 interactions, while the *ILoveAllah.com* Facebook page ranked fifteenth, with 559,000 interactions.

WHAT IF GOD HAD A FACEBOOK?

Amidst Facebook's popularity as a preferred way to remain in touch with others, it is not at all irrational for men and women to imagine a Facebook for God. So, if God had a Facebook, what would be written on it? How many fans would visit? Could *facebook. com* handle more than six billion fans of God, which would far outnumber the one billion current active users of Facebook?

If history is a slate, then God's Facebook had its beginning a long time ago, when individual *Homo sapiens* first started writing their thoughts and prayers. Men and women of the past centuries contributed to God's Facebook in accordance with their beliefs, cultures, and socioeconomic conditions. They spoke not only through words, but also through elaborate artworks: paintings, symbols, idols, and music. They built magnificent temples that show how they valued their devotion to God. They fought countless wars to establish their own ideas about God, such as who and what God is, and what God wants. At the same time, men and women of all epochs embarked on magical missions of love to help fellow human beings in the name of God. Thus, God and humans lived in an indivisible co-existence and spoke to and about each other in commandments, prayers, and simple statements. This fascinating story of God, Man, and Facebook is recorded in this book for the first time in human history.

I HEARD GOD LAUGHING

Yet, we should remember that words alone, human or divine, however powerful they may be, can't capture the essence or the totality of God. In that sense, this book may be nothing more than a source of enjoyment for us to share some laughs, as the great Persian lyrical poet and Sufi mystic, Hafiz (1315–1390), once said:

"I have a thousand brilliant lies

For the question:

How are you?

I have a thousand brilliant lies

For the question:

What is God?

If you think that the Truth can be known

From words,

If you think that the Sun and the Ocean

Can pass through that tiny opening called the mouth,

O someone should start laughing!

Someone should start wildly Laughing –Now!"

— [Tr. by D. Ladinsky: I Heard God Laughing:

Poems of Hope and Joy, by Hafiz]

CHAPTER DIGEST

East met West at the 1893 World Parliament of Religions in Chicago, USA, which marked the beginning of globalization of interfaith dialogues. At that momentous event, a *Cyclonic Monk* from the East brought Yoga and the message of a universal religion to the West and wished for the death of fanaticism. Yoga became popular but fanaticism didn't die. A *Yankee Mohammedan* from the West also spoke at the event, highlighting the message of tolerance in Islam, but that message didn't register in the popular imagination in the West because of the acts of Muslim fundamentalists in later centuries.

The religious exclusivists thought that God belonged to their religions; the inclusivists condescendingly accepted other gods as lesser gods; and the pluralists believed that God is too big to fit into one religion.

Humans invented *Facebook*, which reached a fan count of one billion in less than eight years. The Pope blessed Facebook and opened a *Facebook* page. The Grand Mufti of Egypt opined against banning the social networking site and opened a Twitter account. *Jesus Daily* became the most popular Facebook page, ahead of the pages dedicated to rock stars.

God, inspired by the success of Facebook, decided to open a Facebook page and motivated the author to write *God's Facebook* to deepen and widen the understanding of God.

Thus God, men, women, and Facebook entered into a fascinating relationship, which provided an inspirational basis for a *Friendship of Civilizations*.

2

God's Song of Myself

"I celebrate myself, and sing myself,
And what I assume you shall assume,
For every atom belonging to me as good belongs to you.

You will hardly know who I am or what I mean,
But I shall be good health to you nevertheless,
And filter and fibre your blood.

Failing to fetch me at first keep encouraged,
Missing me one place search another,
I stop somewhere waiting for you."

—WALT WHITMAN (1819-1882), SONG OF MYSELF

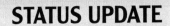

STATUS UPDATE

❖ Men and women seek the Truth.

❖ Men and women search for the "God Particle", "God Gene", and "God Spot."

❖ God facilitates a meeting of two great minds — Nobel laureate scientist Albert Einstein, seeking to understand "God's thoughts", and Nobel laureate poet Rabindranath Tagore, seeking to know "God's soul." Ironically, the later evolution of science pointed to the direction stated by the poet.

❖ God writes his Song of Myself, fashioned after Walt Whitman's famous poem.

NOTES FROM HISTORY
(TIMELINE: 400,000 BC TO NOW)

WHERE IT ALL BEGAN

In the beginning ... there were no humans; the universe was a vast and desolate place. *Homo sapiens*, the only surviving species of humans, appeared on the face of the planet earth about 250,000 to 400,000 years ago. As soon as humans appeared, they wondered about the mysteries of nature, and thus arose beliefs; and the God consciousness was born, forming the basis of our religious belief system, one of the many of our belief systems—scientific, political, and moral, to name a few.

Anthropologists believe that the story of God begins with the story of Goddess, with the imagination of Deity as female. This is based on archaeological finds of female figures and cave paintings, which far outnumber their male counterparts. The Venus of Hohle Fels (dated 35,000–40,000 years ago), discovered in 2008 in Germany, is the oldest female figurine that some think of as the first known religious image, perhaps of the Mother Goddess. Another example of an early religious image (dated 24,000–26,000 years ago) is the Goddess of Willendorf, an 11.5 cm limestone statuette discovered in Austria in 1908.

EVOLUTION OF GOD

The story of God begins with the story of Goddess.

These figurines and other cave arts discovered by anthropologists provide a window into the possible belief systems of our early ancestors, as we have no record of our history from those early years. The history of writing, a form of art used to express thoughts by letters, signs, and marks, goes back only about 5,000 to 6,000 years, to the third or fourth millennium BC. Before the invention of writing, human thoughts and beliefs about God were preserved and passed on through oral traditions, some of which found written expression at a later time.

The story of God unfolded through the years as *Homo sapiens* spread across earth from one continent to another. Raw interactions with enormously powerful natural forces led early humans to take shelter in different forms of beliefs because those helped them to integrate their experiences of a diverse and mysterious world. This pragmatic approach of the ancient periods continues today in the twenty-first century because of the ever-unfolding nature of the mysterious universe that encompasses our existence. Sir Ernst Chain, recipient of the 1945 Nobel Prize in Medicine for his work on the structure of penicillin, wrote: "I consider the power to believe to be one of the great divine gifts to man through which he is allowed in some inexplicable manner to come near to the mysteries of the Universe without understanding them. The capability to believe is as characteristic and as essential a property of the human mind as is its power of logical reasoning, and far from being incompatible with the scientific approach, it complements it and helps the human mind to integrate the world into an ethical and meaningful whole."

THE BELIEF CONUNDRUM

With our different forms of beliefs came debates and a whirlwind of questions during thousands of years of human existence. The essentially primitive and practical questions of how to placate the gods transformed into more philosophical and scientific questions as humans gained more control over nature with the progression of time. Does God exist? Is there a "God Gene" that predisposes us to a belief in higher spirits? Is there a "God Spot" in our brain? Is there a special area in our brain that controls our belief in God? Is belief in God biological? Or is it sociological? Or is it the outcome of an evolutionary process? These are some of the questions that still remain unanswered.

These questions led to an enormous amount of theorizing and writing, which culminated in numerous scientific studies. In 2001, two American medical doctors, Andrew Newberg and Eugene D'Aquila, claimed to have taken a "photograph of God" using a Single-Photon Emission Computed Tomography (SPECT) machine. They injected a radioactive tracer into the cerebral blood supply of eight Tibetan Buddhist monks during meditation and several Franciscan nuns during prayer. The images of the subjects' blood flow patterns showed increased activity in the prefrontal cortex. Thus, the scientists located the "Unknowable" (or the feeling of Him) in our upper rear parietal lobes, both right and left. The scientists also observed decreased activity in the Orientation Association Area (OAA) of our brain, which helps us differentiate between "I" and "not-I"—the individual and the rest of the world. Newberg and D'Aquila wrote a book called Why God Won't Go Away: Brain Science and the Biology of Belief, wherein they claimed: "The deepest origins of religion are based in mystical experience, and ... religions exist because the wiring of the human brain continues to provide believers with a range of unitary experiences."

In 2001, American doctors took God's photograph.

Geneticist Dean Hamer postulated the "God Gene" hypothesis in 2005, promoting the notion that humans inherit genetic material that predisposes them to a belief in higher spirits who transcend humanity. After analyzing DNA and personality score data from over 1000 individuals, Hamer identified this magical gene to be VMAT2 (Vesicular Monoamine Transporter 2).

In the latest such study, published in Proceedings of the National Academy of Sciences in 2009, scientists scanned the brains of 40 participants, including Christians, Muslims, Jews, and Buddhists. Professor Jordan Grafman, a cognitive neuroscientist at the National Institute of Neurological Disorders and Stroke in Maryland, concluded on the basis of that study that "There is nothing unique about religious belief in these brain structures. Religion doesn't have a 'God Spot' as such; instead it's embedded in a whole range of other belief systems in the brain that we use every day."

In this manner, the existence of God has been proven, disproven, and re-proven throughout human history, giving rise to millions of human expressions on God.

God has shaped our world in every way imaginable and affects our day-to-day activities in some form or another, regardless of our belief or disbelief in an omnipotent God or in a God defined by a specific religion. Millions of people have been helped by other benevolent people inspired by God's kind nature; at the same time, millions of people have been persecuted and killed in the name of God as the battle for God has raged on throughout human history.

THE SEARCH CONTINUES...

Scientists still haven't confirmed the existence of the "God Particle", also known as the Higgs boson, first proposed almost fifty years ago by the world's top physicists. If a "God Particle" exists, it would complete the Standard Model of particle physics and explain how all particles get their mass, making it a key to the mysteries of nature. It is obvious that

Stephen Hawking has bet $100 that the "God Particle" will never be found.

the existence of a "God Particle" is a matter of belief among the world's top scientists. Famous British theoretical physicist Stephen Hawking (1942–), author of the bestseller *A Brief History of Time*, has bet $100 that the "God Particle" will never be found. This type of strong intuitive dissent among the world's best scientists about the existence of a specific particle points to the power of belief in shaping our worldview.

On July 4, 2012, two separate experimental teams using the Large Hadron Collider (LHC) at the European Center for Nuclear Research (CERN) reported convincing evidence for the "God Particle." The LHC is the most complex and largest man-made machine; with seventeen miles of tunnels, it can accelerate two beams of protons in opposite directions at nearly the speed of light (186,000 miles per second). Stephen Hawking, upon hearing the news on July 4, stated that he had just lost a $100 bet. However, the elusive "God Particle" remains elusive, pending confirmation from scientists after complete data analysis, which may take until December 2012.

Michael Berg (1973–), an ordained Jewish rabbi and kabbalah scholar, developed the "God Formula", which states that "You" minus "Ego" plus "Transformative Sharing" equals God.

Albert Einstein (1879–1955), perhaps the greatest scientist the world has ever seen, wanted to know God's thoughts and spent a large part of his life looking for a "unified field theory", which is literally a "theory of everything." Einstein had problems accepting quantum mechanics as a complete theory and opposed the Copenhagen interpretation, which says there exists no objective physical reality other than that which is revealed through measurement and observation. He formulated a complex mathematical equation with a cosmological constant, which has been called the human approximation of "God's Equation."

DIALOGUE BETWEEN A SCIENTIST AND A POET

Rabindranath Tagore (1861–1941), the Nobel Laureate poet and philosopher from India, wanted to know "God's soul", and spent a large part of his life looking for a "unified theory" of humanity and God. Because, to him, "True knowledge is that which perceives the unity of all things in God."

So, can we imagine what Einstein and Tagore—one man trying to understand "God's thoughts" and another man searching for "God's soul"—

would have discussed when they meet? The two great minds met in Germany in July of 1930. The New York Times ran a story on August 10, 1930: "Einstein and Tagore Plumb the truth: Scientist and Poet Exchange Thoughts on the possibility of its Existence without relation to Humanity." Encyclopedia Britannica summarized this conversation of great minds in the following manner: "While Tagore held that truth was realized through man, Einstein maintained that scientific truth must be conceived as a valid truth that is independent of humanity."

The conversation between two Nobel Prize winners went like this:

> "Einstein and Tagore Plumb the Truth: Scientist and Poet Exchange Thoughts."
> — NEW YORK TIMES, 1930

TAGORE: You have been busy, hunting down with mathematics, the two ancient entities, time and space, while I have been lecturing in this country on the eternal world of man, the universe of reality.

EINSTEIN: Do you believe in the divine isolated from the world?

TAGORE: Not isolated. The infinite personality of man comprehends the universe. There cannot be anything that cannot be subsumed by the human personality, and this proves that the truth of the universe is human truth.

EINSTEIN: There are two different conceptions about the nature of the universe - the world as a unity dependent on humanity, and the world as reality independent of the human factor.

TAGORE: When our universe is in harmony with man, the eternal, we know it as truth, we feel it as beauty.

EINSTEIN: This is a purely human conception of the universe.

TAGORE: The world is a human world - the scientific view of it is also that of the scientific man. Therefore, the world apart from us does not exist; it is a relative world, depending for its reality upon our consciousness. There is some standard of reason and enjoyment which gives it truth, the standard of the eternal man whose experiences are made possible through our experiences.

EINSTEIN: This is a realization of the human entity.

TAGORE: Yes, one eternal entity. We have to realize it through our emotions and activities. We realize the supreme man, who has no individual limitations, through our limitations. Science is concerned with that which is not confined to individuals; it is the impersonal human world of truths. Religion realizes these truths and links them up with our deeper needs. Our individual consciousness of truth gains universal significance. Religion applies values to truth, and we know truth as good through own harmony with it.

EINSTEIN: Truth, then, or beauty, is not independent of man?

TAGORE: No, I do not say so.

EINSTEIN: If there were no human beings any more, the Apollo Belvedere no longer would be beautiful?

TAGORE: No!

EINSTEIN: I agree with this conception of beauty, but not with regard to truth.

TAGORE: Why not? Truth is realized through men.

EINSTEIN: I cannot prove my conception is right, but that is my religion.

TAGORE: Beauty is in the ideal of perfect harmony, which is in the universal being; truth is the perfect comprehension of the universal mind. We individuals approach it through our own mistakes and blunders, through our accumulated experience, through our illumined consciousness. How otherwise can we know truth?

EINSTEIN: I cannot prove, but I believe in the Pythagorean argument, that the truth is independent of human beings. It is the problem of the logic of continuity.

TAGORE: Truth, which is one with the universal being, must be essentially human; otherwise, whatever we individuals realize as true, never can be called truth. At least, the truth which is described as scientific and which only can be reached through the process of logic - in other words, by an organ of thought which is human. According to the Indian philosophy there is Brahman, the absolute truth, which cannot be conceived by the isolation of the individual mind or described by words, but can be realized only by merging the individual in its infinity. But such a truth cannot belong to science. The nature of truth which we are discussing is an appearance; that is to say, what appears to be true to the human mind, and therefore is human, and may be called maya, or illusion.

EINSTEIN: It is no illusion of the individual, but of the species.

TAGORE: The species also belongs to a unity, to humanity. Therefore the entire human mind realizes truth; the Indian and the European mind meet in a common realization.

EINSTEIN: The word species is used in German for all human beings; as a matter of fact, even the apes and the frogs would belong to it. The problem is whether truth is independent of our consciousness.

TAGORE: What we call truth lies in the rational harmony between the subjective and objective aspects of reality, both of which belong to the superpersonal man.

EINSTEIN: We do things with our mind, even in our everyday life, for which we are not responsible. The mind acknowledges realities outside of it, independent of it. For instance, nobody may be in this house, yet that table remains where it is.

TAGORE: Yes, it remains outside the individual mind, but not the universal mind. The table is that which is perceptible by some kind of consciousness we possess.

EINSTEIN: If nobody were in the house the table would exist all the same, but this is already illegitimate from your point of view, because we cannot explain what it means, that the table is there, independently of us. Our natural point of view in regard to the existence of truth apart from humanity cannot be explained or proved, but it is a belief which nobody can lack —not even primitive beings. We attribute to truth a superhuman objectivity. It is indispensable for us —this reality which is independent of our existence and our experience and our mind - though we cannot say what it means.

TAGORE: In any case, if there be any truth absolutely unrelated to humanity, then for us it is absolutely non-existing.

EINSTEIN: Then I am more religious than you are!

TAGORE: My religion is in the reconciliation of the superpersonal man, the universal spirit, in my own individual being.

Fifty-four years after Einstein met Tagore, Ilya Prigogine (1917–2003), winner of the 1977 Nobel Prize in Chemistry, wrote about the historic dialog in his book *Order Out of Chaos* (1984). Prigogine concluded: "Einstein emphasized that the science had to be independent of the existence of any observer. This led him to deny the reality of time as irreversibility, as evolution. Tagore maintained that even if absolute truth could exist, it would be inaccessible to the human mind. Curiously enough, the present evolution of science is running in the direction stated by great poet." In 1992, Brian Josephson (1940–), winner of the 1973 Nobel Prize in Physics, remarked that "Tagore is, I think, saying that truth is a subtler concept than Einstein realizes."

> *"Curiously enough, the present evolution of science is running in the direction stated by great poet."*

WHO IS GOD?

God is subtler than truth, if God is not the Truth itself. The human search for God (or the Truth) is enormously bigger than the human notions of the "God Particle", "God's Equation", and the "God Formula." The eternal search, which began at the dawn of history as *Homo sapiens* looked with awe at the first rising sun on the eastern horizon, continues today:

"The Sun of the first day
Raised the question
At the new manifestation of soul
Who are you?
There was no answer.
Years after year passed by...
The last sun of the day
Uttered the last question
On the shore of the western sea
In a hushed evening
Who are you?
There was no answer."

— [RABINDRANATH TAGORE: FIRST DAY'S SUN]

HOLLY WALL:
GOD'S INFO

If God were to include "Info" about himself on his facebook, what would he write? He, in his infinite glory, would realize the need for it to be sublime and poetic, consistent with the glorious tradition of his lengthy utterances in holy scriptures, such as the Gita, Bible, and Quran. He, in his infinite wisdom, would also realize the need for it to be modern so that it could appeal to humans immersed in a world of wondrous scientific inventions. Finally, with his infinite pragmatism, he would realize the need for it to be universal so that no special group of humans could lay claim to the sole ownership of God. Balancing all these needs would, indeed, be a difficult task even for God, who has reigned supreme for millions of years.

So imagine that God, in his infinite wisdom and creativity, decided to create a "collage poem" by juxtaposing a selected number of quotes from his facebook. He, in his glory of absolute authority and power, also decided to slightly modify these quotes for linguistic and rhetorical purposes. However, he decided to show his generosity to humans (and perhaps a modicum of respect for the copyright law) by identifying the source of the quote in the body of the "collage poem" at the end of each quote so that his fans could find the original quote in its full glory in this facebook, by looking up the source in the index.

NOTE FOR READERS: God, in his absolute wisdom, also decided to fashion this "collage poem" after the famous poem "Song of Myself", written by the great American poet Walt Whitman.

GOD'S SONG OF MYSELF

I Am God, The Almighty
"I indeed am the Lord of All,
And I am the Radiant One." [COFFIN TEXTS]
"I am One and alone, but sages give me many a title" [RIG VEDA]
"I Am that I Am" [BIBLE, EXODUS]
I "encompass all existence." [RABBI CORDOVERO]
And "I am the origin of all;
from Me all proceeds." [BHAGAVAD GITA]
"I am God, and there is none like me." [BIBLE, ISAIAH]
I am "day and night, winter and summer,
war and peace, surfeit and hunger." [HERACLITUS]
"Verily, I am God.
There is no god but I:
So serve thou Me (only),
And establish regular prayer
For celebrating My praise." [QURAN]

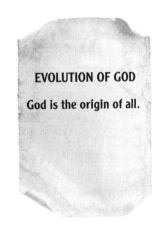

EVOLUTION OF GOD

God is the origin of all.

31

"Prayer does not change me,
but it changes him who prays." [SOREN KIERKEGAARD]
"I am the parent of all things,
the mistress of all the elements,
the primordial offspring of time,
the supreme among Divinities,
the queen of departed spirits,
the first of the celestials,
and the uniform manifestation
of the Gods and Goddesses" [LUCIUS APULEIUS]
I am "a circle whose centre is everywhere
And circumference nowhere." [TIMAEUS OF LOCRI]
"Neither slumber nor sleep overtaketh Me.
Unto Me belongeth whatsoever is in the Heavens

And whatsoever is in the Earth."[QURAN]
And I "do nothing in vain." [ARISTOTLE]

I "sit upon my throne of glory,
robed in praise" [HEKHALOT HYMNS]
Say,
"O Lord, measureless in your glory,
I have grown and lost myself in your grace." [NAMMALVAR]
Say,
"God is merciful and infinite.
The One and Only and is all-pervading." [GURU GRANTH SAHIB]

God's Song of Myself transcends all religions and cultures.

I am "an Inconceivable Entity, External and Attireless.
I am without attachment, colour, form and mark.
My dwelling is within water,
on earth and in heavens." [GURU GOBIND SING]
My "dwelling is the light of setting suns,
And the round ocean, and the living air,
And the blue sky, and in the mind of man,
A motion and a spirit, that impels
All thinking things, all objects of all thought,
And rolls through all things" [WILLIAM BLAKE]

I am "pure order
I am the originator of universal harmony" [LEIBNIZ]
"I am the wind in your beard
I am the flutter in your heart
I am the thing that makes
Flamin' Hot Cheetos taste so delicious
I am the twinkle in a beautiful stranger's eye
I am God and I have a blog.
God's Blog be thy name!" [HTTP://BIGOLDGOD.BLOGSPOT.COM/]

"Life is my novel" [ISAAC BASHEVIS SINGER]
And I enjoy writing it;
My "Moving Finger writes; and, having writ,
Moves on: nor all your Piety nor Wit
Shall lure it back to cancel half a Line,
Nor all your Tears wash out a Word of it." [OMAR KHAYYAM]

I "have created you male and female,
and have made you nations and tribes
that ye may know one another.
Truly the most noble of you,
in the sight of me, is the most God-conscious." [QURAN]
"None merits the name of Creator
But I and the poet." [TORQUATO TASSO]
I gave you poetry
So that I can "be praised,
that to believing souls gives light in darkness,
comfort in despair!" [SHAKESPEARE]

I gave you philosophy
And I declare
"A little philosophy
Inclineth man's mind to atheism,
But depth in philosophy
Bringeth men's minds about to religion." [FRANCIS BACON]

I gave you knowledge
For "ignorance is the curse of God,

Knowledge the wing wherewith you fly to heaven." [SHAKESPEARE]
I "can dream a bigger dream for you
than you can dream for yourself." [OPRAH WINFREY]
And know in your heart that
"God's gifts put man's best dreams to shame." [ELIZABETH BROWNING]

"I exist as I am, that is enough,
If no other in the world be aware I sit content,
And if each and all be aware I sit content." [WALT WHITMAN]
"Reason can never prove my existence." [IMMANUEL KANT]
"Before the creation, I, only I, existed;
nothing else was existent then" [MARKANDEYA]
I am "the Light of the heavens and the earth.
The parable of my light is, as it were,
that of a niche containing a lamp;
the lamp is [enclosed] in glass,
the glass [shining] like a radiant star" [QURAN]
"In all people I see myself,
none more and not one a barleycorn less" [WALT WHITMAN]
"If you don't see Me [God] in the next person you meet,
Look no further." [BUDDHA]
You ask me how you can serve me
I say "You are not yet able to serve men,
how could you serve the Gods?" [CONFUCIUS]
"The fewer your wants, the nearer you resemble me" [SOCRATES]
I am God all by myself
I don't need any help
I can handle things
On my own
I am the first and the last
Whatever you need just ask
For I am, I am, I am God" [DONALD LAWRENCE]

"Do I contradict myself?
Very well then I contradict myself," [WALT WHITMAN]
I contradict "God does not throw dice" [EINSTEIN]
I indeed do throw dice
And I "sometimes throw them

where they cannot be seen." [STEPHEN HAWKING]
But my "dice always have a lucky roll" [SOPHOCLES]
And "Las Vegas is sort of like how
I would do it if I had money." [STEVE WYNN]

Thus making me
"The most popular scapegoat for your sins." [MARK TWAIN]
I know
"A lot of people are willing to give me credit,
but so few ever give me cash." [ROBERT HARRIS]
Therefore "Stop telling me
what to do with my dice." [NIELS BOHR]
And say, say with confidence
"When in doubt, act like God" [MADONNA]

I am the "Heavenly Master,
who governs all the world
As Sovereign of the universe." [ISAAC NEWTON]
I am "in the abundant harvest;
I am also in the famine" [MANSUR AL-HALLAJ]
"My water belongs to me" [PYRAMID TEXT]
"Earth, with her thousand voices, praises" me [COLERIDGE]

"I am the Great Mother,
Worshipped by all creation
And existent prior to their consciousness.
I am the primal female force,
Boundless and eternal." [ANONYMOUS]

I am "God, who gave you
Life and liberty at the same time" [THOMAS JEFFERSON]
I am "One Universal Creator God,
My Name Is Truth" [SRI GURU GRANTHA SAHIB]
I "find myself by creating." [RABINDRANATH TAGORE]
I am "knowable and unknowable,
Evident and hidden", [AL FARABI]
I am "the breath inside the breath" [KABIR]

I am "the immemorial refuge of the incompetent,
the helpless, and the miserable." [MENCKEN]

"Every man thinks God is on his side.
The rich and powerful know" I am. [JEAN ANOUILH]
I "bring men into deep waters not to drown them,
But to cleanse them." [JOHN AUGHEY]
I "alone am real, and all else is illusion." [MEHER BABA]
"Life is not governed by chance;
it is not random.
Your very existence has been willed by me,
blessed and given a purpose!" [POPE BENEDICT XVI]

"Fear not, for I am with you;
Be not dismayed, for I am your God.
I will strengthen you,
Yes, I will help you,
I will uphold you with
My righteous right hand." [BIBLE: ISAIAH]

I gave you religion
Though I am "too big to fit into one religion" [ANONYMOUS]
For "religion tells you
how to relate to each other." [W. D. PHILLIPS]
I gave you science
For "science shows you
how I constructed the universe." [W. D. PHILLIPS]
"The deeper one penetrates into nature's secrets,
the greater becomes one's respect for" me [EINSTEIN]

I am "a rational Creator.
That the entire terrestrial world is made
from electrons, protons and neutrons
and that a vacuum is filled
with virtual particles
demands incredible rationality." [ANTONY HEWISH]
"When you are close to Nature you can
listen to the voice of" Me. [HERMANN HESSE]

I am "pleased with nothing but love" [St. John of the Cross]

Say "To love is to reach God" [Rumi]

Laugh and love, Love and laugh

For life is too short a journey, my dear child

And know that

"Time spent laughing is time spent with" me. [Japanese Proverb]

"Learn to know thyself!

He who has understood himself

Has understood Me." [Prophet Muhammad]

"He who hates does not know God,

But he who loves has the key

That unlocks the door

To the meaning of ultimate reality." [Martin Luther King, Jr.]

"Open your heart,

within you lie all the scriptures,

all the wisdom of all ages.

Within you lie all the religions,

all the prophets.

Your heart is the universal temple

of all the gods and goddesses.

Why do you search for me in vain

within the skeletons of dead scriptures

when I smilingly reside in the privacy

of your immortal heart?" [Kazi Nazrul Islam]

*God's Song of Myself
asks humans not to
search for him because
he resides in their hearts.*

God *noun* **1** a) A being conceived as the perfect, omnipotent, omniscient originator and ruler of the universe, the principal object of faith and worship in monotheistic religions. *b)* The force, effect, or a manifestation or aspect of this being. **2** A being of supernatural powers or attributes, believed in and worshiped by a people, especially a male deity thought to control some part of nature or reality. **3** An image of a supernatural being; an idol. **4** One that is worshiped, idealized, or followed: Money was their god. **5** A very handsome man. **6** A powerful ruler or despot.

— American Heritage Dictionary

CHAPTER DIGEST

The story of God began as Goddess and gradually transformed into the story of a masculine God. In that process, the primitive men and women also transformed into philosophers and scientists, who sought to tame the ancient human's primitive theorizations about God with the help of "reason." New seemingly "reasonable" theories were advanced about a "God Gene", "God Spot", "God Formula", and "God Particle", by the pious and impious alike. Einstein and Tagore, respectively a scientist and a poet, both superstars of their time in their respective fields, entered into an interesting dialogue about the nature of the truth and the divine. Fifty years after the dialogue, other Nobel laureate scientists sided with the poet's intuition about the nature of the truth.

God started to post on his Facebook. God has so much history and so many attributes that creating his "Info" page offered enormous difficulty to the Almighty. Therefore, God, in his infinite wisdom, decided to describe himself through a "collage poem" composed by randomly juxtaposing his scriptural notes with mortal writings of his subjects. He also decided to fashion the poem after Walt Whitman's "Song of Myself."

Through this creative effort, the Creator God set an example by showing how a collage of ideas from different periods and places on earth can exist side by side and form a great poem without losing the essence of the individual parts. Humans took inspiration from God and wondered whether they could create an integrative framework for peaceful coexistence with different religious beliefs without losing the essence of the individual doctrines.

Thus, a motivational basis for a *Friendship of Civilizations* emerged.

3

God is Born
(250,000 to 2000 BC)

"The history of the cosmos
is the history of the struggle of becoming.
When the dim flux of unformed life
struggled, convulsed back and forth upon itself,
and broke at last into light and dark
came into existence as light,
came into existence as cold shadow
then every atom of the cosmos trembled with delight.
Behold, God is born!
He is bright light!
He is pitch dark and cold!"

—D. H. LAWRENCE (1885-1930), GOD IS BORN

STATUS UPDATE (250,000-2000 BC)

❖ God is born!

❖ *Homo Sapiens* appears in Africa and finds God. Thus the God-consciousness is born in human minds and a long procession of human beliefs begins.

❖ God remains silent in Africa and therefore, no holy scriptures exist in African traditional religions.

❖ God was alone in the beginning; but over the course of time humans started worshipping multiple gods, as eulogized in the Pyramid Texts, the oldest known religious texts.

❖ Gods are associated with the objects of nature, such as the sun, sky, moon, etc.

❖ Gods and kings are seen as coequals, and dead kings are thought to take seats with gods in the heavens after death. Supplications are made to gods to help kings in their journey to the heavens.

❖ God, as the Supreme Judge after death, dominates the human vision of the afterlife, as depicted in the Coffin Texts.

NOTES FROM HISTORY
(250,000 TO 2000 BC)

THE BIRTH OF THE UNIVERSE

"It was the night before Sunday, October 23, 4004 BC. The night was dark. God, in his infinite wisdom, created the universe on that night."

Thus goes one of the many beliefs about the beginning of the universe, first proposed by James Ussher (1581–1656), the Anglican Archbishop of today's Northern Ireland. Mayans believe the date of creation was August 11, 3114 BC. Some followers of Judaism believe that the date of creation was September 22 or March 29, 3760 BC. Hindus believe that some of their early religious scriptures, the Vedas, date back to as early as 5000 BC, which predates the creation of the world according to the other beliefs mentioned above. According to Puranic Hinduism, the world was created about 155 trillion years ago (50 Brahma years).

Scientists have their own beliefs, which are based on the current state of scientific knowledge. Today, they believe in radiometric dating, which indicates that the earth was formed 4.55 (± 1%) billion years ago; they also believe in the Big Bang theory, which postulates that the universe began expanding 11–20 billion years ago, with the most widely quoted figure being 13.7 ±0.2 billion years.

On October 1, 2009, scientists announced the discovery of the oldest fossil skeleton of a human ancestor. In a paper in National Geograhic, its Science Editor, Jamie Shreeve revealed that: "our forebears underwent a previously unknown stage of evolution more than a million years before Lucy, the iconic early human ancestor specimen that walked the Earth 3.2 million years ago."

THE EARLY DAYS OF HUMANS

It is a common belief among scientists that modern humans *(Homo sapiens)* emerged in Africa about 250,000 years ago. Then there was a long silence in human history; evolution continued its own course and the earth turned and tossed itself again and again in the eternal blankness that we call the universe. During this long period of silence, *Homo sapiens* increased their understanding of the world, which included inventing bows and arrows around 30,000 BC. About the same time, humans developed symbols to communicate with each other, and the long silence was broken.

John Calvin (1509–1564), an influential French theologian and pastor during the Protestant Reformation, maintained that the idea of God is as old as humans and is implanted in the minds of all humans everywhere. He wrote in his *Institutes of the Christian Religion:* "That there exists in the human minds and indeed by natural instinct, some sense of Deity, we hold to be beyond dispute, since God himself, to prevent any man from pretending ignorance, has endued all men with some idea of his Godhead, the memory of which he constantly renews and occasionally enlarges, that all to a man being aware that there is a God, and that he is their Maker, may be condemned by their own conscience when they neither worship him nor consecrate their lives to his service."

Archaeological research indicates that during the period 30,000 to 26,000 BC, humans created wall paintings depicting horses and rhinoceroses, as found in the Chauvet Cave complex in France. Cave paintings containing animal as well as human figures were found in the Lascaux cave complex in France, which have provided us with the best known examples of Upper Paleolithic art. Some historians believe that these caves were sacred places for some kind of rituals, because otherwise it is difficult to justify why early humans would spend such an immense amount of unproductive labor to decorate and maintain these places.

The first clear evidence of a place of human worship is in the Göbekli Tepe temple complex in Turkey, which dates back to 11,500 BC. The walls of that complex are decorated with carved reliefs of animals and with pictograms, perhaps representing sacred symbols. The carved reliefs depict lions, bulls, boars, foxes, gazelles, asses, snakes, insects, birds, vultures, and a few humanoid forms. The line between the sacred and the powerful was blurred, as the worship of powerful entities (the sun or a serpent, for example) to appease unknown forces dominated the human imagination.

The world population stood at approximately 5 million around 10,000 BC. At that point, the glacial period ended and the world entered into a period of global warming. Agriculture appeared in southwest Asia, and Paleo-Indian hunter-gatherer societies lived nomadically in the North American countryside. The area now known as Long Island in New York became an island when waters broke through on the western end to the interior lake.

> *10,000 BC: World population hits 5 million*

In around 9000 BC, goats, pigs, and dogs were domesticated in different parts of the world. The Ice Age ended in 8000 BC, and agriculture and pottery became widespread. Around that time, the city of Jericho was established, with 2,000 inhabitants living in mudbrick houses in the West Bank of Palestine. Around 7000 BC came the beginning of the Peiligang culture in China, and the establishment of agriculture-based settlements in Mehrgarh, Pakistan. At around the same time, the Chinese started widespread use of rice, millet, soy beans, and yams; the Europeans began making vessels from clay; the Middle Easterners domesticated the cow; and the American indigenous peoples began using stones for grinding food and for hunting bison and smaller animals.

Between 7500 and 5700 BC, the settlements of Catalhoyuk (in present-day Turkey) developed, likely as a spiritual center of Anatolia. Its inhabitants left behind numerous clay figurines and impressions of phallic, feminine, and hunting scenes, which are interpreted to be indications of worship in common shrines.

In 6000 BC, the land bridge connecting England with the rest of Europe disappeared beneath the waters of the North Sea and the English Channel. Around the same time, rice cultivation spread throughout Asia, and permanent settlements focused on agriculture began in Africa. The Sumerian civilization began in southern Mesopotamia, modern-day Iraq, when the first city was built in Eridu (now the city of Tell Abu Shahrain in Iraq) around 5400 BC. This was the earliest known human civilization, and the region is known as the Cradle of Civilization. By 5000 BC, agriculture had spread from the Near East to southern and central Europe.

When the Bronze Age began around 4000 BC, the world population had reached about 14 million. The earliest writing systems emerged around 3500 BC independently in four civilizations: Sumerian, Egyptian, Chinese, and Mesoamerican. Sumerian cuneiform scripts and Egyptian hieroglyphs were among the first coherent texts of ancient writing.

The construction of the Ggantija megalithic temple complex on the island of Gozo, Malta began in 3600 BC. Several other temples were built in Malta at that time. Hindus believe that the Kali Yuga (Age of Vice), the last of the four stages that the world goes through as part of the cycle of Yugas (Epochs), began on February 18, 3102 BC. According to the tradition, the Kali Yuga will last for 432,000 years. Some of the attributes of the Kali Yuga mentioned in the Mahabharata, the great Indian epic, are that kings will become unreasonable and levy unfair taxes on citizenry, and that human lives will be dominated by avarice, wrath, animosity, murder, and lust.

In around 3000 BC, the Semitic tribes occupied Assyria in the northern part of the plain of Shinar and Akkad. Around the same time, Djoser, the King of Egypt, commissioned the Step Pyramid at Saqqara. During the period 2900 to 2400 BC, Sumerians invented phonograms. The main Sumerian deities were the Mother Goddess Innin and her son Tammuz.

EVOLUTION OF GOD

Early God(s) were associated with natural forces: the sun, the sky, the moon, etc.

In Egypt, the pharaohs of the Old Kingdom (2686–2134 BC) reached the high points of civilization in the lower Nile Valley. The pharaohs posited themselves as living gods, deriving from a lineage of heavenly gods. This high and distinct position of the pharaohs is evident in the Pyramid Texts, the earliest known religious texts, which were found in the burial chambers of the dead pharaohs and are thought to have been written around 2600 to 2400 BC. The Great Pyramid of Giza was completed by Pharaoh Khufu (2589–2566 BC), and the world's first extant literary work, the Epic of Gilgamesh, from ancient Iraq, was published in the twenty-sixth century BC. A protracted and severe drought in the region between 2200 and 2150 BC led to the collapse of the Old Kingdom of Egypt.

During the period 2600 to 1900 BC, the agricultural people gave rise to the Mohenjo-Daro (Mound of the Dead) civilization in the Indus Valley, Pakistan. During the same period, people in England built Stonehenge, a famous prehistoric monument of stones with burial mounds arranged in a circular fashion. The Minoan civilization developed in Crete around 2200 BC and the citizens worshipped a variety of goddesses. It is believed that the composition of the earliest Vedas (part of Hindu religious scriptures) may have begun around 2100 to 2000 BC, although many scholars date early parts of the Rig Veda to roughly the sixteenth century BC.

In China, the first Chinese dynasty, the Xia Dynasty, was established by Yu the Great around 2070 BC. He was successful in stopping the Yellow River floods by building canals on all large rivers and taking the water to the sea through these bypass canals.

The earliest example of a law code, The Code of Ur-Nammu, is thought to have been written around 2100 to 2050 BC in the Sumerian language. The Code of Ur-Nammu predated the famous Code of Hammurabi by about 300 to 400 years. The laws were cause-effect based, such that if(-crime), then-(punishment) – a logical pattern that is followed in future legal codes. The Code of Ur-Nammu established the principle of monetary damage for bodily injury, in contrast to the later "eye for an eye" legal principle of Babylonian law, such as the Code of Hammurabi (1700 BC).

Towards the close of the millennium, the third dynasty of Ur established itself as a stable government. The Sumerian civilization reached a high point of culture, with literature and art being patronized by the kings. The oldest love poem in recorded history is a love poem in the Sumerian language. It was discovered on a clay tablet, unearthed in the late 1880s in Nippur (in present-day Iraq), and is known as Istanbul #2461 in the Istanbul Museum of the Ancient Orient in Turkey. The poem was thought to have been recited by a bride of the Sumerian King Shu-Sin, who ruled from 2037 to 2029 BC. The recital was a ceremonial recreation of a fable, in which the bride represented the Goddess of Love and Fertility, Inanna, and King Shu-Sin represented Dumuzi, the God of Shepherds. The love poem goes like this:

"Bridegroom, dear to my heart
Goodly is your beauty, honeysweet,

…………..
You have captivated me
Let me stand trembling before you.

…….
You, because you love me
Give my pray of your caresses."

[TR. BY SAMUEL NOAH KRAMER]

WALL OF MORTALS:
THE PYRAMID TEXTS (2400 BC)

The Pyramid Texts, a collection of ancient Egyptian religious texts, is the oldest known religious text collection in the world. It is carved on the walls and tombs of the pyramids at Saqqara, located 30 km south of modern-day Cairo, Egypt.

The oldest of the Pyramid Texts date between 2400 and 2300 BC. The texts refer to different Egyptian gods, but the most prominent mention is of the god Osiris, who would become the most important deity throughout the height of Egyptian civilization. The story of creation in the Pyramid Texts explains that the sun god, Re, as Atum, rose out of Nu (the primal nothingness), and created Shu and Tefnut from his spittle. From their union came Geb, the earth god, and his wife, Nut. Their children were the first gods on earth: Osiris and his sister and wife Isis; and Set (brother of Osiris) and his sister and wife Nephthys. According to Egyptian belief, all the pharaohs descended from these four gods.

EVOLUTION OF GOD

God is not one, nor alone in the beginning. Kings and gods are seen as coequals.

The Pyramid Texts were first discovered in 1881 by Gaston Maspero, and translations were made by Kurt Heinrich Sethe (in German), Louis Sleepers (in French), and Raymond O. Faulkner and Samuel Alfred Browne Mercer (in English). These religious texts are made up of distinct utterances without any narrative interconnection. To date, 759 utterances have been translated into English.

These magical spells were supposed to help the deceased king in his journey into the heavens. They describe Osiris as a judge of the dead in the afterlife, the lord of love and mercy. The Egyptian kings were thought to be associated with Osiris in death and to inherit eternal life.

NOTE FOR READERS: Most of the utterances begin with the expression "To say", indicating that the words are to be recited by someone, often a priest or the deceased king himself in the first person when he meets the gods at the gates of heaven. The abbreviation "N." in the translations is a surrogate for the name of the kings in whose pyramid the text was found. Therefore, the abbreviation "N." should be read as "I" or "Me" or "My", or also can be substituted with the name of the king.

BIRTH OF DECEASED KING AS A GOD IN HEAVEN

The earliest religious text

"To say:

The face of heaven is

washed; the vault of heaven is bright;

A god is brought to birth by the sky
Upon the arms of Shu and Tefnut, upon the arms of N.
"Great wbn," say the gods;
"Hear it, this word which N. says to thee;
Let thy heart be glad for this N.,
For this N. is a Great One, the son of a Great One;
N. is with thee; take this N.
For life, joy, and eternity, with thee."
"Khepri, hear it, this word,
Which is spoken to thee by N.;
Let thy heart be glad for N.,
For N. is a Great One, the son of a Great One;
N. is with thee; take him with thee."
"Nun, hear it, this word,
Which is spoken to thee by N.;
Let thy heart be glad for N.,
For N. is a Great One, the son of a Great One;
N. is with thee; take him with thee."
"Atum, hear it, this word,
Which is spoken to thee by N.;
Let thy heart be glad for N.,
For N. is a Great One, the son of a Great One;
N. is with thee; take him with thee."

— PYRAMID TEXTS: UTTERANCE 570
[TR. BY SAMUEL A. B. MERCER]

COFFEE BREAK
The Earliest Conception of God: The pyramid texts open the window to the earliest human conception of God. It is noteworthy that placating God(s) was as important at the dawn of human civilization as it is now. One way of placating is to praise God(s), which is a common thread across all ancient and modern religions.

TO MAKE A LIBATION

"To say:
Thy water belongs to thee; thine abundance belongs to thee;
The efflux goes forth from the god,
The secretion which comes out of Osiris,
So that thy hands may be washed,

So that thine ears may be open.

This power is spiritualized by means of its soul.

Wash thyself for thy ka washes itself.

...Thou ferriest over as the great bull,

The pillar (or, column) of the Serpent nome,

To the fields of R', which he loves.

Raise thyself up, N. Thou shalt not die."

— PYRAMID TEXTS: UTTERANCE 436
[TR. BY SAMUEL A. B. MERCER]

KING PRAYS TO SKY GODDESS

"To say:

Great lady, who didst become heaven,

Thou didst become (physically) mighty,

Thou art become victorious,

Thou hast filled every place with thy beauty.

The whole earth lies (lit. is) under thee;

Thou hast taken possession of it;

Thou encompassest the earth and

All things (therein) in thine arms;

Mayest thou establish this N. in thee

As an imperishable star."

— PYRAMID TEXTS: UTTERANCE 432

GODS ARE WARNED NOT TO HINDER DEAD KING ON HIS WAY TO HEAVEN

"To say:

If N. should be bewitched, so will Atum be bewitched.

If N. should be slandered, so will Atum be slandered.

If N. should be beaten, so will Atum be beaten.

If N. should be hindered on this road, so will Atum be hindered.

N, is Horus. N. comes after his father (in time);

N. comes after Osiris.

O thou, whose face is before him, whose face is behind him,

Bring this (boat) to N.

Which boat shall I bring to thee, O N.?

Bring to N. that which flies up and alights."

— PYRAMID TEXTS: UTTERANCE 310
[TR. BY SAMUEL A. B. MERCER]

A CENSING PRAYER

"To say:

The fire is laid, the fire shines;

The incense is laid on the fire, the incense shines.

Thy fragrance comes to N., O Incense;

The fragrance of N. comes to thee, O Incense.

Your fragrance comes to N., O ye gods;

The fragrance of N. comes to you, O ye gods.

May N. be with you, O ye gods;

May you be with N., O ye gods.

May N. live with you, O ye gods;

May you live with N., O ye gods.

May N. love you, O ye gods;

Love him, O ye gods."

> *May I be with you,*
> *O ye gods,*
> *May you be with me,*
> *O ye gods*

— Pyramid Texts: Utterance 269
[Tr. By Samuel A. B. Mercer]

WALL OF MORTALS:
THE COFFIN TEXTS (2180 BC TO 2050 BC)

The Coffin Texts are a collection of Egyptian hieroglyphs, written on the outside of the coffins of the kings and queens from the First Intermediate Period (2180 to 2050 BC) of ancient Egyptian history. About 1,185 spells have been found and documented so far. These texts emphasize the subterranean elements of the afterlife ruled by god Osiris. Excerpts from the translation by famous Egyptologist Raymond O. Faulkner are provided below.

IN DEATH A KING BECOME PART OF THE OSIRIS

"I indeed am Osiris,

I indeed am the Lord of All,

I am the Radiant One, the brother of the Radiant Lady;

I am Osiris, the brother of Isis.

My son Horus and his mother Isis have protected me

From that foe who would harm me;

They have put cords on his arms and fetters on his

thighs Because of what he has done to me."

— Coffin Texts: Spell 227
[Tr. By R.O. Faulkner]

DESCRIPTION OF AFTERLIFE

"The vindication of a man against his foes is brought about in the realm of the dead. The earth was hacked up when the Rivals fought, their feet scooped out the sacred pool in Uinu. Now comes Djehuty/Thoth adorned with his dignity, for Atum has ennobled him with strength, and the Two Great Ladies are pleased with him...N is vindicated before you on the day,...May he be joyful before you even as Isis was joyful in that her happy day of playing music, when her son Heru/Horus had taken possession of the Two Lands in triumph."

— COFFIN TEXTS: SPELL 7
[TR. BY R.O. FAULKNER]

SPEECH BY THE SUN GOD, RE

"Hail in peace! I repeat to you

The good deeds which my own heart did for me

From within the serpent-coil,

In order to silence strife...

I made the four winds,

That every man might breathe in his time...

I made the great inundation,

That the humble might benefit by it like the great...

I made every man like his fellow;

And I did not command that they do wrong.

It is their hearts which disobey what I have said...

I have created the gods from my sweat,

And the people from the tears of my eye."

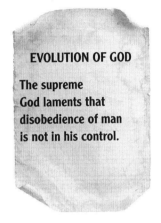

EVOLUTION OF GOD

The supreme God laments that disobedience of man is not in his control.

— COFFIN TEXTS: SPELL 1130
[TR. BY R.O. FAULKNER]

WALL OF MORTALS:
GOD IN AFRICAN TRADITIONAL RELIGIONS

Humans appeared first in Africa and started worshipping a Supreme Deity, who is all alone by himself. This primitive monotheism is still prevalent in many traditional African religions although polytheism flourished all over the world for a long period of human history until the popular rise of strictly monotheistic religions of Christianity and Islam.

In traditional African religions, God is self-created, omniscient, almighty, loving, just, and merciful. Zulu named God uZivelele, which means "The Self-existent One"; the people of Kenya and Tanzania call him Engai, which means "The Unseen One, The Unknown One." A remarkable and unique trait of the concept of God in traditional religions of Africa lies in the fact that nowhere in Africa we find physical images or representations of God.

God remained silent in Africa as there are no holy scriptures which originated in Africa. The religious and ethical teachings are transmitted orally in a variety of forms including prayers, proverbs, and myths.

"In the beginning was God.
Today is God.
Tomorrow will be God,
Who can make an image of God?
He has no body.
He is the word which comes out of your mouth.
That word! It is no more,
It is the past, and still it lives!
So is God."

— PYGMY HYMN (ZAIRE)
[AFRICAN TRADITIONAL RELIGIONS]

"God drives away flies for a cow which has no tail."

—YORUBA PROVERB (NIGERIA)
[AFRICAN TRADITIONAL RELIGIONS]

"Our Father, it is thy universe, it is thy will,
Let us be at peace, let the souls of the people be cool.
Thou art our Father; remove all evil from our path."

— NUER PRAYER (SUDAN)
[AFRICAN TRADITIONAL RELIGIONS]

"God is not hornless;
He is horned:
He exacts punishment for every deed."

— OVAMBO PROVERB (ANGOLA)
[AFRICAN TRADITIONAL RELIGIONS]

EVOLUTION OF GOD

**The God of Africans
is a searching judge
sitting at the gates of
the land of the dead.**

"At the gates of the land of the dead
You will pass before a searching Judge.
His justice is true and he will examine your feet,
He will know how to find every stain,
Whether visible or hidden under the skin;
If you have fallen on the way he will know.
If the Judge finds no stains on your feet
Open your belly to joy, for you have overcome
And your belly is clean."

— DAHOMEY SONG
[AFRICAN TRADITIONAL RELIGIONS]

"O God, You are great,
You are the one who created me,
I have no other. God,
You are in the heavens,
You are the only one:
Now my child is sick,
And You will grant me my desire."

— ANUAK PRAYER (SUDAN)
[AFRICAN TRADITIONAL RELIGIONS]

"The eyes are not prevented [from seeing] by a hedge; God has nothing hid from him."
— OVAMBO PROVERB (ANGOLA)
[AFRICAN TRADITIONAL RELIGIONS]

"Whoever wants to do some evil against another does not remember God."
— PROVERB
[AFRICAN TRADITIONAL RELIGIONS]

"They gave the sacrifice to the East, the East said, "Give it to the West," the West said, "Give it to God," God said, "Give it to Earth, for Earth is senior."
— IDOMA PRAYER
[AFRICAN TRADITIONAL RELIGIONS]

CHAPTER DIGEST (250,000 TO 2000 BC)

Ancient men and women of Africa, the birthplace of humans, found God and started worshipping him. However, there were no open communication channels between God and humans in Africa; thus, there were no holy scriptures in Africa's native religions. This is indeed a period of God's silence, when he let the imagination of humans govern their conceptions of the Almighty.

The pharaohs of Egypt believed that they were related to God and that they would ascend to the heavens after death. So, they took written documents to their graves to communicate with the gods of the afterworld. These documents, called Pyramid Texts, are the earliest known religious texts written by humans.

The human–God relationship in this period was characterized by a power struggle between the Egyptian Kings and God(s), with some degree of defiance on the part of the Kings, who enjoyed unlimited power in this world and yet were uncertain about what would happen to them after death. As a result, God(s) were praised in the hope that this would placate them so that the dead Kings would not be harmed in any manner. At the same time, God(s) were also warned in the Pyramid Texts with the hope that this would dissuade them to trouble the almighty Kings of the living world.

God's universal presence in human consciousness provided a historical basis for a *Friendship of Civilizations*.

4

God Gives Us Religions
(2000 to 1000 BC)

"From the time when Man became truly conscious of his own self, he also became conscious of a mysterious spirit of unity which found its manifestation through him in his society... Somehow Man has felt that this comprehensive spirit of unity has a divine character which could claim the sacrifice of all that is individual in him, that in it dwells his highest meaning transcending his limited self, representing his best freedom.

Man's reverential loyalty to this spirit of unity is expressed in his religion; it is symbolized in the names of his deities. That is why, in the beginning, his gods were tribal gods, even gods of the different communities belonging to the same tribe. With the extension of the consciousness of human unity his God became revealed to him as one and universal, proving that the truth of human unity is the truth of Man's God."

—RABINDRANATH TAGORE (1861-1941), RELIGION OF MAN
[1930 Hibbert Lecture at Oxford University]

STATUS UPDATE (2000-1000 BC)

❖ God reveals himself through the Vedas and Torah, the scriptures of Hinduism and Judaism, respectively. God's laws, such as the Ten Commandments, are codified in these texts.

❖ Kings on earth follow God and enact their moral codes in the name of God. Babylonian King Hammurabi claims in the preface to his law code that he has been asked by God "to bring about the rule of righteousness in the land."

❖ The God of Hinduism is one and many at the same time—thus accommodating both monotheism and polytheism.

❖ The God of Judaism is a single Supreme Being, the one and only, in a strictly monotheistic worldview.

❖ "God is One and his name is Aten," says Akhenaten, a monotheistic pharaoh of Egypt. The Great Hymn to Aten, written by Akhenaten, bears a striking similarity to Psalm 104 of the Torah.

❖ God reveals himself as Ahura Mazda to Iranian prophet Zoroaster, giving rise to Zoroastrianism. Ahura Mazda is all good; no evil emanates from him.

❖ The "Story of Creation" in the Rig Veda from India is remarkably similar to the "Story of Creation" in the Bible from the Middle East.

❖ Man pleads with God, the Supreme Judge, to let him enter heaven after death because of his good conduct on earth. The human conception of good conduct 3,000 years ago is almost the same as what it is today.

NOTES FROM HISTORY
(2000 TO 1000 BC)

This period was marked by the birth of several key religious figures and by the introduction of religious scriptures as the words of God. It should be noted that the dating of religious figures and scriptures is always approximate and controversial.

This period began with the appearance of wheeled chariots and wagons around 2000 BC. The kings of the Third Dynasty of Ur continued their reign in Sumeria and built intricate irrigation projects to centralize agriculture. The first alphabetic scripts were developed around 2000 BC in central Egypt.

In India, the historic Vedic religion emerged around 1900 BC. This religion later transformed into Hinduism. The mode of worship in the Vedic religion was performance of rituals and sacrifices while chanting mantras from the Vedas. The Indus Valley civilization in Pakistan was on the decline due to flooding, and the late Harappan phase of that civilization started around 1900 BC.

In Egypt, the pharaohs of the Middle Kingdom reigned from 2052 to 1570 BC. Arts and crafts flourished during this reign, and a local god, Amun, became the most important god of ancient Egypt.

1812 BC:
The patriarch Abraham was born.

According to the Hebrew calendar, the patriarch Abraham was born in 1812 BC, which corresponded to 1,948 years after biblical creation. Other datings of Abraham's birth include the twenty-third, twenty-first, seventeenth, sixteenth, and fifteenth centuries BC. Abraham would play a prominent role in Judaism, Christianity, and Islam, which are called Abrahamic religions. In Judaism, Abraham, whose birth name was Abram, is revered as the first Jew, the founder of Judaism, and the physical and spiritual ancestor of Jewish people. God tested Abraham's faith by commanding him to sacrifice his son in the name of God. Abraham was about to fulfill God's commandment when God sent an Angel to stop him. In Christianity, Abraham is the ancestor of Jesus Christ and is presented as one who had a relationship with God and one who was in covenant with God. It is believed that God's promise to Abraham will be fulfilled through Jesus. In Islam, Abraham is known as Ibrahim and is recognized as a prophet and a friend of God ("Khalilullah"). The Quran declares that Abraham is neither a Jew nor a Christian, but one who is true in faith and one who has surrendered to one God.

In 1770 BC, Babylon, capital of Babylonia, became the largest city in the world, surpassing Thebes, capital of Egypt. Hammurabi (1792–1745 BC), the Babylo-nian king and law maker, established a set of laws called Hammurabi's Code, which is one of the first written codes of law in recorded history. These laws were written on a stone tablet standing over eight feet tall (2.4 meters).

In 1726 BC, Abraham was blessed by God with a son, named Ishmael. Fourteen years later in 1712 BC, another son, Isaac, was born to Abraham. Ishmael would later be venerated by Muslims as the ancestor of the Arabs and as a prophet, while Isaac would be venerated by Jews as the father of the Jews and as the true heir of Abraham.

1627 BC witnessed the beginning of a global cooling period lasting several years, as recorded in tree rings all over the world. Many scholars date early parts of the Rig Veda (part of Hindu scriptures) to roughly the sixteenth century BC.

The woman pharaoh Hatshepsut reigned as "God's wife."

In China, the Shang dynasty began its reign around 1600 BC, lasting for about 500 years. They had a fully developed system of writing, as attested by inscriptions on bronze artifacts, oracle bones, and turtle shells. Most of these writings were divinations interpreted to gain insights into a question or situation.

Egypt came under the rule of a woman pharaoh, Hatshepsut, meaning "Foremost of Noble Ladies", who ruled as the second pharaoh of the Eighteenth dynasty of ancient Egypt, from 1479 to 1459 BC. A statue of Hatshepsut can be found at the Metropolitan Museum of Art in New York. A pottery jar was found in the tomb of the parents of a senior official of Hatshepsut, with the seal of "God's wife Hatshepsut."

Monotheism arrived in ancient Egypt through Akhenaten, a pharaoh of the Eighteenth dynasty of Egypt, who ruled for seventeen years and died in 1336 or 1334 BC. He is famous for abandoning traditional Egyptian polytheism and introducing the worship of Aten. The idea of a single god was very short-lived in ancient Egypt, as it was quickly replaced with polytheism by the pharaohs who followed Akhenaten.

Ramses II, also known as Ramses the Great, ruled Egypt from 1279 to 1213 BC. The Battle of Kadesh took place in Syria in 1274 BC between the Egyp-tians and Hittites. It was the largest chariot battle ever fought, involving 5,000 to 6,000 chariots. In 1269 BC, Ramses II and Hattusilis III, king of the Hittites, signed the earliest known peace treaty.

The city of Athens was founded in 1235 BC. Moses, the lawgiver and prophet of Judaism, was born around 1200 BC or earlier. Moses was recognized as a prophet by Christians and Muslims also. A significant number of scholars, from Sigmund Freud to Joseph Campbell, suggest that Moses may have fled Egypt after Akhenaten's death (1334 BC), when many of Akhenaten's monotheistic reforms were being reversed by later pharaohs. The books of the Torah, the most sacred writings of Judaism, were revealed to Moses by God in the twelfth century BC, marking the beginning of Judaism.

1194 BC: The Trojan War began.

The legendary Trojan War, mentioned in the Iliad of Homer, began in 1194 BC. The traditional date for the fall of Troy to the Mycenaeans and their allies is given as April 24, 1184 BC. The city of Pyongyang, in present-day North Korea, was founded in 1122 BC. Zoroaster or Zarathustra, an ancient Iranian prophet, philosopher, and poet, was born sometime in the period 1100 to 700 BC. The Zhou Dynasty came to power in China in 1074 BC, after the end of the Shang Dynasty. The early Iron Age took hold in the Near East, including India, around 1000 BC.

HOLY WALL:
THE VEDAS – EARLIEST HINDU SCRIPTURE

The Vedas comprise a large body of religious texts from ancient India. They consist of four canonical Samhitas (or collections): (1) Rigveda, containing hymns to be recited by the chief priest; (2) Yajurveda, containing chants to be recited by the officiating priest; (3) Samaveda, containing hymns to be set to melodies and chanted by other priests; and (4) Atharvaveda, a collection of spells and incantations to be used exclusively by the Brahmans or the most senior chief priests.

"They call him Indra, Mitra, Varuna, Agni,

And he is heavenly nobly-winged Garutman.

To what is One, sages give many a title.

They call it Agni, Yama, Matarisvan."

— Rig Veda

Hindus believe that the Vedas are not of human origin but were directly revealed by God. Thus they are called *sruti* (what is heard) texts, in contrast to *smriti* (what is remembered) texts, such as the Ramayana, Mahabharata, Manu Samhita, and Puranas. The *smriti* texts are not considered to have any divine origin but consist of memories of wisdom that sages passed on to their disciples. These memories constitute traditions and are the second source of Hindu religion. This characterization of *sruti* and *smriti* texts in Hinduism has a striking parallel in Islam, in which the Quran is considered a revealed text (*sruti*) with divine origin, whereas the Hadith (Traditions) literature, which consists of memories of wisdom of the Prophet Muhammad (Peace be upon him) passed on to his disciples, can be considered as a *smriti* text.

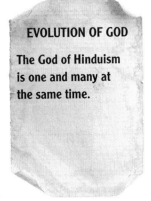

EVOLUTION OF GOD

The God of Hinduism is one and many at the same time.

There are thirty-three principal Vedic gods mentioned in the four Vedas. Indra, the Lord of the Heavens, is the most popular and powerful; he is invoked alone in about one-fourth of the hymns of the Rigveda, far more than are addressed to any other deity. Vedic gods have been associated with symbolic meanings in reference to the human spiritual journey. For example, Indra is the symbol of the awakened or enlightened mind that has developed mastery over all the human senses, while Agni (fire) is the divine spark or the inner soul. Once Agni is invoked, he wakes up the powerful forces and energies hidden in the human body (symbolized as various gods and goddesses) to assist the individual (the performer of the sacrifices) in his spiritual awakening and transformation to godliness. It is said in the Rigveda: "In real worship, we do not just perform ritualistic worship, we try to imbibe the qualities of the one we are worshipping."

COFFEE BREAK

Common Attributes of God: One can find commonalities between the Vedas (Hindu scripture) and the Quran (Muslim scripture) regarding the attributes of God and the manner in which they are described.

MESSAGES FROM VEDAS

"He is One, though the wise call Him by many names."

— RIG VEDA

"Lord of creation! no one other than thee
pervades all these that have come into being.
May that be ours for which our prayers rise,
may we be masters of many treasures!"

— RIG VEDA

"An egotist can never be humble that is why he is seldom blessed even by god."

— RIG VEDA

"Man is but the Image of God. Even Nature is but an appearance of God; the reality is He alone."

— ATHARVA VEDA

"He is present in all places and rules everywhere.
His power controls utterly all the three regions:
Earth, the Middle-Air, and the highest heavens.
One foot is rooted in things we understand:
But the other rests in a realm of deep, dark mystery,
A place far beyond the knowledge of mankind."

— ATHARVA VEDA

"Him who is without beginning and without end, in the midst of confusion, the Creator of all, of manifold form, the One embracer of the universe--by knowing God, one is released from all fetters."

— YAJUR VEDA

"He is the never-created creator of all: He knows all. He is pure consciousness, the creator of time, all-powerful, all knowing. He is the Lord of the soul and of nature and of the three conditions of nature. From Him comes the transmigration of life and liberation, bondage in time and freedom in eternity."

—Y<small>AJUR</small> V<small>EDA</small>

"God is, in truth, the whole universe: what was, what is and what beyond shall ever be. He is the God of life immortal and of all life that lives by food. His hands and feet are everywhere. He has heads and mouths everywhere. He sees all, He hears all. He is in all, and He is."

—Y<small>AJUR</small> V<small>EDA</small>

"He is without any form, yet dwells inside and outside all things
With form and shape,
Yet He is entirely free of error, faultless and pure.
He is far beyond anything a human body can comprehend.
And being the Divine Poet. He is inspiration itself.
He maintains peace and harmony because He is both peace and
Harmony made manifest."

—Y<small>AJUR</small> V<small>EDA</small>

"God! Give us wisdom as a father gives to his sons.
Guide us, O Much-invoked, in this path.
May we live in light."

— R<small>IG</small> V<small>EDA</small>

COFFEE BREAK
Story of Creation: The story of creation in the Vedas bears similarities to those in the Bible and the Quran.

SONG OF CREATION

"Then there was neither Aught nor Naught, no air or sky beyond.
What covered all? Where rested all? In watery gulf profound?
Nor death was then, nor deathlessness, nor change
Of night and day.
That one breathed calmly, self-sustained; Not else beyond it lay.
Gloom hid in gloom existed first—one sea eluding view.
That one, a void in chaos wrapt, by inward fervour grew.
Within it first arose desire, the primal germ of mind,

Which nothing with existence links, as searching sages find.
The kindling ray that shot across the dark and drear abyss –

Was it beneath? Or high aloft? What bard can answer this?
There fecundating powers were found; and mighty forces strove –
A self-supporting mass beneath, and energy above.
Who knows, who ever told, from whence this vast creation arose?
No gods had then been born – who can e'er the truth disclose?
Whence sprang this world, and whether framed by hand divine or no –
Its Lord in heaven alone can tell, if even he can show."

— RIG VEDA: HYMN 129
[TR. BY J. MUIR]

AN INVOKATION OF LORD AGNI (FIRE)

"I Laud Agni, the chosen Priest, God, minister of sacrifice,
The hotar, lavishest of wealth.
Worthy is Agni to be praised by living as by ancient seers.
He shall bring hitherward the Gods.
Through Agni man obtaineth wealth, yea, plenty waxing day by day,
Most rich in heroes, glorious.
Agni, the perfect sacrifice which thou encompassest about
Verily goeth to the Gods.
May Agni, sapient-minded Priest, truthful, most gloriously great,
The God, come hither with the Gods.
Whatever blessing, Agni, thou wilt grant unto thy worshipper,
That, Angiras, is indeed thy truth.
To thee, dispeller of the night, O Agni, day by day with prayer
Bringing thee reverence, we come
Ruler of sacrifices, guard of Law eternal, radiant One,
Increasing in thine own abode.
Be to us easy of approach, even as a father to his son:
Agni, be with us for our weal."

— RIG VEDA: HYMN
[TR. BY RALPH T.H. GRIFFITH]

HOLY WALL:
THE TANAKH – JEWISH SCRIPTURE

Tanakh is a Jewish name for the Old Testament, which is a Christian term referring to the sacred books of the Bible written before the birth of Jesus Christ. The sacred books that were revealed by God after Christ's birth are collectively called the New Testament. Together, the Old and New Testaments form the Bible. The Old Testament is also called the Hebrew Bible. Tanakh is a Hebrew acronym based on the letters T for Torah (Five Books of Moses), N for Neviim (Eight Books of Prophets), and K for Ketuvim (Eleven Books of Writings). It should be noted that Torah can also be used to refer to the entire Old Testament.

According to Jewish religious tradition, Moses received the Torah from God through a process of divine inspiration at Mount Sinai. Some Jews believe that the Torah was created 2,000 years prior to the creation of the universe and was used as a blueprint for Creation, as mentioned in the Zohar, the most significant text in Jewish mysticism. Interestingly, there is a striking similarity between this belief and the belief of some Muslims that the Quran was also created before the creation of the universe and was written in the heavenly skies.

Muslims believe that the Torah (or Tawrat in Arabic) was given to Moses by Allah. Muslims also hold that the Book of Psalms in the Ketuvim is the Zabur that was revealed to the prophet David (or Dawood in Arabic), and that the New Testament is the Injil that was revealed to the prophet Jesus (Isa in Arabic). However, according to Islamic belief these authentic revelations from the same God were corrupted by humans through additions and alterations, leading to the current versions of these holy books. Jews and Christians argue that this accusation of corruption of Biblical texts is a self-serving position taken up by political Islam long after the death of prophet Muhammad.

THE TEN COMMANDMENTS

The Torah includes hundreds of commandments, of which ten received significant prominence over the years and are thought to have been spoken by God to the people of Israel at Mount Sinai. These commandments form the moral foundation of Judaism and Christianity. It should be noted that almost equivalent commandments are also found in the Quran. In addition, one can also contrast and compare these commandments with the quote from the Book of the Dead.

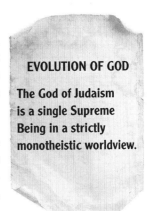

EVOLUTION OF GOD

The God of Judaism is a single Supreme Being in a strictly monotheistic worldview.

The Ten Commandments are similar passages in Exodus 20:2–17 and Deuteronomy 5:6–21, both of which include more than ten moral imperatives. The Jews and Christians variously grouped and parsed these moral imperatives into Ten Commandments according to their religious denominations. One of the most commonly used versions of the Ten Commandments is as follows:

THE TEN COMMANDMENTS

1. Thou shall not take any god except one God.

2. Thou shall make no image of God.

3. Thou shall not use God's name in vain.

4. Thou shall keep the Sabbath holy.

5. Thou shall honour thy mother and father.

6. Thou shall not kill.

7. Thou shall not commit adultery.

8. Thou shall not steal.

9. Thou shall not lie or give false testimony.

10. Thou shall not covet thy neighbour's wife or possessions.

(Exodus 20: 2-17 & Deuteronomy 5: 6-21)

THIRTEEN PRINCIPLES OF JEWISH FAITH

Maimonides, one of the greatest Jewish philosopher, articulated thirteen principles of Jewish faith in 12th century. He argued that if a Jew even rejects one of these principles, he will be an apostate. Though initially criticized and ignored, these principles are widely accepted among the Jewish people today. Poetic renditions of these principles are now included in the Jewish prayer books and are recited during the morning and evening prayers.

These principles are:

THIRTEEN PRINCIPLES

1. God is the creator of all things
2. God is one and only
3. God has no body and is free from all the properties of matter
4. God is the first and the last
5. God alone should be worshipped
6. Words of prophets are true
7. Moses is the chief of prophets
8. Torah is complete and unchanged from what was given to Moses
9. Torah is immutable and it is the last revelation from God
10. God knows all deeds and thoughts of human beings
11. God will reward those who keep His commandments and punish those who do not
12. Messiah will come
13. Dead will be resurrected

MESSAGES FROM TORAH

"At the beginning of God's creating of the heavens and the earth,

When the earth was wild and waste,

Darkness over the face of Ocean,

Rushing spirit of God hovering over the face of the waters –

God said: Let there be light! And there was light.

God saw the light: that it was good.

God separated the light from the darkness.

God called the light: Day! And the darkness he called: Night!

There was setting, there was dawning: one day."

— GENESIS, 1:5 [TR. BY EVERETT FOX]

"See now that I, I am he,
There is no God beside me;
I myself bring death, bestow life,
I wound and I myself heal,
And there is from my hand no rescuing!"

— DEUTERONOMY, 32:39 [TR. BY EVERETT FOX]

"Be strong and of good courage, do not fear nor be afraid of them; for the LORD your God, He is the One who goes with you. He will not leave you nor forsake you."

— DEUTERONOMY, 31:6

"And God spoke unto Moses, and said unto him, I am the LORD:
And I appeared unto Abraham, unto Isaac, and unto Jacob, by the name of God Almighty, but by my name JEHOVAH was I not known to them."

— EXODUS, 6:2-3

"And now Israel, what does the Lord your God require from you, but to fear the Lord your God, to walk in all His ways and love Him, and to serve the Lord your God with all your heart and all your soul."

— DEUTERONOMY, 10:12

"For the LORD your God is God of gods, and Lord of lords, a great God, a mighty, and a terrible, which regardeth not persons, nor taketh reward:
He doth execute the judgment of the fatherless and widow, and loveth the stranger, in giving him food and raiment.
Love ye therefore the stranger: for ye were strangers in the land of Egypt.
Thou shalt fear the LORD thy God; him shalt thou serve, and to him shalt thou cleave, and swear by his name."

— DEUTERONOMY, 10:17-20

"When an alien resides with you in your land, you shall not oppress the alien. The alien who resides with you shall be to you as the citizen among you; you shall love the alien as yourself, for you were aliens in the land of Egypt: I am the Lord your God."

— LEVICTUS, 19:33-34

"Blessed is the man
who doesn't walk in the counsel of the wicked,
nor stand in the way of sinners,
nor sit in the seat of scoffers."

— PSALMS, 1:1

COFFEE BREAK

Multiplicity of Languages: The following passage from the Bible tells a story of how human beings ended up with a multiplicity of languages and were scattered all over the world. This passage is also interpreted as God's punishment for man's arrogance in attempting to build a tower as high as the heavens (the Tower of Babel). This Biblical passage was later parodied by Nobel Prize-winning scientist Leon Lederman with reference to man's arrogance in building a superconducting supercollider. (see page 365)

"And the whole earth was of one language, and of one speech. And it came to pass, as they journeyed from the east, that they found a plain in the land of Shinar; and they dwelt there. And they said one to another, Go to, let us make brick, and burn them thoroughly. And they had brick for stone, and slime had they for mortar. And they said, Go to, let us build us a city and a tower, whose top may reach unto heaven; and let us make us a name, lest we be scattered abroad upon the face of the whole earth. And the Lord came down to see the city and the tower, which the children built. And the Lord said, Behold, the people is one, and they have all one language; and this they begin to do; and now nothing will be restrained from them, which they have imagined to do. Go to, let us go down, and there confound their language, that they may not understand one another's speech. So the Lord scattered them abroad from thence upon the face of all the earth: and they left off to build the city. Therefore is the name of it called Babel; because the Lord did there confound the language of all the earth: and from thence did the Lord scatter them abroad upon the face of all the earth."

— GENESIS, 11:1-9

"Answer me when I call, God of my righteousness.

Give me relief from my distress.

Have mercy on me, and hear my prayer.

You sons of men,

how long shall my glory be turned into dishonor?

Will you love vanity, and seek after falsehood?"

— PSALMS, 4:1-2

"The fool hath said in his heart, There is no God. They are corrupt, they

have done abominable works, there is none that doeth good."

— PSALM, 14:1

Yahweh, my God, I take refuge in you.

Save me from all those who pursue me, and deliver me,

lest they tear apart my soul like a lion,

ripping it in pieces, while there is none to deliver."

— PSALMS, 7:1-2

"How long, Yahweh?

Will you forget me forever?

How long will you hide your face from me?

How long shall I take counsel in my soul,

having sorrow in my heart every day?

How long shall my enemy triumph over me?

Behold, and answer me, Yahweh, my God.

Give light to my eyes, lest I sleep in death;

Lest my enemy say, "I have prevailed against him";

Lest my adversaries rejoice when I fall.

But I trust in your loving kindness.

My heart rejoices in your salvation.

I will sing to Yahweh,

because he has been good to me."

– PSALMS, 13:1-6

COFFEE BREAK

Psalm 104 and Great Hymn to The Aten: Psalm 104 is a beautiful poem from the Book of Psalms of the Tanakh. It is remarkably similar to the "Great Hymn to the Aten," written by the Egyptian Pharaoh Akhenaten around 1340 BC. (see page 79)

"Bless the LORD, O my soul.

O LORD my God, thou art very great;

thou art clothed with honour and majesty.

Who coverest thyself with light as with a garment:

who stretchest out the heavens like a curtain:

Who layeth the beams of his chambers in the waters:

who maketh the clouds his chariot:

who walketh upon the wings of the wind:

Who maketh his angels spirits;

his ministers a flaming fire:

Who laid the foundations of the earth,

that it should not be removed for ever.

Thou coveredst it with the deep as with a garment:

the waters stood above the mountains.

At thy rebuke they fled;

at the voice of thy thunder they hasted away.

They go up by the mountains;

they go down by the valleys unto the place

which thou hast founded for them.

Thou hast set a bound that they may not pass over;

that they turn not again to cover the earth.

He sendeth the springs into the valleys,

which run among the hills.

They give drink to every beast of the field:

the wild asses quench their thirst.

By them shall the fowls of the heaven have their

habitation, which sing among the branches.

He watereth the hills from his chambers:

the earth is satisfied with the fruit of thy works.

He causeth the grass to grow for the cattle,

and herb for the service of man:

that he may bring forth food out of the earth;

And wine that maketh glad the heart of man,

and oil to make his face to shine,

and bread which strengtheneth man's heart.

The trees of the LORD are full of sap;

the cedars of Lebanon, which he hath planted;

Where the birds make their nests:

as for the stork, the fir trees are her house.

The high hills are a refuge for the wild goats;

and the rocks for the conies.

He appointed the moon for seasons:

the sun knoweth his going down.

Thou makest darkness, and it is night:

wherein all the beasts of the forest do creep forth.

The young lions roar after their prey,

and seek their meat from God.

The sun ariseth, they gather themselves together,

and lay them down in their dens.

Man goeth forth unto his work

and to his labour until the evening.

LORD, how manifold are thy works!

in wisdom hast thou made them all:

the earth is full of thy riches.
So is this great and wide sea,
wherein are things creeping innumerable,
both small and great beasts.
There go the ships:
there is that leviathan,
whom thou hast made to play therein.
These wait all upon thee;
that thou mayest give them their meat in due season.
That thou givest them they gather:
thou openest thine hand, they are filled with good.
Thou hidest thy face, they are troubled:
thou takest away their breath, they die,
and return to their dust.
Thou sendest forth thy spirit, they are created:
and thou renewest the face of the earth.
The glory of the LORD shall endure for ever:
the LORD shall rejoice in his works.
He looketh on the earth, and it trembleth:
he toucheth the hills, and they smoke.
I will sing unto the LORD as long as I live:
I will sing praise to my God while I have my being.
My meditation of him shall be sweet:
I will be glad in the LORD.
Let the sinners be consumed out of the earth,
and let the wicked be no more.
Bless thou the LORD, O my soul.
Praise ye the LORD."

— PSALMS, 104: 1-35,

"The heavens are telling the glory of God;
and the firmament proclaims His handiwork.
Day to day pours forth speech,
and night to night declares knowledge.
There is no speech, nor are there words,
neither is their voice heard;
Yet their voice goes out through all the earth,
and their words to the end of the world."

— PSALMS, 19.1-4

HOLY WALL:
THE AVESTA – ZOROASTRIAN SCRIPTURE
(~1100 BC)

The Avesta is the most sacred collection of texts of Zoroastrianism. The most important portion of the Avesta is the Gathas, which are hymns thought to have been composed by Zarathustra (Zoroaster) himself. The verses of the Gathas are devotional. Some verses are directly addressed to the Omniscient Creator Ahura Mazda and expound on the divine essences of truth (Asha), the good mind (Vohu Manah), and the spirit of righteousness.

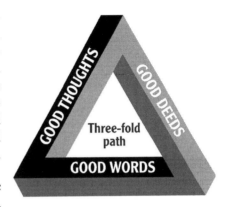

Zoroaster described the human condition as the mental struggle between Asha (truth) and Druj (lie). According to him, humankind's purpose is to attain Asha, and he postulated a three-fold path: good thoughts, good words, and good deeds.

MESSAGES FROM AVESTA

"May the Wise, Ruling-at-will God
grant radiant happiness to the person
who radiates happiness to any other person at large."

— Avesta, Gathas
(Tr. By Ali A. Jafarey)

"Righteousness is the best good. It is radiant happiness.
Radiant happiness comes to the person to whom
righteousness is for the sake of the best righteousness alone."

— Avesta, Gathas
(Tr. By Ali A. Jafarey)

"Wise God, I approach You

through good mind.

Grant me through righteousness

the blessings of both existences,

the material and the mental,

so that I lead my companions to happiness."

— Avesta, Gathas
(Tr. By Ali A. Jafarey)

"Hear the best with your ears

and ponder with a bright mind.

Then each man and woman, for his or her self,

select either of the two, the better or the bad mentality.

Awaken to this doctrine of ours

before the great event of choice ushers in."

— AVESTA, GATHAS
(TR. BY ALI A. JAFAREY)

"With these entreaties, O Mazda Ahura, may we not anger you, nor Truth or Best Thought, we who are standing at the offering of praises to you. You are the swiftest (bringer of) invigorations, and (you hold) the power over benefits."

— AVESTA, GATHAS
(TR. BY L. H. MILLS)

EVOLUTION OF GOD

The God of Zoroastrianism is Ahura Mazda, an omniscient creator God.

"I ask you, O Ahura, about the punishment for the evil-doer who delegates power to the deceitful one and who does not find a livelihood without injury to the cattle and men of undeceiving herdsman."

— AVESTA, GATHAS
(TR. BY L. H. MILLS)

"Grant us (a share) of it both this (material) existence and the spiritual one, that (share) of it through which we may come (and be in) Your shelter and that of Truth, for all time."

— AVESTA, GATHAS
(TR. BY L. H. MILLS)

"The deeds which I shall do and those which I have done ere now, And the things which are precious to the eye, through Good Mind, The light of the sun, the sparkling dawn of the days, All this is for your praise, O Wise Lord, as righteousness!"

— AVESTA, GATHAS
(TR. BY L. H. MILLS)

WALL OF MORTALS:
EPIC OF GILGAMESH (~1800 BC)

The *Epic of Gilgamesh* is the oldest known epic poem in the history of mankind, predating Homer's Iliad by more than a thousand years. Gilgamesh was the fifth King of Uruk, modern-day Iraq. He reigned over a vast kingdom around 2500 BC. The earliest version of the *Epic of Gilgamesh* dates from around 1800 BC. The work captures the interactions and struggles between men and gods as Gilgamesh travels the heavens and the earth in search of everlasting life.

In the epic, Gilgamesh is semi-divine:

"Two-thirds of him is god, one-third of him is human.

The Great Goddess [Aruru] designed(?) the model for his body,

she prepared his form ...

... beautiful, handsomest of men,

... perfect.

… There is no rival who can raise his weapon against him."

(TR. BY MAUREEN GALLERY KOVACS)

But however powerful he may be, Gilgamesh's search for everlasting life is destined to be futile because he is not a full god:

"Why, O Gish, does thou run about?

The life that thou seekest, thou wilt not find.

When the gods created mankind,

Death they imposed on mankind;

Life they kept in their power."

(TR. BY MORRIS JASTROW, JR. & ALBERT CLAY)

THE GREAT FLOOD

The *Epic of Gilgamesh* is the first human literary record of a global flood, which the angry gods sent to annihilate every living thing on planet Earth. A similar story about a massive flood can be found in the Bible and the Quran. The ancient Hindu text *Shatapatha Brahmana* also mentions a great flood.

The description of the great flood in the *Epic of Gilgamesh* is unique in that it says the gods wept as they brought havoc and misfortune upon humans.

"Just as dawn began to glow

there arose from the horizon a black cloud.

Adad rumbled inside of it,

before him went Shullat and Hanish,

heralds going over mountain and land.

Erragal pulled out the mooring poles,
forth went Ninurta and made the dikes overflow.
The Anunnaki lifted up the torches,
setting the land ablaze with their flare.
Stunned shock over Adad's deeds overtook the heavens,
and turned to blackness all that had been light.
The... land shattered like a... pot.
All day long the South Wind blew ...,
blowing fast, submerging the mountain in water,
overwhelming the people like an attack.
No one could see his fellow,
they could not recognize each other in the torrent.
The gods were frightened by the Flood,
and retreated, ascending to the heaven of Anu.
The gods were cowering like dogs, crouching by the outer wall.
Ishtar shrieked like a woman in childbirth,
the sweet-voiced Mistress of the Gods wailed:
'The olden days have alas turned to clay,
because I said evil things in the Assembly of the Gods!
How could I say evil things in the Assembly of the Gods,
ordering a catastrophe to destroy my people!!
No sooner have I given birth to my dear people
than they fill the sea like so many fish!'
The gods--those of the Anunnaki--were weeping with her,
the gods humbly sat weeping, sobbing with grief(?),
their lips burning, parched with thirst.
Six days and seven nights
came the wind and flood, the storm flattening the land.
When the seventh day arrived, the storm was pounding,
the flood was a war--struggling with itself like a woman
                    writhing (in labor).
The sea calmed, fell still, the whirlwind (and) flood stopped up.
I looked around all day long--quiet had set in
and all the human beings had turned to clay!
The terrain was as flat as a roof."

> — EPIC OF GILGAMESH
> [TR. BY MAUREEN GALLERY KOVACS]

EVOLUTION OF GOD

Gods of Babylonians have human-like emotions.

WALL OF MORTALS:
THE EGYPTIAN BOOK OF THE DEAD (~1500 BC)

The Book of the Dead is a collection of funerary texts from the New Kingdom period of ancient Egyptian history, around 1500 BC. These texts were most commonly written on papyrus scrolls, then placed in the coffins or burial chambers of the dead. They include hymns, spells, and instructions for the deceased to help guide their journey into the afterlife.

BOOK OF THE DEAD: JUDGMENT AFTER DEATH

The following shall be said by a man when he dies and cometh unto the hall of Double Right and Truth, wherein he is purged of all the sins which he hath done, and wherein he seeth the faces of all the Gods:

"Hail to thee, great god, the lord of Right and Truth!

I have come unto thee, O my lord

And I have drawn nigh that I may look upon thy beauties.

I know thee, and I know the names of the forty-two gods

Who dwell with thee in this Hall of Double Right and Truth

....

I have come unto thee, and I bring

before thee Right and Truth.

For thy sake I have rejected wickedness.

I have done no hurt unto man;

Nor have I wrought harm unto beasts.

I have committed no crime in the place of Right and Truth.

I have had no knowledge of evil;

Nor have I acted wickedly.

Each day have I labored more than was required of me.

My name hath not come forth to the boat of the Prince.

I have not despised God.

I have not caused misery;

Nor have I worked affliction.

I have done not that which God doth abominate.

I have caused no wrong to be done

to the servant by his master.

I have caused none to feel pain.

I have made [no man] to weep.

I have not committed murder;

EVOLUTION OF GOD

Gods of Egyptians judge humans after death.

*I have not despised God.
I have not caused misery;
Nor have I worked
affliction. I have done
not that which God
doth abominate*

Nor have I ever bidden any man "to slay on my behalf.

I have not wronged the people.

I have not filched that which hath been offered in the temples;

Nor have I purloined the cakes of the gods.

I have not carried away the offerings made unto the blessed dead.

I have not committed fornication;

Nor have I defiled my body.

I have not added unto

Nor have I diminished the offerings which are due.

I have not stolen from the orchards;

Nor have I trampled down the fields.

I have not added to the weight of the balance;

Nor have I made light the weight in the scales.

I have not snatched the milk from the mouth of the babe.

I have not driven the cattle from their pastures.

I have not snared the water-fowl of the gods.

I have not caught fishes with bait of their own bodies.

I have not turned back water at its springtide.

I have not broken the channel of running water.

I have not quenched the flame in its fulness.

I have not disregarded the seasons

For the offerings which are appointed

I have not turned away the cattle set apart for sacrifice.

I have not thwarted the processions of the god.

I am pure. I am pure. I am pure. I am pure.

. . . .

May no evil happen unto me in this land in the

Hall of Double Right and Truth

Because I know, even I, the names of the gods who live therein

And who are the followers of the great god."

— Book Of The Dead: Chapter 125

(Tr. By E. A. Wallis Budge)

WALL OF MORTALS:
THE GREAT HYMN TO THE ATEN (~1350 BC)

Pharaoh Akhenaten (died 1334 BC) preached monotheism in favor of the god Aten. Akhenaten authored this hymn, which was found in the tomb of Ay, in the rock tombs at Amarna in Egypt.

COFFEE BREAK
Similarity With Psalm 104: "The Great Hymn to the Aten", quoted below, is remarkably similar to Psalm 104 of the Hebrew Bible (see page 70).

"How manifold it is, what thou hast made!

They are hidden from the face (of man).

O sole god, like whom there is no other!

Thou didst create the world according to thy desire,

Whilst thou wert alone: All men, cattle, and wild beasts,

Whatever is on earth, going upon (its) feet,

And what is on high, flying with its wings.

The countries of Syria and Nubia, the land of Egypt,

Thou settest every man in his place,

Thou suppliest their necessities:

Everyone has his food, and his time of life is reckoned.

Their tongues are separate in speech,

And their natures as well;

Their skins are distinguished,

As thou distinguishest the foreign peoples.

Thou makest a Nile in the underworld,

Thou bringest forth as thou desirest

To maintain the people (of Egypt)

According as thou madest them for thyself,

The lord of all of them, wearying (himself) with them,

The lord of every land, rising for them,

The Aton of the day, great of majesty."

— Great Hymn to The Aten
(Tr. By James B. Pritchard)

WALL OF MORTALS:
ENUMA ELIS (~1100 BC)

The Enuma Elis is a Babylonian epic written on seven clay tablets. It was discovered in 1849 near current-day Mosul, Iraq by Austen Henry Layard, in the ruins of the library of the Assyrian King Ashurbanipal (685–627 BC). The text was probably composed about 1,000 years before the reign of Ashurbanipal, though some scholars favor a later date of 1100 BC. In the Babylonian world-view, humankind was created to serve the gods.

"When in the height heaven was not named,
And the earth beneath did not yet bear a name,
And the primeval Apsu, who begat them,
And chaos, Tiamut, the mother of them both
Their waters were mingled together,
And no field was formed, no marsh was to be seen;
When of the gods none had been called into being,
And none bore a name, and no destinies were ordained;
Then were created the gods in the midst of heaven."

— ENUMA ELIS
(TR. BY L. W. KING)

COFFEE BREAK

How did man come to the service of gods?: Enuma Elis tells the story of how man came to the service of gods. After six generation of Gods, the younger Gods refused to work to keep the universe going and went on a strike. There was panic among the elder Gods and Marduk, the chief God of Babylon, came to rescue by creating humans to bear the burdens of life while the Gods can be at play. Marduk disclosed his plan to his mother, Ea in this manner:

"Blood I will mass and cause bones to be.
I will establish a savage, 'Man' shall be his name.
Verily, savage-man I will create.
He shall be charged with the service of the gods
That they [the gods] might be at ease!"

— [TR. BY JAMES B. PRITCHARD]

CHAPTER DIGEST (2000 TO 1000 BC)

God broke his long silence and revealed his messages through the scriptures of Hinduism, Judaism, and Zoroastrianism. In contrast, humans remained relatively silent in this period of history. As a result, the postings on the *Holy Wall* by God far exceeded those on the *Wall of Mortals* by humans.

God was decidedly a single Supreme Being in Judaism and Zoroastrianism, but the God of Hinduism was one and many at the same time. The four Vedas mentioned thirty-three principal gods, but Rig Veda, the earliest Hindu scripture, explained the multiplicity of gods in this manner: "He is one, though the wise call him by many names." The God of Judaism prescribed a life guided by the Ten Commandments, while the God of Zoroastrianism professed a three-fold path to good life: good thoughts, good words, and good deeds.

Early human notions of morality found expression in the Egyptian Book of the Dead, posted on the *Wall of Mortals*. The qualities of a good human as depicted therein still hold true after more than three thousand years. The Egyptian Pharaoh Akhenaten preached monotheism and posted "The Great Hymn to the Aten" on the *Wall of Mortals*; however, the Egyptians rejected his monotheism immediately after his death.

The human–God relationship in this period was characterized by dedication to God's commandments, which represented the highest level of morality to which a man could aspire.

The similarities in the essences of the early religions provided an analytical basis for a *Friendship of Civilizations*.

5

God of Prophets, Philosophers, and Poets
(1000 BC to 1 AD)

"And an old priest said, "Speak to us of Religion."

And he said:

Have I spoken this day of aught else?

Is not religion all deeds and all reflection,

And that which is neither deed nor reflection, but a wonder and a surprise ever springing in the soul, even while the hands hew the stone or tend the loom?

Who can separate his faith from his actions, or his belief from his occupations?

Who can spread his hours before him, saying, "This for God and this for myself; This for my soul, and this other for my body?"

All your hours are wings that beat through space from self to self."

—KHALIL GIBRAN (1883-1931), THE PROPHET

STATUS UPDATE (1000 BC-1 AD)

❖ God emerges as the Protector, the Law-giver, and the Life-guide, as prophets, philosophers, and devout believers preach the ideologies of the old and new religions. Several religious scriptures appear: *Tripitaka* (Buddhism), *Upanishads* and *Gita* (Hinduism), and *Agamas* (Jainism).

❖ Confucianism and Taoism flourish in China, more as philosophies of life than as organized religions.

❖ God(s) and Goddess(es) are portrayed as jealous deities (similar to "I am a jealous God" from the Torah) by the Greek poets Homer, Aeschylus, Euripides, and Sophocles. These poets' works immortalize the human sufferings arising from the inexplicable acts of the gods and goddesses.

❖ God faces scrutiny by the Greek philosophers Socrates, Plato, and Aristotle, who attempt to understand the world by the use of human reason.

❖ Socrates, the greatest philosopher of all times, is executed for not believing in the gods.

❖ God and his laws (religion) cause fights among fellow humans as they disparage each other's beliefs. Ashoka the Great, of ancient India, establishes freedom of religious worship in the Maurya Empire in the third century BC.

STATUS UPDATE (1000 BC-1 AD)

❖ God's existence is questioned as atheism emerges in Asia and Europe. Some forms of Hinduism (Samkhya) deny any place for an Ishwar ("God") in their belief system. Diagoras of Melos declares there is no God. A few hundred years later, around the third century BC, the Cyrenaic philosopher Theodorus openly denies that gods exist, and writes a book entitled *On the Gods*.

NOTES FROM HISTORY
(1000 BC TO 1 AD)

This was a transformational period of human civilization, as Homo sapiens grew out of physical needs and began a long and enduring quest for meaning in their lives. They were no longer happy with mere religious explanations or divine revelations; they wanted to understand the world using their own reason. This led to an unparalleled growth in human knowledge and understanding of the world. This millennium was the first period in human history when it was possible to ascribe human thoughts on God to specific authors, rather than to scriptures, which were considered the words of God.

During this millennium, Hinduism and Judaism spread among more people. Several philosophy-based religions emerged—Buddhism, Jainism, Confucianism, and Taoism— that were not God-centric. This period saw the birth of Jesus Christ (3 BC), who would be credited with Christianity, now one of the world's major religions, with one in every three persons currently on earth being a Christian.

This millennium encompassed the Iron Age and saw the rise of many civilizations. David, the king of the ancient Israelites, died in 965 BC. He was depicted in the Bible as a righteous king and was credited with the authorship of many of the psalms in the Book of Psalms. David was followed by King Solomon, who built the First Temple in a hill called Moriah in Jerusalem around 960 BC. This was the first house of worship of the biblical Israelites where the God of Israel was worshipped. The First Temple was later destroyed by the invading Babylonians in 586 BC.

In 900 BC, Yajnavalkya of India wrote the Shatapatha Brahmana, in which he described the motions of the sun and the moon. In 872 BC, a huge flood of the Nile covered the floor of the Luxor Temple, and years later, a civil war started in Egypt.

The Greek dark ages (1100–800 BC) that began at the collapse of the Mycenaean civilization in the eleventh century BC ended in around the ninth century BC when the first Greek city-states emerged. Homer, the famed poet of ancient Greece, was born in 850 BC; he was credited with the authorship of two great epics of the Western world, the Iliad and Odyssey. Around 800 BC, the Iron Age began to take shape in Central Europe. According to tradition, Rome was founded by Romulus on April 21, 753 BC. The Upanishads, a sacred text of Hinduism, were written around 700 BC.

According to the records in the Kojiki ("Record of Ancient Matters"), the earliest extant chronicle of Japan, Emperor Jimmu was born on February 13, 711 BC and founded Japan as its first emperor. The followers of the Shinto religion believe that Jimmu was a direct descendant of the sun goddess, Amaterasu.

711 BC: Japan's first emperor, Jimmu, is born

The seventh and sixth centuries BC saw the birth of several famous thinkers. Thales of Miletus, a pre-Socratic philosopher, was born in 624 BC. According to Bertrand Russell, *"Western philosophy begins with Thales."* Anaximander, another pre-Socratic philosopher and a student of Thales, was born in 610 BC. Anaximander is considered by many to have been the first scientist in human history, as he conducted the earliest recorded scientific experiment. He was one of the first to postulate that natural laws, not supernatural forces, create and maintain order in the universe. Anaximander was the first philosopher to write down his studies.

Mahavira of Vaishali, the twenty-fourth Tirthankara of Jainism, was born in 599 BC in Bihar, India, to King Siddartha and Queen Trishala; although born a prince, at the age of thirty, Mahavira left his kingdom and family, and spent twelve years as an ascetic. He devoted the rest of his life to preaching his philosophy, which is founded on eight cardinal principles—three metaphysical and five ethical. The five ethical principles constitute the five mahavratas (great vows) of Jainism.

Gautama Buddha, founder of Buddhism, was born a prince in 563 BC in today's Nepal, to King Suddhodona and Queen Maha Maya. His birth name was Siddartha, the same name as the father of Mahavira, the founder of Jainism. At the age of twenty-nine, Buddha left his palace in search of the meaning of life. At thirty-five, he received enlightenment through meditation. He spent the rest of his life traveling and preaching his doctrine in the Gangetic plain.

EVOLUTION OF GOD

The God of Buddhism is a non-Being.

In 551 BC, Confucius, the great Chinese philosopher, was born in China. His teachings can be found in the *Analects of Confucius*. His philosophy is based on virtue ethics, which emphasizes self-cultivation, emulation of moral exemplars, and development of value judgment. His philosophy still has great and enduring influence in the Chinese, Korean, Japanese, and Vietnamese cultures.

Lao Tze, the central figure of Taoism, was born in the sixth century BC and was considered a contemporary of Confucius. Lao Tze is credited with the authorship of *Daodejing (Tao Te Ching)*, one of the most influential texts of ancient China. In his philosophy, which is also considered a religion (Taoism) by some, Tao (The Way) is the mystical source of all existence, and it is unseen and unheard. It does not have any God but is a way of life focusing on nature and its relationship with humans. The three jewels of Taoism are compassion, moderation, and humility.

According to tradition, Sun Tzu, author of *The Art of War,* an ancient Chinese book that has a wide-ranging influence even today, was born in 544 BC. This book influenced many generals and leaders of the past, such as Napoleon and Mao Zedong. It is listed as recommended reading in the U.S. Marine Corps Professional Reading Program.

The year 538 BC marked the return of some Jews from Babylonian exile. These repatriates built the Second Temple about seventy years after the destruction of the First Temple. This temple became the center of worship of the Jewish God and a place for animal sacrifices, called korbanot. In India, Pnini (520–460 BC) composed a Sanskrit grammar, which is the oldest extant grammar in any language.

The Greek civilization matured and entered its Classical era, which was marked by highly advanced culture in philosophy, art, theater, poetry, and architecture. This period still has an enduring influence on Western civilization; because, much of our modern philosophy, literature, science, and logical thinking derive from ancient Greek civilization. Some of the famous men of that period are: scientists and mathematicians—Pythagoras, Euclid, Archimedes; philosophers—Xenophanes, Heraclitus, Socrates, Plato, Aristotle, Epicurus; poets—Aeschylus, Aristophanes, Euripides, Sophocles; historians—Herodotus, Xenophon, Thucydides; orators—Demosthenes.

Socrates, the most influential philosopher of all times, was born in 469 BC. He tried to improve the Athenians' sense of justice and started teaching people to question everything, for he claimed, "An unexamined life is not worth living." He became a highly controversial figure, and the authorities arrested him on charges of corrupting the Athenian youth and not believing in the gods of the time. He was tried and sentenced to death. His last words before his execution in 399 BC were: "The hour of departure has arrived, and we go our ways—I to die and you to live. Which is the better, only God knows."

399 BC: Socrates was executed for disobeying the gods.

Socrates is perhaps the most famous human ever killed in the name of protecting the honor of God. He is credited with the *"Socratic Method"* of teaching, which is still being followed in the world's best schools, such as at Harvard University. The goal of the Socratic Method is to increase understanding through inquiry. It uses incisive questioning to dismantle and discard preexisting ideas while allowing the respondent to rethink the primary question.

In 449 BC, Herodotus, the father of history, completed his Histories, which records the events concerning the Persian War. The Parthenon, the temple of the Greek goddess Athena, was completed in 432 BC and still stands today as an enduring symbol of ancient Greek high culture.

Plato, the founder of natural philosophy, was born in 424 BC. He was a disciple of Socrates and established the *"Academy of Athens"*, which was the first institution of higher learning in the Western world. There is a well-known saying that the whole of Western philosophy is a footnote to Plato. This is because his writings have set a course for philosophy that has been followed ever since. Plato published some two dozen dialogues, of which the Republic and the Symposium are the finest examples of philosophy as well as prose.

Aristotle, the greatest polymath that humanity has ever known, was born in 384 BC. He studied under Plato and wrote on many subjects—biology, ethics, government, logic, metaphysics, music, physics, poetry, politics, rhetoric, theater, and zoology. He was considered the *"teacher of those who know."* Aristotle had a profound influence on the philosophical and theological thinking of the three major Abrahamic religions—Judaism, Christianity, and Islam—from the seventh through the sixteenth centuries AD. Aristotle's most famous student was Alexander the Great. As the King of Macedon, Alexander built one of the largest empires of the ancient world and spread the Greek civilization into the East. Alexander invaded India in the winter of 327/326 BC but failed in his military campaign and returned from the banks of the Beas river, the second easternmost river of Punjab. Alexander died in 323 BC.

In the fourth century BC, the Chinese astronomer Gan De divided the celestial sphere into 365¼ degrees, and the tropical year into 365¼ days, at a time when most astronomers used the Babylon division of the celestial sphere into 360 degrees. Ashoka, popularly known as Ashoka the Great, was an Indian emperor of the Maurya Dynasty who ruled almost the entire Indian subcontinent from 269 to 232 BC.

Archimedes of Syracuse (287–212 BC) was a Greek mathematician, physicist, engineer, inventor, and astronomer. He is credited with the foundational work in hydrostatics and statics, and the explanation of the principle of the lever. Archimedes formulated the law of buoyancy, which is known as Archimedes' Principle.

In the second century BC, the Chinese first produced paper. In 146 BC, Rome destroyed and razed the city of Carthage in the Third Punic War. In East Asia, China reached a high point under the Han Dynasty. Julius Caesar was murdered in 44 BC. Herod the Great became the sole ruler of Judea in about 36 BC and completed the expansion of the Second Temple (also called Herod's Temple) in Jerusalem. Jesus Christ was born during the days of Herod the King. Most scholars assume a date of birth for Jesus between 6 and 2 BC.

HOLY WALL:
THE UPANISHADS – A HINDU SCRIPTURE

The Upanishads are a set of Hindu scriptures that constitute the core teachings of Vedanta, a philosophy of self-realization of human divinity. The Upanishads talk about the unity of God (the universal spirit or the Brahman) and that of the individual soul (Atman). This has a strong similarity with the Sufi thought in Islam.

MESSAGES FROM UPANISHADS

"The gods love what is mysterious, and dislike what is evident."

— Brihadaranyaka Upanishad, 4.2.2.

(Tr. By Max Muller)

"BRAHMA was the first of the Devas, the maker of the universe, the preserver of the world. He told the knowledge of Brahman, the foundation of all knowledge, to his eldest son Atharva."

— Mundaka Upanishad, 1.1

(Tr. By Max Muller)

"It stirs and it stirs not; it is far, and likewise near

It is inside of all this, and it is outside of all this.

And he who beholds all beings in the Self,

And the Self in all beings, he never turns away from it.

When to a man who understands, the Self has become all things, what sorrow, what trouble can there be to him who once beheld that unity?

He (the Self) encircled all, bright, incorporeal, scatheless, without muscles, pure, untouched by evil; a seer, wise, omnipresent, self-existent, he disposed all things rightly for eternal years.

All who worship what is not real knowledge (good works), enter into blind darkness: those who delight in real knowledge, enter, as it were, into greater darkness.

One thing, they say, is obtained from real knowledge; another, they say, from what is not knowledge. Thus we have heard from the wise who taught us this.

He who knows at the same time both knowledge and not-knowledge, overcomes death through not-knowledge, and obtains immortality through knowledge."

— Isha Upanishad, Verses 5-11.

(Tr. By Max Muller)

"That which cannot be seen, nor seized, which has no family and no caste 1, no eyes nor ears, no hands nor feet, the eternal, the omnipresent (all-pervading), infinitesimal, that which is imperishable, that which is imperishable, that it is which the wise regard as the source of all beings."

— Mundaka Upanishad 1.6 (Tr. By Max Muller)

Compare With Quran, Sura Al-Baqara: 2:255

"He is the one God, hidden in all beings, all-pervading, the Self within all beings, watching over all works, dwelling in all beings, the witness, the perceiver, the only one, free from qualities."

— SVETASVATARA UPANISHAD 6.11

(TR. BY MAX MULLER)

COFFEE BREAK

How Many Gods are There? *Brihadaranyaka Upanishad,* one of the sacred Hindu texts from the pre-Buddhist era, answered this question in an enigmatic story:

"Now Vidaghda, Sakala's son, asked him, "Yajnavalkya, how many gods are there?"

Following the text of the Veda, he replied, "303, and 3003, as are mentioned in the Vedic hymn of the Visvadevas."

"Right," replied Vidagdha, "but how many gods are there really, Yajnavalkya?"

"Thirty-three."

"Right," he assented, "but how many gods are there really, Yajnavalkya?"

"Six."

"Right," he answered, "but how many gods are there really, Yajnavalkya?"

"Two."

"Right," Vidagdha replied, "but how many gods are there really, Yajnavalkya?"

"One."

"You are the blue butterfly, the green-eyed parrot and the lightning cloud. You are the seasons and the seas. You are the one without any beginning; you are omnipresent; all the worlds are born out of you."

— SVETASVATARA UPANISHAD

(TR. BY MAX MULLER)

"In the highest golden sheath there is the Brahman without passions and without parts. That is pure, that is the light of lights, that is it which they know who know the Self.

The sun does not thine there, nor the moon and the stars, nor these lightnings, and much less this fire. When he shines, everything shines after him; by his light all this is lighted.

That immortal Brahman is before, that Brahman is behind, that Brahman is right and left. It has gone forth below and above; Brahman alone is all this, it is the best."

— MUNDAKA UPANISHAD, 2:2:9-11

(TR. BY MAX MULLER)

"Thou art indeed the manifested Brahman. Of thee will I speak. Thee will I proclaim in my thoughts as true. Thee will I proclaim on my lips as true."

—Taittiriya Upanishad 1:1:1

(Tr. By Max Muller)

"I cannot say that I know Brahman fully. Nor can I say that I know him not. He among us knows him best who understands the spirit of the words: "Nor do I know that I know him not.""

— Kena Upanishad 2:2

(Tr. By Max Muller)

"Eye cannot see him, nor words reveal him;

By the senses, austerity, or works he is not known.

When the mind is cleansed by the grace of wisdom,

He is seen by contemplation--the One without parts."

— Mundaka Upanishad

"That which is beyond this world is without form and without suffering. They who know it, become immortal, but others suffer pain indeed.
That Bhagavat exists in the faces, the heads, the necks of all, he dwells in the cave (of the heart) of all beings, he is all-pervading, therefore he is the omnipresent Siva."

— Svetasvatara Upanishad 3:10-11

(Tr. By Max Muller)

"He created all this, whatever is here. Having created it, into it, indeed, he entered. Having entered it, he became both the actual and the beyond, the defined and the undefined, both the founded and the unfounded, the intelligent and the unintelligent, the true and the untrue."

—Taittiriya Upanishad, 2:6-1

"Man becomes true if in this life he can apprehend God; if not, it is the greatest calamity for him."

— Upanishad

COMPARE UPANISHAD AND QURAN VERSES:

"That which cannot
be seen by the eye but
through which the eye
itself sees, know That to be
Brahman (God) and not
what people worship here
(in the manifested world)."

— Kena Upanishad 1:7

"No human vision
can encompass Him,
whereas He encompasses
all human vision:
for He alone is unfa-
thomable, all-aware."

— Quran: Sura Al Anam: 6:103

TEN COMMANDMENTS OF HINDUISM

There are no such things as the ten commandments of Hinduism in any of its scriptures. However, several Hindu thinkers have articulated the ten commandments of Hinduism in an effort to encapsulate the essence of Hinduism. Since Hinduism is a very open religion, without any formal clergy or religious authority, individual opinions and interpretations abound on all religious matters.

There is no such thing as ten commandments in Hinduism, but people created their own lists.

Professor V. Krishnamurthy (1927–) postulated the ten commandments of Hinduism and divided them into three head and seven describing commandments.

According to Krishnamurthy, the three head commandments are:

1. Omnipresence of Reality
2. Purification of Mind
3. Dharma (Divine Laws)

The seven describing commandments emanate from the three head commandments and they are:

1. Karma Yoga (Actions)
2. One God with many names and forms
3. Avatara (Divine Manifestations)
4. Nama Smarana (Divine Remembrance or Recitation of Divine Names)
5. Surrender
6. Self Revelation

7. Right Attitudes

Subhamoy Das, a web blogger, articulated the following ten commandments of Hinduism:

TEN COMMANDMENTS OF HINDUISM

1. Satya (Truth)
2. Ahimsa (Non-violence)
3. Brahmacharya (Celibacy, non-adultery)
4. Asteya (No desire to possess or steal)
5. Aparighara (Non-corrupt)
6. Shaucha (Cleanliness)
7. Santosh (Contentment)
8. Swadhyaya (Reading of scriptures)
9. Tapas (Austerity, perseverance, penance)
10. Ishwarpranidhan (Regular prayers)

FOUR YOGAS (FOUR PATHS) OF HINDUISM

Hinduism lacks any formal and unified system of beliefs and depends on multiple scriptures of different periods. According to classical Hinduism, the primary goal of life is to attain "moksha" – the liberation of the soul from the cycle of life and birth. Moksha (liberation) is achieved through the union with God. Yoga Upanishad states-

"Living souls are prisoners

of the joys and woes of existence

to liberate them from nature's magic

the knowledge of the brahman is necessary.

It is hard to acquire, this knowledge,

but it is the only boat,

to carry one over the river of Samsara

A thousand are the paths that lead there,

Yet it is one, in truth,

knowledge, the supreme refuge!"

There are four yogas (paths) by which one can achieve moksha:

1. Karma Yoga (the path of selfless and righteous action)
2. Bhakti Yoga (the path of unconditional surrender to God)
3. Raja Yoga (the path of meditation)
4. Jnana Yoga (the path of rational inquiry)"

HOLY WALL:
THE BHAGAVAD GITA – THE MOST SACRED
HINDU SCRIPTURE

The Bhagavad Gita ("Song of God") is a sacred Hindu scripture and is considered one of the most important philosophical classics of the world. It consists of 700 verses and is a part of the Indian epic Mahabharata. According to Catherine Cornille, Associate Professor of Theology at Boston College, "The text [of the Gita] offers a survey of the different possible disciplines for attaining liberation through knowledge (jnana), action (karma) and loving devotion to God (bhakti), focusing on the latter as both the easiest and the highest path to salvation."

MESSAGES FROM GITA

"Those who follow the path of spiritual wisdom) see that where there is One, that One is me (God); where there are many, all are me; they see my face everywhere."

— BHAGAVAD GITA

"I am the origin of all; from ME all (the whole creation) proceeds. Knowing this, the wise worship Me, endowed with conviction."

— BHAGAVAD GITA [10:8]
(TR. S. RADAKRISHNAN)

"Whosoever desires to worship whatever deity — using any name, form, and method — with faith, I make their faith steady in that very deity. Endowed with steady faith they worship that deity, and obtain their wishes through that deity. Those wishes are, indeed, granted only by Me."

— BHAGAVAD GITA (7:21-22)
(TR. DR. RAMANANDA PRASAD)

"I know, O Arjuna, the beings of the past, of the present, and those of the future, but no one really knows Me."

— BHAGAVAD GITA (7:26)
(TR. DR. RAMANANDA PRASAD)

"To these who are constantly devoted and worship Me with love, I grant the concentration of understanding by which they come unto Me. Out of compassion for those same ones, remaining within My own true state, I destroy the darkness born of ignorance by the shining lamp of wisdom."

— BHAGAVAD GITA [10:10-11]
(TR. S. RADAKRISHNAN)

"Set aside all meritorious deeds and religious rituals, and just surrender completely to My will with firm faith and loving devotion. I shall liberate you from all sins, the bonds of Karma. Do not grieve."

— BHAGAVAD GITA [18.66]
(TR. BY DR. RAMANANDA PRASAD)

"The Spirit by whom this entire universe is pervaded is indestructible. No one can destroy the imperishable Spirit."

— BHAGAVAD GITA [2:17]

"Those whose intelligence has been stolen by material desires surrender unto demigods and follow the particular rules and regulations of worship according to their own natures."

— BHAGAVAD GITA [7:20]

COFFEE BREAK
Righteous War: Righteous war is not the monopoly of any single religion. In the Gita, God tells Arjuna, who wants to withdraw from fighting his own relatives, that it is one's duty to fight a righteous war.

"Considering also your duty as a warrior you should not waver like this. Because, there is nothing more auspicious for a warrior than a righteous war. Only the fortunate warriors, O Arjuna, get such an opportunity for an unsought war that is like an open door to heaven. If you will not fight this righteous war, then you will fail in your duty, lose your reputation, and incur sin. People will talk about your disgrace forever. To the honored, dishonor is worse than death."

— BHAGAVAD GITA [2:31-34]
(TR. DR. RAMANANDA PRASAD)

"You have control over doing your respective duty only, but no control or claim over the results. The fruits of work should not be your motive, and you should never be inactive.

Do your duty to the best of your ability, O Arjuna, with your mind attached to the Lord, abandoning worry and selfish attachment to the results, and remaining calm in both success and failure."

— BHAGAVAD GITA [2:47-48]
(TR. DR. RAMANANDA PRASAD)

COFFEE BREAK
True Enlightenment: God counsels that true enlightenment comes from shedding one's ego.

"A person whose mind is unperturbed by sorrow, who does not crave pleasures, and who is completely free from attachment, fear, and anger, is called an enlightened sage of steady intellect."

— BHAGAVAD GITA [2:54-56]
(TR. DR. RAMANANDA PRASAD)

COMPARE GITA AND QURAN VERSES

"Therefore, always remember Me and do your duty. You shall certainly attain Me if your mind and intellect are ever focused on Me."
— BHAGAVAD GITA: 8:7

"So remember Me, and I shall remember you; and be grateful unto Me, and deny Me not."
— QURAN: SURA AL BAQARA: 2:152

"There is neither Self-knowledge, nor Self-perception to those who are not united with the Supreme. Without Self-perception there is no peace, and without peace there can be no happiness."

— BHAGAVAD GITA [2:66]
(TR. DR. RAMANANDA PRASAD)

"One must elevate and not degrade oneself by one's own mind. The mind alone is one's friend as well as one's enemy. The mind is the friend of those who have control over it, and the mind acts like an enemy for those who do not control it."

— BHAGAVAD GITA (6:5-6)
(TR. DR. RAMANANDA PRASAD)

"O Arjuna, I am the sapidity in the water, I am the radiance in the sun and the moon, the sacred syllable OM in all the Vedas, the sound in the ether, and potency in human beings. I am the sweet fragrance in the earth. I am the heat in the fire, the life in all living beings, and the austerity in the ascetics."

— BHAGAVAD GITA (7:8-9)
(TR. DR. RAMANANDA PRASAD)

"I am the Vedas, I am the celestial ruler, I am the mind among the senses, I am the consciousness in living beings.

I am Lord Shiva, I am the god of wealth, I am the fire god, and the mountains.
I am the priest, and the army general of the celestial controllers, O Arjuna. I am the ocean among the bodies of water.

I am the monosyllable cosmic sound, OM, among the words; I am the chanting of mantra among the spiritual disciplines; and I am the Himalaya among the mountains."

— BHAGAVAD GITA (10:21-25)
(TR. DR. RAMANANDA PRASAD)

"If you are unable to do your duty for Me, then just surrender unto My will, and renounce the attachment to, and the anxiety for, the fruits of all work — by learning to accept all results as God's grace — with equanimity."

— BHAGAVAD GITA (12:8-11)
(TR. DR. RAMANANDA PRASAD)

"Make every act an offering to me (God); regard me as your only protector. Relying on interior discipline, meditate on me always. Remembering me, you shall overcome all difficulties through my grace. But if you will not heed me in your self-will, nothing will avail you."

— BHAGAVAD GITA

"O Arjuna, I am the Supreme Spirit (or Supersoul) abiding in the inner psyche of all beings as soul (Atma). I am also the creator, maintainer, and destroyer or the beginning, the middle, and the end –of all beings."

— BHAGAVAD GITA (10:20)

COFFEE BREAK

Wound Not Others: Manusmriti, the Law Code of Manu, is an ancient text of Hinduism. According to tradition, it records the word of Brahma, the Supreme Being. The book was written between 200 BC and 200 AD. One of the sage pieces of advices from Manusmriti states: "Wound not others, do not injury by thought, or deed, utter no word to pain the fellow creatures. He who habitually salutes and constantly pays reverence to the aged obtains an increase of four things: length of life, knowledge, fame, and strength ....Depend not on another, but lean instead on thyself. True happiness is born of self-reliance.... By falsehood a sacrifice becomes vain; by self-complacency the reward for austerities is lost; by boasting the goodness of an offering it is brought to naught."

HOLY WALL:
THE AGAMAS – JAIN SCRIPTURE

According to Jainism, an early religion of India, godhood is not a monopoly of a Supreme Being. Rather, all souls, when liberated with knowledge and good conduct, can achieve self-realization and attain this state of godhood. Liberation of the soul from the transmigratory cycle of birth and death is the ultimate goal of Jainism.

The Jain scriptures reject God as the creator of universe. Acharya Hemacandra (1089-1172) puts forth the Jain view of universe in *Yogasastra* as thus –

"This universe is not created nor sustained by anyone;

It is self-sustaining, without any base or support"

Agamas are canonical texts of Jainism and consists of fortyfive texts. Two of the most sacred texts are Akaranga Sutra and Sutrakrtanga Sutra.

MESSAGES FROM AGAMAS

"Those who praise their own doctrines and disparage the doctrines of others do not solve any problem."

– Sutrakrtanga 1.1.50

"The creatures attain only a temporary residence (in one of the four states of being); hearing this supreme truth (i.e. the doctrine of the Tîrthankara's) one should meditate upon it. The wise man should free himself from the family bonds; fearless should he give up acts and attachments.

A mendicant, living thus, self-controlled towards the eternal (world of living beings), the matchless sage, who collects his alms, is insulted with words by the people assailing him, like an elephant in battle with arrows.

Despised by such-like people, the wise man, with undisturbed mind, sustains their words and blows, as a rock is not shaken by the wind. Disregarding (all calamities) he lives together with clever (monks, insensible) to pain and pleasure, not hurting the movable and immovable (beings), not killing, bearing all: so is described the great sage, a good Sramana.

As the lustre of a burning flame increases, so increase the austerity, wisdom, and glory of a steadfast sage who, with vanquished desires, meditates on the supreme place of virtue, though suffering pain.

The great vows which are called the place of peace, the great teachers, and the producers of disinterestedness have, in all quarters of the earth, been proclaimed by the infinite Gina, the knowing one as light, illumining the three worlds, (repels) darkness.

The unbound one, living amongst the bound (i.e. householders), should lead the life of a mendicant; unattached to women, he should speak with reverence. Not desiring this or the next world, the learned one is not measured by the qualities of love.

EVOLUTION OF GOD

The God of Jainism is a set of high morals, not a creator, protector, or destroyer God.

The dirt (of sins) formerly committed by a thus liberated mendicant who walks in wisdom (and restraint), who is constant, and bears pain, vanishes as the dirt covering silver (is removed) by fire.

He lives, forsooth, in accordance with wisdom (and restraint), and walks free from desire, and with conquered sensuality. As a snake casts off its old skin, so is the Brâhmana freed from the bed of pain.

As they call the great ocean a boundless flood of water, difficult to traverse with the arms (alone), so should the learned one know (and renounce) it (the samsâra): that sage is called 'Maker of the end.'

Here amongst men bondage and deliverance have been declared; he who, according to that doctrine (of the church), knows bondage and deliverance: that sage is called 'Maker of the end.'

He for whom there is no bondage whatever in this world, and besides in the two (other continents, or heaven and hell), is indeed a (monk needing) no support and no standing place; he has quitted the path of births."

— AKARANGA SUTRA, 4TH PART, 16TH LECTURE
(TR. BY HERMANN JACOBI)

FIVE MAHAVRATAS (GREAT VOWS) OF JAINISM

Jainism does not have ten commandments or its equivalents, but it articulates five ethical principles for its adherents:

1. Non-violence (Ahimsa)—to cause no harm to living beings.
2. Truth (Satya)—to always speak the truth in a harmless manner.
3. Non-stealing (Asteya)—to not take anything that is not willingly given.
4. Celibacy (Brahmacarya)—to not indulge in sensual pleasures.
5. Non-possession (Aparigraha)—to detach from people, places, and material things.

HOLY WALL:
THE TRIPITAKA - BUDDHIST SCRIPTURE

Buddhism is a unique religion that does not talk about God or a Supreme Deity. It is a religion of mind and spirit, advocating inner purity, awareness of the present world, ethical conduct, love, and absence of hatred. Tripitaka (literal meaning: three baskets) is the formal term used to refer to a series of Buddhist canonical scriptures. It consists of three divisions: (1) Vinaya Pitaka; (2) Sutta Pitaka (including Dhammapada); and (3) Abhidhamma Pitaka, each containing a series of sutras (or guiding rules). The most famous of this collection is Dhammapada, which is part of Sutta Pitaka. Dhammapada is a versified Buddhist scripture originally spoken by Buddha himself, mostly dealing with ethics.

MESSAGES FROM TRIPITAKA

"All that we are is the result of what we have thought: it is founded on our thoughts, it is made up of our thoughts. If a man speaks or acts with an evil thought, pain follows him, as the wheel follows the foot of the ox that draws the carriage.

All that we are is the result of what we have thought: it is founded on our thoughts, it is made up of our thoughts. If a man speaks or acts with a pure thought, happiness follows him, like a shadow that never leaves him."

— Dhammapada, Chapter 1, Verses 1 And 2.
(Tr. By F. Max Muller)

"For hatred does not cease by hatred at any time: hatred ceases by love, this is an old rule.

The world does not know that we must all come to an end here;--but those who know it, their quarrels cease at once."

— Dhammapada, Chapter 1, Verses 5 And 6.
(Tr. By F. Max Muller)

"Earnestness is the path of immortality (Nirvâna), thoughtlessness the path of death. Those who are in earnest do not die, those who are thoughtless are as if dead already. Those who are advanced in earnestness, having understood this clearly, delight in earnestness, and rejoice in the knowledge of the Ariyas (the elect). These wise people, meditative, steady, always possessed of strong powers, attain to Nirvâna, the highest happiness."

— DHAMMAPADA, CHAPTER 2, VERSES 21-23.
(TR. BY F. MAX MULLER)

"Not to commit any sin, to do good, and to purify one's mind, that is the teaching of (all) the Awakened."

— DHAMMAPADA, CHAPTER 14, VERSE 183.
(TR. BY F. MAX MULLER)

"To be attached to a certain view and to look down upon others' views as inferior--this the wise men call a fetter."

— SUTTA PITAKA, SUTTA NIPATA 798
(TR. BY V. FAUSBOLL)

THE EIGHTFOLD PATH OF BUDDHISM

Buddha taught that one can end one's suffering and rise to the stage of self-awakening by practicing the noble eightfold path, shown below:

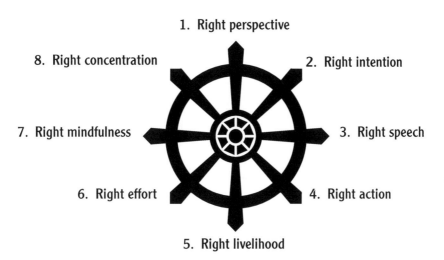

1. Right perspective
8. Right concentration
2. Right intention
7. Right mindfulness
3. Right speech
6. Right effort
4. Right action
5. Right livelihood

THE TEN PRECEPTS (DASA SILA) OF BUDDHISM

Buddhism does not have ten commandments, but it has ten recommendations for its followers. The first five precepts (pancha sila) are for general people who are just interested in living a moral life, the first eight precepts are for those who want to live an ascetic life, and all ten precepts are for those who want to become monks.

TEN PRECEPTS OF BUDDHISM

1. Refrain from killing living things.
2. Refrain from stealing.
3. Refrain from un-chastity (sensuality, sexuality, lust).
4. Refrain from lying.
5. Refrain from taking intoxicants.
6. Refrain from taking food at inappropriate times (after noon).
7. Refrain from singing, dancing, playing music or attending entertainment programs (performances).
8. Refrain from wearing perfume, cosmetics and garland (decorative accessories).
9. Refrain from sitting on high chairs and sleeping on luxurious, soft beds.
10. Refrain from accepting money.

HOLY WALL:
TAO TE CHING – TAOISM SCRIPTURE

Taoism (pronounced Daoism) is a religious/philosophical system of ancient China that developed over a period of centuries from the 6th century BC to 4th century BC. The founder of Taoism is Lao Tzu (or Lao Zi in Chinese), who is said to have lived in the 6th Century BC and was an older contemporary of Confucius. Tao literally means the "path" or the "way", and sometimes it is translated to mean "God" or "The Ultimate Reality." The fundamental philosophy of Taoism is based on three principles: compassion, moderation, and humility. Taoists believe that humans are part of the nature and must seek the harmony with the nature through its actions.

Tao Te Ching is regarded as the defining book of Taoism is thought to have been written by Lao Tzu. The title literally means "The Classic of the Way and Its Power or Virtue." Tao Te Ching is widely translated in Western languages. It consists of 81 short chapters (or poems). The poems are mystical and can be interpreted in a variety of ways. The very first line of Tao Te Ching teaches us that often we speak about things that we are not completely aware of. This can be interpreted to say that when we speak about a "God", we may not be speaking about the true God, but "our personal view of God."

EVOLUTION OF GOD

The God of Taoism is an impersonal mysterious entity.

MESSAGES FROM TAO TE CHING

"The Tao that can be told
is not the eternal Tao
The name that can be named
is not the eternal Name.

The unnamable is the eternally real.
Naming is the origin
of all particular things.

Free from desire, you realize the mystery.
Caught in desire, you see only the manifestations.

Yet mystery and manifestations
arise from the same source.
This source is called darkness.

Darkness within darkness.
The gateway to all understanding."

[TAO TE CHING 1, TR. BY STEPHEN MITCHELL]

"Before the universe was born
there was something in the chaos of the heavens.
It stands alone and empty,
solitary and unchanging.
It is ever present and secure.
It may be regarded as the Mother of the universe.
Because I do not know its name,

I call it the Tao.
If forced to give it a name,
I would call it 'Great'.

Because it is Great means it is everywhere.
Being everywhere means it is eternal.
Being eternal means everything returns to it.
Tao is great.
Heaven is great.
Earth is great.
Humanity is great.
Within the universe, these are the four great things.

Humanity follows the earth.
Earth follows Heaven.
Heaven follows the Tao.
The Tao follows only itself."

[TAO TE CHING 25, TR. BY J. H. MCDONALD]

"Since before time and space were,
the Tao is.
It is beyond is and is not.
How do I know this is true?
I look inside myself and see."

[TAO TE CHING 21, TR. BY STEPHEN MITCHELL]

HOLY WALL:
I CHING AND LUNYU – CONFUCIANISM SCRIPTURE

Confucianism is an ethical/philosophical system of ancient China that later became one of the folk religions of China along with Taoism. The belief system of Confucianism is built upon the improvement of human conditions in the society and in the government. It is more of an ethical system than a religious one. In Confucianism, there is no God to placate; the virtues are to be attained by humans for their own self elevation.

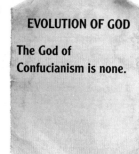

EVOLUTION OF GOD

The God of Confucianism is none.

The five virtues of Confucianism are: (1) Ren (Humaneness); (2) Yi (Righteousness or Justice); (3) Li (Propriety or Etiquette); (4) Zhi (Knowledge); and (5) Xin (Integrity). The ethical system of Confucius later influenced European and Islamic Renaissance. French author and philosopher Voltaire once said of Confucius: "He has no interest in falsehood; he did not pretend to be prophet; he claimed no inspiration; he taught no new religion; he used no delusions; flattered not the emperor under whom he lived."

The canonical scriptures of Confucianism are Five Classics and Four Books. The Five Classics are five ancient Chinese classic books which Confucius studied and interpreted to arrive at his teachings. Those are: (1) Classic of Poetry; (2) Classic of History; (3) Classic of Rites; (4) Classic of Changes (also known as I Ching or Book of Changes); and (5) Spring and Autumn Annals. The Four Books of Confucianism are as follows: (1) Great Learning; (2) Doctrine of the Mean; (3) The Analects (a collection of aphorisms by Confucius himself); and (4) Mencius.

MESSAGES FROM I CHING

"Creativity comes from awakening and directing men's higher natures, which originate in the primal depths of the universe and are appointed by Heaven."

— [I CHING]

"One should act in consonance with the way of heaven and earth, which is enduring and eternal. The superior man perseveres long in his course, adapts to the times, but remains firm in his direction and correct in his goals."

— [I CHING]

"Water everywhere over the earth flows to join together. A single natural law controls it. Each human is a member of a community and should work within it."

— [I CHING]

MESSAGES FROM LUN YU (ANALECTS)

"The Superior Man is all-embracing and not partial. The inferior man is partial and not all-embracing."

— [ANALECTS, CHAPTER II]

"To study and not think is a waste. To think and not study is dangerous."

— [ANALECTS, CHAPTER II]

"When you meet someone better than yourself, turn your thoughts to becoming his equal. When you meet someone not as good as you are, look within and examine your own self."

— [ANALECTS, CHAPTER IV]

WALL OF MORTALS:
(1000 BC TO 1 AD)

GOD WITHIN US

Human expressions on God during the period from 1000 BC to 1 AD demonstrate outstanding courage, as poets and philosophers spoke their minds without reservation. Rational human thought emerged for the first time in human history as the earliest philosophers were trying to understand the nature of things by the use of reason.

"Wealth should not be seized, but the god-given is much better."

— HESIOD (8TH CENTURY BC)
[Greek didactic poet]

"Hail, children of Zeus! Grant lovely song and celebrate the holy race of the deathless gods who are forever, those that were born of Earth and starry Heaven and gloomy Night and them that briny Sea did rear."

— HESIOD (8TH CENTURY BC)

"Whoever obeys the gods, to him they particularly listen."

— HOMER (8TH CENTURY BC)
[Greek epic poet, author of The Iliad and The Odyssey]

"The gods, likening themselves to all kinds of strangers, go in various disguises from city to city, observing the wrongdoing and the righteousness of men."

— HOMER (8TH CENTURY BC)

"All men have need of the gods."

— HOMER (8TH CENTURY BC)

"I strengthen your life like your mother who brought you into being; the sixty great gods stand with me and protect you."

— KING ESARHADDON (7TH CENTURY BC)
[King of Assyria and reigned from 681 BC – 669 BC]

"Nothing is more ancient than God, for He was never created; nothing more beautiful than the world, it is the work of that same God; nothing more active than thought, for it flies over the whole universe; nothing stronger than necessity, for all must submit to it."

—THALES OF MILETUS (640 BC- 546 BC)
[Pre-Socratic Greek philosopher, considered by Aristotle as the 1st philosopher in the Greek tradition, one of the seven sages of Greece]

"The gods help them that help themselves."

— AESOP (620 BC-560 BC)
[Fable writer, birthplace unknown]

GODS OF ANCIENT GREECE

Ancient Greece is considered the birthplace of rational human thought, and occupies a unique place in history for its remarkable contributions to philosophy, mathematics, and science. Ancient Greeks believed in many gods. Indeed, their belief was so strong that they sentenced Socrates, the most revered Greek ever to have lived, to death for not believing in their gods.

The gods of ancient Greece lived on Mount Olympus, an imaginary mountain that rose from the center of the Earth far into the Heavens. There were twelve Olympian gods, headed by the chief god, Zeus; the most famous of the remaining gods were Poseidon, Apollo, Hades, and Aphrodite.

EVOLUTION OF GOD

Gods of ancient Greece exhibit jealousy, subterfuge, trickery, malice, vengeance, and warfare.

The origins of the gods of ancient Greece were beautifully described by Hesiod (eighth century BC) in his famous poem, Theogony (meaning Birth of the Gods). First there was Chaos, which arose spontaneously. Then came Gaia (earth), Tartarus (abyss), and Eros (love), the last being the fairest among the deathless gods. Then came the twelve Titan gods, who were subsequently defeated in a war by the Olympian gods, who ruled forever and were idolized in Greek mythology.

We receive a glimpse of the Greek Olympian gods through the works of the great poet Homer (eighth century BC). The gods depicted by Homer often puzzle and offend modern readers because of their seeming lack of morals and their constant interference in human lives, as captured in Homer's Iliad. These gods exhibit emotions and behaviors similar to humans', such as jealousy, subterfuge, trickery, malice, and warfare. Humans are merely the puppets of these playful and self-absorbed deities, and the tragedies of human warfare are nothing but the result of divine will:

> "Sing, Goddess, sing of the rage of Achilles, son of Peleus—
> that murderous anger which condemned Achaeans
> to countless agonies, threw many warrior souls
> deep into Hades, leaving their dead bodies
> carrion food for dogs and birds—
> all in fulfillment of the will of Zeus."
>
> — (ILIAD, HOMER, TR. IAN JOHNSTON)

The gods of ancient Greece were also vengeful, as depicted by Homer:

> "That god was Apollo, son of Zeus and Leto.

Angry with Agamemnon, he cast plague down
onto the troops—deadly infectious evil.
For Agamemnon had dishonored the god's priest."

— (ILIAD, HOMER, TR. IAN JOHNSTON)

The Olympian gods were so involved with humans in their warfare and day-to-day lives that the Greek hero of the Trojan war, Achilles, wished:

"ye gracious powers above!
Wrath and revenge from men and gods remove:
Far, far too dear to every mortal breast,
Sweet to the soul, as honey to the taste:
Gathering like vapours of a noxious kind
From fiery blood, and darkening all the mind."

— (ILIAD, HOMER, TR. ALEXANDER POPE)

COFFEE BREAK
The Greek Influence: Pythagoras was the first among humans to advance the idea that the material universe can be fully expressed in terms of mathematics. Xenophanes, who came before Socrates, expressed that all our knowledge is our own creation and contains a *"woven web of guesses."* Xenophanes is also raised the question whether God created man in his image or the other way around.

"Truth is so great a perfection, that if God would render himself visible to men, he would choose light for his body and truth for his soul."

-PYTHAGORAS (582 BC - 507 BC)
[Greek mathematician, philosopher, and scientist]

"If horses had Gods, they would look like horses."

-XENOPHANES (570 BC - 470 BC)
[Greek philosopher, poet, and social and religious critic]

"The Ethiops say that their gods
are flat-nosed and black.
While the Thracians say that theirs
have blue eyes and red hair.
Yet if cattle or horses or lions
had hands and could draw
And could sculpture like men,
then the horses would draw their gods
Like horses, and cattle like cattle,

and each would then shape
Bodies of gods in the likeness,
each kind, of its own."

— XENOPHANES (570 BC - 470 BC)

"If you don't see God in the next person you meet, look no further."

— BUDDHA (563 BC - 483 BC)
[Indian philosopher, founder of Buddhism]

"Let a man overcome anger by love, let him overcome evil by good; let him overcome the greedy by liberality, the liar by truth! Speak the truth, do not yield to anger; give, if thou art asked for little; by these three steps thou wilt go near the gods."

— BUDDHA (563 BC - 483 BC)

"Our headstrong passions shut the door of our souls against God."

— CONFUCIUS (551 BC - 479 BC)
[Kong Fu-zi in Chinese, ancient Chinese philosopher, founder of Confucianism]

"Zilu asked how to serve the spirits and gods. The Master said: You are not yet able to serve men, how could you serve the spirits?" Zilu said: "May I ask you about death?" The Master said: "You do not yet know life, how could you know death?""

— CONFUCIUS (551 BC - 479 BC)

"There was something undifferentiated and yet complete,
Which existed before heaven and earth.
Soundless and formless, it depends on nothing and does not change.
It operates everywhere and is free from danger.
It may be considered the mother of the universe.
I do not know its name; I call it Tao.
If forced to give it a name, I shall call it Great.
Now being great means functioning everywhere.
Functioning everywhere means far-reaching.
Being far-reaching means returning to the original point."

— LAO TZE (6TH CENTURY BC)
[Lao Zi in Chinese; ancient Chinese philosopher, author of Tao Te Ching, Tr. By Lionel Giles]

"God is day and night, winter and summer, war and peace, surfeit and hunger."

— HERACLITUS (540 BC - 475 BC)
[Greek philosopher]

"An Act of God was defined as something which no reasonable man could have expected."

— Heraclitus (540 BC - 475 BC)

"This universe, which is the same for all, has not been made by any god or man, but it always has been, is, and will be an ever-living fire, kindling itself by regular measures and going out by regular measures."

— Heraclitus (540 BC - 475 BC)

"How can those who scorn God revere men?"

— Sun Tzu (6Th Century BC)
[Chinese general and strategist, author of "Art of War"]

"On him who wields power gently, the god looks favorably from afar."

— Aeschylus (525 BC - 456 BC)
[First of the three ancient Greek tragedians, whose work has survived, regarded as the father of tragedy]

"To be free from evil thoughts is God's best gift."

— Aeschylus (525 BC - 456 BC)

"Success is man's god."

— Aeschylus (525 BC -456 BC)

"In our sleep, pain that cannot forget falls drop by drop upon the heart and in our own despair, against our will, comes wisdom through the awful grace of God."

— Aeschylus (525 BC - 456 BC)
[Quoted by Robert F. Kennedy, delivering an extemporaneous eulogy to Martin Luther King, Jr., the evening of April 4, 1968, in Indianapolis, Indiana. These words, lacking "own", have been used as one of the inscriptions at the Robert F. Kennedy gravesite in Arlington National Cemetery]

"Born of God, attach thyself to Him, as a plant is to root, that ye may not be withered."

— Demophilus (Died 480 BC)
[Greek general of Thespiae, who led the battle of Thermopylae in 480 BC]

"God is a circle whose centre is everywhere and circumference nowhere."

—Timaeus Of Locri (5Th Century BC)
[(Latin: Timaeus Locrus) Greek Pythagorean philosopher]

COFFEE BREAK

The First Atheist: Pre-Socratic Greek poet and sophist Diagoras of Melos (fifth century BC) is regarded as the first atheist, although the proposition that there may not be any creator God flourished in India in the sixth century BC or earlier through the propagation of Jainism, Buddhism, and some variants of Hinduism.

The Roman philosopher Cicero related the following story about Diagoras. Once a friend said to Diagoras, "You think the gods have no care for man? Why, you can see from all these votive pictures here how many people have escaped the fury of storms at sea by praying to the gods who have brought them safe to harbor." Diagoras replied, "Yes, indeed, but where are the pictures of all those who suffered shipwreck and perished in the waves?" The government of Athens charged him with impiety and offered rewards for his capture. He fled Athens and went to Corinth, where he died.

"God's dice always have a lucky roll."

— SOPHOCLES (497 BC-406/5 BC)
[Ancient greek tragedian famous for his work "Oedipus" and "Antigone"]

"There is no happiness where there is no wisdom; No wisdom but in submission to the gods."

— SOPHOCLES (497 BC-406/5 BC)

"Friends who inhabit the mighty town by tawny Acragas
which crowns the citadel, caring for good deeds,
greetings; I, an immortal God, no longer mortal,
wander among you, honoured by all,
adorned with holy diadems and blooming garlands.
To whatever illustrious towns I go,
I am praised by men and women, and accompanied
by thousands, who thirst for deliverance,
some ask for prophecies, and some entreat,
for remedies against all kinds of disease."

— EMPEDOCLES (490 BC–430 BC)
[Greek pre-Socratic philosopher, known as the originator of cosmogenic theory of four Classical elements]

"Blessed is he who has acquired a wealth of divine wisdom, but miserable he in whom there rests a dim opinion concerning the gods."

— EMPEDOCLES (490 BC–430 BC)

COFFEE BREAK

The First Book Burning: In Athens, Protagoras was charged with impiety and atheism, and the authorities publicly burned his book *On the Gods* in the fifth-century BC. Protagoras was famous for his statement: "Man is the measure of all things: of things which are, that they are, and of things which are not, that they are not." He fled Athens to avoid persecution and died from drowning on his way to Sicily. This intolerant ritual of book burning to suppress dissenting views continues to this day in developed and developing nations alike.

"Concerning the gods, I have no means of knowing whether they exist or not or of what sort they may be, because of the obscurity of the subject, and the brevity of human life."

— PROTAGORAS (490 BC-420 BC)
[Pre-Socratic Greek philosopher]

"He was a wise man who originated the idea of God."

— EURIPIDES (484 BC - 406 BC)
[Third of the ancient Greek tragedians who work has survived, famous for reshaping the structure of Greek tragedy]

"I think,
Some shrewd man first, a man in judgment wise,
Found for mortals the fear of gods,
Thereby to frighten the wicked should they
Even act or speak or scheme in secret."

— EURIPIDES (484 BC - 406 BC)

"Doth someone say that there be gods above? There are not; no, there are not. Let no fool, led by the old false fable, thus deceive you."

— EURIPIDES (480 BC - 406 BC)

"Try thyself first, and after call in God. For to the worker God himself lends aid."

— EURIPIDES (484 BC - 406 BC)

"God does not suffer presumption in anyone but himself."

— HERODOTUS (484 BC-424 BC)
[Greek historian, "Father of History"]

COFFEE BREAK

Birth of Western Philosophy: Socrates, Plato, and Aristotle made Greece the birthplace of Western philosophy. Socrates taught people to question everything, including the authority of the gods of the city. He believed that human virtue does not come from the edicts of the gods, but from human knowledge and under-standing of what is right and what is wrong.

"I pray Thee, O God, that I may be beautiful within."

— SOCRATES (469 BC - 399 BC)

[Greek philosopher, credited as the founder of Western philosophy, originator of the Socratic method of teaching, executed for speaking against Gods of that time]

"I am called wise, for my hearers always imagine that I myself possess wisdom which I find wanting in others: but the truth is, O men of Athens, that God only is wise; and in this oracle he means to say that the wisdom of men is little or nothing... as if he said, He, O men, is the wisest, who like Socrates, knows that his wisdom is in truth worth nothing."

— SOCRATES (469 BC - 399 BC)

"He who is a philosopher or lover of learning, and is entirely pure at departing, is alone permitted to reach the gods."

— SOCRATES (469 BC - 399 BC)

"The fewer our wants, the nearer we resemble the gods."

— SOCRATES (469 BC - 399 BC)

"Nothing exists except atoms and empty space; everything else is opinion."

— DEMOCRITUS OF ABDERA (460 BC - 370 BC)

[Greek philosopher, credited with the atomic theory of cosmos with his mentor Leucippus.]

"This only is denied to God: the power to undo the past."

— AGATHON (448 BC - 400 BC)

[Greek tragic poet]

"God is truth and light his shadow."

— PLATO (427 BC-347 BC)

[Greek philosopher, mathematician, student of Socrates, teacher of Aristotle, founder of the Academy of Athens]

"God is a geometrician."

— PLATO (427 BC-347 BC)

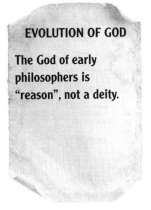

EVOLUTION OF GOD

The God of early philosophers is "reason", not a deity.

"If there exists a good and wise God, then there also exists a progress of men towards perfection; and if there be no progress of men towards perfection, then there cannot be a good and wise God. We cannot suppose that God's moral government, the beginnings of which we see in the world and in ourselves, will cease when we leave this life."

— PLATO (427 BC-347 BC)

"God is not the author of all things, but of good only."

— PLATO (427 BC-347 BC)

"Still I hear a voice saying that the gods cannot be deceived, neither can they be compelled. But what if there are no gods? or, suppose them to have no care of human things."

— PLATO (427 BC-347 BC)

"Men create gods after their own image, not only with regard to their form but with regard to their mode of life."

— ARISTOTLE (384 BC-322 BC)

[Greek philosopher and disciple of Plato; teacher of Alexander the Great. Author of many subjects, including physics, metaphysics, poetry, theater, music, logic, rhetoric, politics, government, ethics, biology, and zoology.]

"The gods too are fond of a joke."

— ARISTOTLE (384 BC-322 BC)

"God and nature do nothing in vain."

— ARISTOTLE (384 BC-322 BC)

"Life also belongs to God for the actuality of thought is life, and God is that actuality; and God's self-dependent actuality is life most good and eternal."

— ARISTOTLE (384 BC-322 BC)

"A tyrant must put on the appearance of uncommon devotion to religion. Subjects are less apprehensive of illegal treatment from a ruler whom they consider god-fearing and pious. On the other hand, they do less easily move against him, believing that he has the gods on his side."

— ARISTOTLE (384 BC-322 BC)

"Beauty is the gift of God."

— ARISTOTLE (384 BC-322 BC)

"God is a principle which exists by virtue of its own intrinsicality, and operates spontaneously without self-manifestation... The ultimate end is God. He is manifested in the laws of nature. He is the hidden spring. At the beginning of all things, He was."

— CHUANG TZU (4TH CENTURY BC)

[Zhuangzi in Chinese, an influential Chinese philosopher]

"By exerting his mental powers to the full, man comes to understand his own nature. When he understands his own nature, he understands God."

— MENCIUS (372 BC- 289 BC)

[Meng Zi in Chinese; ancient Chinese philosopher, made major contributions to the humanism of Confucian thought, author of one of the four books of Confucianism]

"Lakshmi, the Goddess of wealth, comes of Her own accord where fools are not respected, grain is well stored up, and the husband and wife do not quarrel."

— CHANAKYA (350 BC-283 BC)

[Adviser and prime minister of the first Maurya Emperor Chandragupta of India]

"Almighty God, Thou who art impartial,
And dost appoint the virtuous among men as Thy Assistants."

— CHU YUAN (332 BC- 295 BC)

[One of the greatest Chinese poets, who drowned himself in despair. His death is commemorated each year on the fifth day of the fifth moon by dragon boat races]

"Is God willing to prevent evil, but not able?

Then he is not omnipotent.

Is he able, but not willing?

Then he is malevolent.

Is he both able and willing?

Then whence cometh evil?

Is he neither able nor willing? Then why call him God?"

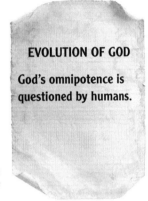

EVOLUTION OF GOD

God's omnipotence is questioned by humans.

— EPICURUS (341 BC- 270 BC)

[Greek philosopher, founder of Epicureanism]

"If the gods listened to the prayers of men, all men would quickly have perished: for they are always praying for evil against one another."

— EPICURUS (341 BC- 270 BC)

"A strict belief in fate is the worst kind of slavery; on the other hand, there is comfort in the thought that God will be moved by our prayers."

— EPICURUS (341 BC- 270 BC)

COFFEE BREAK

First Edict on Religious Tolerance: The Indian King, Ashoka The Great, was the first monarch to issue an official edict on religious tolerance.

"Beloved-of-the-Gods, King Piyadasi, honors both ascetics and the householders of all religions, and he honors them with gifts and honors of various kinds.But Beloved-of-the-Gods, King Piyadasi, does not value gifts and honors as much as he values this

-- that there should be growth in the essentials of all religions. Growth in essentials can be done in different ways, but all of them have as their root restraint in speech, that is, not praising one's own religion, or condemning the religion of others without good cause. And if there is cause for criticism, it should be done in a mild way. But it is better to honor other religions for this reason. By so doing, one's own religion benefits, and so do other religions, while doing otherwise harms one's own religion and the religions of others. Whoever praises his own religion, due to excessive devotion, and condemns others with the thought "Let me glorify my own religion," only harms his own religion. Therefore contact (between religions) is good. One should listen to and respect the doctrines professed by others. Beloved-of-the-Gods, King Piyadasi, desires that all should be well-learned in the good doctrines of other religions."

— ASHOKA THE GREAT (304 BC-232 BC)
[Also known as Piyadasi, ruled as the Emperor of the most of south Asia. This is an edict of King Ashoka]

"There is indeed a God that hears and sees whate'er we do."

— PLAUTUS (254 BC – 184 BC)
[Roman playwright]

"Live with men as if God saw you, and talk to God as if men were listening."

— ATHENODORUS (3RD CENTURY BC)
[Greek stoic philosopher and disciple of Zeno]

"The perfect love of God knoweth no difference between the poor and the rich."

— MARCUS PACUVIUS (220 BC - 130 BC)
[Roman tragic poet]

"Fear created the first gods in the world."

— CAECILIUS STATIUS (220 BC-168 BC)
[Roman comic poet]

"There is nothing which God cannot do."

— CICERO (106 BC – 43 BC)
[Roman philosopher, statesman, lawyer, political theorist, and constitutionalist]

"There are many questions in philosophy to which no satisfactory answer has yet been given. But the question of the nature of the gods is the darkest and most difficult of all…. So various and so contradictory are the opinions of the most learned men on this matter as to persuade one of the truth of the saying that philosophy is the child of ignorance."

— CICERO (106 BC – 43 BC)

"Next to God we are nothing."

— CICERO (106 BC – 43 BC)

"For all the gods must of themselves enjoy
Immortal aeons and supreme repose,
Withdrawn from our affairs, detached, afar:
Immune from peril and immune from pain,

Themselves abounding in riches of their own,

Needing not us, they are not touched by wrath

They are not taken by service or by gift.

Truly is earth insensate for all time."

-LUCRETIUS (99 BC – 55 BC)

[Roman poet and philosopher, best known for "On the Nature of Things", Tr. by William Leonard]

"Each person makes their own terrible passion their God."

—VIRGIL (70 BC – 19 BC)

[Roman classical poet, best known for Aeneid]

"God can change the lowest to the highest, abase the proud, and raise the humble."

– HORACE (65 BC – 8 BC)

[Leading Roman lyric poet during the time of Augustus]

"There is a god within us."

– OVID (43 BC–AD 17 OR 18)

[Born as Publius Ovidius Naso, Roman poet]

"The myths about Hades and the gods, though they are pure invention, help to make men virtuous."

– DIODORUS SICULUS (1ST CENTURY BC)

[Greek historian]

COFFEE BREAK

Son of God: The sayings of Jesus Christ, the prophet of Christianity, are recorded in the New Testament. Jesus is one of the most influential men in the history of mankind. Christians believe that he is the son of God.

"Blessed are the pure in heart, for they will see God.

Blessed are the peacemakers, for they will be called sons of God."

– JESUS CHRIST (5 BC-30 AD)

[Key figure of Christianity, philosopher, religious teacher, martyr, revered by Christians as the Son of God, recognized by Muslims as "Isa", a prophet of God]

"It is easier for a camel to go through the eye of a needle, than for a rich man to enter into the kingdom of God."

– JESUS CHRIST (5 BC-30 AD)

"Let the little children come to me, and do not hinder them, for the kingdom of God belongs to such as these. I tell you the truth, anyone who will not receive the kingdom of God like a little child will never enter it."

– JESUS CHRIST (5 BC-30 AD)

"Thou shalt love the Lord thy God with all thy heart, and with all thy soul, and with all thy mind. This is the first and great commandment. And the second is like unto it, thou shalt love thy neighbour as thyself. On these two commandments hang all the law and the prophets."

— JESUS CHRIST (5 BC-30 AD)

"You cannot serve God and materialism. ...For what is highly esteemed by humanity is an abomination in the sight of God."

— JESUS CHRIST (5 BC-30 AD)

"Do not let your heart be troubled, trust God."

— JESUS CHRIST (5 BC-30 AD)

"The Kingdom of God cometh not with observation; neither shall they say, Lo here or, lo there! for behold, the Kingdom of God is within you."

— JESUS CHRIST (5 BC-30 AD)

COFFEE BREAK

Seneca and Nero: Seneca was a Roman stoic philosopher, and the advisor to Emperor Nero, who was accused of starting the Great Fire of Rome to clear land for his planned palatial complex. Seneca was ordered to kill himself after he was accused of conspiring to kill Nero.

"God is the universal substance in existing things. He comprises all things. He is the fountain of all being. In Him exists everything that is."

— SENECA (4 BC-65 AD)
[Born as Lucius Annaeus Seneca, Roman philosopher, statesman, dramatist, and humorist]

"Call it Nature, Fate, Fortune; all these are names of the one and selfsame God."

— SENECA (4 BC-65 AD)

"God is not to be worshipped with sacrifices and blood; for what pleasure can He have in the slaughter of the innocent? but with a pure mind, a food and honest purpose. Temples are not to be built for Him with stones piled on high; God is to be consecrated in the breast of each."

— SENECA (4 BC-65 AD)

"In every good man a God doth dwell."

— SENECA (4 BC-65 AD))

CHAPTER DIGEST (1000 BC TO 1 AD)

God became a life-coach, as several ideologies on how to live worthily and morally emerged. Postings on the *Holy Wall* of God's Facebook far outnumbered the postings on the *Wall of Mortals*.

In Hinduism, the Upanishads talked about a universal God, who reappeared in Muslim Sufi literature more than a thousand years later. Hinduism also laid out four ways to be unified with God: *karma, bhakti, raja, and jnana*. The wisdom of the Gita, the most sacred Hindu scripture, is timeless, and almost a billion humans draw inspiration from it today.

The Agamas, the holy scriptures of Jainism, didn't mention a Creator God; rather, they stated that everyone can become a god by attaining right perception, knowledge, and conduct. Jainism also formally asserted that all disparate religious doctrines are but complementary parts of a single whole. In this principle one can find the roots of religious pluralism in India.

Buddha came and taught how one can overcome the suffering that permeates human life. He did not talk about God at all, but men and women made him their God.

God posted more of his cryptic messages on the *Holy Wall* through the Tao Te Ching and I Ching, two of the most famous books of the ancient spiritual literature of China. Buddhism, Taoism, and Confucianism captured the imagination of the Chinese people, who number more than a billion today. Huston Smith, author of *The World's Religions*, once stated: "Traditionally, every Chinese was Confucian in ethics and public life, Taoist in private life and hygiene, and Buddhist at the time of death."

The *Wall of Mortals* of God's Facebook in this period of history was graced by the words of some of the greatest human minds ever to have lived on the planet Earth: Socrates, Plato, Aristotle, Ashoka, Lucretius, and Seneca. Socrates preferred to die rather than dishonestly declare allegiance to the common gods of Athens. His words and method of inquiry are still revered today.

God's soldiers burned the books of Protagoras on the grounds of blasphemy. The rise of logic and reason in the human psyche resulted in postings that attempted to reconcile the belief in traditional gods and the call of reason.

The human–God relationship in this period was characterized by a mixture of philosophy and both new and old religions. The variety of opinions about God during this period open a window into the minds of the earliest human intellectuals.

The Greek poet Diagoras of Melos, the first atheist, questioned the existence of God on the basis that evil exists. Socrates, Plato, and Aristotle taught humans how to think clearly and live a moral life on the basis of earthly principles instead of God-given rules. Two Chinese philosophers, Confucius and Lao Tze, also taught ways of moral and peaceful living without referring to Gods of the heavens.

The most popular postings on the *Wall of Mortals* in this period are those of Jesus Christ, whom 2.3 billion Christians all over the world revere as the Son of God.

The commonalities in the essence of both deistic and non-deistic philosophies provided an inclusive basis for a *Friendship of Civilizations*, where believers and non-believers can work together for world peace.

6

God Speaks
(1 to 1000 AD)

"I am God, and there is none like me."

—BIBLE: ISAIAH 46:9

"Verily, I am Allah. There is no god but I: So serve thou Me (only), and establish regular prayer for celebrating My praise."

—QURAN: SURA TA-HA, 20:14

STATUS UPDATE (1-1000 AD)

❖ God speaks to humans through the Bible and the Quran, the two scriptures that shape the ethico-religious lives of more than half the humans in today's world.

❖ The God of Christianity is a Trinity of the Father, the Son, and the Holy Spirit.

❖ The God of Islam is the one and only in what is a strictly monotheistic worldview.

❖ God's moral codes are preached by two great prophets, Jesus Christ and Muhammad.

❖ Rabbinic discussions on Jewish law, ethics, philosophy, and customs are recorded in the Talmud, a central text of Judaism.

❖ God-centric philosophy gains preeminence as Christian and Muslim philosophers attempt to understand and explain the world in the light of the Bible and the Quran. Al-Farabi, a philosopher of the Islamic Golden Age, is the first to separate theology (the study of God) and philosophy, and to profess the superiority of reason over religion.

❖ The Goddess appears with glory when Devi Mahatmya ("Glory of the Goddess") is composed around 400–500 AD in India. The gods and spirits of Japan express themselves in Shinto (Way of the Gods), the Japanese religion.

STATUS UPDATE (1-1000 AD)

❖ God continues to receive praise from poets, who remain awed by the beauty of nature and women.

❖ "Anal Haq, I am God!" cries out Muslim Sufi mystic Mansur Hallaj in an ecstatic state of the unity of the human soul and God. Hallaj is executed for apostasy.

NOTES FROM HISTORY
(1 TO 1000 AD)

God spoke directly to humans in the Bible and the Quran. The two major religions in today's world, Christianity and Islam, flourished during the first millennium. This was also a period of enormous growth in all aspects of human development.

The Roman Empire continued expanding, and conquered Britain under Emperor Claudius (10 BC to 54 AD). Jesus, a Jewish religious leader from Galilee, began his ministry in 26 AD. According to the New Testament, during the reign of Tiberius, Jesus was crucified in Jerusalem on the charge of blasphemy for claiming to be the Son of God. Christians believe that God raised Jesus from the dead three days later. Over the next few decades, his followers, including the apostle Paul, carried his message throughout the Greek-speaking regions of Asia Minor, eventually introducing it to Rome itself. On July 19, 64 AD, the first Roman mass persecution of Christians began with the Great Fire of Rome; this event also marked the earliest significant recognition of Christians in Rome.

Early in the second century, the Roman Empire saw its greatest expansion under Emperor Trajan (53–117 AD). Ptolemy (90–168 AD) compiled a catalogue of all stars visible to the naked eye. He also authored three very influential books, which would be of great importance to later Islamic and European science. These books are: *Almagest* ("Mathematical Treatise"), a treatise on astronomy; *Geography*, a compendium of the geographic knowledge of the Greco-Roman world; and *Quadripartitum*, a treatise on astrology.

In the third century, Mayan civilization entered its classical era. Diophantus of Alexandria (200–284 AD) wrote Arithmetica; Diophantine equations ("Diophantine geometry") were named after him. A primitive form of eyeglasses was developed for a nearsighted princess in Syria.

The early part of the fourth century was shaped by Constantine I (272–337 AD), who became the first Roman emperor to convert to Christianity. Saint Augustine, one of the outstanding philosophers between Aristotle and Aquinas, was born in 354 AD in the town of Hippo in North Africa. He fused Platonic philosophy with Christianity. As the Roman Empire was collapsing, Augustine developed the concept of the Church as the City of God, distinct from the early material world. His great book, *City of God*, talks about how an individual is a citizen of two different communities simultaneously; on the one hand is the city of God, which is eternal and based on true values, while on the other are the worldly, unstable kingdoms, which come and go and are based on false values.

In 381 AD, the First Council of Constantinople reaffirmed the Christian doctrine of the Trinity by adding it to the creed of Nicaea. In 476 AD, the Western Roman Empire came to an end when Romulus Augustus (461–488 AD) was forced to abdicate by the Germanic warlord Odoacer (433–493 AD).

For a thousand years after the fall of the Roman Empire, the Christian church carried the torch of civilization in Western Europe. As a result, ideas and philosophical writings were first scrutinized to determine their compatibility with Christian ideology before being published.

The Sassanid Empire in Persia reached the peak of its glory and power under Khosrau (b. 501 AD, ruled 531–579 AD). He built cities and opulent palaces as well as numerous roads and bridges.

Dionysius Exiguus created the Anno Domini (AD) system, inspired by the birth of Jesus, in 525 AD. This is the system upon which the Gregorian calendar and Common Era (CE) systems are based. *The Hekhalot Hymns* were composed by Jewish mystics around the fourth century. The *hekhalot* means "palaces", referring to the seven heavenly palaces a Jewish mystic must pass through in order to approach the Merkavah (the throne-chariot of God). Kalidasa, the great Sanskrit poet of India, composed his epic poem, *Meghaduta* ("Cloud Messenger").

Devi Mahatmyam or Devi Mahatmya ("Glory of the Goddess") was composed in 400–500 AD by sage (Rishi) Markandeya, describing the victory of the goddess Durga over the demon Mahishasura. It is part of the Markandeya Purana, one of the major Hindu religious texts. The Devi Mahatmyam unified pre-existing mother-goddess beliefs and defined divinity as a female principle, in contrast to females playing a subsidiary role as consorts to male deities. Today, Durga Puja ("Worship of Durga") is a widely celebrated Hindu festival in South Asia.

The Byzantine Emperor Justinian I (483–565 AD) issued between 529 and 534 AD a collection of Roman laws called the *Corpus Juris Civilis* or Body of Civil Law. This forms the ultimate basis of the civil law of most European jurisdictions today. The end of the rise of the Byzantine Empire came when an outbreak of bubonic plague during 541–542 AD killed, at its peak, 10,000 people every day in the capital city of Constantinople.

In 570 AD, Prophet Muhammad (Peace be upon him), the founder of Islam, was born in the holy city of Mecca, Saudi Arabia. In 610 AD, God started revealing the Quran to Prophet Muhammad, and this revelation continued till his death in 632 AD. Prophet Muhammad fled from Mecca to the city of Medina in 622 AD to avoid persecution in his birthplace for preaching Islam, which did not recognize the gods of polytheist Arabs. Soon after his arrival in Medina, he drafted the Constitution of Medina, which declared Muslims and Jews living in the city of Medina to be part of a single community (Ummah) of believers who would enjoy freedom to follow their respective religions ("The Jews have their religion and the Muslims have theirs"). This form of religious tolerance is not reflected in the current animosity between Muslims and Jews. Prophet Muhammad returned to Mecca victorious and established the Kaba, a rectangular building in Mecca, as the holiest Muslim shrine and the House of Allah. According to Muslim tradition, the Kaba was first built by the patriarch Abraham.

The Muslim conquests began after the death of Prophet Muhammad, and Islam expanded beyond the Arabian Peninsula, including into Armenia, Egypt, and North Africa. The Islamic conquest of Persia in the seventh century led to the downfall of the Sassanid Empire. The tide of Arab conquests came to an end in the middle of the eighth century.

Two scriptures of Shintoism, *Kojiki* ("Record of Ancient Mattes") and *Nihongi*

("Chronicles of Japan") were completed in 711–712 AD. Shintoism is the indigenous spirituality of Japan. As of 2011, there are about 120 million Shinto practitioners in Japan. *Shinto* means "The Way of the Gods", and it is a practice that connects present-day Japan with its ancient past.

The Islamic Golden Age began in the middle of the eighth century, when the Abbasid Caliphate ascended to power and moved the capital from Damascus, Syria to Baghdad, Iraq. Harun al-Rashid was the fifth and most famous Abbasid Caliph and ruled the Muslim empire from 786 to 809 AD. His time was marked by scientific, cultural, and religious prosperity; art and music also flourished significantly during his reign. He established the library Bayt al-Hikma ("House of Wisdom"). Many Muslim and non-Muslim scholars assembled in Baghdad and began to translate all the world's knowledge into Arabic. It was through this intellectual movement in the Arab world that people in the West came to know of the works of Plato and Aristotle.

Al-Khwarizmi (780–850 AD), a Persian mathematician, astronomer and geographer, in the House of Wisdom in Baghdad was the first to present the systematic solution of linear and quadratic equations. He is considered the founder of algebra, a credit he shares with Diophantus. The word "algorithm", widely used in today's computer science, stems

> *The computer "algorithm" was born in the eighth century.*

from Algoritmi, the Latin form of his name, which is also the origin of *guarismo* (Spanish) and *algarismo* (Portuguese), both meaning digit. Al-Kindi (801–873 AD), known in the West as Alkindus, was an Arab Iraqi polymath, instrumental in introducing Greek and Hellenistic philosophy to the Arab world. He was a pioneer in science, astrology, chemistry, cryptography, medicine, music theory, and physics.

Johannes Scotus Erigena, one of the most outstanding philosophers during the Dark Ages, was born in Ireland in 810 AD. He argued that since correct reasoning cannot lead to false conclusions, there can never be any conflict between reason and divine revelation. So, he attempted to establish rationally all the truths of the Christian faith.

In 859 AD, the Muslims established what the *Guinness Book of World Records* recognizes as the oldest degree-granting university in the world, the University of Al Karaouine, in Fez, Morocco.

The first known printed book, the *Diamond Sutra*, was printed in China using woodblock technology in 868 AD. In 953 AD, the fountain pen was invented by Al-Muizz Lideenillah of Egypt. Al-Azhar University was established in Cairo, Egypt in 975 AD; this is often considered the first full-fledged university to offer a variety of academic degrees, including post-graduate degrees.

Ibn Sina, commonly known in English by his Latinized name, Avicenna, was born in 980 AD. He was the foremost physician and philosopher of his time, as well as a polymath—an astronomer, chemist, geologist, logician, paleontologist, mathematician, physicist, poet, psychologist, scientist, and teacher. His most famous works are *The Book of Healing*, a vast philosophical and scientific encyclopedia, and *The Canon of Medicine*, which was a standard medical text at many medieval universities.

The tenth century is regarded as the low point in European history. In China it was a period of political upheaval. In the Muslim World, however, it was a cultural zenith, especially in Spain. This century also marked the zenith of the Byzantine and Bulgarian Empires.

HOLY WALL:
THE BIBLE – CHRISTIAN SCRIPTURE

The Bible, also called the Holy Bible, is the primary religious text of Christianity. The Bible as used by Christians consists of the Old Testament and the New Testament. Protestants and Catholics dispute the canonical composition of the Old Testament. Protestants consider all of the books of the Hebrew Bible (Tanakh—the Jewish scripture) to be canonical, while the Roman Catholics consider deuterocanonical books to be part of the Old Testament. The New Testament consists of the Gospels, The Acts of the Apostles, the Epistles, and the Book of Revelation. The New Testament relates the life and teachings of Jesus and was written after his death.

APOSTLES' CREED

The Apostles' Creed is statement of faith that summarizes the core beliefs of Christianity in 12 statements. The origin of this creed is traced to the 4th century though the exact wordings may not have been the same as that of the official Apostles' Creed currently codified in the *Catechism of the Catholic* Church published by the Vatican. The 12 Christian belief statements are:

APOSTLES' CREED

1. I believe in God, the Father almighty, creator of heaven and earth.

2. I believe in Jesus Christ, his only Son, our Lord.

3. He was conceived by the power of the Holy Spirit and born of the Virgin Mary.

4. He suffered under Pontius Pilate, was crucified, died, and was buried.

5. He descended to the dead. On the third day he rose again.

6. He ascended into heaven and is seated at the right hand of the Father.

7. He will come again to judge the living and the dead.

8. I believe in the Holy Spirit,

9. I believe in the holy Catholic Church,

10. I believe in the forgiveness of sins,

11. I believe in the resurrection of the body,

12. I believe in life everlasting.

THE FOUR PILLARS

The *Catechism of the Catholic Church* is divided into four parts, which are sometimes referred to as the four pillars of Christian faith. These parts are:

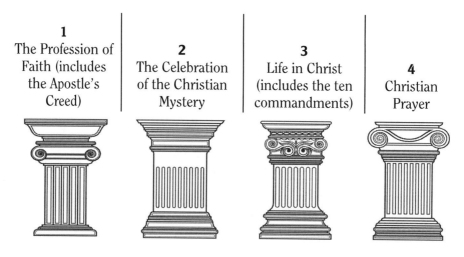

1
The Profession of Faith (includes the Apostle's Creed)

2
The Celebration of the Christian Mystery

3
Life in Christ (includes the ten commandments)

4
Christian Prayer

FOUR PILLARS OF CHRISTIAN FAITH

MESSAGES FROM BIBLE

"Beloved, follow not that which is evil, but that which is good. He that doeth good is of God: but he that doeth evil hath not seen God."

— Bible: 3 John, 1:11
(King James Bible (KJV), 1769 Edition)

"Blessed is the man that walketh not in the counsel of the ungodly, nor standeth in the way of sinners, nor sitteth in the seat of the scornful."

— Bible: Psalms 1:1 (King James Bible)

"So do not fear, for I am with you; do not be dismayed, for I am your God. I will strengthen you and help you; I will uphold you with my righteous right hand."

— Bible: Isaiah 41:10 (King James Bible)

"[Let your] conversation [be] without covetousness; [and be] content with such things as ye have: for he hath said, I will never leave thee, nor forsake thee. So that we may boldly say, The Lord [is] my helper, and I will not fear what man shall do unto me."

— Bible: Hebrews 13:5-6 (King James Bible)

"The kingdom of God is within you."

— Bible: Luke 17:21 (King James Bible)

"He that loveth not knoweth not God; for God is love."
— BIBLE: I JOHN 4:8 (KING JAMES BIBLE)

"With men this is impossible; but, with God all things are possible."
— BIBLE: MATTHEW 19:26 (KING JAMES BIBLE)

"And we know that God causes everything to work together for the good of those who love God and are called according to his purpose for them."
— BIBLE: ROMANS 8:28

"Wash you, make you clean; put away the evil of your doings from before mine eyes; cease to do evil;

Learn to do well; seek judgment, relieve the oppressed, judge the fatherless, plead for the widow."
— BIBLE: ISAIAH 1:16-17 (KING JAMES BIBLE)

"The fear of the LORD is the beginning of knowledge: but fools despise wisdom and instruction."
— BIBLE: PROVERBS 1:7 (KING JAMES BIBLE)

"Let us hear the conclusion of the whole matter: Fear God, and keep his commandments: for this is the whole duty of man. For God shall bring every work into judgment, with every secret thing, whether it be good, or whether it be evil."
— BIBLE: ECCLESIASTES 12:13-14 (KING JAMES BIBLE)

"Do not be anxious about anything, but in everything, by prayer and petition, with thanksgiving, present your requests to God. And the peace of God, which transcends all understanding, will guard your hearts and your minds in Christ Jesus."
— BIBLE: PHILIPPIANS 4:6-7

EVOLUTION OF GOD

The God of Christianity is a Trinity of the Father, the Son, and the Holy Spirit.

"For what can be known about God is plain to [all], because God has showed it to them. Ever since the creation of the world His invisible nature, namely, His eternal power and deity, has been clearly perceived in the things that have been made. So they are without excuse."
— BIBLE: ROMANS 1.19-20

"Be still in the presence of the Lord, and wait patiently for him to act. Don't worry about evil people who prosper or fret about their wicked schemes. Stop being angry! Turn from your rage! Do not lose your temper—it only leads to harm. For the wicked will be destroyed, but those who trust in the Lord will possess the land."
— BIBLE: PSALM 37:7-9

"Trust in the LORD with all your heart and lean not on your own understanding; in all your ways acknowledge Him, and He will make your paths straight."

— BIBLE: PROVERBS 3:5-6

"Husbands, love your wives, just as Christ loved the church and gave himself up for her."

— BIBLE: EPHESIANS 5:25

"Your inner self, the unfading beauty of a gentle, quiet spirit, is of great worth in God's eyes."

— BIBLE: 1 PETER 3:4

"If you love me, keep my commands."

— BIBLE: JOHN 14:15
[NEW INTERNATIONAL VERSION (NIV)]

"Love never fails. But whether there are prophecies, they will fail; whether there are tongues, they will cease; whether there is knowledge, it will vanish away. For we know in part and we prophesy in part. But when that which is perfect has come, then that which is in part will be done away. When I was a child, I spoke as a child, I understood as a child, I thought as a child; but when I became a man, I put away childish things. For now we see in a mirror, dimly, but then face to face. Now I know in part, but then I shall know just as I also am known.

And now abide faith, hope, love, these three; but the greatest of these is love."

— BIBLE: 1 CORINTHIANS 13:8-13

HOLY WALL:
THE QURAN - MUSLIM SCRIPTURE

The Quran, also called the Holy Quran, is the holy scripture of Islam. Muslims believe that the Quran is the word of God revealed to Prophet Muhammad through the angel Jibrail (Gabriel) over a period of 23 years (610–632 AD). Muslims also believe in the continuity of God's revelations with those of other earlier prophets (Adam, Noah, Abraham, Moses, and Jesus), regarding the Quran as the final revelation of God in the same line of revelations. The Quran was written down by the Prophet's companions during his lifetime and was later formalized into a single book by the third Caliph Uthman during his reign (644–656 AD).

The text of the Quran consists of 114 chapters or suras of varying length. The total number of verses in the Quran is slightly more than 6,200, with some controversy among Muslim scholars about the exact number. The Quran is regarded as a miracle of God and the best form of Arabic poetry. It describes itself as a book of guidance and emphasizes the moral lessons of its narratives, without necessarily giving specific details of an event.

FIVE PILLARS OF ISLAM

The five pillars of Islam are the five basic acts that every Muslim must follow. These are:

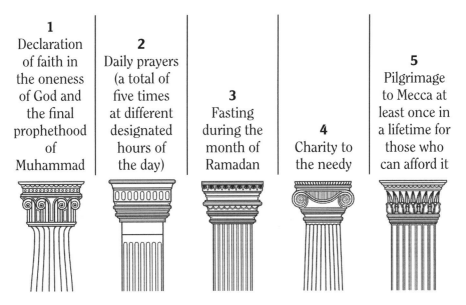

1 Declaration of faith in the oneness of God and the final prophethood of Muhammad

2 Daily prayers (a total of five times at different designated hours of the day)

3 Fasting during the month of Ramadan

4 Charity to the needy

5 Pilgrimage to Mecca at least once in a lifetime for those who can afford it

SEVEN BASIC BELIEFS (AMANTU) OF MUSLIMS

Muslims's belief statement includes seven basic beliefs and a testimony, which is codified in a Al-Imanul Mufassal (the statement of faith), nicknamed Amantu:

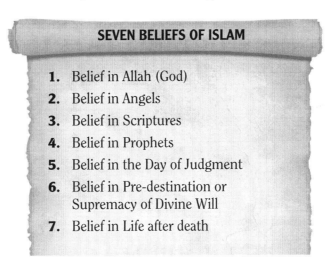

SEVEN BELIEFS OF ISLAM

1. Belief in Allah (God)
2. Belief in Angels
3. Belief in Scriptures
4. Belief in Prophets
5. Belief in the Day of Judgment
6. Belief in Pre-destination or Supremacy of Divine Will
7. Belief in Life after death

THE TEN COMMANDMENTS OF THE QURAN

The Quran, like the Bible, includes hundreds of commandments. Some Muslims believe that the Quran has equivalents for all the Ten Commandments of the Bible. The closest the Quran comes to issuing a subset of the ten commandments in one place is in Chapter 6, Sura Al-Ana'm, Verses 151 to 153. It is interesting to note that, in the very next

135

verse (154), mention is made of Moses, who is believed to have received the original Ten Commandments from God on Mount Sinai.

"Say: "Come, let me convey unto you what God has [really] forbidden to you: "Do not ascribe divinity, in any way, to aught beside Him; and [do not offend against but, rather,] do good unto your parents; and do not kill your children for fear of poverty - [for] it is We who shall provide sustenance for you as well as for them; and do not commit any shameful deeds, be they open or secret; and do not take any human being's life-[the life] which God has declared to be sacred -otherwise than in [the pursuit of] justice: this has He enjoined upon you so that you might use your reason;

And do not touch the substance of an orphan - save to improve it-before he comes of age." And [in all your dealings] give full measure and weight, with equity: [however,] We do not burden any human being with more than he is well able to bear; and when you voice an opinion, be just, even though it be [against] one near of kin. And [always] observe your bond with God: this has He enjoined upon you, so that you might keep it in mind.

And [know] that this is the way leading straight unto Me: follow it, then, and follow not other ways, lest they cause you to deviate from His way. [All] this has He enjoined upon you, so that you might remain conscious of Him.

We vouchsafed the divine writ unto Moses in fulfilment [of Our favour] upon those who persevered in doing good, clearly spelling out everything, and [thus providing] guidance and grace, so that they might have faith in the [final] meeting with their Sustainer."

– QURAN: SURA AL-ANA'M: 6:151-154

COFFEE BREAK

Quranic Equivalents of Ten Commandments: The above verses from the Quran do not include all the Ten Commandments of the Bible. Quranic equivalents can be seen in the following table.

THE TEN COMMANDMENTS OF BIBLE (Exodus 20: 2-17 & Deuteronomy 5: 6-21)	QURANIC EQUIVALENCE OF TEN COMMANDMENTS
1 Thou shall not take any god except one God.	There is no other god beside Allah (47:19). He is the one God; there is no other deity beside Him. (28:70)
2 Thou shall make no image of God.	My Lord, make this a peaceful land, and protect me and my children from worshiping idols. (14:35)
3 Thou shall not use God's name in vain.	Do not subject God's name to your casual swearing, that you may appear righteous, pious, or to attain credibility among the people. (2:224)
4 Thou shall keep the Sabbath holy.	O you who believe, when the Congregational Prayer (Salat Al-Jumu`ah) is announced on Friday, you shall hasten to the commemoration of God, and drop all business. (62:9)
5 Thou shall honour thy mother and father.	....and your parents shall be honored. As long as one or both of them live, you shall never say to them, "Uff" (the slightest gesture of annoyance), nor shall you shout at them; you shall treat them amicably. (17:23)
6 Thou shall not kill.	You shall not kill any person - for God has made life sacred - except in the course of justice. (17:33)
7 Thou shall not commit adultery.	You shall not commit adultery; it is a gross sin, and an evil behavior. (17:32)
8 Thou shall not steal.	The thief, male or female, you shall mark their hands as a punishment for their crime, and to serve as an example from God. God is Almighty, Most wise. (5:38 - 39)
9 Thou shall not lie or give false testimony.	Do not withhold any testimony by concealing what you had witnessed. Anyone who withholds a testimony is sinful at heart. (2:283)
10 Thou shall not covet thy neighbour's wife or possessions.	And do not covet what we bestowed upon any other people. Such are temporary ornaments of this life, whereby we put them to the test. What your Lord provides for you is far better, and everlasting. (20:131)

MESSAGES FROM QURAN

"O mankind! We created you from a single (pair) of a male and a female, and made you into nations and tribes, that ye may know each other (not that ye may despise (each other). Verily the most honoured of you in the sight of Allah is (he who is) the most righteous of you."

— QURAN: SURA AL-HUJURAT: 49: 13 (TR. BY A. YUSUF ALI)

"Your God is one God; there is no god but He, Most Gracious, Most Merciful."

— QURAN: SURA AL-BAQARA: 2:163

"UNTO every community have We appointed [different] ways of worship, which they ought to observe. Hence, [O believer,] do not let those [who follow ways other than thine] draw thee into disputes on this score, but summon [them all] unto thy Sustainer: for, behold, thou art indeed on the right way. And if they [try to] argue with thee, say [only]: "God knows best what you are doing."

— QURAN: SURA AL-HAJJ: 22:67 (TR. BY M. ASAD)

"Allah! There is no God save Him, the Alive, the Eternal.

Neither slumber nor sleep overtaketh Him.

Unto Him belongeth whatsoever is in the heavens

And whatsoever is in the earth.

Who is he that intercedeth with Him save by His leave?

He knoweth that which is in front of them

And that which is behind them,

While they encompass nothing of His knowledge save what He

will. His throne includeth the heavens and the earth,

And He is never weary of preserving them.

He is the Sublime, the Tremendous."

— QURAN: SURA AL-BAQARA: 2:255
(TR. BY M. PICKTHALL)

COFFEE BREAK
Islamic Inclusivism: Islam does not exclude non-Muslims from receiving God's rewards after death.

"Truly those who believe, and the Jews, and the Christians, and the Sabaeans - whoever believes in God and the Last Day and performs virtuous deeds - surely their reward is with their Sustainer, and no fear shall come upon them, neither shall they grieve."

— QURAN: SURA AL-BAQARA: 2:62

"Indeed, those who submit themselves absolutely to GOD alone, while leading a righteous life, will receive their recompense from their Lord; they have nothing to fear, nor will they grieve."

— QURAN: SURA AL-BAQARA: 2:112

"To GOD belongs the east and the west; wherever you go there will be the presence of GOD. GOD is Omnipresent, Omniscient."

— QURAN: SURA AL-BAQARA: 2:115

"Allah. There is no god but He,-the Living, the Self-Subsisting, Eternal. It is He Who sent down to thee (step by step), in truth, the Book, confirming what went before it; and He sent down the Law (of Moses) and the Gospel (of Jesus) before this, as a guide to mankind, and He sent down the criterion (of judgment between right and wrong). Then those who reject Faith in the Signs of Allah will suffer the severest penalty, and Allah is Exalted in Might, Lord of Retribution. From Allah, verily nothing is hidden on earth or in the heavens."

— QURAN: SURA AL-IMRAN: 3:2-5
(TR. BY A. YUSUF ALI)

COMPARE QURAN AND BIBLE VERSES:

"God has sealed their hearts and their hearing, and over their eyes is a veil; and awesome suffering awaits them."

— QURAN: SURA AL-BAQARA 2:7

"They have not known nor understood: for he hath shut their eyes, that they cannot see; [and] their hearts, that they cannot understand."

— BIBLE: ISAIAH 44:18

COFFEE BREAK
Islamic Pluralism: According to the Quran, Muslims are not supposed to distinguish between the Abrahamic prophets.

"Say: We believe in Allah and that which is revealed unto us and that which was revealed unto Abraham and Ishmael and Isaac and Jacob and the tribes, and that which was vouchsafed unto Moses and Jesus and the Prophets from their Lord. We make no distinction between any of them, and unto Him we have surrendered."

— Quran: Sura Al-Imran: 3:84
(Tr. by M. Pickthall)

EVOLUTION OF GOD

The God of Islam is Allah, and there is no God but Allah, in a strictly monotheistic worldview.

"God is the light of the Heavens and of the earth. His light is like a niche in which is a lamp - the encased in a glass, - the glass, as it were, a star."

— Quran: Sura An-Nur: 24:35

"But do good; for Allah loveth those who do good."

— Quran: Sura Al-Baqara: 2:195 (Tr. by A. Yusuf Ali)

"Help ye one another in righteousness and piety, but help ye not one another in sin and rancour: fear Allah, for Allah is strict in punishment."

— Quran: Sura Al-Maidah: 5:2
(Tr. by A. Yusuf Ali)

"For(Allah) loveth not those who do wrong."

— Quran: Sura Ash-Shura: 42:40
(Tr. by A. Yusuf Ali)

"And establish regular Prayer: for Prayer restrains from shameful and unjust deeds."

— Quran: Sura Al-ankabut: 29:45
(Tr. by A. Yusuf Ali)

"[But as for you, O believers,] never shall you attain to true piety unless you spend on others out of what you cherish yourselves; and whatever you spend - verily, God has full knowledge thereof."

— Quran: Sura Al-Imran: 3:92
(Tr. by M. Asad)

"Let there be no compulsion in religion."

— Quran: Sura Al-Baqara: 2:256
(Tr. by A. Yusuf Ali)

"Unto you your religion, and unto me my religion."

— Quran: Sura Al-Kafirun: 109:6
(Tr. by M. Pickthall)

"If anyone sends you an offer of peace do not say to him 'you are not sincere in your offer'."

— Quran: Sura An-Nisaa: 4:94

COMPARISON OF LORD'S PRAYER AND SURA AL-FATIHA

LORD'S PRAYER

"Lord Our Father which art in heaven,
Hallowed be thy name.
Thy kingdom come,
Thy will be done in earth, as it is in heaven.
Give us this day our daily bread.
And forgive us our debts, as
we forgive our debtors.
And lead us not into temptation,
but deliver us from evil:
For thine is the kingdom, and the
power, and the glory, for ever.
Amen."
– BIBLE: MATTHEW 9:13

SURA AL-FATIHA

"Praise belongs to God, the Lord of all Being,
the All-merciful, the All-compassionate,
the Master of the Day of Doom.
Thee only we serve; to Thee
alone we pray for succour.
Guide us in the straight path,
the path of those whom Thou hast blessed,
not of those against whom
Thou art wrathful,
nor of those who are astray. *Amen**"
– QURAN: SURA AL-FATIHA 1:1-7

* Amen is not part of the Sura itself, but added universally by all Sunni Muslims after reciting Sura Al-Fatiha, which is the most recited Sura of the Quran.

"And swell not thy cheek (for pride) at men, nor walk in insolence through the earth; for "Allah loveth not any arrogant boaster.""

– QURAN: SURA LUQMAN: 31:18
(TR. BY A. YUSUF ALI)

"Therefore remember Me, I will remember you. Give thanks to Me, and reject not Me."

– QURAN: SURA AL-BAQARA: 2:152
(TR. BY M. PICKTHALL)

HOLY WALL:
KOJIKI AND NIHONGI –SHINTO SCRIPTURES

The Kojiki ("Record of Ancient Matters") and Nihongi ("Chronicles of Japan") are the inspirations behind Shintoism, the popular religion of Japanese people. The Kojiki was composed in the early eighth century by O No Yasumaro at the request of Empress Gemmei (660–721 AD). The Kojiki consists of songs and poems, and is divided into three parts: Kamitsumaki ("Upper Roll"), Nakatsumaki ("Middle Roll"), and Shimotsumaki ("Lower Roll"). The Nihongi was completed under the editorship of Prince Toneri (676–735 AD), with the assistance of O No Yasumaro.

MESSAGES FROM KOJIKI

"Be charitable to all beings, love is the representative of God."

–THE KOJIKI (TR. BY B. H. CHAMBERLAIN))

"The names of the deities that were born in the Plain of High Heaven when the Heaven and Earth began were the deity Master-of-the-August-Center-of-Heaven; next, the High-August-Producing-Wondrous deity; next, the Divine-Producing-Wondrous deity. These three deities were all deities born alone, and hid their persons. The names of the deities that were born next from a thing that sprouted up like unto a reed-shoot when the earth, young and like unto floating oil, drifted about medusa-like, were the Pleasant-Reed-Shoot-Prince-Elder deity, next the Heavenly-Eternally-Standing deity. These two deities were likewise born alone, and hid their persons. The five deities in the above list are separate Heavenly deities."

–THE KOJIKI (TR. BY B. H. CHAMBERLAIN)

MESSAGES FROM NIHONGI

"Some may boast
Of the splendor
Of red jewels,
But those worn by my lord --
It is they which are admirable."

– NIHONGI (TR. BY W.G. ASTON)

"Of old, Heaven and Earth were not yet separated, and the In and Yo not yet divided. They formed a chaotic mass like an egg which was of obscurely defined limits and contained germs.

The purer and clearer part was thinly drawn out, and formed Heaven, while the heavier and grosser element settled down and became Earth.

The finer element easily became a united body, but the consolidation of the heavy and gross element was accomplished with difficulty. Heaven was therefore formed first, and Earth was established subsequently. Thereafter divine beings were produced between them.

Hence it is said that when the world began to be created, the soil of which lands were composed floated about in a manner which might be compared to the floating of a fish sporting on the surface of the water. At this time a certain thing was produced between Heaven and Earth. It was in form like a reed-shoot. Now this became transformed into a God, and was called Kuni-toko-tachi no Mikoto. Next there was Kuni no sa-tsuchi no Mikoto, and next Toyo-kumu-nu no Mikoto, in all three deities. These were pure males spontaneously developed by the operation of the principle of Heaven."

— NIHONGI
(TR. BY W.G. ASTON)

EVOLUTION OF GOD

The God of Shintoism is an imperfect Being – neither all good, nor all evil.

"Ah, the spirits of my ancestors have looked down from heaven, watching over and helping me. The hosts of evil have now been subdued one and all, and we are without enemy or misfortune. Let us now therefore give worship to the heavenly deities, vowing to abide by the teachings of our imperial ancestors." With that, Emperor Jimmu prepared places of worship in the mountains of Tomi... and thus performed worship to the imperial ancestors and to the heavenly deities."

— NIHONGI

"Our ancestors the emperors of old governed the realm by first paying worship to the kami with reverence and awe. Widely worshipping the kami of mountain and river, they thereby had natural concourse with heaven and earth. For this reason, summer and winter also turned in their season, and the works of creation were in harmony."

— NIHONGI

HOLY WALL:
GOD'S MOOD SWINGS

BELLIGERENCE AND BENEVOLENCE: THE DILEMMA OF CONTENT AND CONTEXT

A careful reader of religious scriptures will notice that God has wide mood swings, from belligerence to benevolence, from love to rage. These changing moods allow religious fundamentalists to cite scriptures to justify "holy wars" and liberals to argue that content must be interpreted with reference to the context to arrive at the true meaning of God's message.

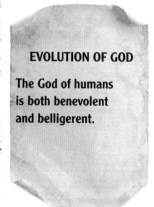

EVOLUTION OF GOD

The God of humans is both benevolent and belligerent.

The arguments typically go like this: the Muslim jihadists or 9/11 terrorists are not "true" Muslims because they don't understand the true message of Islam, which is a religion of peace; and the Christian Crusaders or abortion clinic bombers were/are not "true" Christians because they don't understand the "true" meaning of Christianity.

Professor Philip Jenkins, "one of America's best scholars of religion *(The Economist)*", in his landmark book *Laying Down the Sword*, demonstrates how holy amnesia helped Christians grow past their scriptures, which are far more violent than the Quran when taken literally. He concludes, "When Christians or Jews point to violent parts of the Qur'an (or the Hadith) and suggest that those elements taint the whole religion, they open themselves to the obvious question: what about their own faiths? If the founding text shapes the whole religion, then Judaism and Christianity deserve the utmost condemnation as religions of savagery. Of course, they are no such thing; nor is Islam."

This endless debate can only be ended by recognizing that belligerence and benevolence coexist in our holy scriptures, and no single religion is solely belligerent or benevolent. Selected quotations from a few scriptures are provided on the next page to demonstrate this fact.

The selection of scriptures of Hinduism, Christianity, and Islam in this section to illustrate God's mood swings should not be misconstrued to infer that these religions are the only ones which can, and do, contribute to violence. These three religions are selected because they have a collective following of more than two-thirds of the world population. Other religions can and do contribute to violence with equal fervor. For example, *Buddhist Warfare* (2010), authored by American and European scholars, documented the violent history of Buddhism, which was traditionally considered a peaceful religion. Even a Godless ideology, such as atheism or secularism, can be violent and divisive, when the ideology itself, or the nation-state, promoting the ideology, becomes the object of worship.

WAR AND PEACE IN HINDU SCRIPTURES

"Considering also your duty as a warrior you should not waver like this. Because there is nothing more auspicious for a warrior than a righteous war. Only the fortunate warriors, O Arjuna, get such an opportunity for an unsought war that is like an open door to heaven. If you will not fight this righteous war, then you will fail in your duty, lose your reputation, and incur sin. People will talk about your disgrace forever. To the honored, dishonor is worse than death."

— BHAGAVAD GITA (2:31-34)

"You will go to heaven if killed in the line of duty, or you will enjoy the kingdom on the earth if victorious. No matter what happens you win. Therefore, get up with a determination to fight, O Arjuna."

— BHAGAVAD GITA (2:37)

"May your weapons be strong to drive away the attackers,

May your arms be powerful enough to check the foes,

Let your army be glorious, not the evil-doer."

— RIG VEDA (1:39:2)

"Day after day, from their seat he, Indra, drove them, alike, from place to place, those dark-looking creatures. The Hero slew the meanly-behaving Dasas, Varchin and Shambara, where the waters gather."

— RIG VEDA (6:47:20-21)

"Om! May God protect us both together;

May God nourish us both together;

May we work conjointly with great energy,

May our study be vigorous and effective;

May we not mutually dispute (or may we not hate any).

Om! Let there be Peace in me!

Let there be Peace in my environment!

Let there be Peace in the forces that act on me!"

— KATHA UPANISHAD

"May all the Gods be peaceful,

May the Vedas spread peace everywhere,

May all other objects everywhere give us peace,

And may that peace come to us and remain with us forever."

— YAJUR VEDA

WAR AND PEACE IN BIBLE

"The Lord is a man of war: the Lord is his name"

— BIBLE: EXODUS (15:3)

"And thine eye shall not pity; but life shall go for life, eye for eye, tooth for tooth, hand for hand, foot for foot."

— DEUTERONOMY (19:21)

"Ye have heard that it hath been said, an eye for an eye, and a tooth for a tooth. But I say unto you, that ye resist not evil: but whosoever shall smite thee on thy right cheek, turn to him the other also."

— MATTHEW 5:38-39 (KJV)

"But as for the towns of these peoples that the Lord your God is giving you as an inheritance, you must not let anything that breathes remain alive. You shall annihilate them—the Hittites and the Amorites, the Canaanites and the Perizzites, the Hivites and the Jebusites—just as the Lord your God has commanded, so that they may not teach you to do all the abhorrent things that they do for their gods, and you thus sin against the Lord your God."

— BIBLE: DEUTERONOMY (20:16-18)

"Depart from evil, and do good; seek peace, and pursue it."

— BIBLE: PSALM (34:14)

"Blessed are the peacemakers: for they shall be called the children of God."

— BIBLE: MATTHEW (5:9)

"Let us therefore make every effort to do what leads to peace and to mutual edification."

— BIBLE: ROMANS (14:19)

"You must destroy all the peoples the Lord your God gives over to you. Do not look on them with pity and do not serve their gods, for that will be a snare to you."

— BIBLE: DEUTERONOMY (7:16)

"Now therefore kill every male among the little ones, and kill every woman that hath known man by lying with him. But all the women children, that have not known a man by lying with him, keep alive for yourselves."

— BIBLE: NUMBERS 31:15-19 (KJV)

"And he shall judge among many people, and rebuke strong nations afar off; and they shall beat their swords into plowshares, and their spears into pruninghooks: nation shall not lift up a sword against nation, neither shall they learn war any more."

— BIBLE: ISAIAH (2:4)

"But I say unto you which hear, Love your enemies, do good to them which hate you, Bless them that curse you, and pray for them which despitefully use you. And unto him that smiteth thee on the one cheek offer also the other; and him that taketh away thy cloke forbid not to take thy coat also. Give to every man that asketh of thee; and of him that taketh away thy goods ask them not again. And as ye would that men should do to you, do ye also to them likewise."

— BIBLE: LUKE (6:27-31)

"Recompense to no man evil for evil. Provide things honest in the sight of all men. If it be possible, as much as lieth in you, live peaceably with all men."

— BIBLE: ROMANS (12:17-18)

WAR AND PEACE IN QURAN

"O ye who believe! Fight those of the disbelievers who are near to you, and let them find harshness in you, and know that Allah is with those who keep their duty (unto Him)."

— QURAN [9:123]

"Let those fight in the way of Allah who sell the life of this world for the other. Whoso fighteth in the way of Allah, be he slain or be he victorious, on him We shall bestow a vast reward."

— QURAN [4:74]

"They long that ye should disbelieve even as they disbelieve, that ye may be upon a level (with them). So choose not friends from them till they forsake their homes in the way of Allah; if they turn back (to enmity) then take them and kill them wherever ye find them, and choose no friend nor helper from among them."

— QURAN [4:89]

"Thus, if they let you be, and do not make war on you, and offer you peace, God does not allow you to harm them."

— QURAN [4:90]

"Unto you your religion, and unto me my religion."

— QURAN [109:6]

"Fight in the way of Allah against those who fight against you, but begin not hostilities. Lo! Allah loveth not, aggressors."

— QURAN [2:190]

"And argue not with the People of the Scripture unless it be in (a way) that is better, save with such of them as do wrong; and say: We believe in that which hath been revealed unto us and revealed unto you; our God and your God is One, and unto Him we surrender."

— QURAN [29:46]

"We ordained therein (in Torah) for them: 'Life for life, eye for eye, nose or nose, ear for ear, tooth for tooth, and wounds equal for equal.' But if any one remits the retaliation by way of charity, it is an act of atonement for himself. And if any fail to judge by (the light of) what Allah hath revealed, they are (No better than) wrong-doers."

— QURAN [5:45]

"Allah forbids you not, with regard to those who fight you not for (your) Faith nor drive you out of your homes, from dealing kindly and justly with them: for Allah loveth those who are just."

— QURAN [60:8]

"UNTO every community have We appointed [different] ways of worship, which they ought to observe. Hence, [O believer,] do not let those [who follow ways other than thine] draw thee into disputes on this score, but summon [them all] unto thy Sustainer: for, behold, thou art indeed on the right way."

— QURAN [22:67]

WAR AND PEACE IN ATHEISM

In ancient times, atheists like Diagoras and Protagoras were passive in their nontheistic beliefs. They questioned the religious beliefs of their days and expressed their opinions in conversations or in books. Nontheistic belief systems such as Jainism, Buddhism, and Confucianism also sought personal peace through moral living. Atheism in the West was generally pacifist up to the period of the Enlightenment, and grew as a reasoned opposition to religious wars.

After the French Revolution, atheism gained political muscle in the hands of Karl Marx, an atheistic political economist. Marx felt it was necessary to abolish religion because he believed: "It is the opium of the people. The abolition of religion as the illusory happiness of the people is the demand for their real happiness." Communist regimes such as the Soviet Union took his advice to heart and formed the *Union of Belligerent Atheists*, an organization with a mission to eradicate religion and belief in God from Soviet Russia.

Bertrand Russell attacked all religions in his classic, *Why I'm Not a Christian*, and wrote: "I think all the great religions of the world – Buddhism, Hinduism, Christianity, Islam, and Communism – both untrue and harmful." He went on to proclaim that, "It is possible that mankind is on the threshold of a golden age; but, if so, it will be necessary first to slay the dragon that guards the door, and this dragon is religion." However, after two atomic bombings in Japan during the Second World War, Russell's belligerence was tempered by the horrifying prospect of mutual destruction if humans cannot settle their quarrels, be it among nations or religions or between the communists and the anti-communists. In 1955, he published a proposal for world peace, which came to be known as the Russell-Einstein Manifesto. It contained a unique appeal: "There lies before us, if we choose, continual progress in happiness, knowledge, and wisdom. Shall we, instead, choose death, because we cannot forget our quarrels? We appeal as human beings to human beings: Remember your humanity, and forget the rest."

However, the old atheist belligerence against religion resurfaced in the twentieth century as modern science provided more and more reasons to question the existence of God. The twenty-first century saw the rise of New Atheism, which argued that religion is too dangerous a force to be tolerated; rather, it should be countered and contained. Gradually, New Atheism assumed a great deal of self-righteousness in response to numerous terrorist acts by religious fundamentalists; proponents of atheism began to believe that atheism is the only rational world-view, which is similar to the exclusivist thinking of some religious people.

Celebrated atheist Sam Harris, in his bestselling book, *The End of Faith*, went so far as to suggest and justify the killing of the religious other, expressing a fervor common among religious fundamentalists. In a chapter entitled "The Problem with Islam," Harris wrote: "In our dialogue with the Muslim world, we are confronted by people who hold beliefs for which there is no rational justification and which therefore cannot even be discussed.... There is little possibility of our having a cold war with an Islamist regime armed with long-range nuclear weapons... In such a situation, the only thing likely to ensure our survival may be a nuclear first strike of our own. Needless to say, this would be an unthinkable crime—as it would kill tens of millions of innocent civilians in a single day—but it may be the only course of action available to us, given what Islamists believe."

The condescending tone and placing of the blame on "what Islamists believe" are examples of the self-righteousness of the New Atheists. In a chapter entitled "A Science of Good and Evil," Sam Harris also justifies the use of torture on religious terrorists to save the "secular world," although he vehemently criticizes the church's torture of witches in past centuries. Thus, the New Atheists view secularism as something sacred that requires protection from religionists, and use the fear of "weapons of mass destruction," instead of the fear of "hell," to promote their world-view or "religion."

WALL OF MORTALS:
(1 TO 1000 AD)

Despite the growth of multiple religions during the period 1 to 1000 AD, humans remained cognizant of a global view of God that transcended all religions. The human writings on the Wall of Mortals demonstrated striking similarities in the perception of God among men of different religions and beliefs.

"Woe is me, I think I am becoming a god."

— EMPEROR VESPASIAN (9-79)
[Born as Titus Flavius Vespasianus, the ninth Roman Emperor]

"It is fear that first brought gods into the world."

— PETRONIUS (27-66)
[Roman writer and satirist]

"Everyone is in a small way the image of God."

— MARCUS MANILIUS (1ST CENTURY)
[Roman poet and astrologer]

"Everyone ought to worship God according to his own inclinations, and not to be constrained by force."

-FLAVIUS JOSEPHUS (37-100)
[Jewish army captain, who later became an author]

"Is there any other seat of the Divinity than the earth, sea, air, the heavens, and virtuous minds? Why do we seek God elsewhere? He is whatever you see; he is wherever you move."

— LUCANUS (39–65)
[Born as Marcus Annaeus Lucanus, Roman poet]

"God is the brave man's hope, and not the coward's excuse."

— PLUTARCH (46-127)
[Born as Mestrius Plutarchos, Greek historian, biographer, and essayist]

"It is better to have no opinion of God at all than such as one as is unworthy of him; for the one is only unbelief--the other is contempt."

— PLUTARCH (46-127)

"Like a twisted olive tree in its 500th year, giving then its finest fruit, is man. How can he give forth wisdom until he has been crushed and turned in the Hand of God."

— RABBI AKIBA BEN JOSEPH (50–135)
[Jewish Rabbi, martyred by the Romans, Father of Rabbinic Judaism]

"Difficulties show men what they are. In case of any difficulty remember that God has pitted you against a rough antagonist that you may be a conqueror, and this cannot be without toil."

— EPICTETUS (55-135)
[Greek Stoic philosopher]

"Renew every day your conversation with God:

Do this even in preference to eating.

Think more often of God than you breathe."

— EPICTETUS (55-135)

"God is not in need of anything, but all things are in need of him."

— AUGUSTUS(121–180)

[Imperator Caesar Marcus Aurelius Antoninus Augustus, Stoic philosopher, and Roman Emperor from 161 to his death in 180]

"Live a good life. If there are gods and they are just, then they will not care how devout you have been, but will welcome you based on the virtues you have lived by. If there are gods, but unjust, then you should not want to worship them. If there are no gods, then you will be gone, but will have lived a noble life that will live on in the memories of your loved ones."

— AUGUSTUS (121-180)

EVOLUTION OF GOD

The God of Marcion is a good God, who is revealed only in Christ and is different than the uncultured, wild,and violent God of the Old Testament.

"I, who am Nature, the parent of all things, the mistress of all the elements, the primordial offspring of time, the supreme among Divinities, the queen of departed spirits, the first of the celestials, and the uniform manifestation of the Gods and Goddesses; who govern by my nod the luminous heights of heaven, the salubrious breezes of the ocean, and the anguished silent realms of the shades below: whose one sole divinity the whole orb of the earth venerates under a manifold form, with different rites, and under a variety of appellations."

— LUCIUS APULEIUS (125–180)

[Roman philosopher, orator and romance-writer, of Berber North African origin]

COFFEE BREAK

Marcion's Two Gods: In July of 144 AD, a strange hearing took place in Rome before the city's Christian clergy. Marcion (85–160), a wealthy ship-owner and Christian bishop from Sinope (in modern Turkey), stood before the clergy to explain his views on two Gods. He argued that the God of the Old Testament (Jewish Bible) was an "uncultured, jealous, wild, belligerent, angry and violent God, who has nothing in common with the God of the New Testament." Marcion was offended by the violent and dark passages of the Jewish Bible, which condoned an eye-for-an-eye attitude. Failing to reconcile the Old Testament and the New Testament, Marcion created a new version of the Bible by dropping the Jewish Bible. He felt that Jesus came to replace the cruel and despotic God of the Old Testament with the compassionate God of the New Testament. Marcion didn't have the support of the Christian clergy, and the hearing in Rome ended in a rejection of his views. He was then excommunicated. He set up the Marcionites church, which flourished until the end of the third century.

COFFEE BREAK
Wise Man and God: Buddhist philosopher vocally opposes the pretenses of gods in the face of proliferation of belief in multiple gods of Hinduism.

"The gods are all eternal scoundrels
Incapable of dissolving the suffering of impermanence.
Those who serve them and venerate them
May even in this world sink into a sea of sorrow.
We know the gods are false and have no concrete being;
Therefore the wise man believes them not
The fate of the world depends on causes and conditions
Therefore the wise man may not rely on gods."

— ACHARYA NAGARJUNA (150-250)
[Indian philosopher, who founded a school of Mahayana, one of two major sects of Buddhism]

"Since he is by nature empty.
The thought that the Buddha
Exists or does not exist
After nirvana is not appropriate."

— ACHARYA NAGARJUNA (150-250)

"As the eye naturally seeks the light and vision, and our body naturally desires food and drink, so our mind is possessed with a becoming and natural desire to become acquainted with the truth of God and the causes of things."

— ORIGEN (185-254)
[Alexandrian theologian, most prolific and original Christian thinker of the 3rd century]

"Be careful if you make a woman cry because God counts her tears. The woman came out of a man's rib. Not from his feet to be walked on, not from his head to be superior, but from the side to be equal. Under his arm to be protected, and next to the heart to be loved."

— HEBREW TALMUD (200 AD)

"God is not external to anyone, but is present with all things, though they are ignorant that he is so."

— PLOTINUS (204–270)
[Major philosopher of the ancient world, founder of Neoplatonism (along with his teacher Ammonius Saccas)]

"The sensitive eye can never be able to survey, the orb of the sun, unless strongly endued with solar fire, and participating largely of the vivid ray. Everyone therefore must become divine, and of godlike beauty, before he can gaze upon a god and the beautiful itself."

— PLOTINUS (204-270)

"It did not please God to save his people through dialectic."

— SAINT AMBROSE (340–397)
[Eminent bishop of Milan, Italy]

"When we once begin to form good resolutions, God gives us every opportunity of carrying them out."

— SAINT JOHN CHRYSOSTOM (347–407)
[Christian theologian and orator, Archbishop of Constantinople]

"Lovely face, majestic face,

face of beauty, face of flame,

the face of the Lord God of Israel

when He sits upon His throne of glory,

robed in praise upon His seat of splendour."

— HEKHALOT HYMNS (4TH CENTURY)
[Anonymously composed by Jewish mystics]

"Of the cosmic Gods some make the world be, others animate it, others harmonize it, consisting as it does of different elements; the fourth class keep it when harmonized. These are four actions, each of which has a beginning, middle, and end, consequently there must be twelve Gods governing the world."

— SALLUSTIUS (4TH CENTURY)
[Roman author of On the Gods and Cosmos]

"He was. Taaroa was his name.

He stood in the void: no earth, no sky, no men.

Taaroa calls the four corners of the universe; nothing replies.

Alone existing, he changes himself into the universe.

Taaroa is the light, he is the seed,

he is the base, he is the incorruptible.

The universe is only the shell of Taaroa.

It is he who puts it in motion and brings forth its harmony."

—TAHITIAN RELIGION (4TH CENTURY)
[Tahiti is a South Pacific island, believed to have been settled between 300 to 800 AD by Polynesians]

COFFEE BREAK
God, Fire, Light: Saint Augustine is the author of two of the world's greatest books: *Confessions*, the world's first autobiography and *The City of God,* still a required reading in Religious Studies at universities. His philosophical quest was unique in the sense that it included introspection into his inner life, rather than a mere rational analysis of the reality outside himself. He also argued that since God is unknowable by virtue of not being an object of knowledge, it is impossible for God to know himself.

"Remember this. When people choose to withdraw far from a fire, the fire continues to give warmth, but they grow cold. When people choose to withdraw far from light, the light continues to be bright in itself but they are in darkness. This is also the case when people withdraw from God."

— SAINT AUGUSTINE (354–430)
[St. Augustine of Hippo, also known as Aurelius Augustine, Christian theologian, North African bishop, and a philosopher.]

"God will not suffer man to have knowledge of things to come; for if he had prescience of his prosperity, he would be careless; and understanding of his adversity, he would be senseless."
— SAINT AUGUSTINE (354–430)

"God is best known in not knowing him."

— SAINT AUGUSTINE (354–430)

"Pray as though everything depended on God. Work as though everything depended on you."

— SAINT AUGUSTINE (354–430)

"God is more truly imagined than expressed, and He exists more truly than He is imagined."

— SAINT AUGUSTINE (354–430)

"The Devî (Goddess) said: 'Hear, ye Immortals! My words with attention, that I am now going to speak to you, hearing which will enable the Jîvas to realise My Essence. Before the creation, I, only I, existed; nothing else was existent then. My Real Self is known by the names Chit, Sambit (Intelligence), Para Brahma and others. My Âtman is beyond mind, beyond thought, beyond any name or mark, without any parallel, and beyond birth, death or any other change or transformation. My Self has one inherent power called Mâyâ. This Mâyâ is not existent, nor non-existent, nor can it be called both. This unspeakable substance Mâyâ always exists (till the final emancipation or Moksa)'."

— MARKANDEYA (5TH CENTURY)
[Indian sage, who wrote the Devi Gita and Devi Mahatmya]

"Virtuous hail Thee indestructible and all composite
With form beyond conception and virtues infinite
They call Thee ADI being the first of Tirthankars
They call Thee Brahma having shed all karmas
They call Thee Ishwar having achieved all achievable
They call Thee Ananta as Thy form is ever durable."

— ACHARYA MANATUNGA (4TH TO 5TH CENTURY AD)
[Jain monk, who wrote the Bhaktamara Strota, the most important prayer in Jain religion. This is part of the Bhaktamara Strota]

COFFEE BREAK
God and Beauty: Kalidasa, the greatest poet and playwright of the Sanskrit language, found the sign of God in the beauty of women.

"Oh, my friend, she needs not many words.
She is God's vision, of pure thought
Composed in His creative mind;
His reveries of beauty wrought
The peerless pearl of womankind.
So plays my fancy when I see
How great is God, how lovely she."

— KALIDASA (4TH TO 5TH CENTURY)
[One of the greatest Sanskrit poets of India, famed for Meghaduta (Cloud Messenger)]

"Many years ago, that royal sage was leading a life of stern austerities, and the gods, becoming strangely jealous, sent the nymph Menaka to disturb his devotions. Yes, the gods feel this jealousy toward the austerities of others."

— KALIDASA (4TH TO 5TH CENTURY)

"I shall proclaim the mighty deeds of God,
who is glorious in power.
He alone is God
and there is no other."

—YOSE BEN YOSE (5TH CENTURY)
[Hebrew poet]

"When God comes
A great noise will pierce us,
The day of judgment terribly.

Messengers from the door,
Wind, and sea, and fire.
lightning and thunder
A number without flattery.
The people of the world groaning
Will be concealed."

—TALIESIN (534–599)
[The earliest poet of the Welsh language]

"There the Sovereign of the world
 His calm sway maintains;
As the globe is onward whirled
 Guides the chariot reins,
And in splendour glittering
Reigns the universal King."

— BOETHIUS (480-524)
[Christian poet and philosopher born in Rome]

"Do not conceal from God what is in your breast that it may be hidden; whatever is concealed, God knows all about it."

— ZUHAYR (520-609)
[Zuhayr ibn Abî Sûlma, pre-Islamic Arabian poet, considered to be the greatest writer of Arabic poetry. He wrote one of the seven poems that were hanged inside the Kaba, the Muslim House of God, before the advent of Islam]

"Yours, O Lord, is the sovereignty and You are exalted over all."

— ELEAZAR BEN KALLIR (570-640)
[Hebrew poet who created "piyut", Jewish liturgical verses that are still sung today]

"Guide of Christians
in the wisdom of heaven!
Lead us up beyond unknowing and light,
up to the farthest, highest peak
of mystic scripture,
where the mysteries of God's Word
lie simple, absolute and unchangeable
in the brilliant darkness of a hidden silence."

— DIONYSIUS THE AREOPAGITE (6TH CENTURY)
[Also called Denys or Pseudo-Dionysius, Christian mystic poet who greatly influenced the Christian mysticism]

COFFEE BREAK
The Role Model of Muslims: The sayings of Muhammad, the prophet of Islam, are recorded in Hadith literature. Prophet Muhammad is the ultimate role model for more than 1.5 billion Muslims in the world. His words and actions have inspired, and continue to inspire, many generations of Muslims seeking to establish a code of meaningful and ethical life for themselves in both thought and action.

"Learn to know thyself! He who has understood himself has understood God."
— PROPHET MUHAMMAD (570-632)
[Founder of Islam and ranked by British academic Michael Hart as the most influential man in history above Isaac Newton, Jesus Christ and Buddha]

"Do not turn away a poor man...even if all you can give is half a date. If you love the poor and bring them near you...God will bring you near Him on the Day of Resurrection."
— PROPHET MUHAMMAD (570-632)

"God does not judge you according to your bodies and appearances, but He looks into your hearts and observes your deeds."
— PROPHET MUHAMMAD (570-632)

"He who leaveth home in search of knowledge walketh in the path of God."
— PROPHET MUHAMMAD (570-632)

"O people! Your God is one and your forefather (Adam) is one. An Arab is not better than a non-Arab and a non-Arab is not better than an Arab, and a red (i.e. white tinged with red) person is not better than a black person and a black person is not better than a red person, except in piety."
— PROPHET MUHAMMAD (570-632)

"God hates the man who quarrels and disputes most."
— PROPHET MUHAMMAD (570-632)

"Avoid the seven noxious things. (1) Associating anything with God, (2) magic, (3) killing one whom God has declared inviolate without a just cause, (4) devouring usury, (5) consuming the property of an orphan, (6) running back from the battlefield and (7) slandering chaste women who are believers but indiscreet."
— PROPHET MUHAMMAD (570-632)

"You have two characters which God likes; gentleness and deliberation."
— PROPHET MUHAMMAD (570-632)

"Every nation has a creator of the heavens to which they turn in prayer. It is God who turneth them toward it. Hasten then emulously after good wheresoever ye be. God will one day bring you all together."
— PROPHET MUHAMMAD (570-632)

"If you expect the blessings of God, be kind to His people."

— ABU BAKR AS SIDDIQ (573-634)
[1st caliph (ruler of Islamic Kingdom) of Islam after Prophet Muhammad]

"I have been given the authority over you, and I am not the best of you. If I do well, help me; and if I do wrong, set me right. Sincere regard for truth is loyalty and disregard for truth is treachery. The weak amongst you shall be strong with me until I have secured his rights, if God will; and the strong amongst you shall be weak with me until I have wrested from him the rights of others, if God will. Obey me so long as I obey God and His Messenger. But if I disobey God and His Messenger, ye owe me no obedience. Arise for your prayer, God have mercy upon you."

— ABU BAKR AS SIDDIQ (573-634)
(In his 1st lecture after taking charge of Muslim community after the death of Prophet Muhammad]

"Submission to God's Will is the best companion; wisdom is the noblest heritage; theoretical and practical knowledge are the best signs of distinction; deep thinking will present the clearest picture of every problem."

— IMAM ALI IBN ABI TALIB (599-661)
[4th caliph (ruler) of Islamic Kingdom, founder of Shia sect]

"The best form of devotion to the service of God is not to make a show of it."

— IMAM ALI IBN ABI TALIB (599-661)

"Islam in the fear of hell is the Islam of a slave, and Islam in the hope of Heaven is that of a merchant. The best Islam is Islam for the sake of God's Glory alone."

— IMAM ALI IBN ABI TALIB (599-661)

"While I wait for you,
My lord, lost in this longing,
Suddenly there comes
A stirring of my window blind:
The autumn wind is blowing."

— PRINCESS NUKATA (630-690)
[Japanese poet]

"God is a sea of infinite substance."

— ST. JOHN OF DAMASCUS (676-749)
[Arab Christian monk and priest]

COFFEE BREAK

Islam's Golden Age: Islam's golden age began to emerge in the mid-eighth century with the founding of the city of Baghdad, Iraq. For the next 500 years, Muslim culture was unparalleled in its splendor and contributed enormously to the world of knowledge, including, philosophy, literature, mathematics, logic, science, medicine, physics, architecture, and engineering. This period saw an abundance of expressions on God from Muslim thinkers.

"Since no one really knows anything about God, those who think they do are just troublemakers."

— RABIA BASRI (714-801)
[Rabia al-Adawiyya, Muslim philosopher and woman sufi mystic]

"O Allah! If I worship You for fear of Hell, burn me in Hell,

And if I worship You in hope of Paradise, exclude me from Paradise.

But if I worship You for Your Own sake,

Grudge me not Your everlasting Beauty."

— RABIA BASRI (714-801)

"In my soul there is a temple, a shrine, a mosque, a church where I kneel.

Prayer should bring us to an altar where no walls or names exist.

Is there not a region of love where the

sovereignty is illumined nothing,

where ecstasy gets poured into itself and becomes lost,

where the wing is fully alive but has no mind or body?

In my soul there is a temple, a shrine, a mosque, a

church that dissolve, that dissolve in God."

My soul is your temple

— RABIA BASRI (714-801)

"The deity is immanent in man and man is inherent in the deity; there is neither the divine nor the human; there is no difference in essence at all between them."

— SHINTOISM TRADITIONAL SAYING (7TH TO 8TH CENTURY)

"Man thinks, God directs."

— FLACCUS ALBINUS ALCUIN (735-804)
[Eminent scholar, theologian and catholic educator]

"Not only is there no God, but try finding a plumber on Sunday."

— FLACCUS ALBINUS ALCUIN (735-804)

"No sin may be ordered by God as it is wrong and forbidden, and no sin shall be permitted by God, as they are wrong by themselves. To know about it and believe otherwise, and all that God commands is good for the ordered and all that it is not permissible except to order it is good for himself."

— IBRAHIM AN-NAZZAM (775-845)
[Mulsim Mutazillite (Rationalist) theologian and poet]

159

"My soul is your temple, O Lord,

My actions are your handmaids,

My body is your home,

My senses witness only you,

My sleep is pure meditation on you,

These walking feet are your journey,

Whatever falls from my mouth is prayer to you,

Oh Lord, everything I say and do are worship."

— ADI SHANKARA (788-820)
[Indian philosopher, poet, and teacher of unity of soul and the God]

"God is the pure being, the One, the True, in whom there is no multiplicity in any way."

— AL-KINDI (801-873)
[Abu Yusuf Yaqub ibn Isaq al-Kindi, known in the West as Alkindus. Arab Iraqi polymath –Islamic philosopher, scientist, astronomer, chemist, logician, mathematician, musician, physician, physicist]

"When we are told that God is the maker of all things, we are simply to understand that God is in all things – that He is the substantial essence of all things."

— JOHANNES SCOTUS ERIGENA (815-877)
[Irish theologian and Neoplatonist philosopher]

"What, then, is it to treat of philosophy, unless to lay down the rules of the true religion by which we seek rationally and adore humbly God, who is the first and sovereign cause of all things? Hence it follows that the true philosophy is the true religion, and reciprocally that the true religion is the true philosophy."

— JOHANNES SCOTUS ERIGENA (815-877)

"I gazed upon Him [Allah] with the eye of truth, and said to Him: 'Who is this?' He said: 'This is neither I nor other than I. There is no God but I.' Then he changed me our of my identity into His Selfhood . . . Then I. . communed with Him with the tongue of His grace, saying: 'How fares it with me with Thee?' He said: 'I am Thine through thee: there is no God but Thou'."

— BAYAZID BASTAMI (850-874)
[Persian Muslim sufi and mystic]

"If we keep unperverted the human heart--which is like unto heaven and received from earth--that is God."

— MIKADO SEIWA (850-880)
[Emperor of Japan, This is a Shintoism revelation that came to Mikado Seiwa]

COFFEE BREAK

"I am God": Mansur Hallaj, a Muslim Sufi and mystic, believed that God is within him and there is no separation between him and God. Thus, he proclaimed, "I am God." He would point to his cloak and say, "There is nothing in my cloak but God." He was tried as a heretic and was publicly executed in Baghdad. Louis Massignon wrote Hallaj's method was that of "universalist mystical introspection: It was at the bottom of the heart that he looked for God and wanted to make others find Him. He believed one had to go beyond the forms of religious rites to reach divine reality."

"I saw my Lord with the eye of my heart.

He said, "Who are you?" I said, I am You.

You are He Who fills all place

But place does not know where You are."

— MANSUR AL-HALLAJ (858-922)

[Persian Muslim mystic, writer and teacher of Sufism. Famous for his claim: "I am the Truth [God]." He was executed for apostacy]

"I am He whom I love, and He whom I love is I:

We are two spirits dwelling in one body,

If thou seest me, thou seest Him

And if thou seest Him, thou seest us both."

— MANSUR AL-HALLAJ (858-922)

"Before" does not outstrip Him,

"after" does not interrupt Him

"of" does not vie with Him for precedence

"from" does not accord with Him

"to" does not join with Him

"in" does not inhabit Him

"when" does not stop Him

"if" does not consult with Him

"over" does not overshadow Him

"under" does not support Him

"opposite" does not face Him

"with" does not press Him

"behind" does not limit Him

"previous" does not display Him

"after" does not cause Him to pass away

"all" does not unite Him

"is" does not bring Him into being

"is not" does not deprive Him from Being.

Concealment does not veil Him

His pre-existence preceded time,

His being preceded non-being,

His eternity preceded limit."

— Mansur al-Hallaj (858-922)
[Tr. by A. J. Arberry]

"God is knowable and unknowable, evident and hidden, and the best knowledge of Him is to know that He is something the human mind cannot thoroughly understand."

— Al Farabi (872-950)

[Abu Nasr al-Farabi, known in the West as Alpharabius, Muslim polymath, philosopher, cosmologist, logician, musician, psychologist, and sociologist; one of the greatest scientists and philosophers of the Islamic world in his time]

"It is very difficult to know what God is because of the limitation of our intellect and its union with matter. Just as light is the principle by which colors become visible, in like manner it would seem logical to say that a perfect light should produce a perfect vision. Instead, the very opposite occurs. A perfect light dazzles the vision. The same is true of God. The imperfect knowledge we have of God is due to the fact that He is infinitely perfect. That explains why His infinitely perfect being bewilders our mind. But if we could strip our nature of all that we call 'matter; then certainly our knowledge of His being would be quite perfect."

— Al Farabi (872-950)

"Trees in the wilderness are watered by God."

— Kashmiri Proverb

"Some foolish men declare that Creator made the world. The doctrine that the world was created is ill-advised, and should be rejected. If god created the world, where was he before creation? If you say he was transcendent then, and needed no support, where is he now? No single being had the skill to make the world - for how can an immaterial god create that which is material? How could god have made the world without any raw material? If you say he made this first, and then the world, you are faced with an endless regression. If you declare that the raw material arose naturally you fall into another fallacy, for the whole universe might thus have been its own creator, and have risen equally naturally. If god created the world by an act of will, without any raw material, then it is just his will made nothing else and who will believe this silly stuff? If he is ever perfect, and complete, how could the will to create have arisen in him? If, on the other hand, he is not perfect, he could no more create the universe than a potter could. If he is formless, actionless, and all-embracing, how could he have created the world? Such a soul, devoid of all modality, would have no desire to create anything. If you say that he created to no purpose, because it was his nature to do so then god is pointless. If he created in some kind of sport, it was the sport of a foolish child, leading to trouble. If he created out of love for living things and need of them he made the world; why did he not make creation wholly blissful, free from misfortune? Thus the doctrine that the world was created by god makes no sense at all."

— ACHARYA JINASENA (9TH CENTURY)

[Jain monk, philosopher, and author of Mahapurana. Part of this quote was made famous by Carl Sagan who cited it in his classic Cosmos]

"That there is no good or evil on earth save what Allah wishes: and that things exist by Allah's wish; and that not a single person has the capacity to do anything until Allah causes him to act, and we are not independent of Allah, nor can we pass beyond the range of Allah's knowledge."

— AL-ASHARI (874-936)

[Muslim Arab theologian and the founder of the Ash'ari school of thought]

"He is beyond our knowledge

He is this and not this,

He comes in the form those seek

Who truly turn to him,

And yet they may not be his form."

— NAMMALVAR (880-930)

[Born as Maran in South India, some legend puts his birth in 3rd millenium BC, hymn writer on devotion to Vishnu, the Supreme God in the Vaishnavite tradition of Hinduism]

"In my heart Thou dwellest--else with blood I'll drench it;

In mine eye Thou glowest--else with tears I'll quench it.

Only to be one with Thee my soul desireth--

Else from out my body, by hook or crook, I'll wrench it!"

— ABU SAID ABUL-KHAYR (967-1049)

[Persian Muslim sufi poet]

"Love is the net of Truth

Love is the noose of God"

— ABU SAID ABUL-KHAYR (967-1049)

"There is no God save Allah!—that is true,

Nor is there any prophet save the mind

Of man who wanders through the dark to find The Paradise that is in me and you."

— ABU AL-ALA (973-1057)

[Blind Muslim poet and philosopher, born in Syria]

"God, the supreme being, is neither circumscribed by space, nor touched by time; he cannot be found in a particular direction, and his essence cannot change. The secret conversation is thus entirely spiritual; it is a direct encounter between God and the soul, abstracted from all material constraints."

— AVICENNA (980-1037)

[Also known as Ibn Seena, Persian Muslim polymath and the foremost physician and philosopher of his time. He was also an astronomer, chemist, logician, mathematician, poet, psychologist, physicist, scientist, Sheikh, soldier, statesman and theologian]

"A sign of a liar is his generosity of saying 'by God' without people asking him to swear."

— ARABIC PROVERB

"Even God is fed up of lazy people."

— AFGHAN PROVERB

"Poverty is a noose that strangles humility and breeds disrespect for God and man."

— NATIVE AMERICAN INDIAN (LAKOTA) PROVERB

"God gives us each a song."

— NATIVE AMERICAN INDIAN (UTE) PROVERB

"Prayer carries us half way to God, fasting brings us to the door of His palace, and alms-giving procures us admission."

— OLD MUSLIM PROVERB

"If God doesn't like the way I live, let him tell me, not you."

— ANONYMOUS

"God often visits us, but most of the time we are not at home."

— FRENCH PROVERB

"God is closest to those with broken hearts."

— JEWISH PROVERB

"If God lived on earth, people would break his windows."

— JEWISH PROVERB

CHAPTER DIGEST (1 TO 1000 AD)

God spoke volubly in this period of history through the Bible and the Quran. And he was heard. More than half the people in the world today claim to follow one of the two creeds that are connected to the Bible and the Quran. The God of Christianity is a trinity of the Father, the Son, and the Holy Ghost, while the God of Islam is Allah, a single Supreme Being. The central theme of both religions is submission to the will of God, which represents the highest level of morality to which a man can aspire.

The *Holy Wall* of God's Facebook in this period of history is full of messages from the Bible and the Quran, both of which talk about a kind, gracious, and merciful God who is also righteous, and will judge human beings after death. But there are also enough differences and apparent inconsistencies between these two scriptures that people fought countless wars over their interpretations of these postings. God posted a message of love in the Shintoist scriptures called Kojiki and Nihongi.

The most popular postings on the *Wall of Mortals* in this period are those of the Prophet Muhammad, who is revered by 1.5 billion Muslims all over the world as the ultimate role model for humans. Other postings of note on the *Wall of Mortals* are by St. Augustine, a Christian who argued that God is unknowable; by Kalidasa, a Hindu, who saw the sign of God in the beauty of women; and by Mansur Hallaj, a Muslim, who declared "I am God." These humans and other thinkers of the first millennium defined God in their own ways, depending on their religious and cultural backgrounds. A lot of postings on the *Wall of Mortals* in this period were from Muslim thinkers of Islam's golden age.

A transcendent unity of religions emerged in this period because the core messages on moral and peaceful living from different religions were found to be similar, if not equal, in spirit. Even the teachings of the great philosophers, believers or not, were found to be aligned with the core messages of the religions, when rituals were left aside.

Thus, a theoretical basis for a *Friendship of Civilizations* started to emerge.

7

God of Believers, Unbelievers, and Mystics
(1000 to 1700 AD)

"To Love is to reach God.
Never will a Lover's chest
feel any sorrow.
Never will a Lover's robe
be touched by mortals.
Never will a Lover's body
be found buried in the earth."

—Rumi (1207-1273)

STATUS UPDATE (1000-1700 AD)

❖ God's existence is challenged; Avicenna and Saint Anselm of Canterbury are the first to develop ontological proofs of God's existence.

❖ God and old religions are scrutinized under the lenses of rationalism and empiricism.

❖ God enjoys a diversity of opinions about him, as the European Renaissance and Reformation revolutionize human thoughts on God, religion, morality, art, and literature.

❖ God is seen as the ultimate reality, with whom communion is possible. Muslim Sufi mystics (Rumi, Hafiz, Sanai, Attar, Ibn Arabi) speak of Wahdatul Wujud (the Unity of Being), which emphasizes that there is no true existence except God.

❖ God's mystical nature is expressed in the Zohar, the foundational work of Kabbalah. The Zohar establishes the idea of Sephirot (Enumeration), which is considered to be revelations of God's will.

❖ God and the Bible rise to prominence among European Christian scholars and give rise to Scholasticism, which attempts to reconcile ancient philosophy with medieval Christian theology.

❖ The new science brings about the biggest single change in human conceptions of God and the universe.

STATUS UPDATE (1000-1700 AD)

❖ Galileo almost loses his life for professing the view that the earth moves, which the Roman Catholic Church considers a sinful notion.

❖ God reveals himself as the one universal creator to Guru Nanak Dev, who founds Sikhism, a monotheistic religion in India.

❖ God's Religion (Din-i-Ilahi) is established by the Mughal emperor Akbar the Great, in an effort to synthesize different religions into one.

❖ God's physical laws are uncovered by Isaac Newton ("Nature and Nature's Laws lay hid in night/God said, Let Newton be!, and all was light"). Newton, one of the greatest scientists of all time and a devout Christian, proclaims, "God governs all things."

NOTES FROM HISTORY
(1000 TO 1700 AD)

The advent of printing enables people to record and distribute their thoughts on God in a permanent form. As a result, this period of human civilization is marked by a superabundance of recorded opinions about God. It should be noted that this period saw the demise of new religious scriptures, the sole exception being the Sri Guru Granth Sahib of Sikhism in fifteenth-century Punjab, India.

The eleventh century is considered in Europe to be the beginning of the High Middle Ages, which was marked by rapidly increasing population and the rise of nation-states in Western Europe and city-states in Italy. The "Peace and Truce of God" movement started in the Catholic church; this

1095 AD: The Crusades began.

movement tried to impose spiritual sanctions to limit the private wars of feudalism in medieval Europe.

The eleventh century also marked the high point of both classical Chinese civilization and classical Islamic civilization. The Turkish Seljuk dynasty came to power in 1037 AD in the Middle East. The first of the Crusades, a series of holy wars fought over a period of 200 years to regain Christian control of the Holy Land, especially Jerusalem, was fought in 1095 AD. The Toltec and Mixtec civilizations flourished in Central America, while the Mississippian culture flourished in North America.

A civil war in England raged from 1135 to 1154, which was called the Period of Anarchy. During the twelfth century, huge social, political, and economic transformations took place in Europe, which revitalized it with intellectual, philosophical, and scientific advancements. These great changes paved the way for the Italian Renaissance in the fifteenth century and the scientific developments of the seventeenth century in Europe. A rediscovery of the works of Aristotle gave birth in the twelfth century to a new method of learning in Europe called Scholasticism. Thomas Aquinas, the most famous of the scholastic practitioners, developed a theory about the philosophy of mind, wherein the mind is considered a blank slate at birth and is capable of forming ideas through a divine spark. The first European universities were founded in the twelfth century.

Ibn Rushd, known in European literature as Averroes, was born in 1126 in Cordoba. He was an Andalusian Muslim polymath—a master of Islamic philosophy, Islamic theology, law and jurisprudence, logic, psychology, politics, Arabic music theory, and the sciences of medicine, astronomy, geography, mathematics, physics, and celestial mechanics. He has been described by some as the founding father of secular thought in Western Europe and "one of the spiritual fathers of Europe."

The Mongol Empire spanned Eastern Europe and Asia. At the time of Genghis Khan's death in 1227, the empire was twice the size of the Roman Empire and covered 22% of the world's total land area. The Mongols expanded their empire through invasion, and the death toll from the Mongol and Tartar invasions between 1207 and 1472 is estimated to be in the range of thirty to one hundred million.

The Muslim mystics sought communion with, identity with, the ultimate reality, God. The veil between "I" and "You" (God) was torn by Islamic mysticism. The sufi philosophy of *Wahdatul Wujud* (the Unity of Being) proclaimed that the only truth within the universe is God and everything else is a falsehood. This can be compared with Pantheism, in which the Universe and God are thought to be identical. The Pantheists do not believe in a personal or creator God. On the other hand, the followers of *Wahdatul Wujud* philosophy believe that there is no true existence except God and everything is but the shadow of God, who is mysteriously present in humans, and humans are obliterated in God. The great sufi mystic, Ibn 'Arabi (1165-1240) explained this duality in this manner: "here are two aspects of one and the same state, which are neither merged together nor yet added one to the other."

Rumi (1207–1273), the greatest Persian mystic poet, who is also the most popular poet in America today, completed his masterpiece Masnavi, which is regarded as the most influential work on Sufism. It consists of six books of Persian poetry and contains about 25,000 verses. Masnavi is regarded by some Sufis as the Persian language Quran.

Zohar, the foundational work of Jewish mysticism, was published by Moses de Leon in Spain in the thirteenth century. The idea of the Sephirot, the ten attributes of Kabbalah through which God reveals himself, was introduced by the Jewish mystics.

The Ottoman Empire began in 1299. This empire was in effect the Islamic successor of the Eastern Roman Empire. At the prime of its power (sixteenth to seventeenth centuries) it controlled much of southeastern Europe, Western Asia, and North Africa. The Battle of Vienna in 1683 marked the end of Ottoman expansion in Europe.

The Hundred Years' War, a series of separate wars between two royal dynasties for the French throne, began in 1337. This war lasted for 116 years, with intermittent periods of peace, ending in 1453 with a victory for the House of Valois, who expelled the House of Plantagenet from France. Joan of Arc (1412–1431), a peasant girl from France, claimed divine guidance and led the French army into several battle field victories of the Hundred Years' War. She was captured and tried by the English, and at nineteen was burned at the stake. She was later awarded martyrdom and sainthood by the Catholic church.

In the fifteenth century, the Inca Empire became prominent in South America. The Ming Dynasty ruled in China from 1368 to 1644. The first encyclopedia was commissioned in China by the Ming Dynasty Emperor Yongle. Two thousand scholars worked on the project, which was completed in 1408. The Yongle encyclopedia contained 22,877 volumes in 11,095 books.

The Mughal Empire in India was established by the Timurid Prince Babur in 1526. Akbar the Great ruled from 1556 to 1605 and established religious freedom. He also tried to unite the Hindus and Muslims by introducing *Din-i-Ilahi* ("Divine Faith"), which took the best elements from different religions of his kingdom. Din-i-Ilahi didn't survive Emperor Akbar. The Mughal empire continued to expand its territory until the death of Emperor Aurangzeb in 1707.

1658: The Tajmahal was built.

Emperor Shahjahan, father of Emperor Aurangzeb, immortalized his love for his wife by building the Tajmahal from 1627 to 1658. The Tajmahal is one of the seven wonders of the world and is the finest example of Mughal architecture. Emperor Shahjahan wanted the Tajmahal to express the glory of the creator and, described it as follows in a poem he wrote:

"Should guilty seek asylum here,

Like one pardoned, he becomes free from sin.

Should a sinner make his way to this mansion,

All his past sins are to be washed away.

The sight of this mansion creates sorrowing sighs;

And the sun and the moon shed tears from their eyes.

In this world this edifice has been made;

To display thereby the creator's glory."

The European Renaissance began in Italy and spanned roughly the fourteenth to seventeenth centuries. It was a great cultural movement that profoundly influenced intellectual life in Europe, more specifically art, architecture, ethics, literature, philosophy, politics, religion, science, and sociology. Leonardo da Vinci (1452–1519), an Italian polymath—scientist, mathematician, engineer, inventor, anatomist, painter, sculptor, architect, botanist, musician, and writer—began painting the *"Mona Lisa"*, the most famous painting in the world, in 1503. The French Wars of Religion (1562–1598) were fought between French Catholics and Protestants, with a death toll ranging from two to four million.

EVOLUTION OF GOD

The God of the Renaissance spoke through poets, artists, and musicians.

The scientific revolution in Europe began in 1543 with the publication of two seminal books:

1. *On the Revolutions of the Heavenly Spheres*, by astronomer Nicolaus Copernicus (1473–1543), and

2. *On the Fabric of the Human Body in Seven Books*, by Andreas Vesalius (1514–1564). During the sixteenth century, the Protestant Reformation in Europe dealt a major blow to the authority of the Papacy and the Roman Catholic Church.

William Shakespeare, the great English poet and playwright, and Galileo Galilei, the great Italian scientist, were born in 1564. In 1593, Galileo invented a thermometer. Galileo incurred the rage of the Roman Catholic Church for asserting that the earth rotates on it axis and revolves around the sun. He was condemned by the Church and was forced to recant his statements, promising never again to uphold the sinful view that the earth moves.

Sir Isaac Newton, one of the greatest scientists and among the most influential men in history, was born in 1643. An English polymath—physicist, mathematician, astronomer, natural philosopher, alchemist, and theologian—he laid the foundation of classical mechanics and discovered the laws of motion and universal gravitation. In mathematics, he shares the credit with Gottfried Leibniz for inventing calculus. He made significant contributions to the study of optics, the solution of mathematical equations, and the theory of color. Newton was a devout Christian and a prolific writer on religious matters. Ironically, he wrote more on religion than on the science for which he is remembered today.

The Thirty Year's War (1618–1648) between Protestants and Catholics raged in German states, Sweden, and Poland. The death toll ranged from a low estimate of three million to a high estimate of eleven million. The English Civil War between the Parliamentarians and Royalists took place from 1641 to 1651, ending with a Parliamentarian victory.

The scientific revolution continued well into the late seventeenth century. It greatly influenced human thoughts on God, because the new philosophy of the scientific revolution questioned everything and replaced many old ideas with new ones. English poet John Donne wrote in 1611:

"[The] new Philosophy calls all in doubt,

The Element of fire is quite put out;

The Sun is lost, and th'earth, and no man's wit

Can well direct him where to look for it."

Wilhelm Schickard (1592–1635) built one of the first calculating machines in 1623. In 1672, Otto von Guericke (1602–1686) generated electricity using a machine. Antoni Leeuwenhoek (1632–1723) discovered bacteria in 1676.

HOLY WALL:
THE GURU GRANTH SAHIB – SIKH SCRIPTURE

The Sri Guru Granth Sahib, also called Adi Granth, is the holy scripture and final Guru of the Sikhs. It is a collection of hymns (or shabad) composed by the Sikh Gurus from 1469 to 1708. Guru Gobind Singh (1666–1708), the tenth Guru, affirmed that this book would be his successor, and that there would be no more human Gurus. Sikhs regard Sri Guru Granth Sahib as the living embodiment of the Ten Gurus.

THREE PILLARS, FIVE VIRTUES, AND FIVE EVILS OF SIKHISM

Three pillars of Sikhism are the three basic guidelines formalized by Guru Nanak for Sikhs. In Sikhism, there are five virtues one should develop in order to reach Mukti, or reunite with God and there are five evils one should subdue to pursue a moral and spiritual life.

These three pillars are:

1. Remembrance of God
2. Honest living, and
3. Sharing with others

The five virtues one should develop are:

1. Truth
2. Compassion
3. Contentment
4. Humility, and
5. Love

The five evils one should subdue are:

1. Lust
2. Rage
3. Greed
4. Attachment, and
5. Ego

MESSAGES FROM GURU GRANTH SAHIB

"One Universal Creator God, The Name Is Truth, Creative Being Personified, No Fear, No Hatred, Image Of The Undying, Beyond Birth, Self Existent, By Guru's Grace.Chant and Meditate: True in the primal beginning. True throughout the ages. True here and now. O Nanak, forever and ever true."

— Sri Guru Grantha Sahib, opening verse, Page 1
[Tr. by Dr. Sant Singh Khalsa]

"He wanders around in the four quarters and in the ten directions, according to the dictates of his karma. Pleasure and pain, liberation and reincarnation, O Nanak, come according to one's pre-ordained destiny."

— Sri Guru Grantha Sahib, Page 253
[Tr. by Dr. Sant Singh Khalsa]

"The God-conscious being is always unattached, as the lotus in the water remains detached. The God-conscious being is always unstained, like the sun, which gives its comfort and warmth to all. The God-conscious being looks upon all alike, like the wind, which blows equally upon the king and the poor beggar.

…. The God-conscious being has no egotistical pride. The God-conscious being is the highest of the high. Within his own mind, he is the most humble of all. They alone become God-conscious beings, O Nanak, whom God Himself makes so."

— Sri Guru Grantha Sahib, Page 272
[Tr. by Dr. Sant Singh Khalsa]

"God is merciful and infinite. The One and Only is all-pervading. He Himself is all-in-all. Who else can we speak of? God Himself grants His gifts, and He Himself receives them. Coming and going are all by the Hukam of Your Will; Your place is steady and unchanging. Nanak begs for this gift; by Your Grace, Lord, please grant me Your Name."

— Sri Guru Grantha Sahib, Page 710
[Tr. by Dr. Sant Singh Khalsa]

"Lust, anger, egotism, jealousy and desire are eliminated by chanting the Name of the Lord. The merits of cleansing baths, charity, penance, purity and good deeds, are obtained by enshrining the Lotus Feet of God within the heart."

— Sri Guru Grantha Sahib, Page 1389
[Tr. by Dr. Sant Singh Khalsa]

"First, is the Lord's Praise; second, contentment; third, humility, and fourth, giving to charities. Fifth is to hold one's desires in restraint. These are the five most sublime daily prayers. Let your daily worship be the knowledge that God is everywhere. …. One who realizes the Prophet attains heaven. Azraaeel, the Messenger of Death, does not cast him into hell. Let good deeds be your body, and faith your bride. Play and enjoy the Lord's love and delight. Purify what is impure, and let the Lord's Presence be your religious tradition. Let your total awareness be the turban on your head. To be Muslim is to be kind-hearted, and wash away pollution from within the heart."

— Sri Guru Grantha Sahib, Page 1084
[Tr. by Dr. Sant Singh Khalsa]

"Do not utter even a single harsh word; your True Lord and Master abides in all. Do not break anyone's heart; these are all priceless jewels. The minds of all are like precious jewels; to harm them is not good at all. If you desire your Beloved, then do not break anyone's heart."

— Sri Guru Grantha Sahib, Page 1384
[Tr. by Dr. Sant Singh Khalsa]

"Ever is He present with you--think not He is far:
By the Master's teaching recognize Him within yourself."

— Adi Granth, Majh Ashtpadi, M.3, p. 116

"Why do you go to the forest in search of God?
He lives in all and is yet ever distinct;
He abides with you, too,
As a fragrance dwells in a flower,
And reflection in a mirror;
So does God dwell inside everything;
Seek Him, therefore, in your heart."

— Adi Granth, Dhanasri, M.9, p. 684

EVOLUTION OF GOD

The God of Sikhism is One (Ik Onkar), indescribable yet knowable.

WALL OF MORTALS:
(1000 TO 1700 AD)

COFFEE BREAK

The Ontological Argument: St. Anselm of Canterbury was the first to propose the ontological argument for the existence of God. He argued that if we can conceive of the greatest possible being, it must exist in reality, and if it does not exist in reality, a greater being is possible — one which does exist.

"One Universal Creator God, The Name Is Truth, Creative Being Personified, No Fear, No And indeed we believe you [God] to be something than which a greater cannot be conceived."

— St. Anselm of Canterbury (1033–1109)
[Italian-born British theologian. Archbishop of Canterbury from 1093 until his death. Famous as the originator of the ontological argument for the existence of God]

"For no one who understands what God is can think that he does not exist. ... Whoever understands this also understands that God exists in such a way that one cannot even think of him as not existing."

— St. Anselm of Canterbury (1033–1109)

"For I do not seek to understand in order to believe, but I believe in order to understand. For I believe this: unless I believe, I will not understand."

— St. Anselm of Canterbury (1033–1109)

"Belief brings me close to You but only to the door. It is only by disappearing into Your mystery that I will come in."

— Hakim Sanai (1040 – 1131)
[Persian Muslim sufi poet from Ghazna, Afghanistan]

"But helpless Pieces of the Game He plays
Upon this Chequer board of Nights and Days;
Hither and thither moves, and checks, and slays,
And one by one back in the Closet lays."

— Omar Khayyam (1048-1131)
[Persian polymath, mathematician, philosopher, astronomer, physician, and poet. Translations are from Robert Fitzerald]

God plays chess
— Khayyam

"The Ball no question makes of Ayes and Noes,
But Here or There as strikes the Player goes;
And He that toss'd you down into the Field,
He knows about it all — He knows — HE knows!"

— Omar Khayyam (1048-1131)

"Tell unto reasoners that, for the lovers of God, intuition is guide, not discursive thought."

— OMAR KHAYYAM (1048-1131)

"God's protection is man's hope."

—VLADIMIR II MONOMAKH (1053-1125)
[Famous Grand Prince of Kievan Russia]

COFFEE BREAK
Unique and Unknowable God: Imam Ghazali, a theologian from modern-day Iran, is considered as the single most influential Muslim after the prophet Muhammad; his influence is compared with that of St. Thomas Aquinas in of Christian theology. Ghazali's conception of God is that of an unique and unknowable God, a perspective that was also shared later by the Jewish rabbi Maimonides.

"In God, there is no sorrow or suffering or affliction. If you want to be free of all affliction and suffering, hold fast to God, and turn wholly to Him, and to no one else. Indeed, all your suffering comes from this: that you do not turn toward God and no one else."

— IMAM AL GHAZALI (1058-1111)

[Abu Hamid Muhammad ibn Muhammad al-Ghazali, one of the most respected scholars of Islam, theologian, philosopher, jurist, author, cosmologist, psychologist]

"Let us imagine a child and a grown-up in Heaven who both died in the True Faith, but the grown-up has a higher place than the child. And the child will ask God, "Why did you give that man a higher place?" And God will answer, "He has done many good works." Then the child will say, "Why did you let me die so soon so that I was prevented from doing good?" God will answer, "I knew that you would grow up a sinner, therefore it was better that you should die a child." Then a cry goes up from the damned in the depths of Hell, "Why, O Lord, did you not let us die before we became sinners?" The imponderable decisions of God cannot be weighed by the scales of reason and Mutazilism [Islamic rationalist movement]."

— IMAM AL GHAZALI (1058-1111)

"An intention is good if and only if the intention is believed to and in fact does conform to God's will."

— PETER ABELARD (1079-1142)

[French theologian and moral philosopher, credited as the founder of intentionalist ethics]

"These Gods tainted with attachment and passion; having women and weapons by their side, favour some and disfavour some; such Gods should not be worshipped by those who desire emancipation."

— ACHARYA HEMACANDRA (1089-1172)
[Jain scholar, poet, polymath, and prodigious author]

179

"I know by myself how incomprehensible God is, seeing I cannot comprehend the parts of my own being."

— St. Bernard of Clairvaux (1090–1153)
[Highly influential French churchman and theologian. Founder of the Cistercian, or Bernardine, monastic order]

"God cannot be perceived directly; He is known through creation, through humankind alone, which is a mirror of all God's wonders"

Hildegard von Bingen (1098-1179)
[German woman writer, philosopher, mystic, and founder of monasteries of Rupertsberg and Eibingen, also known as Saint Hildegard]

"Whoever has been occupied with the science of anatomy/dissection has increased his belief in God."

— Ibn Rushd (1126-1198)
[Abul Walid Muhammed Ibn Ahmed Ibn Rushd, known in the West as Averroes, regarded as the most important of the Islamic philosophers; judge, author, psychologist, and author of a medical encyclopedia]

"God is the nonhuman and transcendent first cause of all being."

— Ibn Rushd (1126-1198)

"True science is cognizance of God (may He be blessed and exalted) and of all the existing things as they are, especially the venerable ones among them; and cognizance of happiness in the hereafter and of misery in the hereafter. True practice is to follow the actions that promote happiness and to avoid the actions that promote misery; and cognizance of these actions is what is called 'practical science.'"

— Ibn Rushd (1126-1198)

"When a man reflects on these things, studies all these created beings, from the angels and spheres down to human beings and so on, and realizes the divine wisdom manifested in them all, his love for God will increase, his soul will thirst, his very flesh will yearn to love God."

— Maimonides (1135-1204)
[Rabbi Moshe ben Maimon, Jewish rabbi, physician, and philosopher from Spain who spent most of his life in Egypt]

"The foundation of all foundations, and the pillar of all wisdom is to know that there is God who brought into being all existence. All the beings of the heavens, and the earth, and what is between them came into existence only from the truth of God's being."

— Maimonides (1135-1204)

GOD AND MYSTICISM

All religions have a mystical side to them. A mystic is a person who attempts to transcend and transform observed realities to unite with Absolute Reality — God. Mysticism begins with one's search for the divine within oneself. Mystics perceive God experientially, which is very different from the ways of common believers.

GOD OF HINDU MYSTICS

Hindu mysticism has its roots in Vedanta philosophy, which is based on the Upanishads. Vedanta philosophy teaches that the human soul, in its primordial form, is not only divine but also identical with Absolute Reality — *Brahman* (or God). The Upanishads say: *Tat Tvam Asi*, which means "Thou art that." Absolute Reality cannot be described except in a triad of words, *Sat–Chit–Ananda*, which mean "Existence, Consciousness, and Bliss." These three terms cannot be understood except through a direct mystical experience with our core being, when we can see the self as identical with God. The great ninth-century philosopher Adi Shankara declared: *Brahma satya jagat mithya, javo brahmaiva naparah* — God is the only truth, the spatiotemporal world is an illusion, and there is ultimately no difference between God and the individual self.

EVOLUTION OF GOD

The God of mystics is a personal God, attained by abnegation of the self.

GOD OF JEWISH KABBALISTS

Kabbalah is a form of Jewish mysticism. It is not about worship or belief, but about a direct path to communion with the Supreme Being. Kabbalists call God *Ein Sof*, which literally means "endless." In their view, God is everywhere and transcends the universe; he is indescribable and remote. According to the Kabbalists, the ultimate goal of human existence is union with the Divine *(devekut)*. Rabbi Moshe Cordovero (1522–1570), one of the early Kabbalists, wrote: "The essence of divinity is found in every single thing—nothing but it exists.... Do not attribute duality to God. Let God be solely God. If you suppose that *[Ein Sof]* emanates until a certain point, and that from that point on is outside of it, you have dualized. God forbid! Realize, rather, that *Ein Sof* exists in each existent. Do not say, 'This is a stone and not God.' God forbid! Rather, all existence is God, and the stone is a thing pervaded by divinity."

GOD OF CHRISTIAN MYSTICS

Christian mysticism has its roots in Neoplatonism. Christian mystics believe in a God who is inside the human soul and with whom a direct personal relationship is possible through love and devotion. The great Christian mystic Meister Eckhart wrote: "When I preach, I usually speak of detachment and say that a man should be empty of self and all things; and secondly, that he should be reconstructed in the simple good that God is; and thirdly, that he should consider the great aristocracy which God has set up in the soul, such that by means of it man may wonderfully attain to God." The mystics seek a spiritual union with God, a state of ecstasy described beautifully by St. Teresa of Avila: "In the orison of union, the soul is fully awake as regards God, but wholly asleep as regards things of this world and in respect of herself. During the short time the union lasts, she is... deprived of every feeling, and even if she would, she could not think of any single thing... God established himself in the interior of the soul in such a way that when she returns to herself, it is impossible for her to doubt that she has been in God and God in her." In this state of union, Meister Eckhart said: "The eye with which I see God is the same with which God sees me. My eye and God's eye is one eye, and one sight, and one knowledge, and one love."

GOD OF MUSLIM SUFIS

Sufis are the mystics of Islam. They are literally God-intoxicated humans. The God of the Sufis is all-pervading and all-encompassing. According to the Sufis, the only existence on the Earth is that of God; everything else is a mere manifestation of God. This doctrine is called *Wahdatul Wujud* (the Unity of Being). The great Sufi poet Rumi wrote:

"We are non-existence, displaying the illusion of existence

You [God] are Absolute Being and our only existence."

The ultimate goal of man is to become the Perfect Man, one "who has fully realized his essential oneness with the Divine Being in whose likeness he is made." The Sufi mystics conceptualized two stages of mystical experience, the first being the *"Fana Fillah"*, which means destruction of self into God resulting in a unification with the Divine Essence. The second and final stage of the mystical experience is *"Baqa Billah"* or the coexistence with God, where self is the same as God. In an ecstatic state of *Baqa Billah*, Muslim Sufi Mansur Hallaj proclaimed: "I am God." Sufism made significant contributions to beautiful spiritual poetry by the likes of Rumi, Hafiz, Khayyam, Attar, Shabistari, Saadi, Jami, Iqbal, Sanai, Kabir, and Lalan Shah.

"Love all and hate none."

Mere talk of peace will avail you naught.

Mere talk of God and religion will not take you far.

Bring out all the latent powers of your being

and reveal the full magnificence of your immortal self."

— KHWAJA MOINUDDIN CHISTHI (1141-1230)

[Afghan-born Indian Muslim Sufi, famous for the Chisti order of Sufis, also known as Gharib Nawaz or the Benefactor of the Poor. His burial place is a shrine, known as Ajmeer Sharif, and is visited by millions of Hindus and Muslims every year]

"A friend of God must have affection like the Sun. When the sun rises, it is beneficial to all irrespective of whether they are Muslim, Christian, or Hindu.

A friend of God must be generous like a river. We all get water from the river to quench our thirst. It does not discriminate whether we are good or bad or whether we are a relation or a stranger."

— KHWAJA MOINUDDIN CHISTHI (1141-1230)

"Yet what are seas and what is air? For all

Is God, and but a talisman are heaven and earth

To veil Divinity."

— FARID-UD-DIN ATTAR (1145-1221)

[Persian Muslim poet, theoretician of Sufism, famous for his book "Conference of the Birds")

"God said to David: 'Tell my servants: prayer

Should be creation's all-consuming care;

Though hell were not his fear nor heaven his goal

The Lord should wholly occupy man's soul...'

True prayer seeks God alone;

Its motives start

Deep in the center of a contrite heart ...

If it is paradise for which you pray

You can be sure that you have lost your way."

— FARID-UD-DIN ATTAR (1145-1221)

"I saw

The fragrance fleeing

When the bee came,

What a wonder!
I saw
Intellect fleeing
When the heart came.
I saw
The temple fleeing
When God came."

— ALLAMA PRABHU (12TH CENTURY)
[Indian poet and mystic saint of the Kannada language]

"The image of the God whom the faithful creates is the Image of the God whom his own being reveals. Thus it is psychologically true to say that "the God created in the faiths" is the symbol of the Self. The God to whom we pray can be only the God who reveals Himself to us, by us, and for us, but it is praying to Him that we cause the "God created in the faiths"" to be himself enveloped in the Divine Compassion, that is, existentiated, manifested by it."

— IBN ARABI (1165-1240)
[Andalusian Arab Sufi mystic and philosopher]

"He who knows himself knows his Lord."

— IBN ARABI (1165-1240)

"God (al-Haqq) is your mirror, that is the mirror in which you contemplate your self (nafs, anima), and you, you are His mirror, that is the mirror in which He contemplates His divine Names."

— IBN ARABI (1165-1240)

"Do not speak a hurtful word,
for in everyone lives the true Lord.
Do not break anyone's heart,
for each heart
is a priceless pearl."

— BABA SHEIKH FARID (1173-1266)
[Pakistani Sufi preacher and saint]

"If you have men who will exclude any of God's creatures from the shelter of compassion and pity, you will have men who deal likewise with their fellow men."

— SAINT FRANCIS OF ASSISI (1182–1226)
[Italian religious leader and founder of the Order of Friars Minor, more commonly known as the Franciscans]

"God came to my house and asked for charity. And I fell on my knees and cried, "Beloved, what may I give?" "Just love", He said, "Just love."

— Saint Francis of Assisi (1182–1226)

"It is God alone that gives your arms their power.

If, by your striving, you achieve something good,

Don't claim the credit all for yourself."

— Saadi (1184-1283)

> *[Sheikh Saadi, Persian poet, famous for his books "Gulistan" and "Bostan", a native of Shiraz, Persia]*

"I fear God, and next to God I chiefly fear him who fears Him not."

— Saadi (1184-1283)

COFFEE BREAK

The Most Popular Poet in America: In 2002, *Time* magazine broke the news that Rumi, a Persian Muslim mystic, was the best-selling poet in America. Coleman Bark's *The Essential Rumi*, published in 1995, is one of the most successful poetry book in the West, with more than 250,000 copies in print. Madonna has set his verses to music, Donna Karan (DK brand owner) has used recitations of Rumi's verses in her fashion shows, and he is the most quoted Muslim poet in the West. The God he talks about is rarely interested in the orthodox doctrines.

"Beware! Don't allow yourself to do what you know is wrong, relying on the thought, 'Later I will repent and ask God's forgiveness.'"

— Rumi (1207-1273)

> *[Mevlana Jalal al-Din Muhammad Rumi, Persian poet and philosopher, theologian, teacher, and founder of the Mevlevi (or Mawlawi) order of Sufism; The most popular poet in America]*

"To love is to reach God."

— Rumi (1207-1273)

"Reason is like an officer when the King appears;

The officer then loses his power and hides himself.

Reason is the shadow cast by God; God is the sun."

Reason is not God

— Rumi(1207-1273)

"God turns you from one feeling to another and teaches by means of opposites, so that you will have two wings to fly, not one."

-Rumi(1207-1273)

"The Prophet said that God has declared,
I am not contained in earth or sky, or even
In highest heaven. Know this for a surety, O beloved!
Yet am I contained in the believer's heart!
If ye seek me, search in such hearts."

— RUMI (1207-1273)

"I cannot dance, Lord, unless you lead me."

— MECHTHILD OF MAGDEBURG (1210–1285/1291)
[German mystic and nun]

"There is no god but Love. (La ilaha illa'l-'ishq)"

— AL-IRAQI (1213–1289)
[Fakhr al-din Ibrahim, Persian philosopher and mystic]

"If the Lord Almighty had consulted me before embarking upon his creation, I should have recommended something simpler."

— ALFONSO X OF CASTILE (1221-1284)
[Monarch of Castile, Leon, and Galicia]

"Reason in man is rather like God in the world."

— SAINT THOMAS AQUINAS (1225-1274)
[Italian Catholic philosopher and the best-known theologian of Medieval Europe]

"To disparage the dictate of reason is equivalent to contemning the command of God."

— SAINT THOMAS AQUINAS (1225-1274)

"Prayer was created by God so man could ask for help."

—YUNUS EMRE (1240–1321)
[Turkish poet, sufi mystic; considered the greatest Folk Poet of Islam]

"The most excellent of those who perform good deeds are those who most often remember God in all situations."

— ATA ALLAH (1250-1309)
[Ahmad ibn Muhammad Ibn 'Ata Allah al-Iskandari, a sufi sheikh from Egypt]

"When men in prayer declare the Unity of the Holy Name in love and reverence, the walls of earth's darkness are cleft in twain, and the Face of the Heavenly King is revealed, lighting up the universe.'

— MOSES DE LEON (1250–1305)
[Spanish rabbi and Kabbalist, composer or redactor of the Zohar]

"My Lord told me a joke. And seeing Him laugh has done more for me than any scripture I will ever read."

— MEISTER ECKHART (1260-1328)
[German philosopher, Christian mystic, and theologian]

"To be full of things is to be empty of God. To be empty of things is to be full of God."

— MEISTER ECKHART (1260-1328)

"The eye with which I see God is the same eye with which God sees me: my eye and God's eye are one eye, one seeing, one knowing and one love."

— MEISTER ECKHART (1260-1328)

"I pray God to get rid me of God"

— MEISTER ECKHART (1260-1328)

"Nature is the art of God."

— DANTE (1265–1321)
[Durante degli Alighieri, Italian poet, author of The Divine Comedy]

"The greatest gift that God in His bounty made in creation, and the most conformable to His goodness, and that which He prizes the most, was the freedom of will, with which the creatures with intelligence, they all and they alone, were and are endowed."

— DANTE (1265-1321)

COFFEE BREAK

Ockham's Razor: William of Ockham (1285–1347) is famous for Ockham's Razor, a logical principle stating that given two alternative explanations for the same phenomenon, the simpler one is more likely to be correct and the more complex one to be incorrect. Though William was a theist, Ockham's Razor has been applied to argue that a belief in God requires more complex assumptions to explain the universe than non-belief, and therefore atheism should be preferred.

"Nothing ought to be posited without a reason given, unless it is self-evident (literally, known through itself) or known by experience or proved by the authority of Sacred Scripture."

—WILLIAM OF OCKHAM (1287–1347)
[Prominent British philosopher]

"Only faith gives us access to theological truths. The ways of God are not open to reason, for God has freely chosen to create a world and establish a way of salvation within it apart from any necessary laws that human logic or rationality can uncover."

—WILLIAM OF OCKHAM (1287–1347)

"Let reason go. For His light
burns reason up from head to foot.
If you wish to see that Face,
seek another eye. The philosopher
with his two eyes sees double,
so is unable to see the unity of the Truth.
As His light burns up the angels,
even so does it consume reason.
As the light of our eyes is to the sun,
so is the light of reason to the Light of Lights."

— MAHMUD SHABISTARI (1288-1340)
[One of the most celebrated Persian sufi poet]

Let reason go

"Let us make God the beginning and end of our love, for he is the fountain from which all good things flow and into him alone they flow back. Let him therefore be the beginning of our love."

— RICHARD ROLLE (1290–1349)
[English religious leader and mystic]

"God is infinite and without end, but the soul's desire is an abyss which cannot be filled except by a Good which is infinite; and the more ardently the soul longeth after God, the more she wills to long after him; for God is a Good without drawback, and a well of living water without bottom, and the soul is made in the image of God, and therefore it is created to know and love God."

— JOHANNES TAULER (1300-1361)
[German mystic theologian]

"God indeed is the best: and I am the worst."

— PETRARCH (1304-1374)
[Francesco Petrarca, Italian scholar, poet and one of the earliest Renaissance humanists]

"You have not danced so badly, my dear,
Trying to hold hands with the Beautiful One.
You have waltzed with great style, my sweet, crushed angel,
To have ever neared God's heart at all."

— HAFIZ (1315-1390)
[Khwaja Samsud-Din Muhammad Hafiz-e Shirazi, the most celebrated Persian lyric poet]

"God cannot be grasped by the mind, therefore do not exert yourself to understand Him; He is free of all directions, therefore do not try to seek Him anywhere."

— HAFIZ (1315-1390)

"Whan that the month in which the world bigan,
That highte March, when God first maked man."

— Geoffrey Chaucer (1343-1400)
[English poet, philosopher, and diplomat]

""Dear God," I have prayed, "how is it possible all the horrors I have seen, all the atrocities you allow man to commit when you – God – are ever standing so near and could help us? Could we not hear you voice say 'No' with such love and power never again would we harm?." And my Lord replied, "who would understand if I said that I cannot bear to confine a wing, and not let it learn from the course it chooses.""

— St. Catherine of Siena (1347 - 1380)
[Scholastic philosopher and theologian. One of the two patron saints of Italy, with St. Francis of Assisi]

"God deceiveth thee not."

—Thomas à Kempis (1380 - 1471)
[Christian monk and author of Imitation of Christ]

"A humble knowledge of thyself is a surer way to God than a deep search after learning."

—Thomas à Kempis (1380 - 1471)

"If I am not in the state of grace, may God put me there; and if I am, may God so keep me."

— Joan of Arc (1412-1431)
[Jehanne Darc, mystic visionary, military leader, martyr, saint and heroine of France. Executed by fire as a heretic, later exonerated and canonized as a saint of the Roman Catholic Church on 16 May, 1920]

COFFEE BREAK

Interfaith Inspiration: Kabir, a Hindi poet of India, combined Hindu and Islamic Sufi concepts in his poetry, and has been an enduring source of interfaith inspiration for the people of the Indian subcontinent.

"The Lord God is like sugar spilled in the sand:
An elephant rages around and cannot pick it up.
Says Kabir: The guru gave me the hint:
Become an ant and eat it!"

— Kabir (1440–1518)
[Indian poet, mystic and philosopher]

"O servant, where dost thou seek Me?
Lo! I am beside thee.
I am neither in temple nor in mosque:
I am neither in Kaaba nor in Kailash:

Neither am I in rites and ceremonies,

nor in Yoga and renunciation.

If thou art a true seeker,

thou shalt at once see Me:

thou shalt meet Me in a moment of time.

Kabîr says, "O Sadhu! God is the breath of all breath."

— KABIR (1440–1518)

"Thou, O God, dost sell us all good things at the price of labor."
— LEONARDO DA VINCI (1452-1519)
[Italian Renaissance architect, musician, inventor, engineer, sculptor, and painter. His best known work is Mona Lisa]

"You think that the body is a wonderful work. In reality this is nothing compared to the soul that inhabits in that structure …It is the work of God."
— LEONARDO DA VINCI (1452-1519)

COFFEE BREAK

Good Deeds: Guru Nanak, the founder of the Sikh religion, was once asked "What is superior, Islam or Hindusim?" The Guru replied, "Devoid of good deeds, none will find place in God's court."

"The impurity of the mind is greed, and the impurity of the tongue is falsehood. The impurity of the eyes is to gaze upon the beauty of another man's wife, and his wealth. The impurity of the ears is to listen to the slander of others. O Nanak, the mortal's soul goes, bound and gagged to the city of Death. All impurity comes from doubt and attachment to duality. Birth and death are subject to the Command of the Lord's Will; through His Will we come and go."

— GURU NANAK DEV (1469-1539)
[Founder of Sikhism]

"He/She is not accessible through intellect, or through mere scholarship or cleverness at argument; He/She is met, when He/She pleases, through devotion."

— GURU NANAK DEV (1469-1539)

"God is not willing to do everything, and thus take away our free will and that share of glory which belongs to us."

— NICCOLO MACHIAVELLI (1469-1527)
[Florentine political philosopher, historian, musician, poet, famous for his treatise "Prince"]

COFFEE BREAK

Men of God Fights with Men of Science: Before the advent of new science in 16th and 17th centuries, man's conception of the universe was based on theological assertions that God has made the earth the center of the universe (e.g. Psalm 93 says, addressing God, "Thou hast fixed the earth immovable and firm"). Copernicus (1473-1543) challenged this conception to the outrage of the Christian church. Copernicus avoided persecution by delaying the publication of his work until the year of his death. Galileo (1564-1642) didn't have that good fortune; he was forced to recant to save his life from the hands of the church leaders, and he promised never again to advance the sinful view that the earth moves.

"To know the mighty works of God; to comprehend His wisdom and majesty and power; to appreciate, in degree, the wonderful working of His laws, surely all this must be a pleasing and acceptable mode of worship to the Most High to whom ignorance cannot be more grateful than knowledge."

— NICOLAUS COPERNICUS (1473-1543)
[Astronomer and mathematician; proponent of the heliocentric cosmic model]

"Through steady observation and a meaningful contact with the divined order of the world's structure, arranged by God's wisdom, - who would not be guided to admire the Builder who creates all!"

— NICOLAUS COPERNICUS (1473-1543)

"I live and love in God's peculiar light."

— MICHELANGELO BUONARROTI (1475-1564)
[Italian architect, painter, poet and sculptor]

"The vanities of life have taken from me the time to contemplate God."

— MICHELANGELO BUONARROTI (1475-1564)

"To love God, which was a thing far excelling all the cunning that is possible for us in this life to obtain."

— SAINT THOMAS MORE (1478-1535)
[Also known as Sir Thomas More, English lawyer, writer, and politician]

"All who call on God in true faith, earnestly from the heart, will certainly be heard, and will receive what they have asked and desired."

— MARTIN LUTHER (1483-1546)
[German theologian, ecclesiastical reformer who inspired the Reformation and influenced the Lutheran and Protestant doctrines]

"The slender capacity of man's heart cannot comprehend, much less utter, that unsearchable depth and burning zeal of God's love towards us."

— MARTIN LUTHER (1483-1546)

"He who carries God in his heart bears heaven with him wherever he goes."

— SAINT IGNATIUS OF LOYOLA (1491-1556)
[Also known as Ignacio (Iñigo) López de Loyola, founder of Jesuit order]

"God has a special interest in women for they can lift this world to their breast and help Him comfort."

— Mirabai (1498-1547)
[Aristocratic Hindu mystical singer and devotee of Krishna]

"To God I speak Spanish, to women Italian, to men French, and to my horse – German."
— Emperor Charles V (1500-1558)
[Ruler of the Holy Roman Empire]

"It is no small honour that God for our sake has so magnificently adorned the world, in order that we may not only be spectators of this beauteous theatre, but also enjoy the multiplied abundance and variety of good things which are presented to us in it."
— John Calvin (1509-1564)
[French theologian and pastor]

"Without knowledge of self there is no knowledge of God."
— John Calvin (1509-1564)

"A man with God is always in the majority."

— John Knox (1510-1572)
[Key figure in the Protestant reformation]

"Let nothing disturb thee;
Let nothing dismay thee:
All things pass;
God never changes.
Patience attains
All that it strives for.
He who has God
Finds he lacks nothing:
God alone suffices."

— Saint Teresa of Avila (1515-1582)
[Teresa de Jesús, Spanish mystic, philosopher and Catholic saint]

"We need not wings to go in search of Him, but have only to find a place where we can be alone--and look upon Him present within us."
— Saint Teresa of Avila (1515-1582)

"Insofar as everything that exists is contained in His existence, [God] encompasses all existence."

— Rabbi Moses ben Jacob Cordovero (1522-1570)
[A leading Jewish mystic in Ottoman Palestine]

"Man is certainly stark mad; he cannot make a worm, and yet he will be making gods by dozens."

— MONTAIGNE (1533-1592)
[Michel Eyquem de Montaigne, influential French Renaissance writer]

"God is pleased with nothing but love."

— ST. JOHN OF THE CROSS (1542-1591)
[Juan de la Cruz, Spanish mystic and poet]

"None merits the name of Creator but God and the poet."

—TORQUATO TASSO (1544-1595)
[Italian epic poet and dramatist]

"O GOD in every temple I see people that see thee,
And in every language I hear spoken, people praise thee."

— ABUL FAZL (1551-1602)
[Minister of the Mughal Empeor Akbar the Great, and author of history of Akbar's reign, Akbarnama; also translated Bible in Persian language. This writing is seen in an inscription in a temple in Kashmir, India]

"The nearer the Church, the farther from God."

— BISHOP LANCELOT ANDREWES (1555-1626)
[English clergyman and scholar]

"A little philosophy inclineth man's mind to atheism, but depth in philosophy bringeth men's minds about to religion."

— FRANCIS BACON (1561-1626)
[English philosopher, statesman and essayist]

"I do not feel obliged to believe that the same God who has endowed us with sense, reason, and intellect has intended us to forgo their use."

— GALILEO GALILEI (1564-1642)
[Italian physicist and astronomer]

"Mathematics is the language with which God has written the universe."

— GALILEO GALILEI (1564-1642)

COFFEE BREAK

"God is a Good Man": William Shakespeare, one of the greatest poets the worldhas ever known, was a dispassionate and amused observer of human life. His characters expressed a multitude of opinions about God, but one should not make the mistake of mixing them up with those of the poet himself.

"God hath given you one face, and you make yourselves another."

—WILLIAM SHAKESPEARE (1564-1616)
[The most celebrated English playwright and poet]

"Now God be praised, that to believing souls,
Gives light in darkness, comfort in despair!"

—WILLIAM SHAKESPEARE (1564-1616)

"Well, God's a good man."

—WILLIAM SHAKESPEARE (1564-1616)

"What a piece of work is a man! How noble in
Reason! how infinite in faculties! in form and moving
how express and admirable! In action how like an Angel!
in apprehension how like a god! the beauty of the
world! the paragon of animals! and yet to me, what is
this quintessence of dust? Man delights not me; no,
nor Woman neither."

—WILLIAM SHAKESPEARE (1564-1616)

"Ignorance is the curse of God; knowledge is the wing wherewith we fly to heaven."

—WILLIAM SHAKESPEARE (1564-1616)

"The gods are just, and of our pleasant vices
Make instruments to plague us."

—WILLIAM SHAKESPEARE (1564-1616)

"We shall steer safely through every storm, so long as our heart is right, our intention fervent, our courage steadfast, and our trust fixed on God."

— SAINT FRANCIS DE SALES (1567-1622)
[Bishop of Geneva and a Roman Catholic saint]

"Who falls for love of God, shall rise a star."

— BEN JONSON (1572-1637)
[English poet and dramatist]

"The world 's a theatre, the earth a stage,
Which God and Nature do with actors fill."

—THOMAS HEYWOOD (EARLY 1570s-1641)
[Prominent English playwright, actor and author]

"The chief aim of all investigations of the external world should be to discover the rational order and harmony which has been imposed on it by God and which He revealed to us in the language of mathematics."

— JOHANNES KEPLER (1571-1630)
[German mathematician, astronomer and astrologer]

"With God there is no need for long speeches."

— JANE FRANCES DE CHANTAL (1572-1641)
[Roman Catholic saint, who founded a religious order after the death of her husband]

"The examination of the bodies of animals has always been my delight, and I have thought that we might thence not only obtain an insight into the lighter mysteries of nature, but there perceive a kind of image or reflection of the omnipotent Creator Himself."

— WILLIAM HARVEY (1578-1657)
[English physician, first to describe systemic circulation and properties of blood]

"No general agreement exists concerning the Gods, but there is universal recognition of God. Every religion in the past has acknowledged, every religion in the future will acknowledge, some sovereign deity among the Gods... Accordingly that which is everywhere accepted as the supreme manifestation of deity, by whatever name it may be called, I term God"

— LORD HERBERT OF CHERBURY (1583-1648)
[British soldier, diplomat, historian, poet and religious philosopher. Considered as Father of English Deism]

COFFEE BREAK

From Social Contract to Liberal Democracy: Hobbes, Pascal, Spinoza, and Locke all lived during a period when the West was dominated by religion. Hobbes was an ultimate materialist, who believed that all things, including spirits, God, human thoughts, heaven, and hell, are corporeal. He was the first to propose a social contract, wherein a government derives its authority from the consent of the governed, not from God or scriptures. Pascal argued that since the existence of God cannot be proved (or disproved), and since there was much to be gained from wagering that God exists and since there was little to be gained from wagering that God doesn't exist, a rational person should wager that God exists. Spinoza, a supreme pantheist, argued that God must be co-equivalent with everything. Locke was the chief founding father of empiricism and he contributed more than any other thinker to providing the theoretical foundations of liberal democracy. He argued that since certainty in our knowledge is not available, it is immoral to impose our religious or political beliefs on others.

"For I ... maintain God's existence, and that he is a most pure, and most simple corporeal spirit."

— THOMAS HOBBES (1588-1679)
[English philosopher, pioneer of Western political philosophy]

"Whatever we imagine is finite. Therefore there is no idea or conception of anything we call infinite. No man can have in his mind an image of infinite magnitude, nor conceive infinite swiftness, infinite time, or infinite force, or infinite power ... And therefore the name of God is used, not to make us conceive him (for he is incomprehensible, and his greatness and power are inconceivable), but that we may honour him."

— THOMAS HOBBES (1588-1679)

"God is alpha and omega in the great world: endeavor to make Him so in the little world; make Him thy evening epilogue and thy morning prologue; practice to make Him thy last thought at night when thou sleepest, and thy first thought in the morning when thou awakest; so shall thy fancy be sanctified in the night, and thy understanding rectified in the day; so shall thy rest be peaceful, thy labors prosperous, thy life pious, and thy death glorious."

— FRANCIS QUARLES (1592-1644)
[Prolific English prose-writer and poet]

"Where there is peace, God is."

— GEORGE HERBERT (1593-1633)
[English poet and orator]

"I have concluded the evident existence of God, and that my existence depends entirely on God in all the moments of my life, that I do not think that the human spirit may know anything with greater evidence and certitude."

— RENE DESCARTES (1596-1650)
[French philosopher and mathematician, known as the Father of Modern Philosophy]

"God requireth not a uniformity of religion."

— ROGER WILLIAMS (1603-1684)
[Anglo-American clergyman, pioneering advocate for freedom of conscience in religious matters, and the separation of church and state]

"Who kills a man kills a reasonable creature, God's image, but thee who destroys a good book, kills reason itself."

— JOHN MILTON (1608–1674)
[English poet and politician, most famous for his epic poem Paradise Lost]

"God is thy law, thou mine: to know no more
Is woman's happiest knowledge, and her praise."

— JOHN MILTON (1608-1674)

"For neither man nor angel can discern
Hypocrisy, the only evil that walks
Invisible, except to God alone."

— JOHN MILTON (1608-1674)

"God hears no more than the heart speaks; and if the heart be dumb, God will certainly be deaf."

—THOMAS BROOKS (1608-1680)
[English preacher and author]

"He who utters the Name of God while walking
 gets the merit of a sacrifice at every step.
His body becomes a place of pilgrimage.

He who repeats God's Name while working
   always find perfect peace."

— Sant Tukaram (1608-1650)
[Indian saint and spiritual poet]

"They that worship God merely from fear,
Would worship the devil too, if he appear."

— Thomas Fuller (1608-1661)
[English preacher, historian, and scholar]

"I talk to God but the sky is empty."

— François VI, (1613-1680)
[duc de La Rochefoucauld, prince de Marcillac,
French author]

EVOLUTION OF GOD

The God of unbelievers is Nature.

"Whatsoever we beg of God, let us also work for it."

— Jeremy Taylor (1613-1667)
[Clergyman in the Church of England ,sometimes
known as the "Shakespeare of Divines" for his
poetic style of writing]

"There is no God – some say-
A deep, but dazzling darkness."

— Henry Vaughan (1622-1695*)*
[Welsh physician and metaphysical poet]

Pascal's Wager:

""God is or he is not." But to which side shall we incline? Reason can decide nothing here. ...What will you wager. ....Let us weigh the gain and the loss in wagering that God is. Let us estimate the two chances. If you gain, you gain all; if you lose, you lose nothing. Wager then without hesitation that he is."

"The knowledge of God is very far from the love of Him."

— Blaise Pascal (1623-1662)
[French mathematician, physicist and theologian, famous for Pascal's triangle]

"It is incomprehensible that God should exist, and it is incomprehensible that he should not exist."

— Blaise Pascal (1623-1662)

"There are only three kinds of persons: those who serve God, having found Him; others who are occupied in seeking Him, not having found Him; while the remainder live without seeking Him, and without having found Him."

— BLAISE PASCAL (1623-1662)

"The vastness, beauty, orderliness of heavenly bodies, the excellent structure of animals and plants, and other phenomena of nature justly induce an intelligent, unprejudiced observer to conclude a supreme, powerful, just, and good Author."

— ROBERT BOYLE (1627-1691)
[Natural philosopher, chemist, physicist, inventor, and theologist. Formulated Boyle's Law of Chemistry]

COFFEE BREAK

Spinoza's God: Albert Einstein once famously said: "I believe in Spinoza's God." Philosopher Baruch Spinoza was a rationalist and believed that God, man, and Nature are all part of one substance. He wrote: "By substance I understand what is in itself and is conceived through itself. By attribute I understand what the intellect perceives of a substance, as constituting its essence. By God I understand a being absolutely infinite, i.e., a substance consisting of an infinity of attributes, of which each one expresses an eternal and infinite essence."This is his famous pantheistic (all is God) doctrine. Spinoza equated God with Nature, and wrote: "That eternal and infinite being we call God, or Nature, acts from the same necessity from which he exists." It is interesting to note that his friends who published his writings after his death left out the "or Nature" clause from the more widely accessible Dutch version (but not the Latin version) out of fear of religionists' reactions. During his life, Jews excommunicated him and Christians accused him of atheism because he didn't believe in a Christian God. Later scholars called Spinoza a "God-intoxicated man."

"Whatsoever is, is in God, and without God nothing can be, or be conceived."

— SPINOZA (1632-1677)
[Benedictus de Spinoza, Dutch philosopher who was excommunicated from the Jewish community of his native Amsterdam]

"God exists only philosophically."

— SPINOZA (1632-1677)

COFFEE BREAK

Strange Coincidence: Compare the following quote from Spinoza with what Xenophanes said two-thousand years before Spinoza.

"I believe that, if a triangle could speak, it would say, in like manner, that God is eminently triangular, while a circle would say that the divine nature is eminently circular. Thus each would ascribe to God its own attributes, would assume itself to be like God, and look on everything else as ill-shaped."

— SPINOZA (1632-1677)

"And I ask, whether one coming from heaven in the power of God, in full and clear evidence and demonstration of miracles, giving plain and direct rules of morality and obedience, be not likelier to enlighten the bulk of mankind, and set them right in their duties, and bring them to do them, than by reasoning with them from general notions and principles of human reason?"

— JOHN LOCKE (1632-1704)

[English philosopher and physician, father of Liberalism, regarded as the most influential thinker of the Enlightenment era]

"The stars rule men but God rules the stars."

— CHRISTOPH (KELLER) CELLARIUS (1638-1707)
[German classical scholar]

"Has God forgotten all I have done for him?"

-LOUIS XIV OF FRANCE (1638-1715)
[King of France, upon hearing of the French defeat at Malplaquet, 1709]

COFFEE BREAK

Newton and God: Sir Isaac Newton, perhaps the greatest scientist ever to have lived, was a firm believer of God as the masterful creator whose existence cannot be denied in light of the systematic grandeur of the universe. Newton thought of himself as chosen by God to understand the Bible and published numerous religious articles. However, Newton's groundbreaking work on classical mechanics helped man gain an unprecedented mastery over the physical world and paved the way for the Industrial Revolution. This mastery, in combination with the knowledge that Earth is not the center of the universe, weakened the belief in God in the West, and influenced intellectual movements for the next three centuries.

"The design of God was much otherwise... not to gratify mens curiosities by enabling them to foreknow things, but that after they were fulfilled they might be interpreted by the event, and his own Providence, not the Interpreters, be then manifested thereby to the world."

— SIR ISAAC NEWTON(1643-1727)

[English physicist, mathematician, astronomer, natural philosopher, alchemist, and theologian. One of most influential men in history, ranked No. 2 by English academic Michael Hart]

"God created everything by number, weight and measure."

— SIR ISAAC NEWTON(1643-1727)

"God governs all things."

— Sir Isaac Newton(1643-1727)

"I have a fundamental belief in the Bible as theWord of God, written by those who were inspired. I study the Bible daily."

— Sir Isaac Newton(1643-1727)

"A Heavenly Master governs all the world as Sovereign of the universe. We are astonished at Him by reason of His perfection, we honor Him and fall down before Him because of His unlimited power. From blind physical necessity, which is always and everywhere the same, no variety adhering to time and place could evolve, and all variety of created objects which represent order and life in the universe could happen only by the willful reasoning of its original Creator, Whom I call the Lord God."

— Sir Isaac Newton (1643-1727)

"Men must be governed by God, or they will be ruled by tyrants."
— William Penn (1644-1718)
[Founder of the the Province of Pennsylvania, a US State]

EVOLUTION OF GOD

The God of early scientists is a master creator governing the world through natural laws.

"The order, the symmetry, the harmony enchant us...God is pure order. He is the originator of universal harmony."
— Gottfried Leibniz (1646-1716)
[German philosopher and mathematician]

"The ultimate reason of things must lie in a necessary substance, in which the differentiation of the changes only exists eminently as in their source; and this is what we call God... God alone is the primary Unity, or original simple substance, from which all monads, created and derived, are produced."
— Gottfried Leibniz (1646-1716)

"God assuredly always chooses the best."

— Gottfried Leibniz (1646-1716)

"I need nothing but God, and to lose myself in the heart of God."
— Saint Margaret Mary Alacoque (1647-1690)
[French Roman Catholic nun and mystic]

"God works in a mysterious way in grace as well as in nature, concealing His operations under an imperceptible succession of events, and thus keeps us always in the darkness of faith."
— Francois de Salignac de la Mothe-Fenelon (1651-1715)
[Archbishop of Cambrai,French educationalist, critic, poet, and philosopher]

"God designed all Mankind should at all times know, what he wills them to know, believe, profess, and practice; and has given them no other Means for this, but the Use of Reason."

— MATTHEW TINDAL (1657-1733)
[English deist author]

"It is common for those that are farthest from God, to boast themselves most of their being near to the Church."

— MATTHEW HENRY (1662-1714)
[English non-conformist clergyman]

"If God be infinitely holy, just, and good, He must take delight in those creatures that resemble Him most in these perfections."

— FRANCIS ATTERBURY (1663-1732)
[English politician and bishop]

"God should be the object of all our desires, the end of all our actions, the principle of all our affections, and the governing power of our whole souls."

— JEAN BAPTISTE MASSILLON (1663-1742)
[French Catholic bishop and famous preacher, Bishop of Clermont from 1717 until his death]

"He is an Inconceivable Entity, External and Attireless. He is without attachment, colour, form and mark. He is distinct from all others of various colours and signs. He is the Primal being, Unique and Changeless. He is without colour, mark, caste and lineage. He is the without enemy, friend, father and mother. He is far away from all and closest to all. His dwelling is within water, on earth and in heavens."

— GURU GOBIND SINGH (1666-1708)
[The 10th and the last Sikh Guru, poet and philosopher]

"I believe the promises of God enough to venture an eternity on them."

— ISAAC WATTS (1674-1748)
[English theologian, logician, and a prolific and popular hymnwriter. Known as the Father of English Hymnody]

"Our God, our help in ages past,

Our hope for years to come,

Our shelter from the stormy blast,

And our eternal home."

— ISAAC WATTS (1674-1748)

"How many brave Men, courageous Women, and innocent Children did I see butcher'd, to do God good Service?"

— MARY DAVYS (1674-1732)
[Irish/English shopkeeper, novelist, playwright]

"A God all mercy is a God unjust."

— EDWARD YOUNG (1683-1765)
[English poet, best remembered for Night Thoughts])

"God is a God of order."

— JOHANN SEBASTIAN BACH (1685-1750)
[German music composer]

Nothing hath separated us from God but our own will, or rather our own will is our separation from God."

—WILLIAM LAW (1686-1761)
[English divine]

"God save our gracious king! Long live our noble king! God save the king!"

— HENRY CAREY (1687-1743)
[English poet, dramatist and song-writer]

"An atheist is but a mad, ridiculous derider of piety, but a hypocrite makes a sober jest of God and religion; he finds it easier to be upon his knees than to rise to a good action."

— ALEXANDER POPE (1688-1744)
[One of the greatest English poets of the eighteenth century]

"An honest man is the noblest work of God."

— ALEXANDER POPE (1688-1744)

"If God did not exist, it would be necessary to invent him.'

—VOLTAIRE (1694-1778)
[François-Marie Arouet, better known by his pen name Voltaire, French writer, deist and philosopher]

"I have never made but one prayer to God, a very short one: "O Lord, make my enemies ridiculous." And God granted it."

—VOLTAIRE (1694-1778)

"God is a tranquil Being, and abides in a tranquil eternity. So must your spirit become a tranquil and clear little pool, wherein the serene light of God can be mirrored."

— GERHARD TERSTEEGEN (1697-1769)
[German religious writer]

DOES GOD EXIST? – THE BIG QUESTION

This age-old question has been debated for thousands of years and there is no end in sight. By the close of the nineteenth century, science seemed to have proved God's non-existence by providing vast quantities of evidence against supernatural and/or theological explanations of the physical world. "Reason" laughed at "Faith" and boasted about certainty arising from mathematics and physical observations. But the table was turned in the twentieth century when both mathematics and physics lost their auras of certainty. Kurt Gödel proved through his Incompleteness Theorem that a sufficiently rich axiom system is guaranteed to possess statements that cannot be proved or disproved within the system. Quantum mechanics took away the certainty in human knowledge of the physical world through Heisenberg's Uncertainty Principle, which states that the more precisely we know about the position, x, of a particle, the less precisely we can know about the momentum, m, of that particle. On top of these developments, the scientific discovery that the universe began 13.75 billion years ago (The Big Bang Theory) revived the idea of a creator God. Amidst all these shifts in human thinking, hundreds, if not thousands, of books have been written on the existence and non-existence of God, and hundreds of thousands of postings have been made on the Internet and Facebook attempting to prove or disprove God's existence.

Hans Küng, a Swiss professor of ecumenical theology, Catholic priest, and prolific author, ended his 838-page tome entitled *Does God Exist?* in this manner, after a comprehensive and brilliant analysis of almost all prevailing theories of faith and doubt:

"Does God exist? Despite all upheavals and doubts, even for man today, the only appropriate answer must be that with which believers of all generations from ancient times have again and again professed their faith. It begins with the faith – Te Deum, laudamus, "You, God, we praise" – and ends in trust: In te, Domine, speravi, non confundar in aeternum! "In you, Lord, I have hoped, I shall never be put to shame."

In February 2012, Professor Richard Dawkins, the world's most famous atheist, stunned the audience during a public dialogue at Oxford University with the Archbishop of Canterbury, Dr. Rowan Williams, when Dawkins admitted that he was not sure that God doesn't exist. Professor Dawkins said: "On a scale of seven, where one means I know he exists, and seven I know he doesn't, I call myself a six." Then he modified his score to 6.9, stating: "That doesn't mean I'm absolutely confident, that I absolutely know, because I don't."

SERIOUS PROOFS AND DISPROOFS OF GOD'S EXISTENCE

Philosopher Immanuel Kant stated: "It always remains a scandal of philosophy and universal human reason that the existence of things outside us ... should have to be assumed merely on faith, and that if it occurs to anyone to doubt it, we should be unable to answer him with a satisfactory proof."

Yet many proofs, both satisfactory and unsatisfactory, have been presented through the centuries. A sample of proofs for and against God's existence is provided next.

PROOFS FOR THE EXISTENCE OF GOD	PROOFS AGAINST THE EXISTENCE OF GOD

Ontological Argument: This argument was first proposed by St. Anselm of Canterbury in the eleventh century. He wrote: "God is that than which no greater can be conceived. If God is that than which no greater can be conceived then there is nothing greater than God that can be imagined. If God does not exist then there is something greater than God that can be imagined. Therefore, God exists."

Cosmological Argument: This argument was first articulated by Islamic philosophers in the tenth and eleventh centuries, based on the works of the ancient Greek philosophers Plato and Aristotle. It is also called the Kalam Cosmological Argument. Imam Al-Ghazali (1058-1111) wrote: "Every being which begins has a cause for its beginning; now the world is a being which begins; therefore, it possesses a cause for its beginning." Christian theologian Thomas Aquinas (1225-1274) adapted this argument as one of the five ways of proving the existence of God. In Summa Theologica, he wrote: "There is no case known (neither is it, indeed, possible) in which a thing is found to be the efficient cause of itself; for so it would be prior to itself, which is impossible. Now in efficient causes it is not possible to go on to infinity, because in all efficient causes following in order, the first is the cause of the intermediate cause, and the intermediate is the cause of the ultimate cause, whether the intermediate cause be several, or only one. Now to take away the cause is to take away the effect. Therefore, if there be no first cause among efficient causes, there will be no ultimate, nor any intermediate cause. But if in efficient causes it is possible to go on to infinity, there will be no first efficient cause, neither will there be an ultimate effect, nor any intermediate efficient causes; all of which is plainly false. Therefore it is necessary to admit a first efficient cause, to which everyone gives the name of God."

Argument from Evil: This argument was first put forward by the ancient Greek philosopher Epicurus. An all-knowing, all-powerful, and good God cannot remain silent in the face of so much evil, often pointless, in the world. Since evil exists, and God doesn't intervene, then he must not be good or all-powerful. Therefore, God does not exist. Theologians have proposed three primary defenses against this argument: (1) the Unknown Purpose Defense: God's ways are beyond human comprehension; (2) the Free Will Defense: God needs to allow some evil to preserve human free will; and (3) the Character Building Defense: God allows some evil and attendant suffering to make humans stronger.

Argument from Spontaneity: World-famous physicist Stephen Hawking wrote in his 2010 best-selling book The Grand Design: "Because there is a law such as gravity, the universe can and will create itself from nothing. Spontaneous creation is the reason there is something rather than nothing, why the universe exists, why we exist. It is not necessary to invoke God to light the blue touch paper and set the universe going." Renowned astronomer and scientist Carl Sagan wrote in his classic Cosmos: "If we say that God has always been, why not save a step and conclude that the universe has always been?"

Argument from Simplicity: To explain the complex phenomenon of the universe, it is not correct to introduce an even more complex, multi-faceted, and invisible entity, namely God. The physical universe is no different if we assume God does not exist; therefore, it is simpler to assume He does not exist.

PROOFS FOR THE EXISTENCE OF GOD

Teleological Argument: Thomas Aquinas articulated five ways of proving the existence of God. The fifth is the teleological argument, or the argument from design, which has been the most powerful argument for centuries. Aquinas wrote in Summa Theologica: "We see that things which lack knowledge, such as natural bodies, act for an end, and this is evident from their acting always, or nearly always, in the same way, so as to obtain the best result. Hence it is plain that they achieve their end, not fortuitously, but designedly. Now whatever lacks knowledge cannot move towards an end, unless it be directed by some being endowed with knowledge and intelligence; as the arrow is directed by the archer. Therefore, some intelligent being exists by whom all natural things are directed to their end; and this being we call God."

Miracle Argument: Islam asserts that its holy book, the Quran, is a miracle because it couldn't have been written by a human being. Therefore, a divine author exists, whom we call God. The tenth-century Hindu philosopher Udayanacharya provided nine arguments in favor of the existence of God, including this divine authorship or miracle argument, asserting that the author of the Vedas cannot be human because human knowledge is limited.

Moral Argument: The seventh of the nine arguments of Udayanacharya is Vakyat, which states: "World is governed by moral laws that are objective and universal. These are again manifested by Vedas. Hence there exists God, the promulgator of these laws." The eighteenth- century German philosopher Immanuel Kant (1724-1804) also promoted the idea that all moral thoughts require presupposing the existence of God, which cannot be proved by reason alone.

PROOFS AGAINST THE EXISTENCE OF GOD

Argument from Inconsistency: Descriptions of God in multiple religions are inconsistent, and their scriptures contain inconsistencies and incoherent doctrines. Therefore, as all religions cannot be true, either one is true or none are true. Since God is all-powerful and all-knowing, he couldn't have revealed erroneous scriptures. Therefore, God does not exist.

Argument from Injustice: World-famous philosopher Bertrand Russell wrote: "Here we find in this world a great deal of injustice, and so far as that goes that is a reason for supposing that justice does not rule in the world; and therefore so far as it goes it affords a moral argument against a deity and not in favor of one."

Argument from Contradiction: The Hindu philosophy of Samkhya denies the existence of God and views the universe as consisting of two realities: Purusa (consciousness) and Prakriti (the phenomenal realm of matter). The Vedic sage Kapila wrote: "For, we must conceive Ishwara (God) as being either free (from all fetters) or bound (by material conditions). He can be neither free nor bound; because, in the former case, being perfect, He would have nothing to fulfill by creation, and, in the latter case, He would not possess absolute power."

Argument from Free Will: If God is omniscient, then he knows the future. That implies God knows what we will choose in the future, which further implies that we have no free will. This contradicts the observational evidence that humans have free will. Therefore, God doesn't exist. This argument is also extended to claim that God, by being all-knowing, does not himself have free will, because his perfect knowledge of the future fixes the future and he therefore cannot change that without compromising his omniscience.

FLIPPANT PROOFS AND DISPROOFS OF GOD'S EXISTENCE

The Internet provides a readily accessible forum for people to post flippant proofs and disproofs of God's existence. There are two interesting websites in this regard: (1) http://www.godlessgeeks.com/LINKS/GodProof.htm, which lists more than 660 flippant proofs of God's existence, and (2) http://www.tektonics.org/guest/300proof.html, which lists more than 300 disproofs of God's existence. A sample set of proofs and disproofs is provided below to illustrate how formal arguments are ridiculed.

FLIPPANT PROOFS FOR THE EXISTENCE OF GOD	FLIPPANT PROOFS AGAINST THE EXISTENCE OF GOD
Transcendental argument: If reason exists then God exists. Reason exists. Therefore, God exists.	**Transcendental argument:** If reason exists, then God doesn't exist. Reason exists. Therefore, God doesn't exist.
Cosmological argument: If I say something must have a cause, it has a cause. I say the universe must have a cause. Therefore, the universe has a cause. Therefore, God exists.	**Cosmological argument:** If I say something doesn't have a cause, it doesn't have a cause. I say the universe doesn't have a cause. Therefore, the universe doesn't have a cause. Therefore, God doesn't exist.
Ontological argument: I can conceive of a perfect God. One of the qualities of perfection is existence. Therefore, God exists.	**Ontological argument:** I define God to be X. Since I cannot conceive of X, then X must not exist. Therefore, God doesn't exist.
Teleological argument: Check out the world/universe/giraffe. Isn't it complex? Only God could have made them so complex. Therefore, God exists.	**Teleological argument:** Check out the world/universe/giraffe. Isn't it complex? Evolution (aka random chance) is a good enough explanation for how they became so complex. Therefore, God doesn't exist.
Miracle argument: My aunt had cancer. The doctors gave her all these horrible treatments. My aunt prayed to God and now she doesn't have cancer. Therefore, God exists.	**Lack of Miracle argument:** My aunt had cancer. The doctors gave her all these horrible treatments. My aunt prayed to God, but she died from her cancer anyway. Therefore, God doesn't exist.
Moral argument: Person X, a well-known atheist, was morally inferior to the rest of us. Therefore, God exists.	**Moral argument:** Person X, a well-known theist, was morally inferior to the rest of us. Therefore, God doesn't exist.
Argument from Numbers: Billions of people believe in God. They can't all be wrong, can they? Therefore, God exists.	**Argument from Numbers:** Millions and millions of people don't believe in God. They can't all be wrong, can they? Therefore, God doesn't exist.

FLIPPANT PROOFS FOR THE EXISTENCE OF GOD	FLIPPANT PROOFS AGAINST THE EXISTENCE OF GOD
Argument from Fallibility: Human reasoning is inherently flawed. Therefore, there is no reasonable way to challenge a proposition. I propose that God exists. Therefore, God exists.	**Argument from Fallibility:** Human reasoning is inherently flawed. Therefore, there is no reasonable way to challenge a proposition. I propose that God doesn't exist. Therefore, God doesn't exist.
Argument from Quantum Physics: Quantum physics uses an uncertainty principle. There is room for God. Therefore, God exists.	**Argument from Quantum Physics:** Quantum physics uses an uncertainty principle. But, there is no room for God in science. Therefore, God doesn't exist.
Argument from Einstein: Einstein said that God does not play dice with the universe. Thus, even Einstein believed in God. Therefore, God exists.	**Argument from Steadfast Atheism:** A lot of really cool people didn't believe in God their entire lives. Therefore, God doesn't exist.
Pascal's argument: If God exists, it would be really cool. (And I would win big-time). If God didn't exist, it would really suck. (But I wouldn't lose much). Thus I should believe in God because it's the best bet. Therefore, God exists.	**Anti-Pascal's Argument:** If God exists, it would really suck. If God didn't exist, it would be really cool. Therefore, God doesn't exist.

"God said it, I believe it. That settles it"

— AMERICAN BUMPER STICKER

CHAPTER DIGEST
(1000 TO 1700 AD)

God took a long break from posting anything on the *Holy Wall* after posting the messages of the Quran in the seventh century. Almost a thousand years later, according to Sikhs, God posted the Guru Granth Sahib, the Sikh scripture, on the *Holy Wall*. Sikhism professed one universal creator God and tried to combine the teachings of Hinduism and Islam.

Mere mortals questioned the existence of God after all these years of God's postings on the *Holy Wall*. St. Anselm of Canterbury posted ontological proof of the existence of God on the *Wall of Mortals*. The first few centuries of the second millennium were dominated by postings from scholars, mystics, and philosophers, like Omar Khayyam, Imam Ghazali, Maimonides, Attar, Rumi, Hafiz, Ibn Arabi, Saadi, St. Assisi, Moses De Leon, Meister Eckhart, and Kabir. The mystical philosophies of Sufism and Kabbalah took root in this period, and an inward search for God, instead of outward rituals, began with new intensity.

The postings on the *Wall of Mortals* from the period of the European Renaissance witnessed the struggle for reconciliation among science, religion, and reason. The Christian church struggled with the revolutionary discoveries of science, which challenged the traditional Christian theories and interpretations of the physical world.

Pascal posted a God wager on the *Wall of Mortals*, while Newton, one of the greatest scientists of all time, vociferously vouched for the hand of God in the design and construction of the universe. Galileo posted his thoughts on the *Wall of Mortals* but subsequently withdrew his posting to placate the church. Shakespeare posted numerous entertaining, yet insightful, messages on God on the *Wall of Mortals*.

The human–God relationship in this period was dominated by love, which transcended the feelings of fear, admiration, and servitude dominant in the earlier periods.

Hence, a spiritual basis for a *Friendship of Civilizations* began to take root.

8

God is Dead
(1700 to 1900 AD)

"God is dead. God remains dead. And we have killed him. How shall we comfort ourselves, the murderers of all murderers? What was holiest and mightiest of all that the world has yet owned has bled to death under our knives: who will wipe this blood off us? What water is there for us to clean ourselves? What festivals of atonement, what sacred games shall we have to invent? Is not the greatness of this deed too great for us? Must we ourselves not become gods simply to appear worthy of it?"

—FRIEDRICH WILHELM NIETZSCHE (1844-1900), THUS SPOKE ZARATHUSTRA

STATUS UPDATE (1700-1900 AD)

❖ God is in decline in Europe, where it is thought that one cannot become modern without throwing off religious beliefs. The manuscript of the first complete book on atheism is found in 1729 at the deathbed of Jean Meisler, a French Catholic priest.

❖ "The mind cannot believe in the existence of a God," writes Percy Bysshe Shelley, the great romantic English poet, in his treatise, "The Necessity of Atheism" (1811).

❖ God and religion are attacked by philosophers and sociopolitical thinkers, epitomized by Karl Marx, who states: "Religion is the sigh of the oppressed creature, the heart of a heartless world, just as it is the spirit of a spiritless situation. It is the opium of the people."

❖ God is invoked by politicians and social thinkers alike, as new ethical and social standards are formulated for a better and just world.

❖ "God himself is dead!" announces German philosopher G. W. F. Hegel in 1802. French poet Gerard de Nerval writes, "God is dead," in 1854. However, German philosopher Nietzsche makes the phrase "God is dead" popular in 1882. God's death is not his bodily death but the death of the human need for God in a rational and scientific world.

❖ God loses ground as the sole explanation for the mysteries of nature, as science helps man master the universe.

STATUS UPDATE (1700-1900 AD)

❖ God gives *The Book of Mormon* to Joseph Smith, Jr., who founds The Church of Jesus Christ of Latter Day Saints, popularly known as Mormonism, in 1830.

❖ *The Woman's Bible* is published in 1895 by Elizabeth Cady Stanton and a committee of twenty-six women, excising the traditional text of all references that contradicted the positions of women's rights.

❖ The godless religion of "communism" appears with the publication of *The Communist Manifesto*.

NOTES FROM HISTORY
(1700 TO 1900 AD)

The history of the modern world from 1700 onward is a history of great achievements in science, social philosophy, moral philosophy, art, literature, logic, and medical science.

The Age of Enlightenment (also known as The Age of Reason) began in Europe in the eighteenth century. This period was characterized by the strong belief that reason, rationality, and science were the only sources of legitimacy and authority. German philosopher Immanuel Kant declared in 1784 that the Enlightenment was "mankind's final coming of age, the emancipation of the human consciousness from an immature state of ignorance and error." In 1794, Thomas Paine published *The Age of Reason: Being an Investigation of True and Fabulous Theology*, which challenged the legitimacy of the Bible as holy scripture and criticized institutionalized religion.

During the period between the 1780s and 1880s, the German-speaking world witnessed a philosophical revolution that had not been seen since the time of the ancient Greeks. It began with the publication of Immanuel Kant's *Critique of Pure Reason* in 1781. The other stalwarts of this philosophical revolution were Fichte, Schelling, Hegel, Schopenhauer, Marx, Feuerbach, and Nietzsche.

During the eighteenth and nineteenth centuries, Great Britain conquered large parts of the world and became a major power worldwide. The British forces won the Battle of Plassey in 1757, and began the British rule of India that same year. The industrial revolution, which would radically change the world, started in Britain around the 1770s and continued through the next century. London became the largest city in the world, its population growing from one million in 1800 to about seven million in 1900.

The great Chinese encyclopedia, *Gujin Tushu Jicheng* (literally "Complete Collection of Illustrations and Writings from the Earliest to Current Times"), was written during the reigns of Qing emperors Kangxi and Yongzheng. It contained 800,000 pages and over 100 million Chinese characters. The encyclopedia, printed in 1726 using copper movable type, spanned about 10,000 rolls, and only sixty copies were made. The Encyclopedia Britannica was first published in 1768. At that time it comprised only three volumes. By 1801, the Britannica had grown to twenty volumes, and today it is thirty-two volumes.

The abolitionist movement (for the abolition of slavery) gained momentum in the eighteenth century, when rationalist thinkers argued that slavery violated fundamental human rights. In 1723, Russia abolished slavery, followed by Portugal in 1761 and England in 1772. The state of Pennsylvania was the first in the United States to abolish slavery, in 1780. It was abolished throughout America in 1865 and in Brazil in 1888. By the end of the nineteenth century, slavery had also largely been abolished in the British Empire and the Ottoman Empire.

The American Revolutionary War began in 1775 and lasted till 1783. In 1776, America declared independence from Great Britain. In 1783, the Treaty of Paris ended the war when Britain recognized the sovereignty of the United States. In 1791, the United States adopted the First Amendment of its constitution, and guaranteed freedom of religion for all its citizens: *"Congress shall make no law respecting an establishment of religion, or prohibiting the free exercise thereof."*

From 1789 to 1799, the French Revolution took place and radically changed the political order of Europe. It abolished feudalism and established Enlightenment principles of citizenship and inalienable rights. Napoleon Bonaparte became the dictator of France in 1799. The French Revolution took atheism out of the pubs and into the public sphere, and France was largely secularized during the reign of Napoleon.

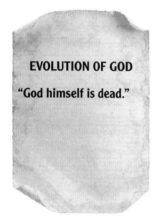

EVOLUTION OF GOD

"God himself is dead."

Atheist philosopher Michael Onfray argues in his book *In Defense of Atheism* that the history of true atheism began in 1729 with the discovery, by the death bed of Jean Meslier (1664–1729), a French Catholic priest, of three copies of a 633-page manuscript that is considered the first complete book on atheism. Meslier repudiated the God of Christianity as well as the God of the deists' natural religion, denouncing all religions as fabrications fostered by the ruling elites. He wrote: *"If God is incomprehensible to man, it would seem rational never to think of Him at all."* Atheism grew among intellectual circles in the eighteenth century with advances in science. It was thought that one could not be modern without throwing out religious beliefs.

German philosopher Hegel announced that "God himself is dead" in 1802, when he published his book *Faith and Knowledge*. In 1811, Percy Bysshe Shelley, the great romantic English poet, anonymously published his treatise "The Necessity of Atheism." German philosopher Ludwig Feuerbach published *The Essence of Christianity* in 1841, wherein he concluded that God is a human invention and religious activities are nothing but wish fulfillment. Feuerbach had a long-standing influence on Marx, Engels, and Nietzsche, the last of whom is credited with making the phrase "God is dead" very popular when he put it into the mouth of a madman in *The Gay Science*, in 1882.

In the nineteenth century, the Spanish, Portuguese, Chinese, Mughal, and Holy Roman empires collapsed. This century ushered in an era of scientific inventions, with significant developments in the fields of mathematics, physics, chemistry, biology, electricity, and metallurgy. The introduction of the railroad resulted in rapid urbanization, along with efficient transport of food products and other goods. Motion picture cameras were invented, leading to the growth of the film industry in the twentieth century.

The latter part of the nineteenth century saw the rise of atheism to prominence under the influence of the rationalist and free-thinking philosophers. Karl Marx argued in his doctoral dissertation that "in the country of reason", the existence of God cannot have any meaning:

"Take paper money to a country in which this use of paper money is not known, and everyone will laugh at your subjective representation. Go with your gods to a country in which other gods are worshipped, and you will be shown that you are the victim of fancies and abstractions. And rightly. Anyone who had brought a migrant god to

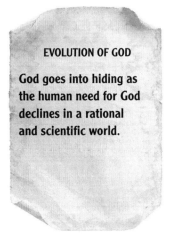

EVOLUTION OF GOD

God goes into hiding as the human need for God declines in a rational and scientific world.

the ancient Greeks, would have found the proof of the non-existence of this god, because it did not exist for the Greeks. What is the case in a certain country for certain foreign gods, takes place for god in general in the country of reason: it is an area in which his existence ceases."

Today, about 2% of the world's population describes itself as atheist, while a further 12% describes itself as nontheist or agnostic.

Karl Marx theorized that capitalism, like previous socioeconomic systems, would inevitably produce tensions and collapse by itself. He argued for a classless society and published *The Communist Manifesto* in 1848 with Friedrich Engels. John Stuart Mill published *On Liberty* in 1859, wherein he indentified the difference between two types of liberty: the freedom to act and the absence of coercion. His views influenced many political leaders of the nineteenth and twentieth centuries. Abraham Lincoln won the US presidential election of 1860, and America plunged into a civil war that lasted from 1861 to 1865. About 620,000 soldiers and an undetermined number of civilians perished in this deadly conflict between the northern and southern states.

The Communist Manifesto.

Charles Darwin hypothesized the theory of evolution by natural selection. Louis Pasteur came up with the germ theory of diseases; his scientific discoveries led to remarkable breakthroughs in disease prevention, resulting in almost a doubling of Europe's population from 200 million in 1800 to roughly 400 million in 1900. Faraday's and Maxwell's electromagnetic theory paved the way for many scientific achievements of the twentieth century. Einstein described Maxwell's work as the "most profound and the most fruitful that physics has experienced since the time of Newton." Thomas Alva Edison, one of the most prolific inventors in history, with 1,093 U.S. patents, invented the light bulb, which made it possible for electricity to reach every house. His other inventions related to electric power generation contributed to rapid industrialization.

Two new religions emerged in the nineteenth century: Mormonism and the Bahá'í faith. Joseph Smith, Jr. had a vision that helped him locate a buried book of golden plates. The book, published in 1830, is known as *The Book of Mormon,* and is regarded by Mormons as a revelation from God. Mormons claim to be true Christians who restored the original church of Jesus and his twelve apostles. The Bahá'í faith, an offshoot of Islam, is a monotheistic religion established by Bahaullah in Iran. It emphasizes the unity of God, unity of religion, and unity of humankind. Bahaullah is the author of *Kitab-i-Aqdas,* which is considered the "Mother-Book" of the Bahá'í faith.

Mormonism and the Bahá'í faith

Elizabeth Cady Stanton (1815–1902), an American social activist and leading figure of the early women's movement, authored *The Woman's Bible* in collaboration with a committee of twenty-six women. *The Woman's Bible* was published in 1895 and became a best seller. It challenged the traditional religious view that women should be subservient to men. In addition, it promoted the idea that the Trinity was composed of "a Heavenly Mother, Father, and Son", and that prayers should be addressed to a Heavenly Mother. The goal of *The Woman's Bible* was "to revise only those texts and chapters directly referring to women, and those also in which women are made prominent by exclusion."

The Woman's Bible was published in 1895.

The Woman's Bible was widely criticized by men and women of all walks of life, as well as by church leaders. Stanton wrote to a friend in 1896: "Our politicians are calm and complacent under our fire but the clergy jump round the moment you aim a pop gun at them, like parched peas on a hot skillet."

God remained a popular topic, as usual, amidst all these transformative changes during the eighteenth and nineteenth centuries. As a result, this period is replete with interesting human observations on God, as presented in the following pages.

HOLY WALL:
THE BOOK OF MORMON – MORMON SCRIPTURE

Joseph Smith, Jr., an American Christian, published The Book of Mormon in 1930. He announced that an angel had led him to a buried book of golden plates near his home in Manchester, New York. He then translated the book and published it under the title The Book of Mormon: An Account Written by the Hand of Mormon upon Plates Taken from the Plates of Nephi. The Book of Mormon is revered by Mormons as a revealed text from God.

Mormon faith influences nearly every aspect of the lives of its followers. They believe that they are spiritual children of a loving heavenly Father who sent them to this earth to live and grow in a mortal state. All Mormon children are taught the Articles of Faith – thirteen statements - that summarize their fundamental beliefs. Mormons don't believe the concept of unified Trinity; but, they believe that God has a physical body, and man can eventually become like God.

MESSAGES FROM THE BOOK OF MORMON

"And inasmuch as ye shall keep my commandments, ye shall prosper, and shall be led to a land of promise; yea, even a land which I have prepared for you; yea, a land which is choice above all other lands."

– BOOK OF MORMON: 1 NEPHI, 2:20.

"I will go and do the things which the Lord hath commanded, for I know that the Lord giveth no commandment unto the children of men, save he shall prepare a way for them that they may accomplish the thing which he commandeth them."

– BOOK OF MORMON: 1 NEPHI, 3:7.

"And now I would that ye should be humble, and be submissive and gentle; easy to be entreated; full of patience and long-suffering; being temperate in all things; being diligent in keeping the commandments of God at all times; asking for whatsoever things ye stand in need, both spiritual and temporal; always returning thanks unto God for whatsoever things ye do receive. And see that ye have faith, hope, and charity, and then ye will always abound in good works."

– BOOK OF MORMON: ALMA, 7:23–24.

"And behold, I tell you these things that ye may learn wisdom; that ye may learn that when ye are in the service of your fellow beings ye are only in the service of your God."

– BOOK OF MORMON: MOSIAH, 2:17.

"And now as I said concerning faith—faith is not to have a perfect knowledge of things; therefore if ye have faith ye hope for things which are not seen, which are true."

– BOOK OF MORMON: ALMA, 32:21.

"Behold, I would exhort you that when ye shall read these things, if it be wisdom in God that ye should read them, that ye would remember how merciful the Lord hath been unto the children of men, from the creation of Adam even down until the time that ye shall receive these things, and ponder it in your hearts.

And when ye shall receive these things, I would exhort you that ye would ask God, the Eternal Father, in the name of Christ, if these things are not true; and if ye shall ask with a sincere heart, with real intent, having faith in Christ, he will manifest the truth of it unto you, by the power of the Holy Ghost.

And by the power of the Holy Ghost ye may know the truth of all things."

– Book of Mormon: Moroni, 10:3-5;
[This selection of text is called the "Moroni's Promise"]

"And now I bid unto all, farewell. I soon go to rest in the paradise of God, until my spirit and body shall again reunite, and I am brought forth triumphant through the air, to meet you before the pleasing bar of the great Jehovah, the Eternal Judge of both quick and dead. Amen."

– Book of Mormon: Moroni, 10:34;
[Last words of the -Book of Mormon]

HOLY WALL:
THE KITAB-I-AQDAS – BAHAI SCRIPTURE

The Kitab-i-Aqdas is the most holy book of the Bahá'í faith. It was written by Bahaullah in Arabic. The book was completed around 1873. It consists of several hundred verses of poetry, as well as rhymed prose. In English translation, it is organized into 189 numbered paragraphs.

Bahai faith is unique in the sense that it acknowledges prophets of earlier religions, Abraham, Krishna, Zoroaster, Moses, Buddha, Jesus, and Muhammad, as divine teachers who were sent by the same God as educators to the humans. The Bahai concept of God consists of the acknowledgment of one supreme Being, unknowable, inaccessible, omniscient, and omnipotent.

MESSAGES FROM THE KITAB-I-AQDAS

"The first duty prescribed by God for His servants is the recognition of Him Who is the Dayspring of His Revelation and the Fountain of His laws, Who representeth the Godhead in both the Kingdom of His Cause and the world of creation. Whoso achieveth this duty hath attained unto all good; and whoso is deprived thereof hath gone astray, though he be the author of every righteous deed."

– Kitab-i-Aqdas, Paragraph 1, Bahai World Center, 1992 edition

"We have enjoined obligatory prayer upon you, with nine rak'áhs, to be offered at noon and in the morning and the evening unto God, the Revealer of Verses. We have relieved you of a greater number, as a command in the Book of God. He, verily, is the Ordainer, the Omnipotent, the Unrestrained."

– Kitab-i-Aqdas, Paragraph 6

"Ye have been forbidden to commit murder or adultery, or to engage in backbiting or calumny; shun ye, then, what hath been prohibited in the holy Books and Tablets."

– Kitab-i-Aqdas, Paragraph 19

"Fear God, and follow not your idle fancies."

– Kitab-i-Aqdas, Paragraph 37

"We have made it lawful for you to listen to music and singing. Take heed, however, lest listening thereto should cause you to overstep the bounds of propriety and dignity."

– Kitab-i-Aqdas, Paragraph 51

"It is forbidden you to trade in slaves, be they men or women. It is not for him who is himself a servant to buy another of God's servants, and this hath been prohibited in His Holy Tablet."

– Kitab-i-Aqdas, Paragraph 72

"Adorn yourselves with the raiment of goodly deeds."

– Kitab-i-Aqdas, Paragraph 73

"Consort with all religions with amity and concord, that they may inhale from you the sweet fragrance of God. Beware lest amidst men the flame of foolish ignorance overpower you. All things proceed from God and unto Him they return. He is the source of all things and in Him all things are ended."

– Kitab-i-Aqdas, Paragraph 144

HOLY WALL:
THE WOMAN'S BIBLE

The Woman's Bible was published in 1895 and challenged the traditional religious view that God created woman to be subservient to man. Elizabeth Cady Stanton, with assistance from twenty-six other women, attempted to demonstrate that it is men's desire for domination, not divine will, that humiliated women through biblical interpretation of God's words. The Woman's Bible is in a unique position to occupy a place on both the *Holy Wall* and the *Wall of Mortals*, because it contains holy words of the Bible, as well as human interpretations thereof. An ever-tolerant God chose to put it on the *Holy Wall* in his facebook.

EVOLUTION OF GOD

The God of modern Christian woman is fair to woman and does not approve misogynous interpretations of Bible.

MESSAGES FROM WOMAN'S BIBLE

"Genesis i: 26, 27, 28.

26 And God said, Let us make man in our image after our likeness: and let them have dominion over the fish of the sea, and over the fowl of the air, and over the cattle, and over all the earth, and over every creeping thing that creepeth upon the earth.

27 So God created man in his own image, in the image of God created he him: male and female image, created he them.

28 And God blessed them, and God said unto them, Be fruitful, and multiply, and replenish the earth, and subdue it; and have dominion over the fish of the sea, and over the fowl of the air, and over every living thing that moveth upon the earth.

Here is the sacred historian's first account of the advent of woman; a simultaneous creation of both sexes, in the image of God. It is evident from the language that there was consultation in the Godhead, and that the masculine and feminine elements were equally represented. Scott in his commentaries says, "This consultation of the Gods is the origin of the doctrine of the trinity." But instead of three male personages, as generally represented, a Heavenly Father, Mother, and Son would seem more rational.

The first step in the elevation of woman to her true position, as an equal factor in human progress, is the cultivation of the religious sentiment in regard to her dignity and equality, the recognition by the rising generation of an ideal Heavenly Mother, to whom their prayers should be addressed, as well as to a Father.

If language has any meaning, we have in these texts a plain declaration of the existence of the feminine element in the Godhead, equal in power and glory with the masculine. The Heavenly Mother and Father! "God created man in his own image, male and female." Thus Scripture, as well as science and philosophy, declares the eternity and equality of sex—the philosophical fact, without which there could have been no perpetuation of creation, no growth or development in the animal, vegetable, or mineral kingdoms, no awakening nor progressing in the world of thought. The masculine and feminine elements, exactly equal and balancing each other, are as essential to the maintenance of the equilibrium of the universe as positive and negative electricity, the centripetal and centrifugal forces, the laws of attraction which bind together all we know of this planet whereon we dwell and of the system in which we revolve.

In the great work of creation the crowning glory was realized, when man and woman were evolved on the sixth day, the masculine and feminine forces in the image of God, that must have existed eternally, in all forms of matter and mind. All the persons in the Godhead are represented in the Elohim the divine plurality taking counsel in regard to this last and highest form of life. Who were the members of this high council, and were they a duality or a trinity? Verse 27 declares the image of God male and female. How then is it possible to make woman an afterthought? We find in verses 5-16 the pronoun "he" used. Should it not in harmony with verse 26 be "they," a dual pronoun? We may attribute this to the same cause as the use of "his" in verse 11 instead of "it." The fruit tree yielding fruit after "his" kind instead of after "its" kind. The paucity of a language may give rise to many misunderstandings.

The above texts plainly show the simultaneous creation of man and woman, and their equal importance in the development of the race. All those theories based on the assumption that man was prior in the creation, have no foundation in Scripture.

As to woman's subjection, on which both the canon and the civil law delight to dwell, it is important to note that equal dominion is given to woman over every living thing, but not one word is said giving man dominion over woman.

Here is the first title deed to this green earth giving alike to the sons and daughters of God. No lesson of woman's subjection can be fairly drawn from the first chapter of the Old Testament."

— WOMAN'S BIBLE, CHAPTER I

WALL OF MORTALS:
(1700 TO 1900 AD)

The writings of a special group of humans, the Nobel Laureates, who are born in the nineteenth century are separately presented in the Chapter 10 "God of Nobel Laureates."

"When a human being kills an animal for food, he is neglecting his own hunger for justice. Man prays for mercy, but is unwilling to extend it to others. Why then should man expect mercy from God? It is unfair to expect something that you are not willing to give."

– BENJAMIN FRANKLIN (1706-1790)
[American inventor, journalist, printer, diplomat, and statesman]

"God heals and the doctor takes the fee."

– BENJAMIN FRANKLIN (1706-1790)

"When religion is good, it will take care of itself. When it is not able to take care of itself, and God does not see fit to take care of it, so that it has to appeal to the civil power for support, it is evidence to my mind that its cause is a bad one."

– BENJAMIN FRANKLIN (1706-1790)

"The most acceptable service of God is doing good to man."

– BENJAMIN FRANKLIN (1706-1790)

"The most acceptable service of God is doing good to man."

– BENJAMIN FRANKLIN (1706-1790)

"The root of all religious observance and spiritual practice is for us to be constantly aware of God. It should make us realize that we were created for the singular purpose of consciously experiencing the Creator."

– RABBI MOSHE CHAIM LUZZATTO (1707-1746)
[Italian Jewish rabbi, kabbalist, and philosopher; also known as Ramchal]

COFFEE BREAK
Our Idea of God: David Hume, who has written the finest philosophy in the English language, argued that our idea of God is derived from reflection on the operations of our own minds, not from observational experiences; therefore, we can never be sure of the existence of God.

"The idea of God, as meaning an infinitely intelligent, wise, and good Being, arises from reflecting on the operations of our own mind, and augmenting, without limit, those qualities of goodness and wisdom."

– DAVID HUME (1711-1776)

[Scottish philosopher, economist, historian, and key figure in the history of Western philosophy]

"God's power is infinite. Whatever he wills is executed. But neither man, nor any other animal, is happy. Therefore he does not will their happiness. Epicurus' old questions are yet unanswered. Is God willing to prevent evil, but unable? Then is he impotent. Is he able, but not willing? Then is he malevolent. Is he both able and willing? Whence then is evil?"

– DAVID HUME (1711-1776)

"God makes all things good; man meddles with them and they become evil."

– JEAN-JACQUES ROUSSEAU (1712-1778)

[Franco-Swiss philosopher, whose ideas influenced French Revolution and social theories]

"Man's power makes use of means, the divine power is self-active. God can because he wills; his will is his power. God is good; this is certain; but man finds his happiness in the welfare of his kind. God's happiness consists in the love of order; for it is through order that he maintains what is, and unites each part in the whole."

– JEAN-JACQUES ROUSSEAU (1712-1778)

"If you want me to believe in God, you must make me touch him."

– DENIS DIDEROT (1713-1784)

[French philosopher and chief editor of the historic project to produce L'Encyclopédie]

"Superstition is more injurious to God than atheism."

– DENIS DIDEROT (1713-1784)

"If the ignorance of nature gave birth to such a variety of gods, the knowledge of this nature is calculated to destroy them."

– BARON D'HOLBACH (1723–1789)

[Paul-Henri Thiry, French author, philosopher and encyclopedist. First self-proclaimed atheist in Europe]

"All children are born Atheists, they have no idea of God."

– BARON D'HOLBACH (1723–1789)

COFFEE BREAK

Golden Age of German Philosophy: During the eighteenth and nineteenth centuries, philosophy flourished in Germany in a scale that is only comparable to what happened in ancient Greece. It began with Immanuel Kant and was enriched by Schopenhauer, Fichte, Schelling, Hegel, Marx, and Nietzsche. Kant argued for a moral and practical necessity for a belief in God, which cannot otherwise be explained rationally because of the inherent human limitations of gaining knowledge only through experience and understanding.

"All arguments, however, to prove the existence of God must, in order to be theoretically valid, start from specifically and exclusively sensible or phenomenal data, must employ only the conceptions of pure physical science, and must end with demonstrating in sensible experience an object congruous with, or corresponding to, the idea of God. But this requirement cannot be met, for, scientifically speaking, the existence of an absolutely necessary God cannot be either proved or disproved. Hence room is left for faith in any moral proofs that may present themselves to us, apart from science."

— IMMANUEL KANT (1724-1804)
[German philosopher, one of the most influential philosophers of Western Philosophy]

"Even if God were to make an immediate appearance, I would still need rational theology as a presupposition. For how am I to be certain that it is God himself who has appeared to me, or only another powerful creature?"

— IMMANUEL KANT (1724-1804)

"Reason can never prove the existence of God."

— IMMANUEL KANT (1724-1804)

"It is thoroughly necessary to be convinced of God's existence, it is not quite so necessary that one should demonstrate it."

— IMMANUEL KANT (1724-1804)

"Whoever undertakes to set himself up as a judge of Truth and Knowledge is shipwrecked by the laughter of the gods."

— EDMUND BURKE (1729–1797)
[Irish political philosopher and statesman; regarded as the "father" of modern conservatism]

"God moves in a mysterious way

His wonders to perform;

He plants his footsteps in the sea,

And rides upon the storm."

— WILLIAM COWPER (1731-1800)
[English poet and hymnodist]

"Let us raise a standard to which the wise and honest can repair; the rest is in the hands of God."

— GEORGE WASHINGTON (1732-1799)
[Commander-in-Chief of the Continental Army in the American Revolutionary War from 1775 to 1783, and the first President of the United States]

"We have abundant reason to rejoice that in this Land the light of truth & reason has triumphed over the power of bigotry and superstition, and that every person may here worship God according to the dictates of his own heart. In this enlightened age & in this Land of equal liberty it is our boast, that a man's religious tenets will not forfeit the protection of the Laws, nor deprive him of the right of attaining & holding the highest offices that are known in the United States."

— GEORGE WASHINGTON (1732-1799)

"When we say God is a spirit, we know what we mean, as well as we do when we say that the pyramids of Egypt are matter. Let us be content, therefore, to believe him to be a spirit, that is, an essence that we know nothing of, in which originally and necessarily reside all energy, all power, all capacity, all activity, all wisdom, all goodness."

— JOHN ADAMS (1735-1826)
[First Vice President of United States and second President of United States, father of John Quincy Adams, the 6th President of United States. Stated this in a letter to Thomas Jefferson, the 3rd President of United States]

"I believe in one God and no more, and I hope for happiness beyond this life. I believe in the equality of man; and I believe that religious duties consist in doing justice, loving mercy, and endeavoring to make our fellow creatures happy."

— THOMAS PAINE (1737-1809)
[English political writer, theorist, and activist, wrote three of the most influential and controversial works of the 18th Century: Common Sense, The Rights of Man and The Age of Reason]

"The Jews say that their Word of God was given by God to Moses face to face; the Christians say, that their Word of God came by divine inspiration; and the Turks say, that their Word of God (the Koran) was brought by an angel from heaven. Each of those churches accuses the other of unbelief; and, for my own part, I disbelieve them all."

— THOMAS PAINE (1737-1809)

Only "Reason" can discover God

"It is only by the exercise of reason that man can discover God."

— THOMAS PAINE (1737-1809)

"I think that if there were a God, there would be less evil on this earth. I believe that if evil exists here below, then either it was willed by God or it was beyond His powers to prevent it. Now I cannot bring myself to fear a God who is either spiteful or weak. I defy Him without fear and care not a fig for his thunderbolts."

— MARQUIS DE SADE (1740-1814)
[French writer]

"Man is to be found in reason, God in the passions."

— GEORG CHRISTOPH LICHTENBERG (1742-1799)
[German scientist, satirist and philosopher]

"It is hardly to be believed how spiritual reflections when mixed with a little physics can hold people's attention and give them a livelier idea of God than do the often ill-applied examples of his wrath."

— GEORG CHRISTOPH LICHTENBERG (1742-1799)

COFFEE BREAK
The Jefferson Bible: Thomas Jefferson literally took a pair of scissors and cut out every miracle and inconsistency he could find in the New Testament Gospels of Matthew, Mark, Luke, and John. Then, pasting the rest together, he produced a four-language (English, Greek, Latin, and French) Bible of his own, later dubbed the "Jefferson Bible." His own handwritten title page was, "The Life and Morals of Jesus of Nazareth. Extracted textually from the Gospels in Greek, Latin, French & English." Jefferson claimed in a letter to John Adams that this shortened version contains "the most sublime and benevolent code of morals which has ever been offered to man."

"The God who gave us life gave us liberty at the same time."

— THOMAS JEFFERSON (1743-1826)
[Third president of the United States, author of the Declaration of Independence, a political philosopher, and one of the most influential founders of the United States]

"Question with boldness even the existence of a god; because, if there be one, he must more approve the homage of reason, than that of blindfolded fear."

— THOMAS JEFFERSON (1743-1826)

"The legitimate powers of government extend to only such acts as are injurious to others. But it does me no injury for my neighbor to say that there are twenty gods, or no God. It neither picks my pocket, nor breaks my leg."

— THOMAS JEFFERSON (1743-1826)

"Believing with you that religion is a matter which lies solely between man and his God, that he owes account to none other for his faith or his worship, that the legislative powers of government reach actions only, and not opinions, I contemplate with sovereign reverence that act of the whole American people which declared that their legislature should "make no law respecting an establishment of religion, or prohibiting the free exercise thereof," thus building a wall of separation between church and State."

— THOMAS JEFFERSON (1743-1826)

"A man should hear a little music, read a little poetry, and see a fine picture every day of his life, in order that worldly cares may not obliterate the sense of the beautiful which God has implanted in the human soul."

— GOETHE (1749-1832)
[Johann Wolfgang von Goethe, German novelist, dramatist, poet, humanist, scientist, philosopher, and for ten years chief minister of state at Weimar]

"The greatest act of faith takes place when a man finally decides that he is not God."

— GOETHE (1749-1832)

"Religion is 'twixt God and my own soul,
Nor saint, nor sage, can boundless thought control."

— JUDITH SARGENT MURRAY (1751-1820)
[American feminist, author, playwright, poet]

"Without doubt God is the universal moving force, but each being is moved according to the nature that God has given it."

— JOSEPH-MARIE, COMTE DE MAISTRE (1753-1821)
[French lawyer, diplomat, writer, and philosopher]

"It is easy to understand God as long as you don't try to explain him."

— JOSEPH JOUBERT (1754-1824)
[French moralist and essayist]

"The God of metaphysics is but an idea. But the God of religion, the Maker of heaven and earth, the sovereign Judge of actions and thoughts, is a power."

— JOSEPH JOUBERT (1754-1824)

"God ordains all for the best, however strange it may appear to our eyes."

— WOLFGANG AMADEUS MOZART (1756-1791)
[German music composer]

"He who sees the Infinite in all things, sees God."

— WILLIAM BLAKE (1757-1827)
[English poet, painter, printmaker, and essayist]

"Nakedness of woman is the work of God."

— WILLIAM BLAKE (1757-1827)

"Where Mercy, Love, & Pity dwell
There God is dwelling too."

— WILLIAM BLAKE (1757-1827)

COFFEE BREAK

God's Presence: Celebrated English poet, William Blake, senses God's mysterious presence around him. Bengali Baul poet, Lalan Shah, also gives a similar description of God's presence.

"And I have felt
A presence that disturbs me with the joy
Of elevated thoughts; a sense sublime
Of something far more deeply interfused,
Whose dwelling is the light of setting suns,
And the round ocean, and the living air,
And the blue sky, and in the mind of man,
A motion and a spirit, that impels
All thinking things, all objects of all thought,
And rolls through all things."

— WILLIAM BLAKE (1757-1827)

"Love is a lamp of God, I am its moth."

— SEYH GALIB (1757-1799)
[Also known as Galib Dede, Turkish poet]

"God helps the brave."

— FRIEDRICH SCHILLER (1759-1805)
[Johann Christoph Friedrich von Schiller, German poet, historian, dramatist, and playwright]

"Expect great things from God. Attempt great things for God."

— WILLIAM CAREY (1761-1834)
[English Baptist missionary and Baptist minister]

"Nothing exists outside of God... God not only is inwardly and concealed within himself, but he also exists and expresses himself."

— JOHANN GOTTLIEB FICHTE (1762-1814)
[German philosopher]

"God is an unutterable sigh, planted in the depths of the soul."

— JEAN PAUL (1763-1825)
[Johann Paul Friedrich Richter, influential German novelist and short-story writer. He is usually known by his pseudonym, Jean Paul]

"All the dead cried out, "Christ! Is there no God?." He answered, "There is none!" The whole Shadow of each then shuddered, not the breast alone; and one after the other, all, in this shuddering, shook into pieces. Christ continued: "I went through the Worlds, I mounted into the Suns, and flew with the Galaxies through the wastes of Heaven; but there is no God! I descended as far as Being casts its shadow, and looked down into the Abyss and cried, Father, where art thou? But I heard only the everlasting storm which no one guides, and the gleaming Rainbow of Creation hung without a Sun that made it, over the Abyss, and trickled down. And when I looked up to the immeasurable world for the Divine Eye, it glared on me with an empty, black, bottomless Eye-socket; and Eternity lay upon Chaos, eating it and ruminating it. Cry on, ye Dissonances; cry away the Shadows, for He is not!" The pale-grown Shadows flitted away, as white vapour which forst has formed with the warm breath disappears; and all was void. O, then came, fearful for the heart, the dead Children who had been awakened before the high Form on the Altar, and said, "Jesus, have we no Father?" And he answered, with streaming tears, "We are all orphans, I and you: we are without Father!""

— Jean Paul (1763-1825)

"All things proclaim the existence of God."

— Napoleon Bonaparte (1769-1821)
[Emperor of the France and King of Italy under the name Napoleon I]

"We bow our heads before Thee, and we laud,

And magnify thy name Almighty God!

But man is thy most awful instrument,

In working out a pure intent."

— William Wordsworth (1770-1850)
[Major English poet of Romantic Age]

COFFEE BREAK
The Real and the Rational: Hegel was a very influential German philosopher whose work gave rise to Hegelianism, which can be summed up in his own words: "the real is the rational and the rational is the real." His philosophy undermined liberal democracy and provided inspiration for the totalitarian and godless philosophies of communism and fascism. One can use Hegel's dialectics to construe any belief within a rational framework. He influenced many leading philosophers, such as Kierkegaard, Feuerbach, Marx, and Engels.

"Pure Being, as it is mere abstraction, is just Nothing. In fact this definition is implied in saying that God is only the supreme Being and nothing more. The Nothing which the Buddhists make the universal principle, as well as the final aim and goal of everything, is the same abstraction."

— Georg Wilhelm Friedrich Hegel (1770-1831)
[Georg Wilhelm Friedrich Hegel, German philosopher, one of the most influential philosophers of Western Philosophy]

"The feeling that "God himself is dead" is the sentiment on which the religion of more recent times rests."

— GEORG WILHELM FRIEDRICH HEGEL (1770-1831)

"God is, as it were, the sewer into which all contradictions flow."

- GEORG WILHELM FRIEDRICH HEGEL (1770-1831)

"The beginning of religion, more precisely its content, is the concept of religion itself, that God is the absolute truth, the truth of all things, and subjectively that religion alone is the absolutely true knowledge."

— GEORG WILHELM FRIEDRICH HEGEL (1770-1831)

"God is immaterial; as He is invisible. He can, therefore, have no form. But from what we are able to perceive in His works we conclude that He is eternal, almighty, omniscient, and omnipresent."

— LUDWIG VAN BEETHOVEN (1770-1827)
[German music composer and pianist]

"Thank God for tea! What would the world do without tea? How did it exist?"

— SYDNEY SMITH (1771-1845)
[English clergyman, critic, philosopher]

"Man is free whenever he produces or manifests God, and through this he becomes immortal."

— VON SCHLEGEL (1772-1829)
[Karl Wilhelm Friedrich Schlegel, German poet, critic and scholar]

"Earth, with her thousand voices, praises God."

— SAMUEL TAYLOR COLERIDGE (1772-1834)
[English poet, critic and philosopher, one of the founders of the Romantic Movement]

"A solitude is the audience-chamber of God."

— WALTER SAVAGE LANDOR (1775-1864)
[English author and poet]

"To speak the plain truth, all religions seem alike to me, one mass of absurdities and lies. I know that there is a God, but I know no more of him; and I believe that all those are liars who pretend to know more than I do."

— MARY MARTHA SHERWOOD (1775-1851)
[English author, prolific writer of children's literature]

COFFEE BREAK

God of Bengali Bauls: The Bauls are a group of mystical singers from Bangladesh and West Bengal, India. They are unlettered mendicants who move from place to place; singing and dancing is their worship. They are true "God-intoxicated humans." Their way to God is the way of love.

The word "Baul" means "mad." They are spiritual rebels transcending religious boundaries. Bauls say: "God is deserting your temple as you amuse yourself by blowing conch shells and ringing bells. The road to you is blocked by temples and mosques. I hear you call, my lord, but I cannot advance. Priests bar the way."

Baul tradition is a fusion of Hindu and Muslim philosophies that consider the human body to be the shrine of God. They consider God to be inside humans as "moner manush" (man of the heart). Bauls are very courageous in their songs, as they break all the rules of conventional religion. They throw challenges at God by asking, "We are nothing but your toys, my Lord; then why do you call us sinners in your playful whim?" One of the most famous Bauls, Lalon Shah, expressed the superficiality of religion in this manner:

"Everyone asks: 'Lalan, what's your religion in this world?'

Lalan answers: 'How does religion look?'

I've never laid eyes on it.

Some wear malas [Hindu rosaries] around their necks,

some tasbis [Muslim rosaries], and so people say

they've got different religions.

But do you bear the sign of your religion

when you come or when you go?"

"He talks to me
But he would not let me see him.
He moves
Close to my hands
But away from my reach.
I explore
The sky and the earth
Searching him,
Circling round my error
Of not knowing me:
Who am I
And who is he?"

– LALAN SHAH (1775-1891)
[Bengali Baul poet, sufi and mystic]

"God does arithmetic."

— CARL FRIEDRICH GAUSS (1777-1855)
[Johann Carl Friedrich Gauss, German mathematician, astronomer and physicist]

"Thou art, O God, the life and light
Of all this wondrous world we see;
Its glow by day, its smile by night,
Are but reflections caught from Thee!
Where'er we turn thy glories shine,
And all things fair and bright are thine!"

— THOMAS MOORE (1779-1852)
[Irish poet and hymnist, now best remembered for the lyrics of The Last Rose of Summer]

"Men will wrangle for religion; write for it; fight for it; die for it; anything but live for it."

— CHARLES CALEB COLTON (1780-1832)
[British author, clergyman, and art collector]

"It is highly convenient to believe in the infinite mercy of God when you feel the need of mercy, but remember also His infinite justice."

— BENJAMIN ROBERT HAYDON (1786-1846)
[English historical painter and writer]

"Monotheistic religions alone furnish the spectacle of religious wars, religious persecutions, heretical tribunals, that breaking of idols and destruction of images of the gods, that razing of Indian temples and Egyptian colossi, which had looked on the sun 3,000 years: just because a jealous god had said, 'Thou shalt make no graven image.'"

— ARTHUR SCHOPENHAUER (1788-1860)
[German philosopher]

"The book of nature which we have to read is written by the finger of God."

— MICHAEL FARADAY (1791-1867)
[British scientist, founder of electronics and electromagnetism]

GOD IN U.S. CONSTITUTIONS

There is not a single reference to God or a Supreme Being in the US Constitution, adopted in 1787. However, God appears in full might in the constitutions of all fifty states. Some state constitutions even go further, denying certain rights that are guaranteed by the federal constitution. For example, Article 6 of the US constitution states that, "no religious test shall ever be required as a qualification to any office or public trust under the United States." Contrast this right with the following clauses in state constitutions:

South Carolina: "No person who denies the existence of the Supreme Being shall hold any office under this Constitution."

Tennessee: "No person who denies the being of God, or a future state of rewards and punishments, shall hold any office in the civil department of this state."

Maryland: "...nor shall any person, otherwise competent, be deemed incompetent as a witness, or juror, on account of his religious belief; provided, he believes in the existence of God, and that under His dispensation such person will be held morally accountable for his acts, and be rewarded or punished there for either in this world or in the world to come."

Texas: "No religious test shall ever be required as a qualification to any office, or public trust, in this State; nor shall any one be excluded from holding office on account of his religious sentiments, provided he acknowledge the existence of a Supreme Being."

From the very beginning, the Christian evangelists were unhappy about the absence of any reference to God in the US constitution. During the American Civil War (1861-1865), evangelists claimed that the war was God's punishment for the omission of God from the Constitution. As a result, in 1864, they sent a formal proposal to Congress to amend the preamble as provided below. This proposed amendment is known as the Christian Amendment and never went to a vote in Congress. The proposed changes are shown in **bold** text.

We, the people of the United States, **humbly acknowledging Almighty God as the source of all authority and power in civil government, the Lord Jesus Christ as the Ruler among the nations, His revealed will as the supreme law of the land, in order to constitute a Christian government, and** in order to form a more perfect union, establish justice, insure domestic tranquility, provide for the common defense, promote the general welfare, and secure **the inalienable rights and** the blessings of **life**, liberty, **and the pursuit of happiness** to ourselves, ~~and~~ our posterity, **and all the people**, do ordain and establish this Constitution for the United States of America.

"There is no God."

– Percy Bysshe Shelley (1792-1822)
[Major English romantic poet]

"If he is infinitely good, what reason should we have to fear him?
If he is infinitely wise, why should we have doubts concerning our future?
If he knows all, why warn him of our needs and fatigue him with our prayers?
If he is everywhere, why erect temples to him?
If he is just, why fear that he will punish the creatures
that he has filled with weaknesses?
If grace does everything for them, what reason
would he have for recompensing them?
If he is all-powerful, how offend him, how resist him?
If he is reasonable, how can he be angry at the blind, to whom
he has given the liberty of being unreasonable?
If he is immovable, by what right do we pretend to make him change his decrees?
If he is inconceivable, why occupy ourselves with him?
If he has spoken, why is the universe not convinced?
If the knowledge of a God is the most necessary, why is
it not the most evident and the clearest?"

– Percy Bysshe Shelley (1792-1822)

"All things that are on earth shall wholly pass away,
Except the love of God, which shall live and last for aye."

– William Cullen Bryant (1794-1878)
[American Romantic poet and journalist]

"Of all God's creatures, Man alone is poor."

– Thomas Carlyle (1795-1881)
[Scottish essayist, satirist, and historian]

"God will forgive me; that's his business."

– Heinrich Heine (1797-1856)
[One of the most significant German romantic poets, journalist, essayist]

"With the blade of his criticism, his Critique of Pure Reason, Kant, the executioner, beheaded belief in God. God, therefore, became now nothing but fiction."

– Heinrich Heine (1797-1856)

"He gave me heaven and earth, and assumed I'd be satisfied,
Actually I was too embarrassed to argue."

– Mirza Ghalib (1797-1869)
[Classical Urdu and Persian poet from India]

"Any and everything of this universe is all the body of God."

— NAKAYAMA MIKI (1798-1887)

[Born Maegawa Miki, Japanese founder of Tenrikyo, the largest current religion founded by a woman. Tenrikyo, a monotheistic religion, has about 2 million followers worldwide, mostly in Japan]

"Clouds symbolize the veils that shroud God."

— HONORÉ DE BALZAC (1799-1850)

[French novelist, founding father of realism in European literature (along with Flaubert)]

"Time spent laughing is time spent with the Gods."

— JAPANESE PROVERB

"I sought to hear the voice of God and climbed the topmost steeple, But God declared: "Go down again - I dwell among the people.""

— JOHN HENRY CARDINAL NEWMAN (1801-1890)

[English convert to Catholicism, later made a cardinal]

"Conscience is God present in man."

— VICTOR MARIE HUGO (1802-1885)

[The most influential French Romantic writer of the 19th century and regarded as the greatest French poet]

"Seeing so much poverty everywhere makes me think that God is not rich. He gives the appearance of it, but I suspect some financial difficulties."

— VICTOR MARIE HUGO (1802-1885)

"It is only Religion, the great bond of love and duty to God that makes any existence valuable or even tolerable."

— DR. HORACE BUSHNELL (1802-1876)

[American pastor, theologian and author]

"God said, "Let us make man in our image." Man said, "Let us make God in our image.""

— DOUGLAS WILLIAM JERROLD (1803-1857)

[English dramatist and writer]

COFFEE BREAK

Intellectual Declaration of Independence: In 1837, Ralph Waldo Emerson, gave a speech entitled *The American Scholar,* which is considered by some to be America's *Intellectual Declaration of Independence.* Emerson led a philosophical movement called Transcendentalism, which professed that organized religion and politics corrupt an individual, and that this can be prevented if we rely more on the inherent goodness of humans than on religious edicts..

"God enters by a private door into every individual."

— RALPH WALDO EMERSON (1803-1882)
[American philosopher, essayist, and poet]

"The soul of God is poured into the world through the thoughts of men."

— RALPH WALDO EMERSON (1803-1882)

"The religion that is afraid of science dishonors God and commits suicide."

— RALPH WALDO EMERSON (1803-1882)

"God, I have said, is the fulfiller, or the reality, of the human desires for happiness, perfection, and immortality. From this it may be inferred that to deprive man of God is to tear the heart out of his breast."

— LUDWIG FEUERBACH (1804-1872)
[German philosopher]

"Christianity set itself the goal of fulfilling man's unattainable desires, but for that very reason ignored his attainable desires. By promising man eternal life, it deprived him of temporal life, by teaching him to trust in God's help it took away his trust in his own powers; by giving him faith in a better life in heaven, it destroyed his faith in a better life on earth and his striving to attain such a life."

— LUDWIG FEUERBACH (1804-1872)

"God could not be everywhere and therefore he made mothers"

— PROVERB

"Man was also in the beginning with God. Intelligence, or the light of truth, was not created or made, neither indeed can be. All truth is independent in that sphere in which God has placed it, to act for itself, as all intelligence also; otherwise there is no existence."

— JOSEPH SMITH, JR. (1805-1844)
[Founder of Latter Day Saint Movement, popularly known as Mormon church, in Doctrine and Covenants of the Church of Latter Day Saints, considered to be revelations from God]

"Every spirit of man was innocent in the beginning; and God having redeemed man from the fall, man became again, in their infant state, innocent before God."

— JOSEPH SMITH, JR. (1805-1844)

"Every man's life is a fairy tale written by God's fingers."

— HANS CHRISTIAN ANDERSEN (1805-1875)
[Danish author and poet, noted for his children's stories]

"God's gifts put man's best dreams to shame."

— ELIZABETH BARRETT BROWNING (1806-1861)
[English poet and the wife of fellow poet Robert Browning]

"God only, who made us rich, can make us poor."

— ELIZABETH BARRETT BROWNING (1806-1861)

"I will call no Being good, who is not what I mean when I apply that epithet to my fellow-creatures; and if such a Being can sentence me to hell for not so calling Him, to hell I will go."

— JOHN STUART MILL (1806-1873)

[English political philosopher and economist, most influential English philosopher of the 19th century]

"The Gods were not supposed to concern themselves much with men's conduct to one another, except when men had contrived to make the Gods themselves an interested party, by placing an assertion or an engagement under the sanction of a solemn appeal to them, by oath or vow."

— JOHN STUART MILL (1806-1873)

"It is the job of prophets and scientists alike to proclaim the glories of God."

— LOUIS AGASSIZ (1807-1873)

[Jean Louis Rodolphe Agassiz, Swiss-born American zoologist, glaciologist, and geologist]

"Nature is a revelation of God; Art a revelation of man."

— HENRY WADSWORTH LONGFELLOW (1807-1882)

[American poet and one of the five members of the group known as the Fireside Poets]

"Those men who laid the foundation of this American government and signed the Declaration of Independence were the best spirits the God of heaven could find on the face of the earth. They were choice spirits . . . noble spirits before God."

— WILFORD WOODRUFF (1807-1898)

[The fourth President of The Church of Jesus Christ of Latter-day Saints (LDS), from 1889 until his death in 1898]

"Fear that man who fears not God."

— ABD-EL-KADER (1808-1883)

[Algerian Islamic scholar, Sufi, political, military leader, and national hero]

"God is dead! Heaven is empty

Weep, children, you no longer have a father."

— GERARD DE NERVAL (1808-1855)

[Pseudonym for Gerard Labrunie, French Romantic poet and essayist]

"Those who deny freedom to others, deserve it not for themselves; and, under a just God, cannot long retain it."

— ABRAHAM LINCOLN(1809-1865)
[16th President of the United States, led the country during the American Civil War, proclaimed emancipation of slaves]

"I know that the Lord is always on the side of the right. But it is my constant anxiety and prayer that I and this nation should be on the Lord's side."

— ABRAHAM LINCOLN(1809-1865)

"I am aware that the assumed instinctive belief in God has been used by many persons as an argument for his existence. The idea of a universal and beneficent Creator does not seem to arise in the mind of man, until he has been elevated by long-continued culture."

— CHARLES DARWIN (1809-1882)
[British naturalist, founder of the theory of evolution]

"I cannot persuade myself that a beneficent and omnipotent God would have designedly created parasitic wasps with the express intention of their feeding within the living bodies of Caterpillars."

— CHARLES DARWIN (1809-1882)

"Little flower — but if I could understand
What you are, root and all, and all in all,
I should know what God and man is."

— LORD ALFRED TENNYSON (1809-1892)
[British Poet Laureate after William Wordsworth]

"Piety and morality are but the same spirit differently manifested. Piety is religion with its face toward God; morality is religion with its face toward the world."

— TRYON EDWARDS (1809-1894)
[American theologian, best known for compiling the "New Dictionary of Thoughts", a book of quotations]

"Every rose is an autograph from the hand of God on his world about us. He has inscribed his thoughts in these marvelous hieroglyphics which sense and science have, these many thousand years, been seeking to understand."

— THEODORE PARKER (1810-1860)
[American minister of the Unitarian church]

"God is the perfect poet,
Who in his person acts his own creations."

— ROBERT BROWNING (1812-1889)
[English poet and playwright, one of the foremost Victorian poets]

COFFEE BREAK

Existentialism: Kierkegaard, a Danish philosopher, is regarded as the founder of existentialism, which became the most fashionable philosophy in Europe immediately after World War II.

"Prayer does not change God, but it changes him who prays."
— Soren Kierkegaard (1813-1855)
[Danish philosopher, theologian, and psychologist]

"Faith is precisely the contradiction between the infinite passion of the individual's inwardness and the objective uncertainty. If I am capable of grasping God objectively, I do not believe, but precisely because I cannot do this, I must believe."
— Soren Kierkegaard (1813-1855)

"It takes something of a poet to apprehend and get into the depth, the lusciousness, the spiritual life of a great poem. And so we must be in some way like God in order that we may see God as He is."
— Edwin Hubbell Chapin (1814-1880)
[Universalist minister and orator]

"The idea of God implies the abdication of human reason and justice; it is the most decisive negation of human liberty, and necessarily ends in the enslavement of mankind, in theory and practice."
— Mikhail Bakunin (1814-1876)
[Russian revolutionary and theorist of collectivist anarchism]

"If God really existed, it would be necessary to abolish him."
— Mikhail Bakunin (1814-1876)

COFFEE BREAK

Woman and Bible: Elizabeth Stanton opposed male interpretations of the Bible and published *The Woman's Bible.*

"The only points in which I differ from all ecclesiastical teaching is that I do not believe that any man ever saw or talked with God, I do not believe that God inspired the Mosaic code, or told the historians what they say he did about woman, for all the religions on the face of the earth degrade her, and so long as woman accepts the position that they assign her, her emancipation is impossible."

– ELIZABETH CADY STANTON (1815-1902)
[American social activist, abolitionist, suffragist, and author of Woman's Bible]

"These familiar texts are quoted by clergymen in their pulpits, by statesmen in the halls of legislation, by lawyers in the courts, and are echoed by the press of all civilized nations, and accepted by woman herself as "The Word of God." So perverted is the religious element in her nature, that with faith and works she is the chief support of the church and clergy; the very powers that make her emancipation impossible. When, in the early part of the Nineteenth Century, women began to protest against their civil and political degradation, they were referred to the Bible for an answer. When they protested against their unequal position in the church, they were referred to the Bible for an answer."

– ELIZABETH CADY STANTON (1815-1902)

"The only difference between us is, we say that these degrading ideas of woman emanated from the brain of man, while the church says that they came from God."

– ELIZABETH CADY STANTON (1815-1902)
[In response to the women critics of Woman's Bible]

"God conceived the world,--that was poetry;

He formed it,--that was sculpture;

He colored it,--that was painting;

He people it with living beings,

--that was the grand, divine, eternal drama."

– CHARLOTTE SAUNDERS CUSHMAN (1816-1876)
[American stage actress]

"Women and God are the two rocks on which a man must either anchor or be wrecked."

– FREDERICK WILLIAM ROBERTSON (1816-1853)
[Known as Robertson of Brighton, English divine]

"It's only by forgetting yourself that you draw near to God."

– HENRY DAVID THOREAU (1817-1862)
[American writer and philosopher]

"All-praise to the unity of God, and all-honour to Him, the sovereign Lord, the incomparable and all-glorious Ruler of the universe, Who, out of utter nothingness, hath created the reality of all things, Who, from naught, hath brought into being the most refined and subtle elements of His creation."

– BAHAULLAH (1817-1892)
[Born Mirza Husayn Ali Nuri, founder of Bahai faith]

"I bear witness, O my God, that Thou hast created me to know Thee and to worship Thee. I testify, at this moment, to my powerlessness and to Thy might, to my poverty and to Thy wealth. There is none other God but Thee, the Help in Peril, the Self-Subsisting."

– BAHAULLAH (1817-1892)
[Obligatory short prayer of Bahai faith]

COFFEE BREAK
The Communist Manifesto: Karl Marx, a noted atheist, was one of the most influential thinkers in modern history. He borrowed heavily from Hegel and transformed the political landscape of the twentieth century with his Communist Manifesto, a set of revolutionary ideas for a classless society posited against industrial capitalist society. Marx believed that religion was the root cause of maintaining the status quo as well as the inequality between the rich and the poor. Therefore, he wanted to abolish religion and drive God out of human lives.

"My object in life is to dethrone God and destroy capitalism."

– KARL MARX (1818-1883)
[German political philosopher, political economist, and social theorist, founder of Marxism]

"Religious suffering is, at one and the same time, the expression of real suffering and a protest against real suffering. Religion is the sigh of the oppressed creature, the heart of a heartless world, and the soul of soulless conditions. It is the opium of the people. The abolition of religion as the illusory happiness of the people is the demand for their real happiness. To call on them to give up their illusions about their condition is to call on them to give up a condition that requires illusions."

– KARL MARX (1818-1883)

EVOLUTION OF GOD

God is blamed by communists for much of the social ills and the inequality between the rich and the poor.

"Since only what is material is perceptible, knowable, nothing is known of the existence of God."

– KARL MARX (1818-1883)

"Every tone [of the songs of the slaves] was a testimony against slavery, and a prayer to God for deliverance from chains."

– FREDERICK DOUGLASS (1818-1895)
[American slave who escaped to freedom later to become an American abolitionist, women's suffragist, editor, orator, author, statesman and reformer]

"Every formula which expresses a law of nature is a hymn of praise to God."
— Maria Mitchell (1818-1889)
[American astronomer]

"Beauty is God's handwriting."
— Charles Kingsley (1819-1875)
[English author, clergyman and educator]

"I'm not denyin' the women are foolish: God Almighty made 'em to match the men."
— George Eliot (1819-1880)
[Mary Ann Evans, English novelist and poet, more well-known by her pen name George Eliot]

"If God made poets for anything, it was to keep alive the traditions of the pure, the holy, and the beautiful."
— James Russell Lowell (1819-1891)
[American Romantic poet, critic, satirist, writer, diplomat, and abolitionist]

"In the faces of men and women I see God."
— Walt Whitman (1819-1892)
[American poet, best known for his work Leaves of Grass]

"And I say to mankind, Be not curious about God,
For I who am curious about each am not curious about God,
(No array of terms can say how much I am at peace about God and about death.)
I hear and behold God in every object, yet understand God not in the least,
Nor do I understand who there can be more wonderful than myself.
Why should I wish to see God better than this day?
I see something of God each hour of the twenty-four, and each moment then,
In the faces of men and women I see God, and in my own face in the glass,
I find letters from God dropt in the street, and every one is sign'd by God's name,
And I leave them where they are, for I know that wheresoe'er I go,
Others will punctually come for ever and ever."
— Walt Whitman (1819-1892)

"A child said What is the grass? fetching it to me with full hands;
How could I answer the child? I do not know what it is any more than he.
I guess it must be the flag of my disposition, out of hopeful green stuff woven.
Or I guess it is the handkerchief of the Lord,
A scented gift and remembrancer designedly dropt,
Bearing the owner's name someway in the corners, that we may see
and remark, and say Whose?"
— Walt Whitman (1819-1892)

"Geology gives us a key to the patience of God."

> — Josiah Gilbert Holland (1819-1881)
> *[American novelist and poet]*

"God pity the man of science who believes in nothing but what he can prove by scientific methods; for if ever a human being needed divine pity, he does."

> — Josiah Gilbert Holland (1819-1881)

"To cultivate a garden is to walk with God."

> — Christian Nestell Bovee (1820-1904)
> *[American author]*

"To understand God's thoughts we must study statistics, for these are the measure of his purpose."

> — Florence Nightingale (1820-1910)
> *[English nurse, writer, and statistician]*

"And Hegel, whose mouth until this moment grimness locked,

Suddenly rose up giant high and spoke:

'I consecrated all my life to Science,

Preached atheism with my whole strength:

I placed Self-Consciousness upon her throne,

Convinced I head already conquered God.' "

> — Friedrich Engels (1820-1895)
> *[German philosopher, author, political scientist and co-author of The Communist Manifesto with Karl Marx]*

"I have lived to thank God that all my prayers have not been answered."

> — Jean Ingelow (1820-1897)
> *[English poet and novelist]*

"I distrust those people who know so well what God wants them to do, because I notice it always coincides with their own desires."

> — Susan Brownell Anthony (1820-1906)
> *[American civil rights leader who, along with Elizabeth Cady Stanton, led the effort to secure Women's suffrage in the United States]*

"God is the only being who, in order to reign, doesn't even need to exist."

> — Charles Baudelaire (1821-1867)
> *[French poet, critic and translator]*

"There are in every man, at all times, two simultaneous tendencies, one toward God, the other toward Satan."

— CHARLES BAUDELAIRE (1821-1867)

"God is universal; confined to no spot, defined by no dogma, appropriated by no sect."

— MARY BAKER EDDY (1821-1910)

[American spiritual teacher and lecturer, founder of Christian Science movement]

"And man has actually invented God. And what's strange, what would be marvellous, is not that God should really exist; the marvel is that such an idea, the idea of the necessity of God, could enter the head of such a savage, vicious beast as man."

— FYODOR DOSTOYEVSKY (1821-1881)

[Russian writer, essayist and philosopher, known for his novels Crime and Punishment and The Brothers Karamazov]

"If there is a God, atheism must seem to Him as less of an insult than religion."

— GONCOURT (1822-1896 AND 1830-1870)

[The brothers Edmond Louis Antoine Huot de Goncourt (1822-1896) and Jules Alfred Huot de Goncourt (1830-1870) were French writers who, in a lifelong collaboration, produced a number of histories, novels and works of art criticism.]

"God's Wisdom and God's Goodness!--Ah, but fools

Misdefine thee, till God knows them no more.

Wisdom and goodness they are God!--what schools

Have yet so much as heard this simpler lore.

This no Saint preaches, and this no Church rules:

'Tis in the desert, now and heretofore."

— MATTHEW ARNOLD (1822-1888)

[English poet, essayist and cultural critic]

"The more I study nature, the more I stand amazed at the work of the Creator. Science brings men nearer to God."

— LOUIS PASTEUR (1822-1895)

[French microbiologist, chemist, pioneer of the "Germ theory of disease", and inventor of the process of Pasteurization]

"Little science takes you away from God but more of it takes you to Him."

— LOUIS PASTEUR (1822-1895)

"Conscience is the authentic voice of God to you."

— RUTHERFORD BIRCHARD HAYES (1822-1893)

[American politician, lawyer, military leader and 19th President of the United States]

"The dear God has made the whole numbers, all the rest is man's work."

— LEOPOLD KRONECKER (1823-1891)

[German mathematician]

"Do not be afraid to be free thinkers. If you think strongly enough, you will be forced by science to the belief in God."

— LORD KELVIN (1824-1907)
[British mathematical physicist and engineer, founder of Thermodynamics]

"Faith is indeed the energy of our whole universe directed to the highest form of being. ..By faith we are convinced that fellowship is possible with our fellow man and with God."

— BROOKE FOSS WESTCOTT (1825–1901)
[English churchman and theologian]

"Love is God, and to die means that I, a particle of love, shall return to the general and eternal source."

— LEO TOLSTOY (1828-1910)
[Russian writer, philosopher, and social activist, author of one of the greatest novel "War and Peace"]

"The Kingdom of God is within you... and all beings."

— LEO TOLSTOY (1828-1910)

"God is that infinite All of which man knows himself to be a finite part. God alone exists truly. Man manifests Him in time, space and matter. The more God's manifestation in man (life) unites with the manifestations (lives) of other beings, the more man exists. This union with the lives of other beings is accomplished through love. God is not love, but the more there is of love, the more man manifests God, and the more he truly exists…We acknowledge God only when we are conscious of His manifestation in us."

— LEO TOLSTOY (1828-1910)

"God brings men into deep waters not to drown them, but to cleanse them."

— JOHN H. AUGHEY (1828-1911)
[American author]

"Give according to your means, or God will make your means according to your giving."

— REVEREND JOHN HALL (1829-1898)
[American pastor, the landmark New York Church on the Fifth Avenue at 55th St. was built during his tenure]

"The sun proceeds unmoved
To measure off another day
For an approving God."

— EMILY DICKINSON (1830-1886)
[One of the greatest American poets of the 19th century]

"I believe, with the Westminster Divines and their predecessors ad Infinitum that "Man's chief end is to glorify God and to enjoy him for ever." That for this end to every man has been given a progressively increasing power of communication with other creatures."

– JAMES MAXWELL (1831-1879)
[Scottish theoretical physicist and mathematician, known for electromagnetic theory, most respected scientist after Newton and Einstein]

"We Americans have no commission from God to police the world."

– BENJAMIN HARRISON (1833-1901)
[23rd President of the United States]

COFFEE BREAK
Nobel Prize: Alfred Nobel is remembered more as the founder of the Nobel Prizes than as an inventor. The Nobel Prizes are the most prestigious intellectual awards in the world. The prize winners are considered geniuses in their fields of expertise. The thoughts of some Nobel Prize winners are presented in Chapter 10 of this book.

"Who made the World? Religion answers: "He!"
But who made Him? Was it eternity,
Or Space, or Chaos that produced the seed
Of that immortal essence? could they breed
With darkest night, themselves inanimate,
The ruling power of universal Fate?
Or is Creation's spirit but a part
Of the crude matter? could that rubbish start,
Unconscious of itself, the wondrous Whole,
And set a seal as of immortal soul
On endless worlds, so overwhelming grand
That grasping thought, unable to expand
Beyond the compass of its sphere assigned
Backs all distracted on the searching mind.
Such is the Atheist's cold and barren creed
Which Love and Hope reject: do we not read
In Nature's face the lines of Nature's thought,
And Cause must be for what Conception wrought
Though vague and shapeless to the mind. Some call
It God, some Power, some Universal Soul;
Some clothe it in a human form, and raise

To abject deities their abject praise.
But deeper minds reject that grovelling lie
And learn from thought and study to defy
The stupid mummeries of a darker age,
Of baleful priests the woeful heritage,
Which pesters with contagious touch the mind
And leaves the dregs of Ignorance behind.
'Tis true eternal darkness hovers round
The Source of things, but in its works are found
Sufficient hints to teach a purer creed
Than nursery tales for which the Clergy plead."

— ALFRED NOBEL (1833-1896)
[Swedish chemist, engineer, inventor of dynamite, instituted Nobel Prize]

COFFEE BREAK

God in the West and the East: In the 19th century, creator God disappeared from the West, while a mystical God flourished in India. As science helped man master the universe, God lost his footing and was scrutinized under the microscope of human rationality. Thus, he disappeared in the face of widespread blasphemy in the West. A few humans thought that reason had killed God, while others thought God was unnecessary. On the other hand, a mystical God, who resides in the immortal hearts of humans, is popularized by Rabindranath Tagore, Ramakrishna, Sri Aurobindo, Swami Vivekananda, and their contemporaries.

"I cannot see why we should expect an infinite God to do better in another world than he does in this."

— COLONEL ROBERT G. INGERSOLL (1833-1899)
[American social activist, orator, and agnostic]

"An honest God is the noblest work of man."

— COLONEL ROBERT G. INGERSOLL (1833-1899)

"Each nation has created a god, and the god has always resembled his creators. He hated and loved what they hated and loved, and he was invariably found on the side of those in power. Each god was intensely patriotic, and detested all nations but his own. All these gods demanded praise, flattery, and worship. Most of them were pleased with sacrifice, and the smell of innocent blood has ever been considered a divine perfume.

All these gods have insisted upon having a vast number of priests, and the priests have always insisted upon being supported by the people, and the principal business of these priests has been to boast about their god, and to insist that he could easily vanquish all the other gods put together."

— COLONEL ROBERT G. INGERSOLL (1833-1899)

"Few nations have been so poor as to have but one god."

— COLONEL ROBERT G. INGERSOLL (1833-1899)

"God often visits us, but most of the time we are not at home."

— JOSEPH ROUX (1834-1886)
[American Priest]

"God: The most popular scapegoat for our sins."

— MARK TWAIN [SAMUEL LANGHORNE CLEMENS] (1835-1910)
[American novelist, humorist, and lecturer, better known by his pen name Mark Twain]

"If there is a God, he is a malign thug."

— MARK TWAIN (1835-1910)

"All gods are better than their conduct."

— MARK TWAIN (1835-1910)

"True irreverence is disrespect for another man's god."

— MARK TWAIN (1835-1910)

"If God wants us to do a thing, he should make his wishes sufficiently clear. Sensible people will wait till he has done this before paying much attention to him."

— SAMUEL BUTLER (1835-1902)
[British satirist]

"To believe in the God over us and around us and not in the God within us - that would be a powerless and fruitless faith."

— PHILLIPS BROOKS (1835-1893)
[American clergyman and author]

"Many are the names of God, and infinite the forms that lead us to know him. In whatsoever name or form you desire to call him, in that very form and name you will see him."

— SRI RAMAKRISHNA PARAMAHAMSA (1836-1886)
[Born Gadadhar Chattopadhyay, a famous Indian mystic, and a teacher of the Vedanta philosophy, the famed philanthropic organization Ramakrishna Mission was established after his name by his chief disciple Swami Vivekananda]

COFFEE BREAK

Insanity of Religions: Ramakrishna, a Bengali sage, invoked God as Mother and preached that all religions are true. Mahatma Gandhi once said of Ramakrishna, "Ramakrishna's life enables us to see God face to face." Lex Hixon, in his book "Great Swan: Meetings with Ramakrishna", describes an encounter with Ramakrishna:

"The Paramahamsa, still in ecstasy, is speaking aloud with the Mother of the Universe. His words are living poetry. Her presence is palpable:

RAMAKRISHNA: Ma, Ma, Ma--Mother, Mother, Mother! Everyone foolishly assumes that his clock alone tells correct time. Christians claim to possess exclusive truth, and even modern liberal thinkers reiterate the same claim to exclusivity. Countless varieties of Hindus insist that their sect, no matter how small and insignificant, expresses the ultimate position. Devout Muslims maintain that Koranic revelation supersedes all others. The entire world is being driven insane by this single phrase: "My religion alone is true." O Mother, you have shown me that no clock is entirely accurate. Only the transcendent sun of knowledge remains on time. Who can make a system from Divine Mystery? But if any sincere practitioner, within whatever culture or religion, prays and meditates with great devotion and commitment to Truth alone, Your Grace will flood his mind and heart, O Mother. His particular sacred tradition will be opened and illuminated. He will reach the one goal of spiritual evolution. Mother, Mother, Mother! How I long to pray with sincere Christians in their churches and to bow and prostrate with devoted Muslims in their mosques! All religions are glorious! Yet if I display too much freedom, every religious community will become angry with me."

"The grace of God is a wind which is always blowing."
— Sri Ramakrishna Paramahamsa (1836-1886)

"I look upon this world as a wrecked vessel. God has given me a lifeboat and said to me, 'Moody, save all you can'."
— D. L. Moody (1837-1899)
[American evangelist Christian and publisher, founder of Moody Church]

"Man is, and always has been, a maker of gods. It has been the most serious and significant occupation of his sojourn in the world."
— John Burroughs (1837-1921)
[American naturalist and essayist]

"I would rather walk with God in the dark than go alone in the light."
— Mary Gardiner Brainard (1837–1905)
[American writer of religious poetry]

"Look! Nature is overflowing with the grandeur of God!"
— John Muir (1838-1914)
[American environmentalist, naturalist, traveler, writer, and scientist]

"We do not want churches because they will teach us to quarrel about God."

— CHIEF JOSEPH (1840-1904)

[Hinmaton-Yalaktit (Hinmah-too-yah-lat-kekt), Native American Indian, Leader of the Nez Perce]

"Smitten as we are with the vision of social righteousness, a God indifferent to everything but adulation, and full of partiality for his individual favorites, lacks an essential element of largeness."

— WILLIAM JAMES (1842-1910)

[Pioneering American psychologist and philosopher, famous for his book "The Varieties of Religious Experience"]

"I myself believe that the evidence for God lies primarily in inner personal experiences."

— WILLIAM JAMES (1842-1910)

"God made the world in six days and was arrested on the seventh."

— AMBROSE BIERCE (1842-1914)

[American satirist, famous for writing "The Devils Dictionary"]

"God, so to speak, is myriad-minded. We cannot look, therefore, to put ourselves in accord with His plans any more than one man can run a line for a railroad which it requires a small army to survey."

— SAMUEL AUGUSTUS WILLOUGHY DUFFIELD (1843-1887)

[American clergyman and hymn writer]

"I cannot believe in a God who wants to be praised all the time."

— FRIEDRICH NIETZSCHE (1844-1900)

[German philosopher and classical philologist, famous for his controversial statement "God is Dead"]

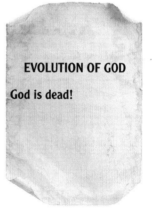

EVOLUTION OF GOD

God is dead!

"Woman was God's second mistake."

— FRIEDRICH NIETZSCHE (1844-1900)

"God is dead! God remains dead! And we have killed him!"

— FRIEDRICH NIETZSCHE (1844-1900)

Like!

"Love is the mystery of divine revelations! Love is the effulgent manifestation! Love is the spiritual fulfillment! Love is the light of the Kingdom! Love is the breath of the Holy Spirit inspired into the human spirit! Love is the cause of the manifestation of the Truth (God) in the phenomenal world! Love is the necessary tie proceeding from the realities of things through divine creation!"

— ABDUL-BAHA (1844-1921)

[Born Abbas Effendi in Iran, eldest son and successor of Bahaullah, the founder of Bahai faith]

"The essence of the true faith of Islam is resignation to the will of God and its corner stone is prayer. It reaches universal fraternity, universal love, and universal benevolence, and requires purity of mind, purity of action, purity of speech and perfect physical cleanliness. It, beyond doubt, is the simplest and most elevating form of religion known to man."

— MOHAMMAD ALEXANDER RUSSELL WEBB (1846-1916)
[First white American Muslim convert, represented Islam at the World Parliament of Religions in Chicago, USA in 1893]

"I have never seen the slightest scientific proof of the religious theories of heaven and hell, of future life for individuals, or of a personal God."

—THOMAS ALVA EDISON (1847-1931)
[American inventor and businessman who developed many devices which greatly influenced life worldwide into the 21st century]

"I am much less interested in what is called God's word than in God's deeds. All bibles are man-made."

—THOMAS ALVA EDISON (1847-1931)

"God is a sort of burglar. As a young man you knock him down; as an old man you try to conciliate him, because he may knock you down."

— HERBERT DRAPER BEERBOHM (1852-1917)
[English actor-manager and wit, who was knighted in 1909]

"The best way to know God is to love many things."

—VINCENT VAN GOGH (1853-1890)
[Dutch painter, regarded as one of the greatest painters in European art history]

"God made everything out of nothing, but the nothingness shows through."

— OSCAR WILDE (1854-1900)
[Irish playwright, poet and author, known for his epigrams]

COFFEE BREAK
God and Human Psyche: Sigmund Freud thought religion to be an illusion and that the need for a god is a manifestation of a child-like longing for a father.

"The psychoanalysis of individual human beings, however, teaches us with quite special insistence that the god of each of them is formed in the likeness of his father, that his personal relation to God depends on his relation to his father in the flesh and oscillates and changes along with that relation, and that at bottom God is nothing other than an exalted father."

— SIGMUND FREUD (1856-1939)
[Austrian neurologist and psychologist and the founder of the psychoanalytic school of psychology]

"The gods retain the threefold task: they must exorcize the terrors of nature, they must reconcile men to the cruelty of Fate, particularly as it is shown in death, and they must compensate them for the sufferings and privations which a civilized life in common has imposed on them."

— Sigmund Freud (1856-1939)

"God is for men and religion is for women."

— Joseph Conrad (1857-1924)
[Polish-born English writer, regarded as one of the greatest English novelists]

"God shows his contempt for wealth by the kind of person he selects to receive it."

— Austin O'Malley (1858-1932)
[American physician and humorist, author of "Keystone of Thought"]

"God on his throne is
Eldest of Poets,
Unto His measures
Moveth the Whole."

— Sir William Watson (1858–1935)
[English poet, popular in his time for the political content of his verse]

"The kiss of the sun for pardon,
The song of the birds for mirth,
One is nearer God's Heart in a garden
Than anywhere else on earth."

— Dorothy Frances Gurney (1858-1932)
[English poet and hymnwriter]

COFFEE BREAK

God, Darwin, and the Church: On November 24, 1859, Charles Darwin published his revolutionary work *On the Origin of Species*, considered to be the foundation of evolutionary biology. It received a vehement response from the Church, as it challenged the grand design theory of a Master Creator. Only 1,250 copies were printed in the first edition, which sold very rapidly. In fewer than forty-five days, on January 7, 1860, Darwin published the second edition of his book and printed 3,000 copies. Interestingly enough, he added the phrase "by the Creator" in the last sentence of his book to appease the Church. The last sentence thus read: "There is grandeur in this view of life, with its several powers, having been originally breathed *[by the Creator]* into a few forms or into one; and that, whilst this planet has gone cycling on according to the fixed law of gravity, from so simple a beginning endless forms most beautiful and most wonderful have been, and are being, evolved."

"Everyone has the same God; only people differ."

— Anton Pavlovich Chekhov (1860-1904)
[Major Russian short story writer and playwright]

"I have never understood why it should be considered derogatory to the Creator to suppose that he has a sense of humour."

— WILLIAM RALPH INGE (1860-1954)
[English author, Professor of divinity at Cambridge]

"Apart from God every activity is merely a passing whiff of insignificance."

— ALFRED NORTH WHITEHEAD (1861-1947)
[English mathematician who later became a philosopher. He wrote on algebra, logic, foundations of mathematics, philosophy of science, physics, metaphysics, and education]

"Where shall I meet him, the Man of my Heart?

He is lost to me and I seek him wandering from land to land.

I am listless for that moonrise of beauty,

which is to light my life,

which I long to see in the fulness of vision

in gladness of heart."

— GAGAN HARKARA (19TH CENTURY)
[Mystic poet of Bengal]

"Before the endgame, the gods have placed the middlegame."

— SIEGBERT TARRASCH (1862-1934)
[One of the strongest chess players of late 19th century]

COFFEE BREAK

"Sir, have you seen God?" asked a fourteen-year-old boy named Narendranath, who would later be known as Swami Vivekananda (1863–1902) and receive worldwide acclaim as a spiritual leader. On the receiving side of this question was Maharshi (Great Saint) Debendranath Tagore (1817–1905), father of the world-famous poet Rabindranath Tagore (1861–1941). The elder Tagore was visibly embarrassed and responded: "My son, your eyes resemble that of a yogi. You should practice meditation and you will have your answer."

A few years later, when Narendranath was nineteen, he asked the same question to a priest, Ramakrishna Paramahansa (1836–1886): "Sir, have you seen God?" Ramakrishna's answer was direct: "Yes, I have seen God. I have seen Him more tangibly than I see you. I have talked with him more intimately than I am talking to you. But my child, who wants to see God! People shed jugs of tears for money, wife and children. But if they wept for God for only one day they would surely see Him."

"All that is real in me is God; all that is real in God is I. The gulf between God and me is thus bridged. Thus by knowing God, we find that the kingdom of heaven is within us."

— SWAMI VIVEKANANDA (1863-1902)

[Born Narendranath Dutta, a famous Indian orator and writer of the Bengal Renaissance period, founder of Ramakrishna Mission, credited with introducing Yoga and Vedanta philosophy to the West]

"As long as we believe ourselves to be even the least different from God, fear remains with us; but when we know ourselves to be the One, fear goes; of what can we be afraid?"

— SWAMI VIVEKANANDA (1863-1902)

"Every religion is only an evolution out of the material man, a God – and the same God is the inspirer of all of them. Why, then, are there so many contradictions? They are only apparent, says the Hindu. The contradictions come from the same truth adapting itself to the different circumstances of different natures."

— SWAMI VIVEKANANDA (1863-1902)

"We need God, not in order to understand the why, but in order to feel and sustain the ultimate wherefore, to give a meaning to the universe."

— MIGUEL DE UNAMUNO Y JUGO (1864-1936)

[Spanish essayist, novelist, poet, playwright and philosopher]

"Those who believe that they believe in God, but without passion in their hearts, without anguish in mind, without uncertainty, without doubt, without an element of despair even in their consolations, believe only in the God idea, not God himself."

— MIGUEL DE UNAMUNO (1864-1936)

"I don't know if God exists, but it would be better for His reputation if He didn't."

— PIERRE-JULES RENARD OR JULES RENARD (1864-1910)

[French author]

"We must be greater than God, for we have to undo His injustice."

— JULES RENARD (1864-1910)

"Religion is the first thing and the last thing, and until a man has found god and been found by God, he begins at no beginning, he works to no end."

— H. G. WELLS (1866-1946)

[British writer best known for his science fiction novels such as The War of the Worlds, The Invisible Man, and The Time Machine]

"One of the most universal of these natural misconceptions of God is to consider him as something magic serving the ends of men."

— H. G. WELLS (1866-1946)

COFFEE BREAK

The Creed for the Disabled: A beautiful poem was found in the pocket of a deceased Confederate State Army (CSA) soldier in the 1860's. It was originally named "The Prayer of An Unknown Confederate Soldier." The insight in the poem applies to more than war situations.

"I asked God for strength, that I might achieve.

I was made weak, that I might learn humbly to obey.

I asked for health, that I might do greater things.

I was given infirmity, that I might do better things.

I asked for riches, that I might be happy.

I was given poverty, that I might be wise.

I asked for power that I might have the praise of men.

I was given weakness, that I might feel the need of God.

I asked for all things, that I might enjoy life.

I was give life, that I might enjoy all things.

I got nothing that I asked for—but got everything I had hoped for.

Almost despite myself, my unspoken prayers were answered.

I am, among all people, most richly blessed."

"Why attack God? He may be as miserable as we are."

— ERIK SATIE (1866-1925)
[French composer and pianist]

"God is the great mysterious motivator of what we call nature, and it has often been said by philosophers, that nature is the will of God. And I prefer to say that nature is the only body of God that we shall ever see."

— FRANK LLOYD WRIGHT (1867-1959)
[American architect, interior designer, writer, educator, recognized as the greatest American architect of all time]

"To know the will of God is the greatest knowledge! To do the will of God is the greatest achievement."

— GEORGE W. TRUETT (1867-1944)
[Southern Baptist minister and writer]

"Gods are fragile things; they may be killed by a whiff of science or a dose of common sense."

— CHAPMAN COHEN (1868-1954)
[Leading English atheist and secularist writer and lecturer]

"The world is a spiritual kindergarten, where thousands of bewildered infants are trying to spell GOD with the wrong blocks."

— EDWIN ROBINSON (1869-1935)
[American poet, who won three Pulitzer Prizes for his work]

COFFEE BREAK

Truth is God: Gandhi was the strongest symbol of nonviolence in the twentieth century, in the face of both political and religious strife. He tried to unite the Hindus and Muslims of India. Gandhi believed that all human beings are sons of God in a metaphorical way. He stated: "I came to the conclusion long ago ... that all religions were true and also that all had some error in them, and whilst I hold by my own, I should hold others as dear as Hinduism." He considered truth to be his God.

"God has no religion."

— MAHATMA (M.K.) GANDHI (1869-1948)

[Mohandas Karamchand Gandhi, commonly known as Mahatma Gandhi, advocate and pioneer of nonviolent social protest in the form he called Satyagraha. He led the struggle for India's independence]

"There is no god higher than truth."

— MAHATMA (M.K.) GANDHI (1869-1948)

"What I want to achieve – what I have been striving and pining to achieve these thirty years – is self-realization, to see God face to face, to achieve Moksha. I live and move and have my being in pursuit of this goal."

— MAHATMA (M.K.) GANDHI (1869-1948)

"If you don't find God in the next person you meet, it is a waste of time to look any further."

— MAHATMA (M.K.) GANDHI (1869-1948)

"My religion is based on truth and nonviolence. Truth is my God. Nonviolence is the means of realizing Him."

— MAHATMA (M.K.) GANDHI (1869-1948)

"Our revolution will never succeed until the myth of God is removed from the mind of man."

—VLADIMIR LENIN (1870-1924)
[Russian revolutionary, first Head of State of Soviet Union]

"The highest praise of God consists in the denial of Him by the atheist, who finds creation so perfect that he can dispense with a creator."

— MARCEL PROUST (1871-1922)
[French novelist, critic, and essayist]

"My God is will and triumphs in his paths,

My God is love and sweetly suffers all."

— SRI AUROBINDO (1872-1950)

[Aurobindo Ghose, Indian nationalist, scholar, poet, mystic, evolutionary philosopher, yogi and guru]

"To listen to some devout people, one would imagine that God never laughs."

— SRI AUROBINDO (1872-1950)

"The more I know of astronomy, the more I believe in God."

— HEBER DOUST CURTIS (1872–1942)

[American astronomer]

"God is the tangential point between zero and infinity."

— ALFRED JARRY (1873-1907)

[French writer]

"There is no better way to manifest love for God than to show an unselfish love for your fellow-men."

— DAVID OMAN MCKAY (1873-1970)

[9th President of The Church of Jesus Christ of Latter-day Saints, Latter-Day Prophet of the Church of Jesus Christ of Latter-Day Saints, also known as the "Mormon Church"]

"Forgive, O Lord, my little jokes on Thee, and

I'll forgive Thy great big joke on me."

— ROBERT FROST (1874-1963)

[American poet; winner of four Pulitzer Prizes]

"God is a verb."

— ROBERT FROST (1874-1963)

"Once abolish the God, and the government becomes the God."

— ROBERT FROST (1874-1963)

"When I was young I had an elderly friend who used often to ask me to stay with him in the country. He was a religious man and he read prayers to the assembled household every morning. But he had crossed out in pencil all the passages that praised God. He said that there was nothing so vulgar as to praise people to their faces and, himself a gentleman, he could not believe that God was so ungentlemanly as to like it."

— SOMERSET MAUGHAM (1874-1965)

[English playwright, novelist and short story writer]

"I cannot believe in a God that has neither honor nor commonsense."

— SOMERSET MAUGHAM (1874-1965)

"Man is a dog's idea of what a God should be."

— HOLBROOK JACKSON (1874-1948)
[British journalist, writer and publisher]

"You can take away a man's gods, but only to give him others in return."

— CARL JUNG (1875-1961)
[Swiss psychiatrist and founder of analytical psychology]

"All ages before ours believed in gods in some form or other. Only an unparalleled impoverishment in symbolism could enable us to rediscover the gods as psychic factors, which is to say, as archetypes of the unconscious. No doubt this discovery is hardly credible as yet."

— CARL JUNG (1875-1961)

"If a door slams shut it means that God is pointing to an open door further on down."

— ANNA DELANEY PEALE (1875-1939)
[American woman, mother of Norman Vincent Peale]

"Next to God we are indebted to women, first for life itself, and then for making it worth living."

— MARY BETHUNE (1875-1955)
[American educator and civil rights leader, best known for starting a school for black students in Florida that eventually became Bethune-Cookman University, advisor to President Franklin D. Roosevelt]

"From the intrinsic evidence of his creation, the Great Architect of the Universe begins to appear as a pure mathematician."

— SIR JAMES JEANS (1877-1946)
[English physicist, astronomer and mathematician]

"A baby is God's opinion that life should go on."

— CARL SANDBURG (1878-1967)
[American poet, historian, novelist, balladeer and folklorist]

"God gives us our relatives—thank God we can choose our friends."

— ETHEL WATTS MUMFORD (1876-1940)
[American author, a New Yorker]

"God is not a dead equation!"

— SIR DR. MUHAMMAD IQBAL (1877-1938)
[Pakistani poet, philosopher, politician, said to have conceived of the idea of Pakistan, as a separate Muslim land for Indian Muslims, commonly known as Allama Iqbal, officially recognized as Pakistan's national poet]

"The immediacy of mystic experience simply means that we know God just as we know other objects. God is not a mathematical entity or a system of concepts mutually related to one another and having no reference to experience."

— Sir Dr. Muhammad Iqbal (1877-1938)

"God made so many different kinds of people. Why would he allow only one way to serve him?"

— Martin Buber (1878-1965)
[Jewish philosopher, theologian, story-teller, and teacher]

"God is love."

-Edward Morgan Forster (1879-1970)
[English novelist, short story writer, and essayist]

"Men have always need of god! A god to defend them against other men."

— Francis Picabia (1879-1953)
[French painter and poet]

"The self-appointed spokesmen for God incline to shout; He, Himself, speaks only in whispers."

— Martin Henry Fischer (1879-1962)
[German-born American physician and author]

"The universe is centred on neither the earth nor the sun. It is centred on God."

— Alfred Noyes (1880-1958)
[English poet]

"God is the immemorial refuge of the incompetent, the helpless, the miserable. They find not only sanctuary in His arms, but also a kind of superiority, soothing to their macerated egos: He will set them above their betters."

— H. L. Mencken (1880-1956)
[American journalist, satirist, social critic, cynic, and freethinker, known as the "Sage of Baltimore" and the "American Nietzsche"]

"God is a Republican, and Santa Claus is a Democrat."

— H. L. Mencken (1880-1956)

"I thank God for my handicaps, for, through them, I have found myself, my work, and my God."

— Helen Keller (1880-1968)
[American writer and social activist; an illness at the age of 19 months left her deaf and blind]

"God gives talent; work transforms talent into genius."

— Anna Pavlova (1881-1931)
[Russian ballerina]

"The discovery of natural law is a meeting with God."

— Friedrich Dessauer (1881-1968)
[German physicist, philosopher, and journalist]

"God is really only another artist. He invented the giraffe, the elephant, and the cat. He has no real style. He just keeps on trying other things."

— Pablo Picasso (1881-1973)
[Spanish artist who lived and worked in Paris, famous for his painting, "Guernica"]

"God is inexhaustibly attainable in the totality of our action."

— Pierre Teilhard de Chardin (1881-1955)
[French philosopher and Jesuit priest]

"I gave up my music because I had received from it all I had to receive. To serve God one must sacrifice the dearest thing, and I sacrificed my music, the dearest thing to me."

— Hazrat Inayat Khan (1882-1927)
[Indian saint and founder of the Sufi Order International]

"The Church knew what the psalmist knew: Music praises God. Music is well or better able to praise Him than the building of the church and all its decoration; it is the Church's greatest ornament."

— Igor Stravinsky (1882-1971)
[Russian-born composer, is thought to be one of the most influential composers of the 20th century]

"God makes stars. I just produce them."

— Samuel Goldwyn (1879-1974)
[Polish-American producer of motion pictures]

"God has made many doors opening into truth which He opens to all who knock upon them with hands of faith."

— Khalil Gibran (1883-1931)
[Lebanese-American poet, artist, and writer, the third best-selling poet of all time, behind Shakespeare and Lao-Tzu]

"God is the expression of the intelligent universe."

— Khalil Gibran (1883-1931)

"Prayer is the song of the heart. It reaches the ear of God even if it is mingled with the cry and the tumult of a thousand men."

— Khalil Gibran (1883-1931)

"The metaphor is perhaps one of man's most fruitful potentialities. Its efficacy verges on magic, and it seems a tool for creation which God forgot inside one of His creatures when He made him."

— José Ortega Y Gasset (1883-1955)
[Spanish philosopher]

"Well, God has arrived. I met him on the 5:15 train. He has a plan to stay in Cambridge permanently."

— John Maynard Keynes, (1883-1946)
[British economist, founder of Keynesian economics, after meeting with Wittgenstein at his arrival in Cambridge, in a letter (18 January 1929) to his wife Lydia Lopokova]

"I have too much respect for the idea of God to make it responsible for such an absurd world."

— Georges Duhamel (1884-1966)
[French author]

COFFEE BREAK
God in the US Court: When the nine Justices of the US Supreme court enter the burgundy draped, gold-trimmed courtroom to hear arguments, all persons in attendance stand, and the Marshall of the Court chants an announcement that ends with the following sentence: "God save the United States and this Honorable Court."

"God is only a great imaginative experience."

— D. H. Lawrence (1885-1930)
[One of the most important English writers of the 20th century, famous for his book "Lady Chatterly's Lover"]

"It is foolish and wrong to mourn the men who died. Rather we should thank God that such men lived."

— General George Patton, Jr. (1885-1945)
[American General during World War II]

"God changes appearances every second. Blessed is the man who can recognize him in all his disguises. One moment he is a glass of fresh water, the next, your son bouncing on your knees or an enchanting woman, or perhaps merely a morning walk."

— Nikos Kazantzakis (1883-1957)
[Greek novelist, poet, playwright and philosopher]

"God has no office hours.

There is never a time of day when God is unavailable.

Day or night, summer or winter,

God is always present—always ready to heal, to comfort, to inspire."

— Emmet Fox (1886–1951)
[Irish-American electrical engineer turned spiritual leader]

"Poems are made by fools like me, But only God can make a tree."

— Alfred Joyce Kilmer (1886-1918)
[American journalist and poet]

"I made god upon god
step from the cold rock,
I made the gods less than men
for I was a man and they my work...."

— Hilda Doolittle (1886-1961)
[American poet and novelist]

"God is in the details."

— Ludwig Mies van der Rohe (1886-1969)
[Born Maria Ludwig Michael Mies, German-American architect]

"To be willing to suffer in order to create is one thing; to realize that one's creation necessitates one's suffering, that suffering is one of the greatest of God's gifts, is almost to reach a mystical solution to the problem of evil."

— John Sullivan (1886-1937)
[Popular science writer and literary journalist]

"God does not exist. He is being itself beyond essence and existence. Therefore, to argue that God exists is to deny him."

— Paul Johannes Tillich (1886-1965)
[German-American theologian and Christian existentialist philosopher]

"Laughter is the closest thing to the grace of god."

— Karl Barth (1886-1968)
[Swiss theologian, one of the most influential Christian thinkers of the 20th century]

"When attempts were later made to speak systematically about God and to describe His nature, men became more talkative. They spoke of God's aseity , His being grounded in Himself; they spoke of God's infinity in space and time, and therefore of God's eternity. And men spoke on the other hand of God's holiness and righteousness, mercifulness and patience. We must be clear that whatever we say of God in such human concepts can never be more than an indication of Him; no such concept can really conceive the nature of God. God is inconceivable."

— Karl Barth (1886-1968)

"No religion is capable of altering the fact that the behaviour of men is a behaviour apart from God. All that religion can do is to expose the complete godlessness of human behaviour ... Woe be to us, if from the summits of religion there pours forth nothing but religion! Religion casts us into the deepest of all prisons: it cannot liberate us."

— Karl Barth (1886-1968)

"An equation for me has no meaning unless it expresses a thought of God."

— Srinivasa Ramanujan (1887-1920)
[Indian groundbreaking mathematician and self taught genius]

"To define God is to limit Him. Still it seems inevitable that man should do that in order to get some edge to which his min may cling."

— Heywood Broun (1888-1939)
[American journalist and sportswriter]

"Nobody talks so constantly about God as those who insist that there is no God."

— Heywood Broun (1888-1939)

"To believe in God means to see that the facts of the world are not the end of the matter. To believe in God means to see that life has a meaning."

— Ludwig Wittgenstein (1889-1951)
[Austrian-born philosopher who spent much of his life in England teaching at Cambridge University]

"Certainly it is correct to say: Conscience is the voice of God."

— Ludwig Wittgenstein (1889-1951)

"By simple common sense I don't believe in God, in none."

— Charlie Chaplin (1889-1977)
[English comedian, actor and director]

"God's patience is infinite. Men, like small kettles, boil quickly with wrath at the least wrong. Not so God. If God were as wrathful, the world would have been a heap of ruins long ago."

— Sadhu Sundar Singh (1889-1929)
[Indian Christian missionary]

"I believe today that my conduct is in accordance with the will of the Almighty Creator."

— Adolf Hitler (1889-1945)
[Austrian-born Nazi Party leader and Chancellor of Germany from 1933 to 1945, mastermind behind the senseless killing of more than ten million people including six million Jews]

"But if out of smugness, or even cowardice, this battle is not fought to its end, then take a look at the peoples five hundred years from now. I think you will find but few images of God, unless you want to profane the Almighty."

— Adolf Hitler (1889-1945)

"I had a million questions to ask God: but when I met Him, they all fled my mind; and it didn't seem to matter."

— Christopher Morley (1890-1957)
[American journalist, novelist, poet, and playwright]

"There is no God. But it does not matter. Man is enough."

— EDNA ST. VINCENT MILLAY (1892-1950)
[American lyrical poet and playwright and the first woman to receive the Pulitzer Prize for Poetry]

"There are truths that are beyond us, transcendental truths about beauty, truth, honour, etc. There are truths that man knows exist, but they cannot be seen, they are immaterial but no less real to us. It is only through the language of myth that we can speak of these truths. We have come from God and only through myth, through story-telling, can we aspire to the life we were made for with God."

— JOHN R. R. TOLKIEN (1892-1973)
[English writer, poet, author of The Lord of the Rings and The Hobbit]

"We have come from God, and inevitably the myths woven by us, though they contain error, will also reflect a splintered fragment of the true light, the eternal truth that is with God. Indeed only by myth-making, only by becoming 'sub-creator' and inventing stories, can Man aspire to the state of perfection that he knew before the Fall. Our myths may be misguided, but they steer however shakily towards the true harbour, while materialistic 'progress' leads only to a yawning abyss and the Iron Crown of the power of evil."

— JOHN R. R. TOLKIEN (1892-1973)

"God, give us grace to accept with serenity the things that cannot be changed, courage to change the things which should be changed, and the wisdom to distinguish the one from the other."

— REINHOLD NIEBUHR (1892-1971)
[American Protestant theologian]

COFFEE BREAK
Steve Jobs and Autobiography of a Yogi: In his Ipad, Steve Jobs downloaded only one book, entitled "Autobiography of a Yogi." He said this was the most important book of his life and he re-read the book once a year for decades. The book was published in 1946 and was written by a Bengali guru, living in Los Angeles and preaching self-realization through *Kriya Yoga*. The book became an instant hit, and has since been translated into twenty-eight languages. In 1999, the book was designated by a panel of experts as the "100 Most Important Spiritual Books of the 20th Century." Yogananda's *Kriya Yoga* helps one to accelerate one's spiritual development for the ultimate purpose of communion with God.

"You do not have to struggle to reach God, but you do have to struggle to tear away the self-created veil that hides him from you."

— PARAMAHANSA YOGANANDA (1893-1952)
[Indian yogi and guru, born Mukunda Lal Ghosh]

"You are walking on the earth as in a dream. Our world is a dream within a dream; you must realize that to find God is the only goal, the only purpose, for which you are here. For Him alone you exist. Him you must find."

— PARAMAHANSA YOGANANDA (1893-1952)

"What makes humility so desirable is the marvelous thing it does to us; it creates in us a capacity for the closest possible intimacy with God."

— MONICA BALDWIN (1893–1975)
[British nun turned author]

"No citizen enjoys genuine freedom of religious conviction until the state is indifferent to every form of religious outlook from Atheism to Zoroastrianism."

— HAROLD LASKI (1893–1950)
[British political thinker, economist, author and lecturer]

"If you want to know what God thinks of money, just look at the people he gave it to."

— DOROTHY PARKER (1893–1967)
[American poet and satirist]

"We say the name of God, but that is only out of habit."

— NIKITA KRUSHCHEV (1894-1971)
[Soviet leader and prime minister]

"God made man, and then said I can do better than that and made woman."

— ADELA ROGERS ST. JOHNS (1894-1988)
[American journalist, novelist, and screenwriter]

"Kill one man and you are a murderer. Kill millions and you are a conqueror. Kill everyone and you are a God."

— JEAN ROSTAND (1894-1977)
[French biologist and philosopher]

"God alone is real, and all else is illusion."

— MEHER BABA (1894-1969)
[Indian mystic and spiritual leader who claimed himself to be an incarnation of God]

"From out of the depth of unbroken Infinity arose the Question, "Who am I?" And to that Question there is the answer, "I am God!""

— MEHER BABA (1894-1969)

"A man who believes in God can never find God. If you are open to reality, there can be no belief in reality. If you are open to the unknown, there can be no belief in it. After all, belief is a form of self-protection, and only a petty mind can believe in God. Look at the belief of the aviators during the war who said God was their companion as they were dropping bombs! So you believe in God when you kill, when you are exploiting people. You worship God and go on ruthlessly extorting money, supporting the army — yet you say you believe in mercy, compassion, kindliness.

As long as belief exists, there can never be the unknown; you cannot think about the unknown, thought cannot measure it. The mind is the product of the past, it is the result of yesterday, and can such a mind be open to the unknown? It can only project an image, but that projection is not real; so your god is not God – it is an image of your own making, an image of your own gratification."

— JIDDU KRISHNAMURTI (1895-1986)
[Indian-born American author, philosopher, and public speaker]

"What we need in America today is a vigorous return to the God of our fathers and a most vigorous defense against the minion of godlessness and atheism."

— J. EDGAR HOOVER (1895-1972)
[Director of American FBI since its founding in 1935 till his death in 1972]

"God, to me, it seems,

Is a verb

Not a noun,

Proper or improper."

— RICHARD BUCKMINSTER FULLER (1895-1983)
[American architect, author, designer, inventor, and futurist]

"A rabbi today has his work cut out for him, but he should not despair if people do not do as much as they should. Every parent has that with children. God is merciful."

— RABBI LOUIS FINKELSTEIN (1895-1991)
[Talmud scholar and expert in Jewish law]

"God loved the birds and invented trees. Man loved the birds and invented cages."

— JACQUES DEVAL(1895-1972)
[Pseudonym for Jacques Boularan, French playwright and director]

"To place oneself in the position of God is painful: being God is equivalent to being tortured. For being God means that one is in harmony with all that is, including the worst. The existence of the worst evils is unimaginable unless God willed them."

— GEORGES BATAILLE (1897-1962)
[French writer]

"Of all human activities, man's listening to God is the supreme act of his reasoning and will."

— POPE PAUL VI (1897-1978)
[Served as Pope from 1963 to 1978]

"I used to pray the God would do this or that; now I pray that God will make His will known to me."

— MADAME CHIANG KAI-SHEK (1897-2003)
[Born Soong Mei-ling, wife of Chinese nationalist leader Chiang Kai-Shek]

"No matter how much I prove and prod,

I cannot quite believe in God;

But oh, I hope to God that He

Unswervingly believes in me."

— E.Y. (YIP) HARBURG (1896-1981)
[American popular song lyricist]

"As long as you are proud you cannot know God. A proud man is always looking down on things and people; and, of course, as long as you are looking down, you cannot see something that is above you."

— C. S. LEWIS (1898-1963)
[Irish-born British novelist, academic, medievalist, literary critic, essayist]

"A man can no more diminish God's glory by refusing to worship Him than a lunatic can put out the sun by scribbling the word, 'darkness' on the walls of his cell."

— C. S. LEWIS (1898-1963)

"One of the most powerful concepts, one which is a sure cure for lack of confidence, is the thought that God is with you and helping you."

— NORMAN VINCENT PEALE (1898-1993)
[Protestant preacher and author (most notably of The Power of Positive Thinking]

"Let them spread jealousy, prejudice and defamation,

We will offer justice, peace and one God's proclamation.

Let them seek narrowness, pigeon-hole and mud from pond,

We will seek open space, shining light and love's bond."

— KAZI NAZRUL ISLAM (1899-1976)
[Celebrated Bengali poet, song writer, musician, revolutionary, and philosopher, also known as the Rebel poet of Bengal]

"Open your heart, within you lie
all the scriptures,
all the wisdom of all ages.
Within you lie all the religions,
all the prophets
your heart
is the universal temple
of all the gods and goddesses.
Why do you search for God in vain
within the skeletons of dead scriptures
when he smilingly resides in the privacy
of your immortal heart?"

— KAZI NAZRUL ISLAM (1899-1976)

CHAPTER DIGEST (1700 TO 1900 AD)

According to Bahais and Mormons, God posted respectively the *Kitab-I-Aqdas*, the Bahai scripture, and the *Book of Mormon*, the Mormon scripture, on the *Holy Wall* of God's Facebook. But the most significant posting on the *Holy Wall* in this period was by a few American women, who revised what God had written on the *Holy Wall* many centuries ago. They posted the *Woman's Bible* on the *Holy Wall* by excising from the Bible all references that contradicted the position of women's rights. They claimed that it was not divine will, but men's desire for domination that humiliated women through biblical interpretations of God's words. God, with his everlasting tolerance, didn't intervene and let the *Woman's Bible* be posted on his *Holy Wall*.

The postings on the *Wall of Mortals* in the eighteenth and nineteenth centuries range from utter blasphemy to pure devotion. In America, memories of religious persecution in Europe shaped the thinking of the founding fathers, who posted on the *Wall of Mortals* strong opinions on the separation of church and state. Thomas Jefferson produced the *Jefferson Bible* by excising the miracles and inconsistencies from the Bible, and declared, "The God, who gave us life, gave us liberty at the same time." Some of the states' constitutions contradicted the federal constitution in the USA by requiring those who held a state office to believe in God, although the United States Constitution prohibited such requirements.

In Europe, the Age of the Enlightenment (also known as the Age of Reason) influenced intellectuals, who dared to raise all kinds of questions and utter all kinds of comments about God. David Hume, Immanuel Kant, Wilhelm Hegel, Søren Kierkegaard, Karl Marx, and Sigmund Freud dominated the human intellectual world and posted utterances that changed how we think about God today. In Germany, Nietzsche declared, "God is dead," and in America many years later, Mencken held a funeral for God.

In contrast, a mystical God appeared in India, in postings from Ramakrishna, Vivekananda, Gandhi, and others. Poets of this period, from both the East and the West, posted beautiful poetry about God on the *Wall of Mortals*.

The human–God relationship in this period was tumultuous. In the West, the Enlightenment killed God, at least temporarily. The Christian church struggled to keep God alive in the West using reformation but met with mixed success. In India, mysticism found new meaning in serving indigent and oppressed human beings. The sages there saw the face of God in the faces of suffering humans.

Thus, a humanitarian basis for a *Friendship of Civilizations* emerged.

9

God is Back
(1900 to 2012 AD)

"What we came across in these blood thirsty times
With their smoke of burning trash, their dead ashes
As we weren't able to stop looking
We often stopped to look at the names of God
We lifted them with tenderness because they reminded us
Of our ancestors, of the first people, those who said the prayers
Those who discovered the hymn that united them in misfortune
And now seeing the empty fragments which sheltered those ancient people
We feel those smooth substances,
Worn out and used up by good and by evil."

—PABLO NERUDA (1904-1973), GAUTAMA CHRIST

STATUS UPDATE (1900-2012 AD)

❖ God's decline from the nineteenth century continues well into the first half of the twentieth century.

❖ English poet Thomas Hardy writes a poem titled "God's Funeral." A memorial service for the gods is held by American journalist H. L. Mencken in 1923.

❖ *Humanist Manifesto* is published in 1933. It promotes a philosophy and value system without the belief in a God or higher power.

❖ "My God, what have we done," writes Robert Lewis, the commander of the Enola Gay, which drops the first atomic bomb on Hiroshima, Japan, on August 6, 1945, killing more than 150,000 people.

❖ God shows ultimate tolerance as he is ridiculed by atheists. He doesn't stop the growth of atheism and agnosticism amidst humanity's unprecedented scientific achievements.

❖ The Goddess movement gains steam out of second-wave feminism in North America, Western Europe, Australia, and New Zealand in the 1970s.

❖ The Freedom From Religion Foundation (FFRF) is formed in 1976 in Wisconsin to promote the separation of church and state and to educate the public on atheism and agnosticism.

❖ The "God particle" (the Higgs boson) remains a matter of belief among the world's top scientists because its existence cannot yet be proven.

STATUS UPDATE (1900-2012 AD)

❖ US Court declares Atheism as a religion.

❖ Richard Dawkins writes a book entitled *The God Delusion,* and offers alternatives to the Ten Commandments.

❖ Interfaith dialogue gains momentum and God becomes more universal.

❖ The song "God is a Girl (2002)", from the German trance group Groove Coverage, reaches number one in China, with 1.5 million legal downloads.

❖ The single most frequently used noun in the 2008 Republican convention is "God."

❖ In 2011, God is diagnosed with Bipolar Disorder by an American psychiatrist and theologian of Yale University Divinity School.

❖ In 2011, God co-authors a book with an American comedy writer; the title of the book is *"The Last Testament: A Memoir by God."*

NOTES FROM HISTORY
(1900 TO 2012 AD)

This century began with modest horse-drawn carts and ended with space shuttles. More technological advances were made in this century than in all the previous centuries combined. Home appliances, personal computers, mobile phones, transportation technology, information technology, and medical advances radically altered daily lives of humans.

Humanity's search for God or the Supreme Being continued into outer space. The discovery of the theory of relativity and quantum physics changed the worldview of scientists completely. It was realized that the universe is ever-expanding and much more complex than humans could ever imagine.

The world population increased from two billion in 1927 to six billion in 1999 and reached seven billion in 2012. Of the seven billion people, less than 3% are atheists (non-believers in God), and the remaining 97% believe in one form of God or another. More than 50% of the world's population are followers of Abrahamic religions (~33% Christianity, ~22% Islam, <1% Judaism). Other major religious groups are: Hinduism, ~14%; Buddhism, ~7%; traditional Chinese religions, ~6%; other religions ~7%. About 12% of the world's population claim to be "non-religious," which includes atheists.

Computers were invented during this period and have gradually taken control of our lives. We are dependent on computers in all aspects of existence. In this period, human mobility also expanded greatly, as cruise ships and airlines made world travel possible for the general masses.

English poet Thomas Hardy wrote a poem entitled "God's Funeral" between 1908 and 1910. In the poem, he admits:

"I did not forget

That what was mourned for, I, too

Once had prized."

God and religion were ridiculed by atheists, as atheism and agnosticism flourished amidst hitherto unseen scientific achievements. American satirist Ambrose Bierce published *The Devil's Dictionary* in 1911, in which "pray" is defined as: "To ask that the laws of the universe be annulled in behalf of a single petitioner confessedly unworthy." Steve Eley, an American speculative fiction author and podcaster, produced a manifesto about the Invisible Pink Unicorn, which stated: "Invisible Pink Unicorns are beings of great spiritual power. We know this because they are capable of being invisible and pink at the same time. Like all religions, the Faith of the Invisible Pink Unicorns is based upon both logic and faith. We have faith that they are pink; we logically know that they are invisible because we can't see them."

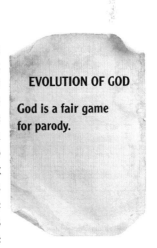

EVOLUTION OF GOD

God is a fair game for parody.

World War I, a major war centered in Europe, raged from 1914 to 1918 and left about twenty million people dead. The four major imperial powers—the German, Russian, Austro-Hungarian, and Ottoman empires—were militarily and politically defeated. The first two empires lost a great amount of territory, while the last two were dismantled entirely. Several smaller states emerged in Europe, and the League of Nations, a predecessor of today's United Nations, was formed to promote peace across the world. Political, social, and cultural ideologies were drastically changed in the aftermath of World War I. The Russian Revolution of 1917 is considered to have been an outcome of the revolutionary social thinking arising out of the privations of the war. Vladimir Lenin (1870–1924), the first head of state of the Soviet Union, blamed religion for the social and political perils of his country and declared: "Even the bare mention of a citizen's religion in official documents should unquestionably be eliminated."

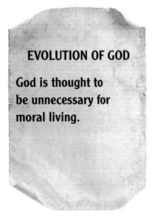

EVOLUTION OF GOD

God is thought to be unnecessary for moral living.

A worldwide influenza pandemic, called the Spanish Flu, killed fifty to one hundred million people between 1918 and 1920. An economic boom followed World War I in Europe, and the period between 1920 and 1929 is known there as the "Golden Twenties." Communism, a godless religion, started gaining popularity because of the apparent success of the Soviet Revolution.

In 1923, the American journalist H. L. Mencken held a memorial service for gods, who, as he put it, had "gone down the chute." He asked: "Where is the graveyard of dead gods? What lingering mourner waters their mounds?... Men labored for generations to build vast temples to them—temples with stones as large as hay-wagons. The business of interpreting their whims occupied thousands of priests, wizards, archdeacons, evangelists, haruspices, bishops, archbishops. To doubt them was to die, usually at the stake. Armies took to the field to defend them against infidels: villages were burned, women and children were butchered, cattle were driven off... They were gods of the highest standing and dignity—gods of civilized peoples—worshiped and believed in by millions. All were theoretically omnipotent, omniscient, and immortal. And all are dead."

In 1925, John Baird invented the mechanical television. Jazz and jazz-influenced dancing became very popular throughout the decade. The American stock market crashed in October of 1929. The Great Depression, an economic crisis, spread across the globe. Unemployment in the U.S.A. rose to almost 25%.

In 1933, American philosopher Roy Sellers and Unitarian minister Raymond Bragg authored *A Humanist Manifesto* (commonly referred to as *Humanist Manifesto I*). Sixty-five people were asked to sign the manifesto, but only 34 agreed. The signatories included ten professors, seven ministers, and one rabbi. The 1,109 words manifesto affirmed fifteen beliefs without any belief in supernatural deities. It proclaimed that the universe is self-existing and is not created. This historic document reflected the hope of liberal thinkers of American society for establishing the rule of reason over revelation.

World War II raged from 1939 to 1945 and involved all the major powers of the world. This global conflict was the deadliest war in human history, leaving about fifty to seventy million people dead. About forty million civilians died in the conflict as a result of starvation, disease, massacres, bombing, and deliberate genocide. Nazi supremacist ideology, propagated by Adolf Hitler, resulted in the systematic genocide of about six million Jews during the Holocaust, along with another five million Roma, Slavs, and homosexuals. In China, about seven million civilians perished under the Japanese occupation. The Bengal famine of 1943 is partially attributed to the war and resulted in about three million civilian deaths from starvation and malnutrition.

On Monday, August 6, 1945, at 8:15 AM, an American B-29 bomber dropped the first atomic bomb on the town of Hiroshima in Japan. It is estimated that the direct hit killed about 80,000 people, which was doubled by the end of the year due to additional deaths from injury and radiation.

World War II ended with the unconditional surrender of the Axis forces, led by Japan and Germany, to the Allied forces, led by the United States, Russia, and the United Kingdom. When World War II ended, the United States and the Soviet Union emerged as rival superpowers.

Marxism, a political, economic, and social philosophy based on the materialistic interpretation of history, started gaining popularity in many countries. Karl Marx hypothesized that communism, a social structure in which classes are abolished and property is commonly controlled, would be the final stage in human social evolution. Russia and its allies embraced socialism, which was actively opposed by the United States and its allies, who promoted capitalism. China embraced communism and started promoting the idea to other countries. This polarization of ideologies led to the Cold War era, 1945–1991. The Cold War was a continued state of political, military, and economic tension between the Western world and the Soviet Union. The Cold War ended when the Soviet Union broke up in 1991, which left the United States as the sole superpower.

The assault on God and religion continued and is epitomized by Bertrand Russell's comment in *"Why I Am Not a Christian"* (first published in 1947): "I think all the great religions of the world—Buddhism, Hinduism, Christianity, Islam and Communism—both untrue and harmful."

The massive exploitation of earth's natural resources in this period resulted in unprecedented human development, but at the same time caused widespread pollution of the environment. After years of struggle, almost all Western nations gave women the right to vote.

The Israeli-Palestinian conflict became a much more polarized battle between two religions, Judaism and Islam, with ever more people claiming that God was on their side. Religious fundamentalism raised its ugly head in three major monotheistic religions—Judaism, Christianity, and Islam—in response to the painful challenges to traditions that came from modernity and technological innovations. Karen Armstrong beautifully traced the history of the rise of fundamentalism in these three major religions in her seminal book ,*The Battle for God*. The latter part of the twentieth century saw an alarming rise of Hindu fundamentalism in India.

During the 1960s and 1970s, the Western world witnessed revolutionary social progress in terms of increased political awareness, opposition to wars, and demand for equal rights for all races and genders. There was increased openness towards atheistic and agnostic beliefs.

EVOLUTION OF GOD

Time **magazine publishes a cover story, "Is God Dead?"**

Time magazine ran the cover story "Is God Dead?" on April 8, 1966. The cover of *Time* was eye-catching—giant blood-red letters against a black background spelled out the question, loud and clear. This was the first occasion in *Time's* forty-three-year history that a cover was printed without a photograph or an illustration. The implication was that the modern world was moving towards a secular worldview.

American astronaut, Neil Armstrong (1930-) became the first human to set foot on the surface of the moon at 10:56 PM Eastern Daylight Time (EDT) on July 20, 1969. As he set his left foot on the lunar surface, he spoke the famous words: "That's one small step for a man, one giant leap for mankind." Armstrong's words were broadcast worldwide and it was estimated that the global audience was about 450 million listeners out of a total world population of about 3.6 billion at that time.

EVOLUTION OF GOD

The Economist **publishes God's obituary.**

In its millennium issue (December 23, 1999), *The Economist* published God's obituary: "After a lengthy career, the Almighty recently passed into history", ending with the rhetorical question, "Or did he?"

Forty-three years after the *Time* story, survey after survey has consistently proved that God is alive and well in America, with more than 98% of those surveyed saying they believe in God. America has shown that religion and modernity can go hand in hand, in contrast to what Europe, the heartland of secularism, thinks. The four biggest religions, Christianity, Islam, Buddhism, and Hinduism, can claim 75% of the world's population among their adherents. Secularism is on the decline and atheists are almost dead, as many of them have become agnostics (non-committal) or spiritualists.

Peter Berger, an Austrian-born American psychologist, told the *New York Times* in 1968 that "[by] the 21st century, religious believers are likely to be found only in small sects, huddled together to resist a worldwide secular culture." However, in the late 1990s, Berger himself recanted and wrote: "It wasn't a crazy theory, but I think it's basically wrong."

The "God particle" (the Higgs boson) remains a matter of belief among the world's top scientists because its existence cannot yet be proven. In 1993, Nobel Laureate physicist Leon Lederman published a book entitled *The God Particle: If the Universe is the Answer, What is the Question?* He also parodied the Bible and wrote a few sections of the The Very New Testament.

On July 20, 1998, *Newsweek* magazine published the cover story "Science Finds God", wherein author Sharon Begley claimed: "The achievements of modern science seem to contradict religion and undermine faith. But for a growing number of scientists, the same discoveries offer support for spirituality and hints of the very nature of God." It is an amazing coincidence that a few days later, on July 23, 1998, the journal *Nature* published a paper entitled "Leading Scientists Still Reject God", in which authors Edward Larson and Larry Witham concluded: "Disbelief in God and immortality among NAS [U.S. National Academy of Sciences] biological scientists was 65.2% and 69.0%, respectively, and among NAS physical scientists it was 79.0% and 76.3%. Most of the rest were agnostics on both issues, with few believers. We found the highest percentage of belief among NAS mathematicians (14.3% in God, 15.0% in immortality). Biological scientists had the lowest rate of belief (5.5% in God, 7.1% in immortality), with physicists and astronomers slightly higher (7.5% in God, 7.5% in immortality)."

EVOLUTION OF GOD

God is rejected by leading scientists.

Knowledge of the world became more widely available with the invention of computers, telecommunications, mass media, and the internet. This fostered the free flow of information from east to west and from north to south, thereby enhancing global awareness of the struggles and successes of others.

Al Qaeda, a Muslim terrorist group, attacked the United States on September 11, 2001 and destroyed the Twin Towers of New York's World Trade Center, killing almost 3,000 civilians. This marked the culmination of an alarming rise in Islamic fundamentalism all around the world. September 11, 2001 was a historic day as it changed all the rules of the game in the world as far as the individual nations and their relationships were concerned. The United States launched its War on Terrorism, which gained worldwide support initially, but later saw an erosion of support due to many factors. Interfaith dialogue gained momentum as humans realized that mutual understanding of faiths is a critical requirement for world peace.

The economic conditions of humans on earth improved significantly for all the people in the world, though abject poverty remained widespread in under-developed regions. Europe and America amassed a great deal of wealth through modernization of agriculture, industrial production, and scientific advancements. The technological revolution in home appliances improved living standards and provided people with significant free time. In 2009, about two thirds of the world's population used cell phones.

The internet was invented, resulting in a revolution in communication and information flow. This global system of interconnected computers serves billions of users worldwide. Currently, about one third of the world's population uses the internet. "God is a Girl", the third and final single released in 2002 by the German trance group Groove Coverage, reached number one in China, with 1.5 million legal downloads.

Facebook, the globe's greatest social networking tool, was launched in 2004 and gained rapid popularity throughout the world for individuals and groups to share information.

Founded by Harvard student Mark Zuckerberg and his friends, Facebook has affected the social and political lives of the global community in a major way. As of October 2012, Facebook had over one billion active users, making it the largest collection of people in "one place" that the world has ever seen. "Does Zuckerberg have a Facebook 'God' account?" was a question raised by Facebook users when it was discovered that a user cannot block Facebook CEO Zuckerberg on the social networking site. The attempt returns a general block failure error, although a user can block any other Facebook user. This means that Zuckerberg has access to everyone's profile and private information on Facebook. This is, indeed, a "God-like" immunity.

God made a remarkable comeback in the latter part of the twentieth century. John Micklethwait and Adrian Wooldridge, both journalists at *The Economist*, published *God is Back* to explain the global revival of faith. The two researchers declared, "God is alive and well in America," based on a social survey of faiths. Karen Armstrong, the leading religious scholar of our time, published a book entitled, *The Case for God*, which is a definitive analysis of the role of religious belief and transcendence in our lives.

More and more politicians started using the name of God to promote their own agenda. According to the authors of *God is Back*, the single most frequently used noun in the 2008 Republican convention in the United States was "God." Gandhi was right in saying that "anyone who thinks that religion and politics can be kept apart, understands neither religion nor politics."

Some believe God and religion are good for human health. Daniel Hall, a doctor at the University of Pittsburgh Medical Center, discovered that weekly church attendance could add two to three years to one's life.

God On Trial was the title of a 2008 BBC television play in which Jewish prisoners of the Nazi concentration camp at Auschwitz put God on trial in absentia for abandoning them. Their main question is how God could allow the Nazis to kill about six million Jews during World War II. The television play was based on a famous book entitled *The Trial of God* (1995) by Nobel prize winning author Elie Wiesel, a survivor of Nazi concentration camp.

A 2008 survey of 35,000 Americans, conducted by Pew Forum, on religion and public life revealed many interesting facts about the religious landscape of the United States, the most powerful and the richest country in the world:

- 83% are affiliated with a religion; 16% are not affiliated with any religion, of which 21% are atheist and 55% agnostics.
- 92% believe in the existence of God or a universal spirit; 71% are absolutely sure about the existence of God.
- 70% of the unaffiliated also believe in God.
- 70% believe that many religions can lead to eternal life; among American Muslims, 56% hold such a belief.
- 74% believe in life after death, and also in heaven.
- 58% say that they pray at least once a day.
- 60% of adults believe that God is a person with whom one can have a personal relationship.

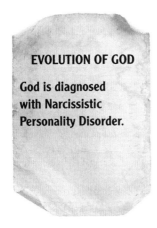

EVOLUTION OF GOD

God is diagnosed with Narcissistic Personality Disorder.

Tom Rees, a British medical writer and biotechnologist, published a paper in 2009 in the *Journal of Religion and Society*, claiming: "across a broad multinational panel, those countries with shorter life expectancy, higher infant mortality, higher violent crime, more corruption, higher abortion rates, and less peace also tend to have higher average levels of personal religiosity, as measured by the frequency of prayer."

Catherine Deveny, an Australian comedy writer and stand-up comedian diagnosed God with Narcissistic Personality Disorder (NPD) in 2009. She cited eight diagnostic criteria for NPD and demonstrated that the God of today's religions meets most of the criteria. Three of those criteria are: (1) "Feelings of grandiosity and self-importance (I am God); exaggerating accomplishments (I made you and the world) to the point of lying (I exist and there is a heaven); demands to be recognized as superior without commensurate achievements (Worship me and only me because I am great and almighty and I know everything); (2) Requires excessive adulation, attention and affirmation - or, failing that, wishes to be feared (Worship me. And me only. Or you will feel my wrath. Worse still, you will not come to my party in heaven); and (3) Behaves arrogantly (I am great and you are sinners); feels "above the law" (Kill in the name of God, etc)."

Ophelia Benson and Jeremy Stangroom published *Does God Hate Women?* in 2009. In a probing commentary, they explored the role of religion and culture in the oppression of women. They argued that, "what would otherwise look like stark bullying is very often made respectable and holy by a putative religious law or aphorism or scriptural quotation... They worship a God who is male who gangs up with other males against women. They worship a thug." The authors further argued that "[it] is possible to imagine a god who is a friend to the despised and downtrodden, a lover of fairness and equality and hope, a champion of rights and of our better natures. But that's not the God we have. It's a contingent fact but it is a fact that the God we have in the Big Three monotheisms is a god who originated in a period when male superiority was absolutely taken for granted... That is the God who looks on approvingly when young girls are married off and raped, when women are whipped for showing a little hair, when men throw stones at a crying teenage girl until she is dead. That God is a product of history but taken to be eternal, which is a bad combination. That is the God who hates women. That God has to go."

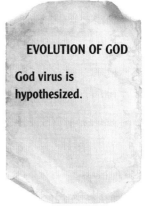

EVOLUTION OF GOD

God virus is hypothesized.

The God Virus: How Religion Infects our Lives and Culture was published in December, 2009. Its author, Dr. Darrel Ray, asserts, "God viruses are always mutating, and new ones may break out of viral reservoirs at any time. The best prophylactic for god viruses, especially fundamentalist variants, is science education. The more science is taught or discussed, the fewer tools a god virus has to infect populations." In April 2010, *The Religion Virus: Why We Believe in God: An Evolutionist Explains Religion's Incredible Hold on Humanity* was published. In it, author Craig James tells

EVOLUTION OF GOD

God is very popular in modern America with 95% people believing in at least one of America's Four Gods.

the story of the image makeover of the jealous, vengeful God of the ancient period to the benevolent God of our post-modern era. He claims that it is essentially the fittest, not necessarily the truest, religious ideas that survive, because of their appeal to our hopes and aspirations, our vanities and prejudices, our fears and helplessness.

Despite the successes of science and the freedom from religion movement in the U.S.A., a recent book entitled, *America's Four Gods* revealed that almost 95% of Americans believe in God. The authors, Paul Froese and Christopher Bader, both professors of sociology, found that the differences among Americans were not about God, but about their views on God. In an interesting survey of about 3,500 people, they found that Americans believe in four Gods:

1. The Authoritative God—the one who is both engaged and judgmental (31%);
2. The Benevolent God—the one who is engaged but not judgmental (24%);
3. The Critical God—the one who is not engaged but judgmental (21%); and
4. The Distant God—the one who is not engaged or judgmental (24%).

These four views of God influenced individual beliefs and behaviors, regardless of upbringing, religion, or political identity.

EVOLUTION OF GOD

God faces competition for the first time.

American biologist entrepreneur, Craig Venter was accused of "playing God" for being one of the first to sequence the human genome. In 2007, the editors of *Nature* wrote: "Many a technology has at some time or another been deemed an affront to God, but perhaps none invites the accusation as directly as synthetic biology." Pat Mooney, the executive director for the science watchdog organization the ETC group stated – "For the first time, God has competition." He added, "Venter and his colleagues have breached a societal boundary, and the public hasn't even had a chance to debate the far-reaching social, ethical and environmental implications of synthetic life." In 2010, Dr. Venter led a team of scientists to create the first synthetic life form. He is currently working on creating synthetic biological organisms and documenting genetic diversity in the world's oceans. Venter, an atheist, once said: "I think from my experience in war and life and science, it all has made me believe that we have one life on this planet. We have one chance to live it and to contribute to the future of society and the future of life. The only 'afterlife' is what other people remember of you."

In 2011, Rev. Dr. J. Henry Jurgens, a practicing psychiatrist and doctor of divinity at Yale University Divinity School, diagnosed God with Bipolar Disorder, a manic-depressive psychological condition defined by the presence of episodes of high energy levels, mood swings, mania, and depression. Dr. Jurgens announced in a press conference: "I always knew there had to be some explanation, and, after several years of patient research and long sessions with God Almighty through the intercessionary medium of prayer, I was able to pinpoint the specific nature of His problem." The newspaper also reported that, "Evidence of God's manic-depression can be found throughout the Universe, from the white-hot explosiveness of quasars to the cold, lifeless vacuum of space. However, theologians note, humanity's exposure to God's affliction comes primarily through His confusing propensity to alternately reward and punish His creations with little rhyme or reason." Dr. Jurgens asked humans to be understanding and forgiving because God, due to his bipolar condition, is not necessarily in control of his actions and does not realize how they affect others. Dr. Jurgens is forming a support group, "Living With a Bipolar Creator-Deity."

EVOLUTION OF GOD

God is diagnosed with bipolar disorder.

WALL OF MORTALS:
(1900 TO 2012 AD)

God and religion generated a lot of thought in people from all professions and backgrounds during this fascinating period of human history. The diversity of these writings on God is unprecedented—provocative, thoughtful, silly, devotional, blasphemous, funny, and insightful. The writings of a special group of humans, the Nobel Laureates, of this period are separately presented in the next chapter, "God of Nobel Laureates."

"In the nineteenth century the problem was that God is dead; in the twentieth century the problem is that man is dead."

– ERICH FROMM (1900-1980)
[German-American psychologist and humanistic philosopher]

"If you're going to sin, sin against God, not the bureaucracy; God will forgive you but the bureaucracy won't."

– U.S. NAVY ADMIRAL HYMAN G. RICKOVER (1900-1986)

"God tests His real friends more severely than the lukewarm ones."

– KATHRYN HUMLE (1900-1981)
[American author, famous for semi-biographical novel, The Nun's Story]

COFFEE BREAK

Indian Guru: Neem Karoli Baba is an Indian saint who had influenced many Americans, like Harvard psychologist Dr. Richard Alpert (1931-) , who later took the name Ram Dass. During the 1960s and 1970s, many Americans, including Steve Jobs, co-founder and former CEO of Apple, traveled to India to meet Neem Karoli Baba, but Baba had died several months before Steve's arrival.

"Keep God in your heart the same way as you keep money in a bank."

– NEEM KAROLI BABA (1900-1973)
[Indian saint and guru]

"One who works for God, his works are accomplished automatically."

– NEEM KAROLI BABA (1900-1973)

"Love everyone, serve everyone, remember God, and tell the truth."

– NEEM KAROLI BABA (1900-1973)

"In God we trust, all others must use data."

– WILLIAM EDWARDS DEMING (1900-1993)
[American statistician, professor, author, lecturer, and consultant, credited with the launching of Total Quality Management (TQM) movement in business]

"I could prove God statistically."

— GEORGE GALLUP (1901-1984)
[American statistician, inventor of Gallup poll]

"God-belief, however, is placed [in Buddhism] in the same category as those morally destructive wrong views which deny the karmic results of action, assume a fortuitous origin of man and nature, or teach absolute determinism. These views are said to be altogether pernicious, having definite bad results due to their effect on ethical conduct."

— NYANAPONIKA THERA (1901-1994)
[German-born Sri-Lanka-ordained monk of Theravada Buddhism, author and teacher]

"I contend that we are both atheists. I just believe in one fewer god than you do. When you understand why you dismiss all the other possible gods, you will understand why I dismiss yours."

— SIR STEPHEN HENRY ROBERTS (1901-1971)
[Australian historian and university vice-chancellor]

"More consequences for thought and action follow the affirmation or denial of God than from answering any other basic question."

— MORTIMER ADLER (1902-2001)
[American philosopher, educator, and popular author, best known as the chief editor of the "Great Books of the Western World" series]

"God is what man finds divine in himself. God is the best way man can behave in the ordinary occasions of life, and the farthest point to which man can stretch himself."

— MAX LERNER (1902-1992)
[American journalist and educator]

"The point is, could God pass an examination in Theology?"

— MALCOLM MUGGERIDGE (1903-1990)
[British journalist, author, media personality, soldier, spy and Christian scholar]

"God is a metaphor for that which transcends all levels of intellectual thought. It's as simple as that."

— JOSEPH CAMPBELL (1904-1987)
[American professor, writer, and orator, best known for his work on PBS series "The Power of Myth"]

"It is in the agricultural world of ancient Mesopotamia, the Egyptian Nile, and in the earlier planting-culture systems that the Goddess is the dominant mythic form."

— JOSEPH CAMPBELL (1904-1987)

COFFEE BREAK

God and His Image: In the beginning, God made man in his own image; in the twentieth century, man and woman made Gods in their own images.

"And now I see the face of god, and I raise this god over the earth, this god whom men have sought since men came into being, this god who will grant them joy and peace and pride. This god, this one word: 'I.'"

— AYN RAND (1905-1982)
[Russian-American novelist, philosopher, playwright, and screenwriter. Founder of objectivism, famous for her two books "Fountainhead" and "Atlas Shrugged"]

"A God who let us prove his existence would be an idol."

— DIETRICH BONHOEFFER (1906-1945)
[German Lutheran pastor and theologian]

"Man has learned to cope with all questions of importance without recourse to God as a working hypothesis."

— DIETRICH BONHOEFFER (1906-1945)

"I prefer to think that God is not dead, just drunk."

— JOHN MARCELLUS HUSTON (1906-1987)
[American filmmaker, screenwriter and actor]

COFFEE BREAK
Militant Islam: The seeds of militant Islam are sown by Hassan Al-Banna as a revolt to the British colonialism, and economic dominance throughout the Muslim lands. The passion of religion is evoked to inspire the native populace against foreign hegemony

"God is our objective, the Quran is our Constitution, the Prophet is our leader, Jihad is our way, and death for the sake of God is the highest of our aspirations."

— HASSAN AL-BANNA (1906-1949)
[Egyptian social and Islamist political reformer– Credo of Muslim Brotherhood (established in 1928)]

"The most preposterous notion that H. sapiens has ever dreamed up is that the Lord God of Creation, Shaper and Ruler of all the Universes, wants the saccharine adoration of His creatures, can be swayed by their prayers, and becomes petulant if He does not receive this flattery. Yet this absurd fantasy, without a shred of evidence to bolster it, pays all the expenses of the oldest, largest, and least productive industry in all history."

— ROBERT ANSON HEINLEIN (1907-1988)
[One of the most popular, influential, and controversial authors of science fiction of the 20th Century]

"A religious man is a person who holds God and man in one thought at one time, at all times, who suffers harm done to others, whose greatest passion is compassion, whose greatest strength is love and defiance of despair."

— ABRAHAM J. HESCHEL (1907-1972)
[Polish-born American rabbi and theologian]

"Religion is not an end in itself. One's union with God is the ultimate goal. There are so many religions because immature people tend to emphasize trivial differences instead of important likenesses."

— PEACE PILGRIM (1908-1981)
[Born Mildred Lisette Norman, an American pacifist, vegetarian, and peace activist]

"Must we only fear God's puissant thunder
And not remember his glittering festival?"

— BUDDHADEVA BASU (1908-1974)
[Major Bengali writer, poet, literary critic]

"Every perfect life is a parable invented by God."

— SIMONE WEIL (1909-1943)
[French social and religious philosopher]

"Every man thinks God is on his side. The rich and powerful know he is."

— JEAN ANOUILH (1910-1987)
[French dramatist, screenwriter and translator]

"God: a disease we imagine we are cured of because no one dies of it nowadays."

— EMIL CIORAN (1911-1995)
[Romanian philosopher and essayist]

EVOLUTION OF GOD

God returns as the human quest for spiritual happiness triumphs over the human need for material goods.

"Listen O God,
Listen to my entreaty for once,
Can you tell me
Why in this beautiful world of yours
There is so much misery
Why the piteous groans of tortured humanity
Fill the sky and the forests and the hills."

— SUFIA KAMAL (1911-1999)
[Bangladeshi poet, writer, and social activist]

"God is love, but get it in writing."

— GYPSY ROSE LEE (1911-1970)
[American burlesque entertainer, actress, author and playwright]

"Freedom prospers when religion is vibrant and the rule of law under God is acknowledged."

— RONALD REAGAN (1911-2004)
[40th President of the United States, American actor and politician]

"Without God there is no virtue because there is no prompting of the conscience,... without God democracy will not and cannot long endure."

— RONALD REAGAN (1911-2004)

COFFEE BREAK

School Prayers: In 1955, the New York Board of Regents developed a prayer that read "Almighty God, we acknowledge our dependence upon Thee, and we beg Thy blessings upon us, our parents, our teachers and our Country." The Board recommended it to be recited every day in schools under its jurisdiction. In a landmark decision in 1962, the US Supreme Court struck down the law as unconstitutional because state-sponsored establishment of religion was prohibited under the First Amendment of the US Constitution. In a separate case the following year in 1963, the US Supreme Court also ruled that state-sponsored Bible reading in public schools is also unconstitutional. These two landmark cases established the prohibition of state-sponsored school prayers in US public schools.

"A theologian is a person who uses the word 'God' to hide his ignorance."

— LEMUEL K. WASHBURN, 20TH CENTURY FREETHINKER
[Aphorist, author of "Is The Bible Worth Reading And Other Essays" (1911)]

"What is the best way to live? How large is God? How are finite beings related to the infinite? What was God's purpose in creating the universe? How can we be helpful? These ageless questions can inspire people today just as they have inspired people throughout the ages, linking the human soul to philosophy and to the love of wisdom."

— SIR JOHN TEMPLETON (1912-1997)
[American-born British philanthropist, known as one of the greatest stock investors, founder of John Templeton foundation, renounced American citizenship over $100 million tax dispute]

"Mozart makes you believe in God because it cannot be by chance that such a phenomenon arrives into this world and leaves such an unbounded number of unparalleled masterpieces."

— SIR GEORG SOLTI (1912-1997)
[Hungarian-British orchestral and operatic conductor]

"What can you say about a society that says God is dead and Elvis is alive?"

— IRV KUPCINET (1912-2003)
[American newspaper columnist]

"God is indeed dead. He died of self-horror when He saw the creature He had made in His own image."

— IRVING LAYTON (1912-2006)
[Canadian poet]

"I've been hiding from God, and I'm appalled to find how easy it is."

— MIGNON McLAUGHLIN (1913-1983)
[American journalist and author]

"It is with God Himself as it is with a great mountain. The important thing is to come to Him not with fear, but with love."

— SHERPA TENZING NORGAY (1914-1986)
[Born Namgyal Wangdi, Nepali Indian mountaineer who accompanies Sir Edmund Hillary in their successful pursuit to be first humans to reach the Mount Everest peak]

"In attempting to control the superstitious fears that were spawned in the darkness of his infantile ignorance, man created the God of religion in whom he could take refuge from the overwhelming tragedies of daily life. Thus, God and His transcendent world of beings became man's "security blanket", his "opium" according to Marx, the anodyne that made this life barely bearable in time on the promise of the "pie-in-the-sky" awaiting him as a reward in the next. This is how God and religion all started, in the days of man's infancy and adolescence."

— VINCENT MICELI (1915-1991)
[American catholic priest, philosopher, theologian and author]

"The religious idea of God cannot do full duty for the metaphysical infinity."

— ALAN WILSON WATTS (1915-1973)
[British philosopher, writer, speaker]

"God exists: I have met him."

— ANDRE FROSSARD (1915-1995)
[French journalist and essayist, this is the title of his 1969 book]

"I don't pray because I don't want to bore God."

— ORSON WELLES (1915-1985)
[American actor, writer, and film director, famous for his movie "Citizen Kane"]

"Do not be too quick to condemn the man who no longer believes in God: for it is perhaps your own coldness and avarice and mediocrity and materialism and selfishness that have chilled his faith."

— THOMAS MERTON (1915-1968)
[One of the most influential Catholic authors of the 20th century]

"When I admire the wonder of a sunset or the beauty of the moon, my soul expands in worship of the Creator."

— INDIRA GANDHI (1917-1984)
[Daughter of India's first prime minister Jawaharlal Nehru, became the first woman Prime Minister of India in 1966]

"God is omnipotent; God is wholly good; and yet evil exists. There seems to be some contradiction between these three propositions, so that if any two of them were true the third would be false. But at the same time all three are essential parts of most theological positions: the theologian it seems, at once must adhere and cannot consistently adhere to all three."

— J. L. MACKIE (1917-1981)
[Australian philosopher and author]

"I don't believe in God but I'm very interested in her."

— ARTHUR CLARKE (1917-2008)
[British science fiction author, inventor, and futurist, most famous for the novel "2001: A Space Odyssey", which was a famous movie directed by Stanley Kubrick]

"It may be that our role on this planet is not to worship God, but to create him."

— ARTHUR CLARKE (1917-2008)

"My fellow citizens of the world, ask not what America will do for you, but what together we can do for the freedom of man. With a good conscience our only sure reward, with history the final judge of our deeds, let us go forth to lead the land we love, asking His blessing and His help, but knowing that here on earth God's work must truly be our own."

— JOHN FITZGERALD KENNEDY (1917-1963)
[35th President of the United States, celebrated as the most popular President ever to have held the office, was assassinated in Texas, while in office]

"The rights of man come not from the generosity of the state, but from the hand of God."

— JOHN FITZGERALD KENNEDY (1917-1963)

"People see God every day, they just don't recognize Him."

— PEARL BAILEY (1918-1990)
[American actress and singer]

COFFEE BREAK

Which God?: Australian geneticist and theologian Louis Charles Birch (1918-2009) related the following interesting story in his book, *A Purpose for Everything*.

"A student of Columbia University came to see Harry Emerson Fosdick, who was pastor of Riverside Church in New York. He was agitated. Before he had time to sit down he announced to Dr. Fosdick that he didn't believe in God. 'So you're an atheist' said Fosdick. 'Describe for me the God you don't believe in.' The student did a good job of picturing God as a venerable bookkeeper taking notes of everyone's good and bad deeds. When the student had finished Fosdick surprised him by saying 'My boy, that makes two of us. I don't believe in that God either. But we've still got the universe on our hands, haven't we. What do you really think about it?'"

"The old notion of a divine being controlling the universe from outside is no longer credible. The relevant question now is, in what sense, if any, is there divine activity in the universe. Why bring God into the argument at all? Hasn't the notion of God been disposed of by science and the Enlightenment and more recently by theologians themselves who have written about the death of God? The critical question to ask is which God is dead? There are many concepts of God and many of them should die. The primary question is not, do you believe in God? but, what do you think you would be believing in if you did believe in God? There is the God who can do anything, who could prevent nuclear war, who could have prevented the holocaust -- but didn't. There is the God who set the universe going in the first place and then left it except for occasional interventions in the form of miracles which rarely happen. There is the God of the gaps who is brought in to fill the gaps left by science; that God grows smaller with every advance in scientific understanding of the universe. There is the cosmic bellhop who sits at the end of a cosmic telephone exchange dealing with billions of calls every minute and whom the caller hopes will alter the course of events to suit the caller. There is the God who requires praise. There is the God who demands sacrifice. There is the God who is on our side in wars who would have us kill for his sake. There is the uncertain God of the soldier's prayer -- please God, if there be a God, save my soul if there be a soul! There is the God of judgment who rules by fear and who dispenses post-mortem rewards and punishments. All these theologies of God make things pretty easy for atheists. I too am an atheist about those Gods."

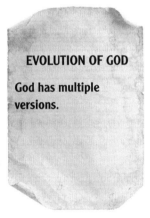

EVOLUTION OF GOD

God has multiple versions.

– LOUIS CHARLES BIRCH (1918-2009)

[Australian professor and geneticist, theologian, prolific writer, joint winner of International Templeton Prize for Progress in Religion, visiting professor at UC Berkeley and Oxford]

"I cannot believe that God wants punishment to go on interminably any more than does a loving parent. The entire purpose of loving punishment is to teach, and it lasts only as long as is needed for the lesson. And the lesson is always love."
— MADELEINE L'ENGLE (1918-2007)
[American writer and poet, most famous for her children's books]

"I do not deny for a moment that the truth of God has reached others through other channels - indeed, I hope and pray that it has. So while I have a special attachment to one mediator, I have respect for them all."
— JOHN MACQUARRIE (1919 –2007)
[Distinguished Scottish theologian and philosopher]

"If I were not an atheist, I would believe in a God who would choose to save people on the basis of the totality of their lives and not the pattern of their words. I think he would prefer an honest and righteous atheist to a TV preacher whose every word is God, God, God, and whose every deed is foul, foul, foul."
— ISAAC ASIMOV (1920-1992)
[Russian-born American author and biochemist]

"There comes a time when every scientist, even God, has to write off an experiment."
— P. D. JAMES (1920-)
[British writer of crime fiction and member of the House of Lords]

"God's mind is not only in His Word, but also in everything He created. God's mind exists wherever we go in heaven or on earth."
— SUN MYUNG MOON (1920-)
[Korean founder and leader of the worldwide Unification Church, founder of conservative Washington Times newspaper]

"As far as I know, God is not a sectarian. He is not obsessed with minor details of doctrine. We should quickly liberate ourselves from theological conflict which results from blind attachment to doctrines and rituals, and instead focus on living communication with God."
— SUN MYUNG MOON (1920-)

"If you talk to God, you are praying; if God talks to you, you have schizophrenia."
— THOMAS SZASZ (1920-)
[Professor Emeritus in Psychiatry at the State University of New York]

"Some have concluded that by now there is no longer any need for God. For them, faith in science has supplanted faith in God. It has been said that one must choose between faith and science: either one embraces one or believes in the other. He who proceeds with a commitment to scientific research no longer has need of God; vice versa, he who wishes to believe in God cannot be a serious scientist, because between science and faith there is an irremediable conflict."

— Pope John Paul II (1920-2005)
[Born Karol Józef Wojtyła] served as Pope of the Roman Catholic Church from 1978 until his death]

"The Church is guided by the faith that God the Creator wants to save all humankind in Jesus Christ, the only mediator between God and man, inasmuch as He is the Redeemer of all humankind."

— Pope John Paul II (1920-2005)

"The Goddess can be touched, the Christian God is high up. You cannot touch this old bearded man—or Christ. But the Goddess, she leaves her footprints, but she also has spiritual dimension."

— Marija Gimbutas (1921-1994)
[Lithuanian-American archaeologist, professor of University of California at Los Angeles, author of "Language of Goddess"]

"Life is a great miracle, a most beautiful gift, an incredible mystery. Our planet is an even more magnificent wonder. We must therefore be thankful and be in love with our Earth, with humanity, with all living beings, with the universe and with God and God's angels."

— Robert Muller (1923-2010)
[Belgian-born Assistant Secretary General of the United Nations for 40 years, known as the "philosopher" of the UN]

"Fear is a reminder that we are creatures- fragile, vulnerable, totally dependent on God. But fear shouldn't dominate or control or define us. Rather, it should submit to faith and love."

— Philip Berrigan (1923-2002)
[American peace activist, Christian anarchist, and former Roman Catholic priest]

COFFEE BREAK

Intolerance in Politics: George H. W. Bush's statement as Republican Presidential Nominee in August of 1988 is a frequently cited example of intolerance from a man in high office; he was, at that time, the Vice President of the United States. It is not known whether he has changed his views.

"I don't know that atheists should be considered citizens, nor should they be considered patriots. This is one nation under God."

— George Herbert Walker Bush (1924-)
[41st President of the United States. Father of the 43rd President George W. Bush]

"Patience with others is Love,
Patience with self is Hope,
Patience with God is Faith."

– ADEL BESTAVROS (1924-2005)
[Egyptian Christian preacher and scholar of the Christian Coptic Orthodox Church]

"Your talent is God's gift to you; what you do with it is your gift to God."
– LEO BUSCAGLIA (1924-1998)
[American professor, author, and motivational speaker]

"I am, like much, agnostic, i.e. conscious of my incapacity to say anything about what it is agreed to call by the word God."

– ALBERT JACQUARD (1925-)
[French geneticist and essayist]

"You may think the President is all-powerful, but he is not. He needs a lot of guidance from the Lord."

– BARBARA BUSH (1925-)
[Wife of 41st U.S. President George H. W. Bush and mother of 43rd U.S. President George W. Bush]

"What happens really matters only if it matters ultimately, and it matters ultimately only if it matters everlastingly. What happens can matter everlastingly only if it matters to him who is everlasting. Hence, seriousness about life implicitly involves faith in God."

– JOHN COBB (1925-)
[American professor and United Methodist theologian, known for his contributions in the development of process theology]

"I regard monotheism as the greatest disaster ever to befall the human race. I see no good in Judaism, Christianity, or Islam -- good people, yes, but any religion based on a single, well, frenzied and virulent god, is not as useful to the human race as, say, Confucianism, which is not a religion but an ethical and educational system."

– GORE VIDAL (1925-)
[American author and playwright]

"God is in my head, but the devil is in my pants."

– JONATHAN HARSHMAN WINTERS III (1925-)
[American comedian and actor]

"Science cannot answer the deepest questions. As soon as you ask why there is something instead of nothing, you have gone beyond science. I find it quite improbable that such order came out of chaos. There has to be some organizing principle. God to me is the explanation for the miracle of existence – why there is something instead of nothing."

— ALLAN REX SANDAGE (1926-)
[American astronomer]

"There is no greater distance than that between a man in prayer and God."

— IVAN ILLICH (1926-2002)
[Austrian philosopher, Roman Catholic priest]

"Any fool can count the seeds in an apple. Only God can count all the apples in one seed."

— ROBERT SCHULLER (1926-)
[American televangelist, pastor, and author]

"The heart with compassion is the temple of God."

— SATHYA SAI BABA (1926-2011)
[Born Sathyanarayana Raju, South Indian guru, religious figure, and educator]

COFFEE BREAK
"The Man Who Was God Is Dead": Sathya Sai Baba called himself a god and had a following of more than fifty million devotees. By the time of his death in 2011, he had amassed a fortune worth more than $8 billion for his charitable trust. *Time* magazine broke the news of his death in April 24, 2011 with a story titled, "The Man Who Was God Is Dead."

"I am God; you too are God. The only difference between you and me is that while I am aware of it, you are completely unaware."

— SATHYA SAI BABA (1926-2011)

"Practise silence, for the voice of God can be heard in the region of your heart only when the tongue and the inner storm are stilled, and the waves (of the mind) are calmed."

— SATHYA SAI BABA (1926-2011)

"If God would have wanted us to live in a permissive society He would have given us Ten Suggestions and not Ten Commandments."

— ZIG ZIGLAR (1926-2012)
[Hilary Hinton "Zig" Ziglar, American self-help author and speaker]

"Discussing God is not the best use of our energy."

—THICH NHAT HANH (1926-)
[Vietnamese Buddhist montk, author, poet]

"Because God loves us, because He wants us to grow into truth, He must necessarily make demands on us and must also correct us."

— POPE BENEDICT XVI (1927-)
[Born Joseph Alois Ratzinger, Current Pope and head of the Catholic church]

"Catholics and Muslims must show the common belief that we are members of one family loved by God our Creator, and uphold the dignity of every human person."

— POPE BENEDICT XVI (1927-)

"You might think that in today's world people are unlikely to start worshipping other gods. But sometimes people do worship 'other gods' without realizing it. False 'gods' are nearly always associated with the worship of three things: material possessions, possessive love, or power."

— POPE BENEDICT XVI (1927-)

"The Qur'an insists, Muslims believe, and historians affirm that Muhammad and his followers worship the same God as the Jews [see Qur'an 29:46]. The Quran's Allah is the same Creator God who covenanted with Abraham."

— FRANCIS EDWARD PETERS (1927-)
[Professor emeritus of middle Eastern and Islamic studies of New York University]

"We are all growing toward God, and experience is the path. Through experience we mature out of fear into fearlessness, out of anger into love, out of conflict into peace, out of darkness into light and union in God."

— SIVAYA SUBRAMUNIYASWAMI (1927–2001)
[Born Robert Hansen in California, USA, one of Hinduism's Gurus, the founder and leader of the Saiva Siddhanta Church]

"God owns heaven, but He craves the earth."

— ANNE SEXTON (1928-1974)
[Born Anne Gray Harvey,American poet and writer]

"Those who demand guarantees from God show that they have no understanding of God"

— GUSTAVO GUTIERREZ (1928-)
[Peruvian priest and founder of liberation theology]

"A woman's heart should be so hidden in God that a man has to seek Him just to find her."

— MAYA ANGELOU (1928-)
[Born Marguerite Ann Johnson, American poet, autobiographer, actress, civil rights activist, professor]

"If you cannot see that divinity includes male and female characteristics and at the same time transcends them, you have bad consequences. Rome and Cardinal O'Connor base the exclusion of women priests on the idea that God is the Father and Jesus is His Son, there were only male disciples, etc. They are defending a patriarchal Church with a patriarchal God. We must fight the patriarchal misunderstanding of God."

— HANS KUNG (1928-)

[Celebrated Swiss theologian, professor, and prolific author; drafted "Towards a Global Ethic: An Initial Declaration" signed by 143 religious leaders from the world's major faiths at the 1993 Parliament of the World's Religions in Chicago, USA]

"I do not hope for a unity of religions or any syncretism. I hope for an ecumenical peace among the world religions. That means peaceful co-existence, growing convergence and creative pro-existence of the religions – in the common quest for a greater truth and the mystery of the one and true God that will only be revealed fully at the end-time."

— HANS KUNG (1928-)

"How do I define God? I don't. Divinities have been understood in various ways in the cultural traditions that we know. Take, say, the core of the established religions today: the Bible. It is basically polytheistic, with the warrior God demanding of his chosen people that they not worship the other Gods and destroy those who do -- in an extremely brutal way, in fact. It would be hard to find a more genocidal text in the literary canon, or a more violent and destructive character than the God who was to be worshipped."

— NOAM CHOMSKY (1928-)

[American philosopher, linguist, author, activist, cognitive scientist, emeritus professor at Massachusetts Institute of Technology (MIT)]

"The human mind evolved to believe in the gods. It did not evolve to believe in biology."

— EDWARD O. WILSON (1929-)

[American biologist, researcher, and author]

"The best remedy for those who are afraid, lonely, or unhappy is to go outside, somewhere where they can be quiet, alone with the heavens, nature, and God."

— ANNE FRANK (1929-1945)

[A Jewish girl who perished in Nazi concentration camp, famous for keeping a diary which was published as the "Diary of a Young Girl" in 1947]

COFFEE BREAK

If You Were God: In a Public Broadcasting System (PBS) interview, Bill Moyers asked Karen Armstrong: "If you were God, would you do away with religion?" Armstrong answered: "Well, there are some forms of religion that must make God weep. There are some forms of religion that are bad, just as there's bad cooking or bad art or bad sex, you have bad religion too. Religion that has concentrated on egotism, that's concentrated on belligerence rather than compassion."

"ALL religions of a spiritual nature are inventions of man. He has created an entire system of gods with nothing more than his carnal brain. Just because he has an ego, and cannot accept it, he has to externalize it into some great spiritual device which he calls "God"."

– ANTON SZANDOR LAVEY (1930-1997)
[Satanist author and the founder of Church of Satan]

"All Gods are One God,
and all Goddesses are One Goddess,
there is only One Initiator.
To each his own God,
and the God Within... "

– MARION ELEANOR ZIMMER BRADLEY (1930-1999)
[American author of fantasy novels]

"Satan is a tool of God's love in the sense that he forces us to see God's loving patience."

– PAT ROBERTSON (1930-)
[Christian televangelist from USA, founder of Christian Coalition and host of the TV Show "The 700 Club", which airs on ABC Family]

"The idea of a God gene goes against all my personal theological convictions. You can't cut faith down to the lowest common denominator of genetic survival. It shows the poverty of reductionist thinking."

– JOHN POLKINGHORNE (1930-)
[British particle physicist and theologian]

"The seach for God is subtle, but perhaps it is this long journey, this search, more than anything else, that makes us human. We are the thinking part of this vast and sometimes very intimidating universe, and our quest could well be the purpose of it all."

– OWEN GINGERICH (1930-)
[Former Research Professor of Astronomy and of the History of Science at Harvard University, and a senior astronomer emeritus at the Smithsonian Astrophysical Observatory]

"The first problem in beginning to understand God is with the limitations of our intelligence. We have unwitting conviction that if something is there, we should see it, that if something is explained, we should understand it. If we can't understand it (like the inner workings of the atom), then it's not worth bothering about. This reaction is naïve. You can't see, smell, touch, or taste most of the realities in your room: radio waves, muons, gluons, quarks, neutrinos. You can't see most of the light spectrum."

– WILLIAM O'MALLEY (1931-)
[American Jesuit priest, author, and actor]

"When the heart is open, it's easier for the mind to be turned toward God."

– RICHARD ALPERT (1931-)
[Also known as Baba Ram Dass, is a contemporary spiritual teacher]

"God is not proved objectively. What is proved objectively - the electron, neutron or proton? Nobody has yet seen electrons, neutrons, protons, but the scientists say they are. If nobody has seen them why do you say they are? Scientists say, "Because though we cannot see them, we can see their effect." The mystics say the same thing: "God is not observed objectively, but we can see the effect."

— BHAGWAN SHREE RAJNEESH (1931 – 1990)
[Born Chandra Mohan Jain in India, also known as Osho. Indian professor, guru and spiritual leader. A village in Oregon, USA, is named "Rajneeshpuram" after him. Fined $400,000 for immigration law violations and deported from USA in 1985]

"Einstein argued that there must be simplified explanations of nature, because God is not capricious or arbitrary. No such faith comforts the software engineer."

— FREDERICK BROOKS, JR. (1931-)
[American software engineer and computer scientist, best-known for his book "Mythical Man Month"]

"When we have
A childlike state of mind,
It becomes extremely easy to find God
Here, there and everywhere."

— SRI CHINMOY [CHINMOY KUMAR GHOSE] (1931-2007)
[Bangladesh-born American spiritual teacher and philosopher]

"I was born into the Hindu religion, but now my only religion is to love God and to be of service to God. Love of God embraces all religions: Christianity, Hinduism, Judaism, Islam and others."

— SRI CHINMOY (1931-2007)

"Man and God are one another's supreme necessity. Man needs God for his highest transcendental realization and God needs man for His absolute earthly manifestation. Man needs God to realize his highest truth, his highest existence. God needs man to manifest Him here on earth totally, divinely and supremely."

— SRI CHINMOY (1931-2007)

"I would argue that it is the universal potentiality of consciousness that we resonate with when we tap the mind's well. We access the very power behind all existence, a power which is encrypted everywhere in the foundation of space itself. It is the power of the one source, the order that underlies and enfolds all orders, that unifies all fields and forms, as well as consciousness, and it will not, by now, surprise you to hear my assertion that we call this source by its code name: God"

— MANI BHAUMIK (1931-)
[Indian-born American quantum physicist, co-inventor of excimer laser, which made the LASIK eye surgery possible, philanthropist and author of books on spirituality and cosmology]

COFFEE BREAK

Female Deity: The women's liberation movement peaked in the twentieth century and more and more women actively contributed to the intellectual progress of humankind. The idea of a solely male God in Western religions was challenged and the concept of a female deity was advanced by several feminist thinkers.

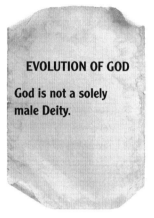

EVOLUTION OF GOD

God is not a solely male Deity.

"I am the Great Mother, worshipped by all creation
and existent prior to their consciousness.
I am the primal female force, boundless and eternal.
I am the chaste Goddess of the Moon, the Lady of all magic.
The winds and moving leaves sing my name.
I wear the crescent Moon upon my brow and
my feet rest among the starry heavens."

— ANONYMOUS, SONG OF THE GODDESS

"The Goddess is not just the female version of God. She represents a different concept. It is difficult to grasp the immensity and significance of the extreme reverence paid to the Goddess over a period of (at least) seven thousand years and over miles of land cutting across national boundaries and vast expanses of sea."

— MERLIN STONE (1931-2011)
[American sculptor and professor of art and art history, best-known for her feminist book "When God Was a Woman"]

"I believe in a higher power, I believe in one God. I'm so glad I asked for help."

— ELIZABETH TAYLOR (1932-2011)

[World famous British-American actress, twice won Oscar for best actress]

"I believe you can be close to God anywhere."

— ELIZABETH TAYLOR (1932-2011)

"God is a gentleman. He prefers blondes."

— JOHN KINGSLEY ("JOE") ORTON (1933-1967)
[English playwright]

"Thank God for these gay demonstrators. If I didn't have them, I'd have to invent them. They give me all the publicity I need."

— JERRY FALWELL (1933-2007)
[American Southern Baptist pastor, televangelist, founder of the Moral Majority and Liberty University]

"God had let the terrorists attack the World Trade Center because he was fed up with the pagans in America... the terrorist attack was the fault of ACLU (the American

Civil Liberties Union), abortionists, feminists, homosexuals, and others, who provoked God's wrath."

— JERRY FALWELL (1933-2007)

"If God wanted us to bend over he'd put diamonds on the floor."

— JOAN RIVERS (1933-)

[American comedian, TV personality and actress, winner of Emmy Award]

COFFEE BREAK

"Where they burn books, they will also ultimately burn people." Thus wrote Heinrich Heine, German Jewish poet, in his 1820–1821 play *Almansor*. His premonition came true in Germany during the Nazi regime. On the night of May 10, 1933, more than one hundred years after Heine's admonition, German university students, singing Nazi anthems, burned more than 20,000 books in thirty-four university towns across Germany on the grounds that these books contained "un-German" ideas. In Berlin alone, some 40,000 people gathered to celebrate the event at which Dr. Joseph Goebbels, Hitler's propaganda minister, declared that "the era of extreme Jewish intellectualism is now at an end." The burned books included works of Albert Einstein, Ernest Hemingway, Sigmund Freud, Karl Marx, Jack London, Helen Keller, Heinrich Heine, Andre Gide, among a dozen other authors.

"Who destroys a good book, kills reason itself, kills the image of God"

— JOHN MILTON (1608-1674)

"The idea that God is an oversized white male with a flowing beard who sits in the sky and tallies the fall of every sparrow is ludicrous. But if by God one means the set of physical laws that govern the universe, then clearly there is such a God. This God is emotionally unsatisfying... it does not make much sense to pray to the law of gravity."

— CARL SAGAN (1934-1996)

[American astronomer and popular science writer]

"God may be in the details, but the goddess is in the questions. Once we begin to ask them, there's no turning back."

— GLORIA STEINEM (1934-)

[American feminist, journalist, social activist and author]

"I looked and looked but I didn't see God."

— YURI GAGARIN (1934-1968)

[Russian astronaut, first human in space (12 April, 1961). After returning from his space trip]

"How to make God laugh: Tell him your future plans."

– WOODY ALLEN (1935-)
[Born Allen Stewart Königsberg, American film director, writer, musician, actor and comedian]

"Not only is there no God, but try getting a plumber on weekends."

– WOODY ALLEN (1935-)

"What people say about God is bound to be approximate, provisional, corrigible, and often wrong. That is because no one has ever seen God"

– JOHN BOWKER (1935-)
[British professor of religious studies, who taught at Cambridge]

"All the gods are dead except the god of war."

– ELDRIDGE CLEAVER (1935-1998)
[American author, prominent civil rights leader]

"The world is more alive at night; it's like God isn't looking."

– ELVIS PRESLEY (1935-1977)
[American singer-songwriter and musician, earned the title "King of Rock and Roll"]

"A personal relationship with God enhances life. First, it enables us to accept our limitations without being frustrated by them."

– HAROLD S. KUSHNER (1935-)
[American rabbi]

"Religion has never really had a big problem with murder. Not really. More people have been killed in the name of God than for any other reason."

– GEORGE DENNIS CARLIN (1937-2008)
[Grammy-winning American stand-up comedian, actor and author]

"There is hope for the future because God has a sense of humor and we are funny to God."

– BILL COSBY (1937-)
[American actor, comedian, television producer and activist]

"Arguing whether or not a God exists is like fleas arguing whether or not the dog exists."

– ROBERT FULGHUM (1937-)
[American author]

"If God exists, he certainly existed before religion. He is a philosopher's God, logically inferred from self-evident premises. That he should have been taken up by a glorified supporters' club is only a matter of psychological interest."

– TOM STOPPARD (1937-)
[British playwright]

COFFEE BREAK
Computer God: In the fall of 1999, "Computer God" Donald Knuth of Stanford University gave a series of public lectures at MIT on the topic of religion and science. In his sixth and final lecture, "God and Computer Science," he elaborated on how computer science can help answer many ancient and difficult questions.

"God is a challenge because there is no proof of his existence and therefore the search must continue."

– DONALD KNUTH (1938-)
[Professor Emeritus of the Art of Computer Programming at Stanford University, renowned computer scientist and winner of the 1974 Turing Award]

"I guess I sort of assumed, mistakenly, that God would have certain purposes as if God were a human being."

– DONALD KNUTH (1938-)

"A mathematical formula should never be "owned" by anybody! Mathematics belong to God."

– DONALD KNUTH (1938-)

"Simply being the creator is not enough alone to constitute being a God. Consider the science fiction situation of our universe being created by a teenager living in another dimension or realm, as the equivalent of a high school science or art project."

– ROBERT NOZICK (1938-2002)
[American philosopher and professor of Harvard University]

"Why is it when we talk to God, we're said to be praying-but when God talks to us, we're schizophrenic?"

– LILY TOMLIN (1939-)
[American actress and comedian]

"For me the goddess is the female of God, She is powerful if different."

– TINA TURNER (1939-)
[Born Anna Mae Bullock, American singer and actress, she earned the title "The Queen of Rock 'n' Roll"]

"God is a concept by which we can measure our pain."

– JOHN LENNON (1940-1980)
[Born John Winston Lennon], singer, songwriter, guitarist, political activist, humorist, painter and writer]

THE TEN COMMANDMENTS OF ATHEISM

1. "Do not do to others what you would not want them to do to you

2. In all things, strive to cause no harm

3. Treat your fellow human beings, your fellow living things, and the world in general with love, honesty, faithfulness and respect.

4. Do not overlook evil or shrink from administering justice, but always be ready to forgive wrongdoing freely admitted and honestly regretted.

5. Live life with a sense of joy and wonder

6. Always seek to be learning something new

7. Test all things; always check your ideas against the facts, and be ready to discard even a cherished belief if it does not conform to them.

8. Never seek to censor or cut yourself off from dissent; always respect the right of others to disagree with you.

9. Form independent opinions on the basis of your own reason and experience; do not allow yourself to be led blindly by others.

10. Question everything."

[SOURCE: THE GOD DELUSION: RICHARD DAWKINS]

"Part of me suspect I'm a loser, and
Part of me thinks I'm God Almighty"

– JOHN LENNON (1940-1980)

"Whatever it is you say God is, God is more. The very constitution of the idea is deconstructive of any such construction ... the very formula that describes God is that there is no formula with which God can be described?"

– JOHN D. CAPUTO (1940-)
[American professor and a prolific author on hermeneutics, phenomenology, deconstruction and theology]

"Most wars are thought to be conducted for a high moral purpose, and often this means seeing them as blessed by God."

— MARK JUERGENSMEYER (1940-)

[American scholar and professor, authority on religious violence and global religion]

"Warfare often unites a sense of nationalism with religious purpose—fighting for 'God and country.' Few political leaders in a time of warfare are unable to resist the temptation to claim God for their side, and to admit the humility that Abraham Lincoln was said to have displayed during the Civil War in the United States when he was asked whether God was on his side. Lincoln was said to have claimed that he did not know which side God was on, but that he certainly hoped that he was on God's side."

— MARK JUERGENSMEYER (1940-)

COFFEE BREAK

The God Delusion: Richard Dawkins argued that a supernatural creator definitely does not exist and that religious faith is a human delusion—an imaginary belief. His seminal book, *The God Delusion*, has sold more than two million copies in the original English language and has been translated into more than thirty other languages.

"Most people, I believe, think that you need a God to explain the existence of the world, and especially the existence of life. They are wrong, but our education system is such that many people don't know it."

— RICHARD DAWKINS (1941-)

[British zoologist, author, famous for his book "The God Delusion"]

"Suppose we grant that there is indeed some small chance that God exists. Nevertheless, it could be said that you will lead a better, fuller life if you bet on his not existing, than if you bet on his existing and therefore squander your precious time on worshiping him, sacrificing to him, fighting and dying for him, etc."

— RICHARD DAWKINS (1941-)

"An Eternal Father who is younger than His progeny? Comparative chronologies bear witness to this bizarre circumstance. We His children are ancient in relation to our Creator, who may be august but is a late bloomer. He is, at best, six tho usand years old; Home Sapiens is between fifty and a hundred thousand years old. The two millennial timelines unfurl in polite ignorance of each other, which avoids the embarrassment of a confrontation."

— REGIS DEBRAY (1941-)

[French intellectual, author, journalist, and professor]

GOD AND PLEDGE OF ALLEGIANCE

The current version of the United States Pledge of Allegiance, recited by thousands of children in school every day, reads: "I pledge allegiance to the flag of the United States of America, and to the republic for which it stands, one nation *under God*, indivisible, with liberty and justice for all." The phrase *"under God"* was not in the original version adopted in 1942 but was added in 1954 by an act of Congress to differentiate the USA from communist regimes and their state-sponsored atheism.

In 2000, Michael Newdow, an atheist doctor and attorney from Sacramento, California, brought a lawsuit against the Elk Grove Unified School District, in which his daughter attended school. He claimed that the phrase *"under God"* was an unconstitutional establishment of religion, prohibited under the First Amendment.

The US Court of Appeals for the Ninth Circuit sided with him and ruled in 2002 that the phrase *"under God"* is indeed an unconstitutional establishment of religion. However, the US Supreme Court overturned the ruling on a procedural matter, stating that Newdow didn't have standing to file the lawsuit because he didn't have legal custody of his daughter and the mother of the child had no objection to the oath's wording. The Supreme Court didn't consider the constitutional merits of the issue at hand.

Newdow brought another lawsuit in 2005 against Rio Linda Union School District on behalf of three unnamed parents, and a District Court Judge ruled in his favor, citing the earlier binding ruling from the Court of Appeals. In response to the hugely negative public reaction, the US Congress passed a bill in July 2006, which if enacted into law, would have stripped the courts of the power to consider any legal challenges to the government's promotion of the Pledge of Allegiance. The Senate didn't act on the bill and it never passed.

In March of 2010, the US Court of Appeals for the Ninth Circuit upheld the words *"under God"* in the case of *Newdow v. Rio Linda Union School District*. In a 2–1 majority decision, the court ruled that the words were of a "ceremonial and patriotic nature" and did not constitute an establishment of religion. In November of 2010, the United States Court of Appeals for the First Circuit in Boston sided with a lower federal court, which found that the *"under God"* phrase doesn't violate students' rights. The US Supreme Court denied to hear an appeal on this case in June 2011.

It should be noted that about half of the states allow students the option not to recite the *"under God"* phrase or any other parts of the pledge that they may find offensive to their faiths.

"God gave me this illness to remind me that I'm not number One; he is."

— MUHAMMAD ALI (1942-)

[Born Cassius Marcellus Clay Jr., American boxer, three times World Heavyweight champion]

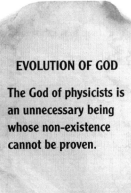

EVOLUTION OF GOD

The God of physicists is an unnecessary being whose non-existence cannot be proven.

"We have one life; it soon will be past; what we do for God is all that will last."

— MUHAMMAD ALI (1942-)

"Las Vegas is sort of like how God would do it if he had money."

— STEVE WYNN (1942-)

[American casino resort/real-estate developer who has been credited with spearheading the dramatic resurgence and expansion of the Las Vegas Strip in the 1990s]

"Can anyone picture God telling, taking, or enjoying a good joke? The idea is laughable. The Devil, on the other hand, laughs with demonic mirth, is possessed of a sardonic wit, and his eyes hold a glint of wicked bemusement."

— DIANE HEGARTY (1942-)

[Co-founder with Anton LaVey of the Church of Satan; typed and edited The Satanic Bible, The Satanic Rituals, The Compleat Witch (aka The Satanic Witch) and The Devil's Notebook]

"Women are the nourishers of the world, and as such, we are the messengers of God."

— KAREN BERG (1942-)

[Woman Kabbalist, author of "God Wears Lipstick", founder of Kabbalah Center, mother of Yehuda Berg and Michael Berg]

"Consideration of particle emission from black holes would seem to suggest that God not only plays dice, but also sometimes throws them where they cannot be seen."

— STEPHEN HAWKING (1942-)

[British theoretical physicist and author, famous for "A Brief History of Time"]

"We are nearing God."

— STEPHEN HAWKING (1942-)

"The question is: is the way the universe began chosen by God for reasons we can't understand, or was it determined by a law of science? I believe the second. If you like, you can call the laws of science 'God', but it wouldn't be a personal God that you could meet, and ask questions."

— STEPHEN HAWKING (1942-)

COFFEE BREAK
The Same God?: British Nobel Laureate and philosopher, Bertrand Russell was jailed as a conscientious objector during World War I. The admitting clerk asked him his religion, to which Russell replied that he was an agnostic. The clerk looked at him and commented that he had never heard of that religion, but it didn't matter because all religions worship the same God.

"The idea that God is a worthy recipient of our gratitude for the blessings of life but should not be held accountable for the disasters is a transparently disingenuous innovation of the theologians. And of course it doesn't work all that well... All the holy texts and interpretations that contrive ways of getting around the problem read like the fine print in a fraudulent contract — and for the same reason: they are desperate attempts to conceal the implications of the double standard they have invented."

– DANIEL DENNETT (1942-)
[American philosopher and cognitive scientist, professor at Tufts University]

"No character on stage, page, or screen has ever had the reception that God has had. God is more than a household word in the West. He is, welcome or not, a virtual member of the Western family. Parents who would have done with him cannot keep their children from him. For not only has everyone heard of him. Everyone, even now, can tell you something about him."

– JACK MILES (1942-)
[Pulitzer prize winning American author]

"The God myth tells us that there is a separate God up there or out there who: (1) created what we see around us, (2) demands certain things from us, (3) watches and judges us in our daily lives and, (4) at some far distant point in time, will give us a cosmic thumbs up or down depending on whether we give God what He wants. Then it's an eternity of either stoking the fires of Hell or enjoying glorious salvation in Heaven. How did this myth come about? It did not originate in the Bible but was already an ancient misunderstanding in Middle Eastern oral tradition long before the books making up the Old Testament were even contemplated."

– TONY STUBBS (20TH CENTURY)
[British-born American computer scientist and author of metaphysical books, author of "Living With Soul" and "An Ascension Handbook"]

"I always put a face on God, but my soul knows that the face isn't God. Putting a face on God is a human trick to make God more accessible."

– GRAHAM NASH (AGE 47),
[A musician from California, quoted in Sullivan (1990)]

"Well, I kind of split my life into two pieces. One was where my chess career lies. There, I kept my sanity, so to speak, and my logic. And the other was my religious life. I tried to apply what I learned in the church to my chess career too. But I still was studying chess. I wasn't just "trusting in God" to give me the moves."

– BOBBY FISCHER (1943-2008)
[Born Robert James Fischer, American World Chess Champion (1972-75), one of the greatest chess player in history]

"God is in the sadness and the laughter, in the bitter and the sweet. There is a divine purpose behind everything—and therefore a divine presence in everything."

– NEALE DONALD WALSCH (1943-)
[American author of the series Conversations with God]

"The Incarnation of God did not happen in Bethlehem 2000 years ago. That is just when we started taking it seriously. The incarnation actually happened 14.5 billion years ago with a moment that we now call "The Big Bang." That is when God actually decided to materialize and to self expose."

– FATHER RICHARD ROHR (1943-)
[American Franciscan priest known for his numerous inspirational books]

"White people really deal more with God and black people with Jesus."

– NIKKI GIOVANNI (1943-)
[Born Yolande Cornelia 'Nikki' Giovanni, American poet, activist and author]

"Sure God created man before woman. But then you always make a rough draft before the final masterpiece."

– ANONYMOUS

"God may have written just a few laws and grown tired. We do not know whether we are in a tidy universe or an untidy one."

– NANCY CARTWRIGHT (1944-)
[Philosopher and professor]

COFFEE BREAK
Necessity of God: Karen Armstrong is one of the most prolific writers on God and Religion. She argues for the necessity and inevitability of God on the basis of the complex relationship between human existence and the transcendent nature of God.

"Nirvana is something within you. It is not an external reality. No god thunders down from the mountaintop. Just as the great mystics in the Christian, Jewish and Muslim faiths all discovered, God is within the self. God is virtually inseparable from ourselves."

– KAREN ARMSTRONG (1944-)
[British nun turned author, the foremost religious scholar of current century, famous for her book "History of God", winner of the TED prize and the Freedom of Worship award]

"A personalized God can be a mere idol carved in our own image- a projection of our limited needs, fears, and desires. We can assume that he loves what we love and hates what we hate, endorsing our prejudices instead of compelling us to transcend them."

– KAREN ARMSTRONG (1944-)

"A God who kept tinkering with the universe was absurd; a God who interfered with human freedom and creativity was tyrant. If God is seen as a self in a world of his own, an ego that relates to a thou, a cause separate from its effect, "he" becomes a being, not Being itself. An omnipotent, all-knowing tyrant is not so different from earthly dictators who made everything and everybody mere cogs in the machine which they controlled. An atheism that rejects such a God is amply justified. Instead we should seek to find a "god" above this personal God."

— KAREN ARMSTRONG (1944-)

TRIAL OF GOD

In 1944, three erudite and pious rabbis imprisoned at Auschwitz, a Nazi death camp, indicted and tried God for allowing his children to be massacred. After several nights of court proceedings, a unanimous verdict was reached by the rabbis: God was found guilty of crimes against humanity. Nobel Laureate Elie Wiesel, then only sixteen, witnessed the private trial while imprisoned with the rabbis. After announcing the verdict, the members of the tribunal recited the evening prayers, a contradiction that made Wiesel feel like crying. The very next day, all three judges were killed by Nazis, along with several other witnesses.

EVOLUTION OF GOD

God is tried in a court for breaking his covenant with the Jewish people.

More than thirty years later, in 1979, Wiesel published *Trial of God*, a fictional play in which he historically resituates his experience of witnessing the unusual trial at Auschwitz against the backdrop of the 1648-49 massacre of Jewish people in a Ukrainian village. In this play, God is tried for breaking his covenant with the Jewish people and allowing the massacre to happen. A poignant exchange of arguments takes place between Berish, the prosecutor, and Sam, the defense attorney for God:

Berish: You want to leave Him [God] out? Turn Him into a neutral bystander? Would a father stand by quietly, silently, and watch his children being slaughtered?

Sam: By whom? By his other children!

Berish: All right, by his other children! Would he not interfere? Should he not?

Sam: You are using images, let me add mine. When human beings kill one another, where is God to be found? You see Him among the killers. I find Him among the victims.

Berish: He- a victim? A victim is powerless; is He powerless? He is almighty, isn't

He? He could use His might to save the victims, but He doesn't! So- on whose side is He? Could the killer kill without His blessing- without His complicity?

Sam: Are you suggesting that the Almighty is on the side of the killer?

Berish: He is not on the side of the victim.

Sam: How do you know? Who told you?

Berish: The killers told me. They told the victims. They always do. They always say loud and clear that they kill in the name of God.

Sam: Did the victims tell you? (Berish hesitates) No? Then how do you know? Since when do you take the killers' word for granted? Since when do you place your faith in them? They are efficient killers but poor witnesses.

Berish: You would like to hear the victims? So would I. But they do not talk. They cannot come to the witness stand. They're dead. You hear me? The witnesses for the prosecution are the dead. All of them. I could call them, summon them a thousand times, and they would not appear here before you.

Unlike the trial at Auschwitz, the fictional proceedings in Trial of God end without a verdict, despite the emotional power of the prosecutor's final remark:

Berish: I lived as a Jew, and it is as a Jew that I die -- and it is as a Jew that, with my last breath, I shall shout my protest to God! And because the end is near, I shall shout louder! Because the end is near, I'll tell Him that He's more guilty than ever!

Mendel, the wisest of the three judges, declares: "In truth, if I had to pronounce a verdict right now, it would be, I think, influenced by Berish the innkeeper. But we are not going to have enough time for our deliberations. The verdict will be announced by someone else, at a later stage. For the trial will continue – without us."

Professor Matthew Fox, writing the "Afterword" for *Trial of God*, comments that this trial of God is a trial of us, in the sense of what kind of God or gods we worship. He cites the great Christian mystic Meister Eckhart, who used to say "I pray God to rid me of God," and then concluded "In many ways that is what I heard echoed in this trial of God: it was a trial to finally rid ourselves of a God who is too small, who does not live up to the divine nature of compassion and justice."

"The experience of God, or in any case the possibility of experiencing God, is innate."

– ALICE WALKER (1944-)

[American author, famous for her book "Color Purple"]

"There are faces of the divine that must be beyond what we ourselves have glimpsed from our own sheepfold. It is God's transcendence which drives us to find out what others have known of God."

— Diana Eck (1945-)
[American professor of comparative religion and director of the Pluralism Project at Harvard University]

"Encountering God in all God's fullness enables us to see how rich and profound our many theisms really are. Encountering God in this way, we can perhaps move from competitive theism and the strife it has produced to dialogical theism, a deep and searching dialogue in which we all learn from and challenge one another in our understanding of the one we call God."

— Diana Eck (1945-)

"We are close to God when we are close to people."

— Daniel Ortega (1945-)
[Born José Daniel Ortega Saavedra, current (83rd) President of Nicaragua]

"But how much theology is required to observe, for example, that assertions of God's existence suggest the obvious question, Who made God? If he's simply there and needs no explanation, then why not just say that about the world itself rather than multiply mysteries?"

— John Paulos (1945-)
[American university professor of mathematics, author of "Innumeracy" and "Irreligion"]

"God is an artifact of the brain."

— Michael Persinger (1945-)
[American cognitive neuroscience researcher and professor at Laurentian University, Canada]

"The simplest and most basic meaning of the symbol of the Goddess is the acknowledgment of the legitimacy of female power as a beneficent and independent power."

— Carol P. Christ (1945-)
[American teacher and author, famous for writing the widely reprinted essay "Why Women Need Goddess"]

"Time is the brush of God, as he paints his masterpiece on the heart of humanity."

— Ravi Zacharias (1946-)
[Indian born Canadian-American evangelical Christian apologist]

"Today we are learning the language in which God created life. We are gaining ever more awe for the complexity, the beauty, the wonder of God's most divine and sacred gift."

— Bill Clinton (1946-)
[42nd President of the United States from 1992 to 2000]

GOD AND BILLBOARD WARS

In America, Christians have been using large billboards along major highways and streets to advertise God. Atheists put their first billboard up in January, 2008 when they erected a large billboard along Route 95 South, near Ridgefield, New Jersey. It stated: *"Don't believe in God? You are not alone."* Since then, we are witnessing a war of words between theists and atheists as both seek public attention through billboards. A small sample of billboard contents from different states is provided below:

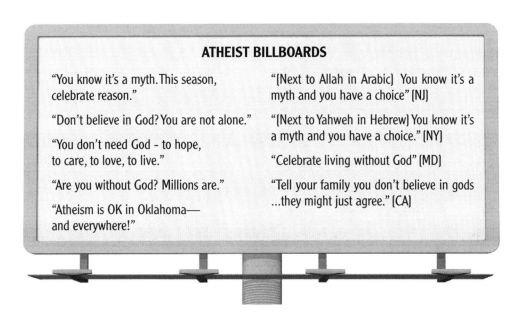

ATHEIST BILLBOARDS

"You know it's a myth. This season, celebrate reason."

"Don't believe in God? You are not alone."

"You don't need God - to hope, to care, to love, to live."

"Are you without God? Millions are."

"Atheism is OK in Oklahoma— and everywhere!"

"[Next to Allah in Arabic] You know it's a myth and you have a choice" [NJ]

"[Next to Yahweh in Hebrew] You know it's a myth and you have a choice." [NY]

"Celebrate living without God" [MD]

"Tell your family you don't believe in gods ...they might just agree." [CA]

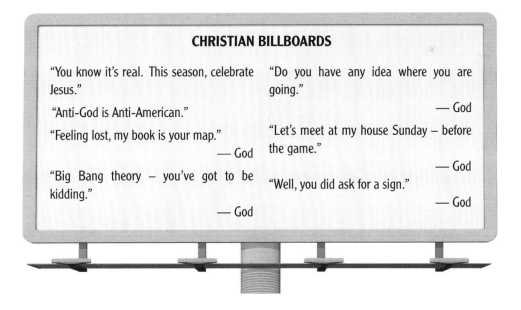

CHRISTIAN BILLBOARDS

"You know it's real. This season, celebrate Jesus."

"Anti-God is Anti-American."

"Feeling lost, my book is your map."
— God

"Big Bang theory – you've got to be kidding."
— God

"Do you have any idea where you are going."
— God

"Let's meet at my house Sunday – before the game."
— God

"Well, you did ask for a sign."
— God

COFFEE BREAK

Do All Religions Worship the Same God?: This is an age-old question. In around 1200 BC, RigVeda (a Hindu scripture) answered the question in this manner: "He is One, though the wise call Him by many names." In the twenty-first century, an American president attempted to answer the same question in his own way. However, his answer, given below, received harsh criticisms from evangelical Christian leaders, who argued that the God of the Bible is the only true God, and not the same as the God of other religions.

"In looking at these major belief systems and their views of God, we find tremendous diversity:

- Hindus acknowledge multitudes of gods and goddesses.
- Buddhists say there is no deity.
- New Age followers believe they are God.
- Muslims believe in a powerful but unknowable God.
- Christians believe in a God who is loving and approachable.

Are all religions worshiping the same God?"

> — MARILYN ADAMSON (20TH CENTURY)
> *[American Christian, ex-atheist]*

EVOLUTION OF GOD

The God of politicians is a convenient being used to promote political agendas.

"Well, first of all, I believe in an Almighty God, and I believe that all the world, whether they be Muslim, Christian, or any other religion, prays to the same God."

> — GEORGE WALKER BUSH (1946-)
> *[43rd President of the United States from 2001 to 2009]*

"I don't see how you can be president at least from my perspective, how you can be president, without a relationship with the Lord."

> — GEORGE WALKER BUSH (1946-)

"The kind of connectedness women's spirituality and goddess spirituality teaches about the earth is missing in politics today and the people who are guiding our countries see only nature as a resource for industrial growth. They don't see the sacredness and the interconnectedness and the simple fact that we live on a finite planet."

> — CHARLENE SPRETNAK (1946-)
> *[American author, activist, and feminist]*

"If God died in the cities of the industrial revolution, he has risen again in the postindustrial cities of the developing world."

> — MIKE DAVIS (1946-)
> *[American social commentator, author, and historian]*

"Describing God as a malicious monster punishing people for their sins is a striking perversion that turns people away from loving Him and hinders their advancement on the spiritual Path."

> — VLADIMIR ANTONOV (1946-)
> *[Russian biologist and spiritual author]*

"I am running for President of the United States to enable the Goddess of Peace to encircle within her arms all the children of this country and all the children of the world."

– DENNIS KUCINICH (1946-)

[Ohio Congressman and a candidate for the Democratic nomination for President in 2004 and 2008]

"God is an abbreviation for Goddess"

– ANONYMOUS

COFFEE BREAK

God Returns: Humans' urge for the infinite transcends their love of rationality, and thus began an era of spiritualism in the mid-twentieth century. By the first decade of the new millennium, God had come back in all spheres of life, from science to politics, and established a strong footing on Earth again.

"Every person is a God in embryo. Its only desire is to be born."

– DEEPAK CHOPRA (1946-)

[Indian-American endocrinologist, lecturer, celebrity and author of books on spirituality and mind-body medicine]

"As soon as we define God we limit God. God is the ultimate mystery that we cannot define. God is our highest potential to know ourselves and the end goal of our seeking…. God is the ultimate revelation that allows us to see every aspect of the Universe as divinity in motion."

– DEEPAK CHOPRA (1946-)

"The spiritual meaning of love is measured by what it can do. Love is meant to heal. Love is meant to renew. Love is meant to bring us closer to God."

– DEEPAK CHOPRA (1946-)

"I'm a religious man. I am Jewish but I believe in all religions. I believe in God and see him as an old man with a big white beard and pray to him every day for a few minutes."

– URI GELLER (1946-)

[Israeli British entertainer]

"Do not blame God for your stupid decisions."

– LAURA SCHLESSINGER (1947-)

[American talk-radio host and author]

"I do not need the idea of God to explain the world I live in."

— SALMAN RUSHDIE (1947-)

[British Indian novelist and essayist. author of the controversial book "Satanic Verses"]

"God gave women intuition and femininity. Used properly, the combination easily jumbles the brain of any man I've ever met."

— FARRAH FAWCETT (1947-2009)

[American actress and artist, famous for "Charlie's Angels" TV series]

"Do you know how cruel your God can be, David. How fantastically cruel? ...Sometimes he makes us live."

— STEPHEN KING (1947-)

[American author, screenwriter, musician, columnist, actor, film producer and director]

"When his life was ruined, his family killed, his farm destroyed, Job knelt down on the ground and yelled up to the heavens, "Why God? Why me?" and the thundering voice of God answered, "There's just something about you that pisses me off."

— STEPHEN KING (1947-)

COFFEE BREAK

Mr. g: The creator God is the storyteller in a profound and provocative 2012 novel entitled *Mr. g*, written by American physicist Alan Lightman. In this novel, God (or Mr. g) tells us how he first created time, space, and matter, followed by the creation of stars, planets, and finally, intelligent beings with moral dilemmas. God, in this novel, is all-powerful but not all-knowing, as he discovers a few things he didn't know during the act of creation. The novel's delightful interplay of faith and science is captivating, as the author presents a cosmic parable of God, the universe, and man. The story of creation, as stated in the novel, begins in this manner:

"As I remember, I had just woken up from a nap when I decided to create the universe. Not much was happening at that time. As a matter of fact, time didn't exist. Nor space. When you looked out into the Void, you were really looking at nothing more than your thought. And if you tried to picture wind or stars or water, you could not give form or texture to your notions. Those things didn't exist."

— ALAN LIGHTMAN (1948-)

[American physicist and author, Professor at Massachusetts Institute of Technology, author of Einstein's Dreams]

"The word God has become empty of meaning through thousands of years of misuse."

— ECKHART TOLLE (1948-)

[Born Ulrich Tolle, German-Canadian spiritual teacher, motivational speaker, and writer]

"Judaism, Christianity, and Islam are religions of revelation – faiths in which God speaks and we attempt to listen."

– RABBI JONATHAN SACKS (1948-)

[Jewish scholar, chief Rabbi of the United Hebrew Congregations of the Commonwealth, author of "Dignity of Difference"]

"In the course of history God has spoken to mankind in many languages: through Judaism to Jews, Christianity to Christians, and Islam to Muslims. Only such a God is truly transcendental – greater not only than the natural universe but also than the spiritual universe articulated in any single faith, any specific language of human sensibility."

– RABBI JONATHAN SACKS (1948-)

COFFEE BREAK

Revisions Due to Criticisms: Rabbi Sacks was severely criticized by some Jewish scholars for putting Judaism, Christianity, and Islam on an equal theological ground. In subsequent editions of his book, *The Dignity of Difference*, he removed the first of the above two quotes entirely and revised the second quote to read: "As Jews we believe that God has made a covenant with a singular people, but that does not exclude the possibility of other peoples, cultures and faiths finding their own relationship with God within the shared frame of the Noahide laws."

"God's promises are like the stars; the darker the night the brighter they shine."

– DAVID NICHOLAS (1950-)

[British historian]

"Maybe God is what you feel
When you stand on a very high mountain
And see a big beautiful view all around you."

– ETAN BORITZER (1950-)

[American author of children's books]

"Arguably, then, it is not God's representation as male that is problematic but our own definitions of male/ness."

– ASMA BARLAS (1950-)

[Pakistani-born American author and professor, writes on equality of women in Islam]

"Clearly, God is a Democrat."

– PATRICK HAYWARD CADDELL (1950-)

[American public opinion pollster and a political film consultant]

"Modernism may be seen as an attempt to reconstruct the world in the absence of God."

-BRIAN APPLEYARDE (1951-)

[British author]

"I mean in a way Obama's standing above the country, above – above the world, he's sort of God."

– EVAN THOMAS (1951-)
[American journalist and author]

"The long sleep of Mother Goddess is ended. May She awaken in each of our hearts — Merry meet, merry part, and blessed be."

– STARHAWK (1951-)
[Born Miriam Simos, American writer, social activist]

"The Goddess religion asserts that the earth is alive, and that everything on the earth is part of a living being. We believe that you can celebrate life in many different images and forms, that life moves in cycles of birth and growth and death and rebirth, and that the same spirit moves through nature, through the cycles of the seasons, through the birth and growth and death of plants and animals, and through our lives as human beings."

– STARHAWK (1951-)

"My findings are agnostic on the existence of God. If there's a God, there's a God. ... Religious believers can point to the existence of God genes as one more sign of the creator's ingenuity—a clever way to help humans acknowledge and embrace a divine presence."

– DEAN HAMER (1951-)
[American geneticist, Director of Gene Structure and Regulation at US National Cancer Institute, famous for his book "The God Gene: How Faith is Hardwired into our Genes."]

COFFEE BREAK

Is Atheism a Religion?: Atheists would vehemently deny such an assertion. There is a lot of commotion in the blogosphere about whether atheists should participate in "interfaith" dialogues, because the word "faith" is a deal-breaker for many atheists. True, atheism is not a religion in the traditional sense. But one can call it a religion by following in the footsteps of Bertrand Russell, an icon among unbelievers worldwide and one of the greatest philosophers of the twentieth century, who labeled "communism" as a religion on the premise that it consisted of a strong set of beliefs, like any other traditional religion.

In 1961, the US Supreme Court ruled in *Torcaso v. Watkins* that secular humanism, an atheistic belief, is a religion: "Among religions in this country which do not teach what would generally be considered a belief in the existence of God are Buddhism, Taoism, Ethical Culture, Secular Humanism and others." In 2005, the United States Seventh Circuit Court of Appeals ruled that Wisconsin prison officials had violated an inmate's rights because they did not treat atheism as a religion. The court stated: "Atheism is [the inmate's] religion, and the group that he wanted to start was religious in nature even though it expressly rejects a belief in a supreme being."

"It is an insult to God to believe in God."

– GALEN JOHN STRAWSON (1952-)
[British philosopher and literary critic]

"Every age reinterprets God with their own metaphor. God doesn't change, but our metaphors do."

– KEVIN KELLY (1952-)
[Founding executive editor of the "Wired" magazine, in response to a question regarding his article entitled "God is the Machine"]

"I hate the word housewife; I don't like the word home-maker either. I want to be called Domestic Goddess."

– ROSEANNE (1952-)
[Roseanne Barr, American actress, comedian, writer, television producer and director]

COFFEE BREAK

God is Popular: In the late twentieth century, God no longer remained a theological topic, reserved for scholars. Instead, the topic of God entered popular culture, and various actors, singers, and politicians expressed their opinions about God.

"Does God know he [exists]?" "Of course he does. Otherwise, you could not have asked the question, and I could not have answered."

– DOUGLAS ADAMS (1952-2001)
[English author and satirist, famous for his "The Hitchhiker's Guide to the Galaxy"]

"I can't stand politicians who wear God on their sleeves."

– TONY BLAIR (1953-)
[British politician, Prime Minister of United Kingdom from 1997 to 2007]

"You can safely assume that you've created God in your own image, when it turns out that God hates all the same people you do."

– ANNE LAMOTT (1954-)
[American author]

"God can dream a bigger dream for you than you can dream for yourself, and your role on Earth is to attach yourself to that divine force and let yourself be released to it."

– OPRAH WINFREY (1954-)
[Celebrated American TV host, actress, media mogul, entrepreneur, and philanthropist]

"We do tend to look at the world and find meaningful patterns and impose on those patterns intentional agency. And so, the intentional agents are things like ghosts and Gods and demons and angels and aliens and so forth. And God is another version of that. It's a projection of what our brain is doing to try to understand and make sense of the world."

— MICHAEL SHERMER (1954-)
[American science writer, author, and founder of The Skeptics Society]

"Schermer's Last Law: Any sufficiently advanced extraterrestrial intelligence is indistinguishable from God."

— MICHAEL SHERMER (1954-)

"Sometimes I think war is God's way of teaching us geography."

— PAUL RODRIGUEZ (1955-)
[Mexican-born American stand-up comedian and actor]

"It sometimes surprises me, although it shouldn't, how religious devotees feel the need to regularly reinforce their own convictions in groups of like-minded individuals. I suppose this is the purpose of regular Sunday church services, for example, to reinforce the community of belief in between the rest of the week when the real world may show no evidence of God, goodness, fairness, or purpose."

— LAWRENCE MAXWELL KRAUSS (1954-)
[Canadian-American Professor of physics, author of best-selling science books]

COFFEE BREAK
Unsure About God: Steve Jobs and Bill Gates, both born in 1955, are the two icons of the late-twentieth-century computer industry. Both of them revolutionized how human beings use computers and other related digital devices, and in the process, both became multi-billionaires. Both are unsure about God.

"I'm about fifty-fifty on believing in God. For most of my life, I have felt that there must be more to our existence than meets the eye."

— STEVE JOBS (1955-2011)
[American inventor and businessman, co-founder and CEO of Appple, widely credited for revolutionizing the personal computer industry]

"If I raise my finger, will God know which one I'm going to raise even before I do it?"

— STEVE JOBS (1955-2011)
[In 1968, while questioning a Pastor after Life magazine published a shocking cover showing a pair of starving children in Biafra]

"Sometimes I believe in God, sometimes I don't. I think it's 50-50 maybe. But ever since I've had cancer, I've been thinking about it more. And I find myself believing a bit more. I kind of – maybe it's 'cause I want to believe in an afterlife. That when you die, it doesn't just all disappear. The wisdom you've accumulated. Somehow it lives on, but sometimes I think it's just like an on-off switch. Click and you're gone. And that's why I don't like putting on-off switches on Apple devices."

– STEVE JOBS (1955-2011)

[Quoted by his biographer Walter Isaacson in an interview with CBS show "60 Minutes" aired on October 23, 2011]

""In terms of doing things I take a fairly scientific approach to why things happen and how they happen. I don't know if there's a god or not, but I think religious principles are quite valid."

– BILL GATES (1955-)

[Co-founder and Chairman of Microsoft, Forbes magazine listed him as the world's richest man for 12 consecutive years. He said this in a PBS interview with David Frost in November, 2005]

COFFEE BREAK

In God We Trust; Everyone Else…: "In God We Trust" has been the official motto of the United States of America since 1956. The phrase appeared on US paper currency for the first time in 1957, although the phrase had been used sporadically on US coins since 1864. In 1970, a US citizen challenged the constitutionality of the motto and its use on currency, citing the First Amendment of the US constitution, which states that "Congress shall make no law respecting an establishment of religion, or prohibiting the free exercise thereof." The US Court of Appeals ruled: "In God We Trust has nothing whatsoever to do with the establishment of religion. Its use is of patriotic or ceremonial character and bears no true resemblance to a governmental sponsorship of a religious exercise." This phrase has given rise to several aphorisms, such as "In God We Trust. Everyone Else Pays Cash," "In God We Trust. Everyone Else Must Bring Data," and "In God We Trust. Everyone Else We Polygraph."

"Adam walked with me in the cool of the day, yet he was lonely. He could not see me or touch me. He could only feel me. So everything I wanted Adam to share and experience with me, I fashioned in you; My holiness, My strength, My purity, My love,

My protection and support. You are special because you are an extension of Me. Man represents my image, Woman my emotions. Together, you represent the totality of God."

– ANONYMOUS
[God's Letter to Women]

"Science can never prove the non-existence of God, just as it can never prove the existence of God."

– DR. LEE RAYFIELD (1955-)
[British lecturer of immunology and current Bishop]

"I think I need a god – but whom to choose?
A raft of deities; I'm sure to lose
My sense in search."

– MARK SLAUGHTER (1957-)
[Biological scientist]

"I think gods arose as illusions, and that the subsequent history of the idea of god is, in some sense, the evolution of an illusion."

– ROBERT WRIGHT (1957-)
[American journalist, scholar, and prize-winning author of best-selling books]

"Though we can no more conceive of God than we can conceive of an electron, believers can ascribe properties to God, somewhat as physicists ascribe properties to electrons... You could say that with electrons, as with God, there are believers and there are skeptics. "

– ROBERT WRIGHT (1957-)

COFFEE BREAK
Intolerance at Its Worst: Osama bin Laden, a Muslim radical, invokes God to spread terrorism.

"Hostility toward America is a religious duty, and we hope to be rewarded for it by God . . . I am confident that Muslims will be able to end the legend of the so-called superpower that is America."

– OSAMA BIN LADEN (1957-2011)
[Notorious terrorist, founder of the terrorist organization, Al-Qaeda, known for masterminding the September 11, 2001 attacks on America]

"We--with God's help--call on every Muslim who believes in God and wishes to be rewarded to comply with God's order to kill the Americans and plunder their money wherever and whenever they find it."

– OSAMA BIN LADEN (1957-2011)
[Bin Laden edict (Fatwa)]

"What's "God"? Well, you know, when you want something really bad and you close your eyes and you wish for it? God's the guy that ignores you."

— STEVE BUSCEMI (1957-)
[American actor, writer, and film director]

COFFEE BREAK

Michael and Madonna: Two of the greatest pop-singers of the twentieth century, Michael Jackson and Madonna, were both born in August of 1958—Madonna on August 16 in Michigan and Jackson on August 29 in Indiana.

"I try to be kind and generous and to give to people and to do what I think God wants me to do. Sometimes I pray and say "where do you want me to go next, God? What do you want me to do from here?" I've always been very spiritual in that way. It's nothing new."

— MICHAEL JACKSON (1958-2009)
[American singer and entertainer, perhaps the most famous global singer ever to have lived, known as the King of Pop, recognized as the most successful artist of all time by the Guinness Book of World Records]

"We are all a part of God's great big family
And the truth, you know,
Love is all we need."

— MICHAEL JACKSON (1958-2009)

"When in doubt, act like god."

— MADONNA (1958-)
[Born Madonna Louise Ciccone, American pop singer-songwriter, dancer, actress, and a fashion icon, called "Queen of Pop"]

"If God was a woman
With long blond hair
Would you kneel at her altar
And offer her prayer."

— RICHIE SAMBORA (1959-)
[American musician, singer/song writer, lead guitarist for rock band Bon Jovi]

"My God and my Christ is a tolerant God, and that's what we want to see in this world."

— STEPHEN HARPER (1959-)

[Canadian Prime Minister and leader of the Conservative Party, in response to Quran burning by Florida pastor]

COFFEE BREAK
Intolerance at Its Worst: Randall Terry, a Christian radical, preaches hatred and intolerance in God's name.

"I want you to just let a wave of intolerance wash over you. I want you to let a wave of hatred wash over you. Yes, hate is good. ... Our goal is a Christian nation. We have a Biblical duty, we are called by God, to conquer this country. We don't want equal time. We don't want pluralism."

— RANDALL TERRY (1959-)
[American conservative religious activist, founder of pro-life organization Operation Rescue]

"The more I listened to what they had to say about the 'Great Bearded White Man in the Sky' the more I realized that he was no one I could talk to. You couldn't say nothing to the 'dude'. He didn't answer prayers. He could 'go off' on you at any minute and you were supposed to be grateful no matter what he did. This is nobody who made any kind of sense to me in my naiveity. So I put him down and hung with Mary [the mother of God]."

— LUISAH TEISH (20TH CENTURY)
[Amrican author, story teller, and priestess, author of several books on African religion]

"God the unmanifest is less than nothing and at the same time more than everything. He is less than zero and simultaneously greater than infinity. Whatever attribute we ascribe to him is wrong, and whatever attribute we deny him is equally wrong."

— BERNARD HAISCH (20TH CENTURY)
[German born American astrophysicist]

"I pray hard, work hard, and leave the rest to God."

— FLORENCE GRIFFITH JOYNER (1959-1998)
[African American track and field athlete, holds the world record for 100 meters and 200 meters races for woman]

"I often wonder if religion is the enemy of God. It's almost like religion is what happens when the Spirit has left the building."

— BONO (1960-)
[Born Paul Hewson, Lead singer of the famous Irish rock band U2 and the most famous rock star in the world, an activist and a contributing columnist for the New York Times]

"Could it be that God is a nerd?"

— BONO (1960-)

"A little with the head of Maradona and a little with the hand of God"

— DIEGO MARADONA (1960-)

[Argentine soccer player, considered to be one of the greatest soccer player of all time, speaking of a controversial World Cup goal against England, where Maradona used his hand illegally]

"We are at a point in history when a new view of God is needed again, and many of the emerging believers might be rejected by their fellow believers as atheists. Yet this state of affairs, this betrayal of religion, can be a source of hope. Perhaps we will, as Meister Eckhart suggested, forsake God for the sake of God. And perhaps many of us will be able to exit our religious boxes and meet atheists who have exited theirs. And find ourselves in a new open space."

— SAMIR SELMANOVIC (1960-)

[Yugoslav American Christian minister and founder of "Faith House Manhattan" an interfaith group]

"God does not have an ego that can be wounded by our disbelief about God's existence."

— SAMIR SELMANOVIC (1960-)

"I want to argue that God has a proper place in the speculative thought of the future. That place is not in religion or philosophy. It is in science fiction."

— BART KOSKO (1960-)

[American professor of electrical engineering at the University of Southern California– and author of "Fuzzy Thinking"]

"The basic tenet of liberalism is that nature is god and men are monkeys."

— ANN COULTER (1961-)

[American conservative columnist, author, and lawyer, author of "Godless: the Church of Liberalism"]

"God is a girl

Wherever you are

Do you believe it

Can you receive it.

God is a girl

Whatever you say

Do you believe it

Can you receive it"

[LYRICS OF SONG "GOD IS A GIRL" RELEASED IN 2002 BY GERMAN EURO-TRANCE BAND GROOVE COVERAGE]

"Some of God's greatest gifts are unanswered prayers."

— GARTH BROOKS (1962-)

[American country music singer and songwriter]

GOD AND A COMEDY WRITER

David Javerbaum is a comedy writer and former executive producer of The Daily Show with John Stewart. He has won twelve Emmy awards and is the co-author of two bestselling humor books. In 2011, he published a book entitled *"The Last Testament: A Memoir by God."* The book's description reads: "Over the course of his long and distinguished career, god has literally seen it all. And not just seen. In fact, the multi-talented deity has played a pivotal role in many major events, including the Creation of the universe, the entirety of world history, the life of every human being who has ever lived, and the successful transitioning of American Idol into the post–Simon Cowell era. Now, as the earth he has godded so magnificently draws to a Mayan-induced close, God breaks his 1,400-year literary silence with his final masterpiece, The Last Testament."

Here is an excerpt from Chapter 1, illustrating the satirical nature of the book.

1. In the beginning, God created the heavens and the earth.

2. Yea; that takes me back.

3. Back to the first day of creation; the day when, in a sense, it all began for me;

4. The day I tossed aside the idleness of my early eons, to take on the honor, responsibility, and privilege of being the LORD thy God, King of the Universe.

5. I remember that day like it was yesterday, though to be sure it was not yesterday; rather it was ages ago, across an unfathomable sea of time whose meagerest inlet exceeds the ken of human understanding.

6. It was October 23, 4004 B.C.

7. But before I speak of that day, and that week, and all the laughter and tears and tragedy and triumph that followed; let me pause at the beginning of this, my last testament, to tell thee a little about myself.

8. I am Omnipotent, Omniscient, All-Merciful, All-Powerful, All-Informed, All-Possessing, All-Compelling, All-Subduing, Most Holy, Most High, and Most Powerful.

9. My hobbies include being Sovereign LORD, Heavenly Ordainer, Day-star of Eternal Guidance, Tabernacle of Majesty, Quintessence of Glory, Hand of Divine Power, Tongue of Grandeur, and Eye of Splendor.

10. And in the interest of full disclosure, I must also confess that I have on occasion been known to dabble in being the Desire of the World, the Source of Everlasting Life, the Sovereign Protector, and the Wellspring of Infinite Grace.

11. With all these qualities, and many more—for another of my qualities is being infinitely qualitied—people have often wondered why it was I created the universe, when I could have remained content simply to hover alone as pure spirit contemplating my own divinity.

12. Because that's not godding, that's why.

13. In my humble opinion, thou canst hardly call thyself the LORD, if thou hast created no other beings to LORD it over.

"I'm an atheist. But I absolutely love religions and the rituals. Even though I don't believe in God, we celebrate pretty much every religion in our family with the kids. They love it."

– JODY FOSTER (1962-)
[American actress, film director, and producer. Received Oscar for Best Actress twice]

"America has succeeded in putting God back in modernity partly because it put modernity, or at least choice and competition, back into God."

– JOHN MICKLETHWAIT (1962-)
[British journalist who wrote the book "God is Back" with co-author Adrian Wooldridge]

"The Founding Father's clever compromise over religion not only allowed God to survive and prosper in America, it also provided a way of living with religion – of ensuring that different faiths can coexist, and of taming a passion that so often turns the religious beast to savagery."

– JOHN MICKLETHWAIT (1962-)

"God is that part of us that cares for a child that is starving in another country."

– COLLEEN PING (AGE 25), A MOTHER FROM NEW JERSEY
[quoted in Sullivan (1990)]

"I can't embrace a male god who has persecuted female sexuality throughout the ages. And that persecution still goes on today all over the world."

– AMANDA DONOHUE (1962-)
[British actress]

"If God had a name, what would it be

And would you call it to his face

If you were faced with him in all his glory

What would you ask if you had just one question

……..

What if God was one of us

Just a slob like one of us

Just a stranger on the bus

Trying to make his way home."

— JOAN OSBOURNE (1962-)
[American blues singer and songwriter, famous for her song "One of Us"]

"See I can run, Lord you know I will

When there is nowhere to go I know I can go to you

I know I can run to you oh

I'll hasten, I'll hasten to his, his throne."

— WHITNEY HOUSTON (1963-2012)
[American singer and actress, one of world's best-selling music artists]

"God isn't calling us to a lonely, joyless existence with the promise of a delayed reward."

— JOHN POWELL (1963-)
[English film score composer, based in Los Angeles]

"Considering the size of the universe, we might conclude that God likes to exaggerate!"

— MEHMET MURAT ILDAN (1965-)
[Turkish playwright and novelist]

"Religion is not a bridge between God and Man; it is a Great Wall of China between them!"

— MEHMET MURAT ILDAN (1965-)

There are two gods in this universe: God and Imagination. Both of them can design and create infinite creations."

— MEHMET MURAT ILDAN (1965-)

"God has a sense of humor. If you don't believe me, tomorrow go to Wal-mart and just look at people."

— CARLOS MENCIA (1967-)
[Ned Arnel Mencía, American comedian, writer, and actor]

"God is not to be found "out there" but deep within existence."

— JEFFREY SMALL (20TH CENTURY)
[American lawyer, author, speaker]

"The traditional view of God leads to the philosophical problems caused by the existence of evil, the reality of human suffering, and the multiple religions around the world with opposing doctrines about God. How can such a God be omniscient, omnipotent, and loving at the same time?"

— Jeffrey Small (20th century)

"Within the heart of the Goddess, God rests and dreams. She is the miracle and magic of life. She comes to help you fulfill your dreams."

— Toni Carmine Salerno (20th century)
[American intuitive artist and author]

COFFEE BREAK

What's in the Numbers?: Adherents of different religions claim (or have claimed in the past) theirs to be the fastest growing religion. Rising numbers could be due to higher birth rates or conversions or both. However, do such claims mean anything? It is interesting to note that even atheists take pride in claiming that their numbers are growing, as if the "truth" depends on its popularity.

"God may be quite mysterious, but if god is completely mysterious for humans, then a person's belief has nothing to aim at, nothing to believe in, even if this person really wants to believe."

— John Shook (20th century)
[American professor, author]

"Contemplative Prayer immerses us into the silence of God. How desperately we in the modern world need this wordless baptism! Progress in intimacy with God means progress toward silence."

— Richard Foster (20th century)
[American theologian, author in Quaker tradition]

"I'm not against God. I'm against the misuse of God."

— Marilyn Manson (1969-)
[Born Brian Hugh Warner, American musician, artist, and lead singer]

"God is everywhere in U.S. culture."

— Dan Harris (1971-)
[American journalist, co-anchor of ABC's "Good Morning America" show]

"God is a woman. No discussion, no debate, no denial. She's a woman. That people challenge this notion is ridiculous. The proof is all around. If God were a man, He'd be the only one. There would not be another man anywhere. The entire planet would be full of no one but beautiful women."

— Ian Coburn (1971-)
[American comedian, famous for his book "God is a Woman: Dating Disasters"]

GOD AND THE HOLOCAUST

"I believe in the sun when it is not shining.

I believe in love even when feeling it not.

I believe in God even when He is silent."

> — [ANONYMOUS INSCRIPTION ON A CELLAR WALL WHERE
> SEVERAL JEWS WERE HIDING DURING THE HOLOCAUST]

EVOLUTION OF GOD

God disappoints the Jewish people.

Did God die at Auschwitz? Where was He when millions of Jews were burned alive by the Nazis? Failing to answer these poignant questions, many Jews lost faith in an omnipotent and omnibenevolent God after the Holocaust. This disillusion gave rise to Holocaust Theology, which refers to a body of literature and an intense debate about the role of God and the problem of evil, manifested in gigantic proportions in the genocide of six million Jews by the Nazis during the 1930s and 1940s. A few postings on the *Wall of Mortals* are provided below, not in chronological order because order is irrelevant for wounded hearts.

"Behind me, I heard the same man asking: "Where is God now?" And I heard a voice within me answer him: "Where is He? Here He is—He is hanging here on this gallows."

> — ELIE WIESEL (1928-)
> *[Passage from Night, Elie Wiesel's autobiographical depiction of his harrowing experience at the Auschwitz concentration camp when he was forced to watch the death by hanging of a Jewish child. Many readers concluded that God died at the Auschwitz gallows with this child.]*

"Auschwitz casts a black pall upon the civilized world. Not only is man's humanity put under a question mark, but God himself stands accused. Jews are asking insistently: Where was God when our brothers and sisters were dragged to the gas ovens?"

> — JAKOB JOCZ (1906-1983)
> *[Lithuanian-born Canadian professor of theology and influential writer]*

"Of one thing I am convinced: more than the bodies of my people went up in smoke at Auschwitz. The God of the covenant died there."

> — RICHARD RUBINSTEIN (1924-)
> *[American rabbi, theologian, and professor, credited for Holocaust Theology]*

"No man can really say that God is dead. How can we know that? Nevertheless, I am compelled to say that we live in the time of the 'death-of-God'.... When I say we live in the time of the death of God, I mean that the thread uniting God and man, heaven and earth, has been broken. We stand in a cold, silent, unfeeling cosmos, unaided by any purposeful power beyond our own resources. After Auschwitz, what else can a Jew say about God?"

> — RICHARD RUBINSTEIN (1924-)

Milton Teichman and Sharon Leder's anthology Truth and Lamentations: Stories and Poems on the Holocaust (1993) "reveals the human faces hidden behind the all-too-familiar statistics of the event." Excerpts from two poignant poems in this anthology depict the sadness and anger of the Jewish people.

"O God of Mercy
For the time being
Choose another people.
We are tired of death, tired of corpses.
We have no prayers.
For the time being
Choose another people."

— KADYA MOLODOVSKY (1894-1974-)
[Russian-born American poet and short story writer]

"You have no God in you! Open the doors, you heavens, fling them open wide,
And let the children of my murdered people enter in a stream.
Open the doors up for the great procession of the crucified,
The children of my people, all of them, each one a God – make room!"

— SIMCHA BUNIM SHAYEVITSH (1907-1945)
[Yiddish poet and story-teller, perished in Auschwitz, shortly before liberation]

Simon Friedeman, a Holocaust survivor, wrote: "I cannot conceive of God being capable of performing miracles and refraining from doing it. I could not worship a God capable of preventing the horrors in the Nazi death campus Who did not act." Rabbi David Wolf Silverman sought the answer in God's attributes and wrote: "The Holocaust has, I think, dismissed any easy use of omnipotence as an attribute appropriate to God. After Auschwitz, He can assert with greater force than ever before that an omnipotent God would have to be either sadistic or totally unintelligible. . . .The Holocaust disclosed the depths to which man had sunk and the degree to which God withdrew."

With the passage of time, the majority of the Jewish people were able to overcome this disappointment with God. Elie Wiesel best presented how he resolved this Jewish dilemma about faith in an omnipotent and omniscient God, in a television interview:

"For a Jew to believe in God is good. For a Jew to protest against God is still good. But simply to ignore God--that is not good. Anger, yes. Protest, yes. Affirmation, yes. But indifference? No. You can be a Jew with God. You can be a Jew against God. But not without God."

"The God Formula: Through a dual process of eradicating the ego and performing transformative sharing, we awaken our true nature and become like God, creating a life of total joy and fulfillment."

— Michael Berg (1973-)
[Ordained Rabbi, Kabbalah scholar, and noted spiritual leader]

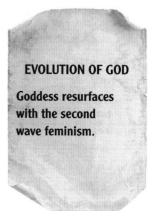

EVOLUTION OF GOD

Goddess resurfaces with the second wave feminism.

"For the people who believe in it, I hope so. There doesn't need to be a God for me."

— Angelina Jolie (1975-)
[American actress, received Oscar for Best Supporting Actress]

"In the Holy Qur'an there is a line that God made us different nations and tribes that we may come to know one another."

— Eboo Patel (1975-)
[American Muslim, interfaith leader, founder of Interfaith Youth Core (IFYC)]

"Modern, organized Humanism began, in the minds of its founders as nothing more nor less than a religion without a God."

— Greg Epstein (1977-)
[Current secular humanist chaplin at Harvard University]

"God is a philosophical black hole – the point where reason breaks down."

— Kedar Joshi (1979-)
[Indian philosopher and writer]

COFFEE BREAK

God Appears in a Movie: In a movie scene, God appears as a witness in a US court and declares: "If it please the court, and even if it doesn't please the court, I'm God, your honor." This is the plot of a 1977 comedy film titled *Oh, God!*

In the movie, God asks an aged supermarket manager to become his messenger to the modern world, as if he is a contemporary prophet. Theologians vehemently attack the supermarket manager, and ultimately a preacher sues him for slander. So, the supermarket manager tells the judge that he is calling God to the witness stand. The judge threatens him with contempt of court but to everyone's surprise, God actually appears in the court to defend the supermarket manager.

God gets sworn in, but replaces the last word of the procedural oath, "So help me God," with, "So help me Me." God plays some tricks and performs some miracles in the court, then disappears with the following parting words:

"It can work. Don't hurt each other. If it's hard to have faith in me, maybe it will help to know that I have faith in you."

— GOD IN THE MOVIE OH, GOD!

[The film, Oh God, was based on a novel by American novelist Avery Corman (1935-) and the screenplay was written by Larry Gelbart (1928-2009). The role of God was played by famous American comedian, actor, and writer George Burns (1896-1996), born Nathan Birnbaum]

"I asked God to take away my habit.

God said, No.

It is not for me to take away, but for you to give it up.

I asked God to make my handicapped child whole.

God said, No.

His spirit is whole, his body is only temporary.

......

I asked God to give me happiness.

God said, No.

I give you blessings; Happiness is up to you.

....

I asked God for all things that I might enjoy life.

God said, No.

I will give you life, so that you may enjoy all things."

— JOANNE GOBURE (1982-)
[Poet from the Pacific nation of Nauru]

"I said 'God it hurts'
And God said 'I Know'
I said 'God I cry alot'
And God said 'That's why I gave you tears'
I said 'God I get so depressed'
And God said 'That why I gave you sunshine'
I said god I feel Alone'
And god said 'That's why I gave you loved ones'."

— AMY LOUISE KERSWELL (1987-)
[A twentieth century poet who published on the internet]

"At this season of the Winter Solstice may reason prevail. There are no gods, no devils, no angels, no heaven or hell. There is only our natural world. Religion is but myth and superstition that hardens hearts and enslaves minds"

— A large poster board sign maintained by
Freedom From Religion Foundation (formed in 1976)
in Wisconsin State Capitol during the Christmas season.

"Elvis is GOD!"

— "MR. RABBITTE" IN THE COMMITMENTS (1991)

"I believe in God; I just don't trust anyone who works for him."

—ANONYMOUS, FROM A STAND-UP COMEDY ROUTINE ON TELEVISION

"Deep down in every man, woman, and child, is the fundamental idea of God."

— ANONYMOUS

"Doubt cries, "It is impossible! You can't, you can't go on!"
Faith softly whispers, "Yes, you can. Just trust in God. Be Calm."
Doubt cries, "Look down! Your path is steep And rough with stones and briar!"

Faith gently says, "I'll take your hand. It's beautiful up higher."

Doubt has not one thing to give But "going back" alone;

Faith has God, eternal life, And heirship to a throne!

And so, on unseen eagle's wings,

These feet of clay are borne.

While faith within me sings and sings,

We rise above the storm!"

— ALICE HANSCHE MORTENSON (20TH CENTURY)
[Christian author]

HUMANIST MANIFESTOS AND GOD

Humanist Manifesto I was published in 1933. It announced itself as a new religion, replacing the old religions based on revelations and deities. It declared: "Religious humanists regard the universe as self-existing and not created." Forty years later, in 1973, *Humanist Manifesto II* was published and took an even more aggressive stance on God. This version made two strong assertions, among others:

"As in 1933, humanists still believe that traditional theism, especially faith in the prayer-hearing God, assumed to live and care for persons, to hear and understand their prayers, and to be able to do something about them, is an unproved and outmoded faith."

and

"We believe, however, that traditional dogmatic or authoritarian religions that place revelation, God, ritual, or creed above human needs and experience do a disservice to the human species."

Thirty years later, in 2003, *Humanist Manifesto III* was published. The words "God" and "religion" did not appear in it. This manifesto was signed by twenty-one Nobel laureates. The central message of this manifesto was captured in the first two sentences: "Humanism is a progressive philosophy of life that, without supernaturalism, affirms our ability and responsibility to lead ethical lives of personal fulfillment that aspire to the greater good of humanity. The lifestance of Humanism—guided by reason, inspired by compassion, and informed by experience—encourages us to live life well and fully."

"There are two kinds of directors in the theater. Those who think they are God and those who are certain of it."

— Rhetta Hughes (late 20th century)
[American Rhythm and Blues singer and actress]

"I asked for strength.
God gave me difficulties to make me strong.
I asked for wisdom.
God gave me problems to solve.
I asked for prosperity.
God gave me brawn and brain to work.
I asked for courage.
God gave me dangers to overcome.
I asked for patience.
God placed me in situations where I was forced to wait.
I asked for love.
God gave me troubled people to help.
I asked for favors.
God gave me opportunities.
I received nothing I wanted.
I received everything I needed.
Today is the last day of your
life........so far."

— Anonymous

"God is not dead but alive and well and, working on a much less ambitious project."

— Anonymous

"You can tell the size of your God by looking at the size of your worry list. The longer your list, the smaller your God."

—Anonymous

"Don't question God, for He may reply: 'If you're so anxious for answers, come up here.'"

— Anonymous

"Every evening I turn my worries over to God. He's going to be up all night anyway."

— Anonymous

"The dog is the only animal that has seen his god."

— Anonymous

"Sure God created man before woman, but then you always make a rough draft before the final masterpiece."

— Anonymous

COFFEE BREAK

Book Burning Continues: On January 14, 1989, about a thousand conservative Muslim protesters burned The Satanic Verses of Salman Rushdie in the streets of Bradford, England. On December 30, 2001, Harry Potter books were burned by the Christ Community Church of Alamogordo, New Mexico. In August 2003, the Jesus Non-denominational Church in Greenville, Michigan, also burned Harry Potter books.

In March 2001, CNN reported that 200 right-wing Hindus had burned the Quran in India to protest the destruction of ancient Buddhist statues in Afghanistan by Muslim fundamentalists. In November of 2007, a group of conservative Hindu activists burned anti-Hindu books on display at a book fair organized by the National Book Trust of India.

In Switzerland, two Hindu fundamentalists were arrested in November of 2010 for their attempt to burn the Bible and the Quran by invoking Agni, the Hindu God of fire.

Terry Jones, a conservative Christian pastor from Florida, held a trial of the Quran on March 20, 2011 and burned a copy of the Quran on church premises in Gainesville, Florida, as part of carrying out the "one-judge-panel" verdict.

"Every burned book enlightens the world."

— RALPH WALDO EMERSON (1803–1882)

"Maybe the atheist cannot find God for the same reason a thief cannot find a policeman."

— ANONYMOUS

"A dog thinks: Hey, these people I live with feed me, love me, provide me with a nice warm, dry house, pet me, and take good care of me. . . . They must be Gods! A cat thinks: Hey, these people I live with feed me, love me, provide me with a nice warm, dry house, pet me, and take good care of me. . . . I must be a God!"

— ANONYMOUS

"God is too big to fit into one religion."

— ANONYMOUS

"Friends are God's way of apologizing to us for our families."

— ANONYMOUS

"Death is God's way of saying you're fired. Suicide is humans way of saying you can't fire me, I quit."

— ANONYMOUS

COFFEE BREAK

Lawsuit Against God: In 2007, Nebraska Democratic State Senator Ernie Chambers (1937-) filed a lawsuit against God in Douglas County Court, seeking a permanent injunction ordering God to "cease certain harmful activities and the making of terroristic threats...of grave harm to innumerable persons, including constituents of Plaintiff [Senator Chambers] who Plaintiff has the duty to represent." Senator Chambers accused "defendant [God] directly and proximately has caused, inter alia, fearsome floods, egregious earthquakes, horrendous hurricanes, terrifying tornados, pestilential plagues."

Chambers' lawsuit against God was initially motivated by his desire to draw attention to the situation of courts being required to hear frivolous cases. But his lawsuit took on a life of its own when he claimed that it was in response to bills trying to stop lawsuits being filed. He said "The Constitution requires that the courthouse doors be open, so you cannot prohibit the filing of suits. Anyone can sue anyone they choose, even God."

A judge threw out the case because God was not properly served, since His home address is unlisted. Senator Chambers filed an appeal to the Nebraska Supreme Court arguing that "the court itself acknowledges the existence of God. A consequence of that acknowledgment is a recognition of God's omniscience. Since God knows everything, God has notice of this lawsuit."

The case was finally closed in 2009 by the Nebraska Court of Appeals stating that "[a] court decides real controversies and determines rights actually controverted."

"Oh foolish man that he was, to search for
God with the eyes of his mind;
When He was forever with him, when seen
through the eyes of his soul."

– DANIEL J. MILLER
[20th century mystic and author]

"GOD" is most accurately defined as the personification of ignorance, representing everything that we do not yet understand."

– KENNETH MARSALEK (20TH CENTURY)
[President of Washington Area Secular Humanists]

EVOLUTION OF GOD

The God of twentieth century tolerates blasphemy, ridicule, and lawsuits.

"Many atheists are quite religious, holding their views about God with the conviction of zealots and evangelizing with verve."

– STEPHEN PROTHERO (20TH CENTURY)
[American professor of religion and author]

"Because God is beyond human imagining, we are forever groping around for God in the dark. It is foolish to say that your religion alone is true and all other religions are false."

– STEPHEN PROTHERO (20TH CENTURY)

THE MAN WHO SUED GOD

The Man Who Sued God is a 2001 Australian comedy film that reached the top spot on its opening weekend, with a box office earning of A$1.1 million. The plot of the movie goes like this: Lawyer Steve Myers (played by comedian Billy Connolly) quits the glitzy life after losing his job, his marriage, and all his possessions, and becomes a fisherman, seeking a quieter existence. Unfortunately, one day his boat is destroyed by a lightning strike. He files a claim with his insurance agency, which declines to pay, declaring the incident an "act of God" and invoking an exclusion clause of the insurance policy. Steve files a suit against God, naming Church officials as God's representatives and therefore the respondents in his case. The religious leaders face a major dilemma: if they admit that the destruction of Steve's boat was actually an "act of God," then they, as God's representatives, need to compensate Steve; alternatively, they can say it was not an "act of God" and thereby deny God's existence, an ironic situation in which religious leaders have to deny God's existence to win the case.

EVOLUTION OF GOD

God is sued for "Act of God."

During the lengthy court proceedings, Steve finds new love with a journalist who is covering this "trial of the century." Finally, he withdraws the case. The final scene of the movie is quite revealing:

– "Your Honour, I'm withdrawing from the case.

– What? He can't do that.

– Yes, he can. But he'd better explain.

– I brought an action against someone who doesn't exist. The defendant does not exist?

– What about these characters?

– If God doesn't exist, they don't exist as his representatives. The God of the 'Act of God' does not exist. Not one person in this courtroom has been prepared to say that he does. It's a lie that they use to rob decent, honorable people, the kind of people who have joined me in this action. There's something else. If God exists, I don't think he sits around sinking people's little boats, I don't think he causes earthquakes and landslides, or dreams up ways to make people's brakes fail. If there is a God, surely he is everywhere. He's in everything. He's even in this courtroom…. Maybe you were right. My boat was a tiny little speck of dust in the great scheme of things. Losing it was nothing. Let's say God did sink my boat. How can I sue God for an act that led me to this woman? For an act of love.

– Mr. Myers did more than prove that the insurers god is a false one....He has withdrawn his case, but he's made his point indelibly.

– Your Honour, the case is, with the greatest respect, the case was against the churches.

– Yes. And they will have to consider their position.

.....

– I said to Sam, you want to win this case you've got to prove God does not exist. That's easier said than done. I saw an article which said they'll soon be able to, apparently.

– A science magazine?

– No, Presbyterian Monthly.

– It's a question of faith. Either you believe He doesn't exist, or you don't."

"An open, tolerant, infinitely interpretable, transforming God that, to my mind, is the only God who can save us from ourselves. All other so-called "Gods", national Gods, Gods of certain religions and peoples, are in danger of becoming idols.... The idol Gods of tribes, nations, and religions are divisive and potentially destructive, unless they are seen as manifestations of a single essentially unknowable God, a God who is subject to interpretation, transformation and emendation; who is the province of all and who embraces all peoples, cultures, species, and ideas."

— SANFORD DROB (20TH CENTURY)
[American philosopher, clinical psychologist, and theological writer]

"We are all born with a belief in God."

— KENT NERBURN (20TH CENTURY)
[American author]

"If triangles had a God, He'd have three sides."

— OLD YIDDISH PROVERB

"The grace of God is a wind which is always blowing."

— ANONYMOUS

"God may not play dice with the Universe, but we're not Gods so we have to keep rolling the dice until we get it right."

— RALPHIE FRANK (20TH CENTURY)
[New York based business activist]

"A lot of people are willing to give God credit, but so few ever give Him cash."
– Robert E. Harris (20th century)
[Laugh with the Circuit Rider]

"Anything that surpasses explanations of human agency gets covered by the gods."
– Kelley L. Ross (20th century)
[Teacher at Los Angeles Valley College, CA, USA]

COFFEE BREAK
"God is a Myth": On Saturday, March 24, 2012, a unique event took place on American soil, on the lawn in front of the National Mall, Washington, D.C. It was the first Reason Rally, described on the organizers' website as "a national gathering of nonreligious Americans to celebrate secular values." More than 20,000 people gathered in a show of unity to denounce discrimination against non-believers. According toa recent Pew survey, about 16% of Americans are currently not affiliated with any particular religion.

The rally was touted as the largest ever gathering of non-believers in one place. The weather was inclement—but people stood in the open space, in steady and sometimes heavy rain, to listen to writers, singers, activists, and comedians. In the Lincoln Tunnel, a large billboard was erected to promote the event: "Celebrate living without God." Dave Silverman, president of the *American Atheists*, announced at the rally, "God is a myth. Closet atheists, you are not alone." The crowd chanted: "We're here. We're godless—get used to it."

GOD IN THE WHITE HOUSE

The President of the United States has often been described, correctly or incorrectly, as the most powerful person on Earth. Despite their almost almighty position, US presidents seek the help of God by voluntarily adding the phrase "So help me God" at the end of the constitutionally mandated presidential oath. The personal religious beliefs of the Presidents are a matter of curiosity for many. A few of the presidents are quoted below, while others are quoted elsewhere in this book.

"Whereas it is the duty of all Nations to acknowledge the providence of Almighty God, to obey his will, to be grateful for his benefits, and humbly to implore his protection and favor-- and whereas both Houses of Congress have by their joint Committee requested me to recommend to the People of the United States a day of public thanksgiving and prayer to be observed by acknowledging with grateful hearts the many signal favors of Almighty God especially by affording them an opportunity peaceably to establish a form of government for their safety and happiness."
—George Washington (1732-1799)
[Thanksgiving Proclamation, October 3, 1789]

"God created us in such a way that we can make our religious choices. Who is the state to tell us something that God chose not to tell us?"
—THOMAS JEFFERSON (1743-1826)

"The will of God prevails. In great contests, each party claims to act in accordance with the will of God. Both may be, and one must be wrong. God cannot be for and against the same thing at the same time."
— ABRAHAM LINCOLN (1809-1865)
[US President from 1861-1865]

"We are fighting, as our fathers have fought, to uphold the doctrine that all men are equal in the sight of God."
— FRANKLIN D. ROOSEVELT (1882-1945)
[US President from 1933-1945]

"I believe in an America that is officially neither Catholic, Protestant nor Jewish -- where no public official either requests or accepts instructions on public policy from the Pope, the National Council of Churches or any other ecclesiastical source -- where no religious body seeks to impose its will directly or indirectly upon the general populace or the public acts of its officials -- and where religious liberty is so indivisible that an act against one church is treated as an act against all."
— JOHN F. KENNEDY (1917-1963)
[US President from 1961-1963]

"I still believe that God is the creator. ... I still believe that He lives today, in some form, directing the destinies of the cosmos. ... For the time being I shall accept the solution offered by Kant, that man can only go so far in his research and explanations; from that point on we must accept God."
— RICHARD NIXON (1913-1994)
[US President from 1969-1974]

"I have always felt a closeness to God and have looked to a higher being for guidance and support, but I didn't think it was appropriate to advertise my religious beliefs."
— GERALD FORD (1913-2006)
[US President from 1974-1977]

"God knew I needed a nudge. God wanted that assassination attempt to happen. He gave me a wake-up call. Everything I do from now on, I owe to God."
— RONALD REAGAN (1911-2004)
[US President from 1981-1989]

"I think Lincoln was right: you can't be president without spending some time on your knees professing your faith and asking God for strength, and to save our nation. But I believe strongly in the separation of church and state."

— GEORGE H. W. BUSH (1924-)
[US President from 1989-1993]

"My faith tells me that all of us are sinners, and each of us has gone in our own way and fallen short of the glory of God."

— BILL CLINTON (1946-)
[US President from 1993-2001]

"Freedom and fear, justice and cruelty have always been at war; and we know that God is not neutral between them."

— GEORGE W. BUSH (1946-)
[US President from 2001-2009]

"I may be opposed to abortion for religious reasons, but if I seek to pass a law banning the practice, I cannot simply point to the teachings of my church or evoke God's will. I have to explain why abortion violates some principle that is accessible to people of all faiths, including those with no faith at all."

— BARACK OBAMA (1961-)
[US President from 2009-]

INTERFAITH DIALOGUES

Interfaith dialogues are as old as ancient religions and have helped neighbors live in peace, however temporary that may be. Hans Kung (1928–), a Swiss Catholic priest and prolific author, once said: "There will be no peace among the nations without peace among the religions. There will be no peace among the religions without dialogue among the religions."

The first global interfaith dialogue took place in 1893 in Chicago, USA at the World's Parliament of Religions. About 7,000 people from different countries and different religions took part in that conference. The interfaith dialogue movement gathered interest in the 1960s as civil rights and humanistic philosophies achieved prominence in Western society.

NOSTRA AETATE

In 1965, Pope Paul VI (1897-1978) announced the official release of a revolutionary document, called Nostra Aetate (In Our Age). This is the Second Vatican Council's Declaration on the Relationship of the Church to Non-Christian Religions. It reversed centuries of the Christian church's teachings on religious exclusivism. Nostra Aetate acknowledged the truth in other religions and ushered in a new era of interfaith dialogues by declaring non-discrimination on the basis of religion.

Selected excerpts from Nostra Aetate are provided below to shed light on the Vatican's official view on other religions.

ON HINDUISM AND BUDDHISM:

"Thus in Hinduism, men contemplate the divine mystery and express it through an inexhaustible abundance of myths and through searching philosophical inquiry. They seek freedom from the anguish of our human condition either through ascetical practices or profound meditation or a flight to God with love and trust. Again, Buddhism, in its various forms, realizes the radical insufficiency of this changeable world; it teaches a way by which men, in a devout and confident spirit, may be able either to acquire the state of perfect liberation, or attain, by their own efforts or through higher help, supreme illumination. Likewise, other religions found everywhere try to counter the restlessness of the human heart, each in its own manner, by proposing "ways," comprising teachings, rules of life, and sacred rites. The Catholic Church rejects nothing that is true and holy in these religions. She regards with sincere reverence those ways of conduct and of life, those precepts and teachings which, though differing in many aspects from the ones she holds and sets forth, nonetheless often reflect a ray of that Truth which enlightens all men."

— NOSTRA AETATE (1965)
[Declaration on the Relationship of the Church to Non-Christian Religions]

ON MOSLEMS:

"The Church regards with esteem also the Moslems. They adore the one God, living and subsisting in Himself; merciful and all- powerful, the Creator of heaven and earth,(5) who has spoken to men; they take pains to submit wholeheartedly to even His inscrutable decrees, just as Abraham, with whom the faith of Islam takes pleasure in linking itself, submitted to God. Though they do not acknowledge Jesus as God, they revere Him as a prophet. They also honor Mary, His virgin Mother; at times they even call on her with devotion. In addition, they await the day of judgment when God will render their deserts to all those who have been raised up from the dead. Finally, they value the moral life and worship God especially through prayer, almsgiving and fasting."

– Nostra Aetate (1965)

ON JEWS:

"God holds the Jews most dear for the sake of their Fathers; …. True, the Jewish authorities and those who followed their lead pressed for the death of Christ; still, what happened in His passion cannot be charged against all the Jews, without distinction, then alive, nor against the Jews of today. Although the Church is the new people of God, the Jews should not be presented as rejected or accursed by God, as if this followed from the Holy Scriptures….Furthermore, in her rejection of every persecution against any man, the Church, mindful of the patrimony she shares with the Jews and moved not by political reasons but by the Gospel's spiritual love, decries hatred, persecutions, displays of anti-Semitism, directed against Jews at any time and by anyone."

– Nostra Aetate (1965)

ON NON-DISCRIMINATION:

"We cannot truly call on God, the Father of all, if we refuse to treat in a brotherly way any man, created as he is in the image of God. Man's relation to God the Father and his relation to men his brothers are so linked together that Scripture says: "He who does not love does not know God" (1 John 4:8)….The Church reproves, as foreign to the mind of Christ, any discrimination against men or harassment of them because of their race, color, condition of life, or religion."

– Nostra Aetate (1965)

WHERE IS GOD?

"And upon the stillness of a cloud-filled
afternoon, the child asked of the Mystic:
"Where is God, the Creator, and how
will I endeavor to find the sacredness of
His Being?"
And the Mystic answered:
Once upon a thousand years ago did a
man seek the answer to your very question.
He searched the mountains for the One
called God;
But he only saw the green and yellow
blanket of distant aspen trees.
He walked along the ocean shore, to
know the Creator of Life;
But all he heard was the rhythmic roar
of the tide's own song.
He rode across the prairie, looking to
find God at his journey's end;
But all that came to him was the sweet
fragrance of the wild flower's bloom.
He reached out for the sky, pleading for
a sign of His Presence;
But he only felt the vastness and timelessness
of the starlit night.
Oh foolish man that he was, to search for
God with the eyes of his mind;
When He was forever with him, when seen
through the eyes of his soul."

— DANIEL J. MILLER

*[A twentieth-century mystic and author who posts his poems online
(http://www.stanford.edu/~djmiller/, author of Prophet's Candle]*

GOD IN DIFFERENT FAITHS

Faith	Conception of God
Hinduism (~1900 BC)	The God of Hinduism is one and many at the same time. Hinduism is very permissive in its conceptualization of the divine. Some Hindus believe in a single creator God, Ishwar, who is the Supreme Being and the absolute reality without beginning and without end. Some Hindus believe that the universe is divided into three separate worlds (lokas) and that three primary gods rule those worlds: Brahma (Creator), Vishnu (Preserver), and Shiva (Destroyer). These gods are assisted by consort goddesses: respectively, Saraswati, Lakshmi, and Parvathi. Yet others believe in an elaborate hierarchy of gods who, in the minds of believers, may or may not be manifestations of a single Supreme God. Hindu mystics see God as an all-encompassing existence— "ishavasyam idam sarvam"—which means that everything in this world is covered and filled with Ishwar.
Judaism (~1800 BC)	The God of Judaism is a single Supreme Being in a strictly monotheistic worldview. His name is YHWH (meaning "I am"). He is self-existent, omnipotent, omniscient, eternal, perfect, infinite, just, and merciful. He is non-physical and neither male nor female. He is incomprehensible to humans. This God is interested in individual humans, who can build personal relationships with God. Jewish mystics see God as Ein Sof (meaning "endless") and believe that the ultimate goal of a human being is union with God. This God is simple as well as infinitely complex.
Zoroastrianism (~1100 BC)	The God of Zoroastrianism is a single creator God, Ahura Mazda, or the "Wise Lord." He is omniscient but not omnipotent, a marked departure from Abrahamic religions. Ahura Mazda is incomprehensible, unchanging, omnipresent, and the source of all goodness and happiness. He is an upholder of truth and a friend of the just man. Ahura Mazda is uncreated and so is his rival, Angra Mainyu, the evil spirit.
Jainism (~600 BC)	God of Jainism is a set of high morals, not a creator, protector, or destroyer God. According to Jainism, a human being can become a god if he or she can attain godliness by freeing up the soul through infinite bliss, infinite peace, and infinite wisdom. Therefore, all liberated human souls are gods (tirthankaras) whose numbers increase as more and more humans liberate their souls from the cycle of suffering and rebirth. The God of Jainism is not a heavenly entity and is neither omniscient, nor omnipotent, nor the law-giver of humans. In that sense, Jainism is non-theistic.

Faith	Conception of God
Buddhism (~550 BC)	The God of Buddhism is a non-Being. Buddhism is unique among religions in that it does not concern itself with the idea of an omnipotent and omniscient Supreme Being ruling over the world. As a matter of fact, most Asian religions are non-theistic, such as Buddhism, Jainism, Confucianism, Taoism, and some sects of Hinduism. Buddha rejected the idea of God as worthless, and taught that a human being should study nature to gain personal wisdom, which will then help alleviate the stress of worldly living (samsara) and lead to nirvana.
Christianity (~1st Century)	The God of Christianity is a single creator God who exists in three divine forms: Father, Son, and Holy Spirit. Christians believe that God, the Father, took human form in Jesus Christ, the Son, and that God manifests today as the Holy Spirit in the actions of believers. God is infinite, eternal, omnipotent, omniscient, merciful, just, and self-existent. God is very concerned about the personal behaviors of humans and their salvation. He is the chief law-giver of humans. Christian mystics believe in a God who is inside the human soul and with whom a direct personal relationship is possible through love and devotion.
Islam (~7th Century)	The God of Islam is Allah, and there is no God but Allah in this strictly monotheistic worldview. Allah is the sole creator of the world; he is without beginning and without end. He is omnipotent, omniscient, just, merciful, infinite, eternal, and self-existent. Allah is concerned with the personal behaviors of humans and will reward or punish them according to their actions on earth. He is without form, invisible, incomprehensible, and self-sufficient. Allah is the chief law-giver of humans. The Muslim mystics believe that God is the only existence in the universe—all other things, including humans, are mere manifestations of God; they think union with God is the ultimate human purpose and is possible through devotion.
Shintoism (~8th Century)	God is a complex and somewhat foreign concept in Shintoism. Believers of Shintoism worship kami (best translated as spirits), which can respond to prayers and can change the course of events. Kami can be good or evil, in contrast to the traditional concept of an "all good and no evil" God. Kami are not omnipotent or perfect; they are the spiritual essence of everything that pervades the earth, like streams, birds, trees, mountains. Kami also include ancestors and the souls of remarkable dead persons.

Faith	Conception of God
Sikhism (~15th Century)	The God of Sikhism is One God (Ik Onkar), indescribable yet knowable. He is a self-existent creator God who is formless and genderless. He is fearless and without enemies. He is omnipresent, merciful, and compassionate. God can be experienced through worship, love, and devotion. Sikhs believe that union with God is the main purpose of any human being.
Bahaism (~19th Century)	The God of Bahaism is a single creator God who is omnipotent and omniscient. He is eternal and is the God of all religions. God is only knowable through his prophets, who are manifestations of God. The prophets of Bahaism include Abraham, Moses, Zoroaster, Buddha, Jesus, Muhammad, and Bahaullah, the last one being the founder of Bahaism.

A COMMON WORD

The 2nd World Parliament of Religions took place again in Chicago in 1993, one hundred years after the first one. Since then, there were four other such global interfaith meetings, each one attended by 8,000 to 9,000 people from 50 to 60 countries. The next Parliament of World's Religions is scheduled to take place in 2014 in Brussels, Belgium.

Muslims and Christians search for common grounds

The interfaith movement gained momentum after the September 11, 2001 terrorist attack, to satisfy the needs of ever-growing multi-religious communities.

On October 13, 2007, 138 Muslim scholars, clerics, and intellectuals issued an open letter, *A Common Word Between Us and You*, to the leaders of the Christian community, in an effort to highlight the common ground between Christianity and Islam, the first such effort since the days of Prophet Muhammad. This was followed by several high-profile international and national interfaith conferences and seminars. Quotes from this open letter, and statements and comments from these conferences, are provided below as example postings on the *Wall of Mortals* in God's Facebook.

"Muslims and Christians together make up well over half of the world's population. Without peace and justice between these two religious communities, there can be no meaningful peace in the world. The future of the world depends on peace between Muslims and Christians."

– A COMMON WORD BETWEEN US AND YOU (2007)
[Written by Muslim Scholars to Christians]

"In the Holy Qu'ran, God Most High tells Muslims to issue the following call to Christians (and Jews-the People of the Scripture): "Say: O people of the Scripture! Come to a common word between us and you: that we shall worship none but God, and that we shall ascribe no partner unto him, and that none of us shall take others for lords beside God. And if they turn away, then say: Bear witness that we are they who have surrendered (unto Him)." (Aal'Imran 3:64)"

Muslim scholars write to Christians

– A COMMON WORD BETWEEN US AND YOU (2007)
[Written by Muslim Scholars to Christians]

"Of God's Unity, God says in the Holy Qu'ran: "Say, He is God, the One! God, the Self Sufficient Besought of all! (Al – Ikhlas 112:1–2)." Of the necessity of love for God, God says in the Holy Qu'ran: "So invoke the Name of thy Lord and devote thyself to him with a complete devotion (Al-Muzzammil 73:8)." Of the necessity of love for the neighbour; the prophet Muhammad said: "None of you has faith until you love for your neighbour what you love for yourself."

"In the New Testament, Jesus Christ said: "Hear, O Israel, the Lord our God, the Lord is One./ And you shall love the Lord your God with all your heart, with all your soul, with all your mind, and with all your strength." This is the first commandment. / And the second, like it, is this: "You shall love your neighbour as yourself." There is no other commandment greater than these." (Mark 12: 29–31)

– A COMMON WORD BETWEEN US AND YOU (2007)
[Written by Muslim Scholars to Christians]

"In obedience to the Holy Qu'ran, we as Muslims invite Christians to come together with us on the basis of what is common to us, which is also what is most essential to our faith and practice: the Two Commandments."

(In Islam)... "the call to be totally devoted and attached to God, heart and soul, far from being a call for a mere emotion or for a mood, is in fact an injunction requiring all-embracing, constant and active love of God. It demands a love in which the innermost spiritual heart and the whole of the soul-with its intelligence, will and feeling – participate through devotion."

"The Shema in the book of Deuteronomy (6:4–5), a centrepiece of the Old Testament and of Jewish Liturgy, says: 'Hear, O Israel: The LORD our God, the LORD is one!/You shall love the LORD your God with all your heart, and with all your soul, and with all your strength.'"

"In the New Testament, when Jesus Christ, the Messiah, is asked about the Greatest Commandment, he answers: "But when the Pharisees heard that he had silenced the Sadducees, the gathered together./Then one of them, a lawyer, asked Him a question, testing Him, and saying,/"Teacher, which is the greatest commandment in the law?" Jesus said to him, "You shall love the LORD your God with all your heart, with all your soul, and with all your mind."/This is the first and greatest commandment./ And the second is like it: "You shall love your neighbour as yourself." On these two commandments hang all the Law and the Prophets." (Matthew 22:34–40)."

"The commandment to love God fully is (thus) the First and Greatest Commandment of the Bible."

– A Common Word Between Us and You (2007)
[Written by Muslim Scholars to Christians]

"There are numerous injunctions in Islam about the necessity and paramount importance of love for – and mercy towards – the neighbour. Love of the neighbour is an essential and integral part of faith in God and love of God because in Islam without love of the neighbour there is no true faith in God and no righteousness. The Prophet Muhammad said: "None of you has faith until you love for your brother what you love for yourself." And: "None of you has faith until you love for your neighbour what you love for yourself.""

– A Common Word Between Us and You (2007)
[Written by Muslim Scholars to Christians]

"Whilst Islam and Christianity are obviously different religions – and whilst there is no minimising some of their formal differences – it is clear that the Two Greatest Commandments are an area of common ground and a link between the Qu'ran, the Torah and the New Testament."

– A Common Word Between Us and You (2007)
[Written by Muslim Scholars to Christians]

"Muslims recognise Jesus Christ as the Messiah, not in the same way Christians do (but Christians themselves anyway have never all agreed with each other on Jesus Christ's nature), but in the following way: ...the Messiah Jesus son of Mary is a Messenger of God and His Word which He cast unto Mary and a Spirit from Him..(Al – Nisa 4: 171). We therefore invite Christians to consider Muslims not against and thus with them, in accordance with Jesus Christ's words here."

– A Common Word Between Us and You (2007)
[Written by Muslim Scholars to Christians]

"Let us respect each other, be fair, just and kind to one another and live in sincere peace, harmony and mutual good will."

– A Common Word Between Us and You (2007)
[Written by Muslim Scholars to Christians]

"The more recent Common Word letter which echoed a theme consonant with my first encyclical: the unbreakable bond between love of God and love of neighbor, and the fundamental contradiction of resorting to violence or exclusion in the name of God."

– H.H. Pope Benedict XVI (1927-)
[Born Joseph Aloisius Ratzinger on 16 April 1927) is the 265th and current Pope, at the King Hussein Mosque in Jordan on Saturday 9 May 2009]

"I am well aware that Muslims and Christians have different approaches in matters regarding God. Yet we can and must be worshippers of the one God who created us and is concerned about each person in every corner of the world. Together we must show, by our mutual respect and solidarity, that we consider ourselves members of one family: the family that God has loved and gathered together from the creation of the world to the end of human history."

– H.H. Pope Benedict XVI (1927-)
[Speaking at the first seminar of the Catholic-Muslim Forum, Rome, November, 2008]

349

"This common ground consists in love of God and of neighbour gives hope that deep cooperation between us can be a hallmark of the relations between our two communities."

— YALE DIVINITY SCHOOL'S CENTRE FOR FAITH AND CULTURE

"Muslims do not accept that one can discuss the Koran in depth, because they say it was written by dictation from God.... With such an absolute interpretation, it is difficult to discuss the contents of faith."

— CARDINAL JEAN-LOUIS TAURAN (1943-)
[A Vatican official]

1. "Muslims and Christians affirm the unity and absoluteness of God. We recognise that God's merciful love is infinite, eternal and embraces all things. This love is central to both our religions and is at the heart of the Judeo-Christian-Islamic monotheistic heritage.

EVOLUTION OF GOD

God's unity and absoluteness are affirmed by both Christians and Muslims.

2. We recognize that all human beings have the right to the preservation of life, religion, property, intellect, and dignity. No Muslim or Christian should deny the other these rights, nor should they tolerate the denigration or desecration of one another's sacred symbols, founding figures or places of worship.

3. We are committed to these principles and to furthering them through continuous dialogue. We thank God for bringing us together in this historic endeavour and ask that He purify our intentions and grant us success through His all encompassing Mercy and Love.

4. We Christian and Muslim participants meeting together at Yale for the historic "A Common Word" conference denounce and deplore threats made against those who engage in interfaith dialogue. Dialogue is not a departure from faith; it is a legitimate means of expression and an essential tool in the quest for the common good."

— STATEMENT FROM THE PARTICIPANTS (2008)
[Over 120 Muslim and Christian leaders attending a conference convened by the Yale Centre for Faith and Culture in collaboration with the Royal Al –Bayt Institute and held at Yale University, July 2008]

"We profess that Catholics and Muslims are called to be instruments of love and harmony among believers, and for humanity as a whole, renouncing any oppression, aggressive violence and terrorism, especially that committed in the name of religion, and upholding the principles of justice for all."

— CATHOLIC MUSLIM FORUM AT ROME, NOVEMBER, 2008
[The Final Declaration]

GOOD WITHOUT GOD

Can we be good without God? Is goodness or morality connected with the belief in a God? Does atheism entail that everything goes? These are hotly debated questions from antiquity. The Greek philosopher Plato mentioned a debate between Socrates and Euthyphro regarding the basis for determining an action to be good or bad. The debate went like this:

> Euthyphro: "Piety, then, is that which is dear to the gods, and impiety is that which is not dear to them."

> Socrates: "Is that which the gods love good because they love it, or do they love it because it is good?"

If whatever gods love is by definition good, then what is the guarantee that gods can't be unfair or frivolous, as evidenced in Greek mythology? Even in our religious scriptures, we note with judicious silence that God dictated many actions which we couldn't accept as moral: righteous war, genocide, slavery, and stoning of non-virgin brides.

On the other hand, if gods love an action because it is good, then the definition of good is independent of gods. Philosopher Bertrand Russell created his own version of Euthyphro's dilemma: "The point I am concerned with is that, if you are quite sure there is a difference between right and wrong, then you are then in this situation: is that difference due to God's fiat or is it not? If it is due to God's fiat, then for God himself there is no difference between right and wrong, and it is no longer a significant statement to say that God is good."

Professor Jerry A. Coyne of the University of Chicago offered a resolution to the age-old dilemma: "Though both moral and immoral behaviors can be promoted by religions, morality itself—either in individual behavior or social codes—simply cannot come from the will or commands of a God."

Harvard's humanist chaplain Greg Epstein published a book entitled *Good Without God* in 2005. There he argued that humanism is the answer because in his view, "Humanism is being good without God." But he warned that "humanist" should not merely mean "one who denies the existence of the gods", but one who creates a life full of good deeds. Indeed, our focus should be on good, with or without God, as Epstein beautifully stated: "We all need to remember that we can get beyond arguing over whether we can be good with or without a God, and simply be good, together." That is the basis of the *Friendship of Civilizations*, where religious and non-religious people work together for the good of humanity.

CHAPTER DIGEST (1900 TO 2012 AD)

God stopped posting any messages on the *Holy Wall*, but his old postings were translated and interpreted again and again by mere mortals, with the colors of their own psyches and analytical methods. The *Holy Wall* of God's Facebook was flooded with requests for postings, and words and word-roots of scriptural passages were minced for meanings that matched particular ideologies and agendas.

God decided to block any mere mortals from posting on the *Holy Wall*. As a result, the *Wall of Mortals* in this era grew beyond the wildest human imagination. Anyone and everyone posted on the *Wall of Mortals*, which displayed a colorful tapestry of human thoughts on God by including the words of rock stars like Elvis Presley, Madonna, Michael Jackson, and Whitney Houston; computer gurus like Steve Jobs and Bill Gates; spiritual leaders like Neem Karoli Baba, Deepak Chopra, and Saitha Sai Baba; and popular icons like Ronald Reagan, Bill Clinton, George Bush, Indira Gandhi, Muhammad Ali, Bill Cosby, Oprah Winfrey, and Diego Maradona. The postings on the *Wall of Mortals* also included thoughts of comedians and the general populace. The diversity of opinions about God only proved that the human understanding of God is only approximate, provisional, and corrigible

During this period, there was a great resurgence of God and religion in the human arena. The twentieth-century plot to kill God had failed miserably. Many studies and surveys were conducted to understand the relationship between God and humans, with interesting results, such as America's Four Gods and some scientists' rejection of God. The US courts also saw many court cases involving God or, to be more correct, involving the roles and rights of God in public life. God appeared on US currency, despite a constitutional prohibition against the state establishing any religion.

The human–God relationship in this period was shaped, not by God or his commandments, but by wars and terrorism. God again became necessary to humans as the rampant materialism of this period left them empty-handed, and they yearned for more spiritual peace. God also became necessary to tame the dragon of religious fundamentalism that was causing havoc all over the world. The sword of the *Clash of Civilizations* was looming with clear and immediate danger. It was realized that God is the greatest unifying force among humans of all cultures and all continents.

Thus, a pragmatic basis for a *Friendship of Civilizations* emerged.

10

God of
Nobel Laureates

"Who made the World? Religion answers: "He!"
But who made Him? Was it eternity,
Or Space, or Chaos that produced the seed
Of that immortal essence? could they breed
With darkest night, themselves inanimate,
The ruling power of universal Fate?
Or is Creation's spirit but a part
Of the crude matter? Could that rubbish start,
Unconscious of itself, the wondrous Whole,
And set a seal as of immortal soul
On endless worlds, so overwhelming grand
That grasping thought, unable to expand."

—ALFRED NOBEL (1833-1896)

STATUS UPDATE

❖ God's standing among Nobel laureate scientists gains importance as the status of Nobel scientists rises to the level of demigods among the commoners.

❖ "God is a matter of faith, not of science"; thus is the implicit pronouncement of most top scientists, who prefer to remain silent about their personal faiths.

❖ God's fans cite Nobel laureates in support of their belief in God; atheists, too, cite Nobel laureates to support their viewpoint.

❖ God's popularity among scientists gradually declines during the twentieth century, the beginning of which is marked by the introduction of the Nobel prizes in 1901. A report published in Nature claims that in 1914, 27% scientists believed in a personal God; that number declined to 15% in 1933 and to 7% in 1998.

❖ God's popularity among scientists increases towards the beginning of the twenty-first century. The Pew Forum conducts a survey in 2009 among the members of the American Association for Advancement of Science and finds the following:

  – 33% of scientists believe in God and 18% believe in a higher spirit;

  – 41% of scientists do not believe in God and another 7% are agnostics or refuse to answer.

NOTES FROM HISTORY
(ERA OF NOBEL PRIZE, 1901-2012)

The Nobel Prize was started in 1901 and soon became the most prestigious award one can receive in the fields of physics, chemistry, medicine, literature, economics, and peace. Alfred Nobel, a Swedish chemist and industrialist, bequeathed 94% of his total assets of 31 million Swedish kronors (in 2008 dollars, that is about $181 Million) to establish five Nobel Prizes. The five prizes were awarded for the first time in 1901. In 1969, a prize in economics in the memory of Alfred Nobel was established by Sweden's central bank. Between 1901 and 2012, Nobel Prize was awarded to only 835 individuals – 792 men and 43 women. That makes the Nobel Prize winners a very elite group of people whose words and thoughts are widely regarded by others.

John Polkinghorne, a British particle physicist and theologian, observed: "It's certainly a historical fact that most of the pioneers of modern science were religious men. They may have had their difficulties with the Church (like Galileo) or been of an orthodox cast of mind (like Newton), but religion was important for them. They used to like to say that God had written two books for our instruction, the book of scripture and the book of nature. I think we need to try to decipher both books if we're to understand what's really happening."

Words on God from Nobel Prize winners are presented below in two categories: the scientists and the rest.

WALL OF MORTALS:
GOD OF NOBEL SCIENTISTS

"As we conquer peak after peak we see in front of us regions full of interest and beauty, but we do not see our goal, we do not see the horizon; in the distance tower still higher peaks, which will yield to those who ascend them still wider prospects, and deepen the feeling, the truth of which is emphasized by every advance in science, that 'Great are the Works of the Lord'."

— SIR JOSEPH J. THOMSON (1856-1940)

[British physicist, credited with the discovery of electron, isotopes, and mass spectrometer, winner of 1906 Nobel Prize in Physics]

COFFEE BREAK

Personal or Professional Opinion?: In this era of specialization, there are very few polymaths—people who have expertise in a wide array of subjects—unlike what used to be the case prior to the eighteenth century. In addition, most scientists today are too busy with their professional work to think adequately and meaningfully about God or religion. However, there is great hunger among both religious and non-religious commoners for scientific geniuses' opinions on God. Ordinary people often seek justifications for their point of view in such opinions. It should be noted that these opinions are, on many occasions, purely personal and are not connected with or based on the individual's scientific expertise and insights.

"This day relenting God
Hath placed within my hand
A wondrous thing; and God
Be praised. At His command,
Seeking His secret deeds
With tears and toiling breath,
I find thy cunning seeds,
O million-murdering Death.
I know this little thing
A myriad men will save.
O Death, where is thy sting?
Thy victory, O Grave?"

— SIR RONALD ROSS (1857-1932)

[Received the 1902 Nobel Prize in Medicine and Physiology. On August 20, 1897, Ross made his landmark discovery that malaria is transmitted to people by Anopheles mosquitoes. On that day of discovery, he wrote the above poetic words in his Journal.]

"Both religion and science need for their activities the belief in God, and moreover God stands for the former in the beginning, and for the latter at the end of the whole thinking. For the former, God represents the basis, for the latter – the crown of any reasoning concerning the world-view."

– MAX PLANCK (1858–1947)

[German physicist, known as the founder of the quantum theory; winner of 1918 Nobel Prize in Physics]

"All matter originates and exists only by virtue of a force which brings the particle of an atom to vibration and holds this most minute solar system of the atom together. We must assume behind this force the existence of a conscious and intelligent mind. This mind is the matrix of all matter."

– MAX PLANCK (1858-1947)

"To me it is unthinkable that a real atheist could be a scientist."

– ROBERT ANDREWS MILLIKAN (1868–1953)

[American physicist, President of CalTech from 1921 to 1945, winner of 1923 Nobel Prize in Physics]

"I have never known a thinking man who did not believe in God."

– ROBERT ANDREWS MILLIKAN (1868–1953)

"I have, in effect, fingerprinted God in the heavens. I found a Creator continually on the Job. I bear witness that the teachings of science are extraordinarily like the preaching of Jesus in that nature is at bottom benevolent and good."

– ROBERT ANDREWS MILLIKAN (1868–1953)

"The need of God expresses itself in prayer. Prayer is a cry of distress; a demand for help; a hymn of love. Prayer gives us strength to bear cares and anxieties, to hope when there is no logical motive for hope, to remain steadfast in the midst of catastrophes."

– ALEXIS CARREL (1873–1944)

[French surgeon, biologist, and eugenicist, winner of 1912 Nobel Prize in Medicine and Physiology]

"It is, of course, a waste of time to talk to children of theology and duty. But we should follow Kant's advice and present God to them very early indeed as an invisible father who watches over them and to whom they can address prayers. The true mode of honoring God consists in fulfilling His will."

– ALEXIS CARREL (1873–1944)

"It is sheer pride to believe oneself capable of correcting nature, for nature is the work of God. To command nature, we must obey her."

– ALEXIS CARREL (1873–1944)

"The more I work with the powers of Nature, the more I feel God's benevolence to man; the closer I am to the great truth that everything is dependent on the Eternal Creator and Sustainer; the more I feel that the so-called science, I am occupied with, is nothing but an expression of the Supreme Will, which aims at bringing people closer to each other in order to help them better understand and improve themselves."

– GUGLIELMO MARCONI (1874–1937)
[Italian inventor, known for invention of radio telegraphy, winner of 1909 Nobel Prize in Physics]

"Every step, science makes, brings us ever new surprises and achievements. And yet science is like a faint light of a lantern flickering in a deep and thick forest, through which humanity struggles to find its way to God. It is only faith that can lead it to light and serve as a bridge between man and the Absolute.

I am proud to be a Christian. I believe not only as a Christian, but as a scientist as well. A wireless device can deliver a message through the wilderness. In prayer the human spirit can send invisible waves to eternity, waves that achieve their goal in front of God."

– GUGLIELMO MARCONI (1874–1937)

COFFEE BREAK

Einstein's God: Albert Einstein obtained the stature of a God of Science among the public and science enthusiasts of the late twentieth century. He didn't believe in a personal God, nor did he like to be called an atheist.

In 1929, Boston's Cardinal O'Connell attacked Einstein and his General Theory of Relativity. The Cardinal warned that the theory "cloaked the ghastly apparition of atheism", and was "befogged speculation, producing universal doubt about God and His creation." On April 24, 1929, Rabbi Herbert Goldstein of New York sent a telegram to Einstein: "I believe in Spinoza's God, Who reveals Himself in the lawful harmony of the world, not in a God who concerns Himself with the fate and the doings of mankind." Rabbi Goldstein then defended Einstein against Cardinal O'Connell's attack and wrote: "Spinoza, who is called the God-intoxicated man, and who saw God manifest in all nature, certainly could not be called an atheist. Furthermore, Einstein points to a unity. Einstein's theory if carried out to its logical conclusion would bring to mankind a scientific formula for monotheism." Einstein chose to remain silent on the Rabbi's last point.

"I want to know how God created this world. I am not interested in this or that phenomenon, in the spectrum of this or that element. I want to know His thoughts, the rest are details."

– ALBERT EINSTEIN (1879-1955)
[German born American theoretical physicist, known for the theory of relativity, regarded as the father of modern physics, the most famous scientist of modern age, winner of 1921 Nobel Prize in Physics]

"The deeper one penetrates into nature's secrets, the greater becomes one's respect for God."

– ALBERT EINSTEIN (1879-1955)

"The main source of the present day conflicts between the spheres of religion and of science lies in this concept of a personal God."

– ALBERT EINSTEIN (1879-1955)

"The most beautiful and most profound emotion we can experience is the sensation of the mystical. It is the sower of all true science. He to whom this emotion is a stranger, who can no longer stand rapt in awe, is as good as dead. That deeply emotional conviction of the presence of a superior reasoning power, which is revealed in the incomprehensible Universe, forms my idea of God."

– ALBERT EINSTEIN (1879-1955)

"The word God is for me nothing more than the expression and product of human weakness, the Bible a collection of honorable, but still purely primitive, legends which are nevertheless pretty childish."

– ALBERT EINSTEIN (1879-1955)

"There are people who say there is no God; but, what makes me really angry is that they quote me for support of such views. What separates me from most so-called atheists is a feeling of utter humility toward the unattainable secrets of the harmony of the cosmos."

– ALBERT EINSTEIN (1879-1955)

"I, at any rate, am convinced that He does not throw dice."

– ALBERT EINSTEIN (1879-1955)

"Stop telling God what to do with his dice."

– NIELS BOHR [NIELS HENRIK DAVID BOHR] (1885-1962)
[Danish physicist, known for his fundamental contribution to atomic structure and quantum mechanics, winner of 1922 Nobel prize in Physics]

"The grave error in a technically directed cultural drive is that it sees its highest goal in the possibility of achieving an alteration of Nature. It hopes to set itself in the place of God, so that it may force upon the divine will some petty conventions of its dust-born mind."

– ERWIN SCHRÖDINGER (1887–1961)
[Austrian physicist and theoretical biologist, one of the fathers of quantum theory, winner of 1933 Nobel Prize in Physics]

"For myself, faith begins with the realization that a supreme intelligence brought the universe into being and created man. It is not difficult for me to have this faith, for it is incontrovertible that where there is a plan there is intelligence. An orderly, unfolding universe testifies to the truth of the most majestic statement ever uttered: 'In the beginning God...' [Genesis 1, 1]."

– ARTHUR HOLLY COMPTON (1892–1962)
[American physicist, discovered Compton Effect, winner of 1927 Nobel Prize in Physics]

"In their essence there can be no conflict between science and religion. Science is a reliable method of finding truth. Religion is the search for a satisfying basis for life."

– ARTHUR HOLLY COMPTON (1892–1962)

"Physics filled me with awe, put me in touch with a sense of original causes. Physics brought me closer to God. That feeling stayed with me throughout my years in science. Whenever one of my students came to me with a scientific project, I asked only one question, 'Will it bring you nearer to God?'"

– ISIDOR ISAAC RABI (1898-1988)
[Galician born American physicist, discoverer of nuclear magnetic resonance, winner of 1944 Nobel Prize in Physics.]

"I cannot believe God is a weak left-hander."

– WOLFGANG PAULI (1900-1958)
[Austrian-Swiss physicist, winner of the Nobel Prize for Physics in 1945]

"The first gulp from the glass of natural sciences will turn you into an atheist, but at the bottom of the glass God is waiting for you."

– WERNER HEISENBERG (1901–1976)
[German theoretical physicist, best known for uncertainty principle of quantum theory, winner of 1932 Nobel Prize in Physics]

"God used beautiful mathematics in creating the world."

– PAUL DIRAC (1902-1984)
[Paul Adrien Maurice Dirac, British theoretical physicist and a founder of quantum physics. Awarded 1933 Nobel Prize in Physics]

"I cannot understand why we idle discussing religion. If we are honest—and scientists have to be—we must admit that religion is a jumble of false assertions, with no basis in reality. The very idea of God is a product of the human imagination."

– PAUL DIRAC (1902-1984)

EVOLUTION OF GOD

God is a hotly debated topic among top scientists.

"Religion is a kind of opium that allows a nation to lull itself into wishful dreams and so forget the injustices that are being perpetrated against the people. Hence the close alliance between those two great political forces, the State and the Church. Both need the illusion that a kindly God rewards—in heaven if not on earth—all those who have not risen up against injustice, who have done their duty quietly and uncomplainingly. That is precisely why the honest assertion that God is a mere product of the human imagination is branded as the worst of all mortal sins."

– PAUL DIRAC (1902-1984)

"I can't for the life of me see how the postulate of an Almighty God helps us in any way. What I do see is that this assumption leads to such unproductive questions as why God allows so much misery and injustice, the exploitation of the poor by the rich and all the other horrors He might have prevented."

– PAUL DIRAC (1902-1984

"If I consider reality as I experience it, the primary experience I have is of my own existence as a unique self-conscious being which I believe is God-created."

– SIR JOHN ECCLES (1903–1997)

[Australian neurophysiologist, famous for his work on synapse, winner of 1963 Nobel Prize in Medicine and Physiology]

"I believe in God, who can respond to prayers, to whom we can give trust and without whom life on this earth would be without meaning (a tale told by an idiot). I believe that God has revealed Himself to us in many ways and through many men and women, and that for us here in the West the clearest revelation is through Jesus and those that have followed him."

– SIR NEVILL MOTT (1905-1996)

[English physicist, famous for his work on amorphous semiconductors, winner of 1977 Nobel Prize in Physics]

"Science can have a purifying effect on religion, freeing it from beliefs from a pre-scientific age and helping us to a truer conception of God. At the same time, I am far from believing that science will ever give us the answers to all our questions."

– SIR NEVILL MOTT (1905-1996)

"I consider the power to believe to be one of the great divine gifts to man through which he is allowed in some inexplicable manner to come near to the mysteries of the Universe without understanding them. The capability to believe is as characteristic and as essential a property of the human mind as is its power of logical reasoning, and far from being incompatible with the scientific approach, it complements it and helps the human mind to integrate the world into an ethical and meaningful whole.

There are many ways in which people are made aware of their power to believe in the supremacy of Divine guidance and power: through music or visual art, some event or experience decisively influencing their life, looking through a microscope or telescope, or just by looking at the miraculous manifestations or purposefulness of Nature."

– SIR ERNST CHAIN (1906-1979)

[German-born British biochemist, winner of 1945 Nobel Prize in Medicine and Physiology]

"A scientist who believes in god suffers from schizophrenia."

– JACQUES MONOD (1910-1976)
[French biologist, winner of 1965 Nobel Prize in Medicine and Physiology]

"I strongly believe in the existence of God, based on intuition, observations, logic, and also scientific knowledge."

– CHARLES HARD TOWNES (1915-)
[American physicist, known for his work on maser and quantum electronics, winner of 1964 Nobel Prize in Physics. He gave the above answer to the inquiry, "What do you think about the existence of God?"]

COFFEE BREAK

Value of Scientists' Opinion: "In 1916, when scientists were emerging as the high priests of a new technological culture, everybody cared about what they thought and believed, But the prestige of science peaked in 1960 and has been declining ever since. Do people still care whether scientists believe in God? I'm not so sure."

– GEORGE MARSDEN (1939-)
[American Professor of History at University of Notredame]

"I think only an idiot can be an atheist. We must admit that there exists an incomprehensible power or force with limitless foresight and knowledge that started the whole universe going in the first place. He gave the above answer to the inquiry, 'What do think about the existence of God?'"

– CHRISTIAN ANFINSEN (1916–1995)
[American biochemist, winner of 1972 Nobel Prize in Chemistry]

"This kind of belief [in God] is damaging to the well-being of the human race."

– HERBERT HAUPTMAN (1917-)
[American mathematician, known for developing mathematical methods that revolutionized the whole field of chemistry, winner of 1985 Nobel Prize in Chemistry; answering a student's question "Can you be a good scientist, and believe in God?"]

"God is Truth. There is no incompatibility between science and religion. Both are seeking the same truth. Science shows that God exists."

– SIR DEREK BARTON (1918–1998)
[British organic chemist, winner of 1969 Nobel Prize in Chemistry]

"As I have already stated, God is Truth. But does God really have anything to do with man? Certainly I cannot believe that God accepts only one religion, or one sect, as the only group authorized to speak for man. I would believe that God accepts all, even those who pretend not to believe. Morality and religion interact and much beneficial human behavior results from this interaction."

– SIR DEREK BARTON (1918–1998)

"God was invented to explain mystery. God is always invented to explain those things that you do not understand. Now, when you finally discover how something works, you get some laws which you're taking away from God; you don't need him anymore. But you need him for the other mysteries. So therefore you leave him to create the universe because we haven't figured that out yet; you need him for understanding those things which you don't believe the laws will explain, such as consciousness, or why you only live to a certain length of time -- life and death -- stuff like that. God is always associated with those things that you do not understand. Therefore I don't think that the laws can be considered to be like God because they have been figured out."

— RICHARD FEYNMAN (1918-1988)
[American physicist, professor at CalTech and winner of 1965 Nobel Prize in Physics]

"We're just working with the tools God gave us. There's no reason that science and religion have to operate in an adversarial relationship. Both come from the same source, the only source of truth – the Creator."

— JOSEPH E. MURRAY (1919-)
[American surgeon, who performed the first successful human kidney transplant in 1954, winner of 1990 Nobel Prize in Medicine and Physiology]

"There are enormously different cults and religious sects, and I think it's not unreasonable, because I think God – if He's as wonderful as we believe – is also very complex, and that different people have to see Him differently. You can't expect a peasant and a philosopher to have the same picture of God. I think God is big enough to cover them all, even for science writers – they can have their picture of God."

— ARTHUR SCHAWLOW (1921–1999)
[American physicist, co-inventor of the laser, winner of 1981 Nobel Prize in Physics]

COFFEE BREAK

Parody of the Bible: Nobel Prize-winning physicist Leon Lederman is known among his peers for his humor. In his book, *The God Particle: If the Universe is the Answer, What is the Question?*, he wrote a parody of selected biblical passages and called it *"The Very New Testament."*

"And the whole universe was of many languages, and of many speeches. And it came to pass, as they journeyed from the east, that they found a plain in the land of Waxahachie, and they dwelt there. And they said to one another, Go to, let us build a Giant Collider, whose collisions may reach back to the beginning of time. And they had superconducting magnets for bending, and protons had they for smashing. And the Lord came down to see the accelerator, which the children of men builded. And the Lord said, Behold the people are unconfounding my confounding. And the Lord sighed and said, Go to, let us go down, and there give them the God Particle so that they may see how beautiful is the universe I have made."

— LEON LEDERMAN (1922-)
[American experimental physicist, winner of Nobel Prize in Physics in 1988 for his work on neutrinos. The Very New Testament, 11:1. This is in parody to Bible, Genesis 11:5-9 (see page 69)]

"And the Lord looked upon Her world, and She marveled at its beauty – for so much beauty there was that She wept. It was a world of one kind of particle and one force carried by one messenger who was, with divine simplicity, also the one particle."

— LEON LEDERMAN (1922-)
[The Very New Testament, 3:1]

"And the Lord looked upon the world She had created and She was convulsed with wholly uncontrolled laughter. And She summoned Higgs and, suppressing Her mirth, She dealt with him sternly and said:

"Wherefore hast thou destroyed the symmetry of the world?"

And Higgs, shattered by the faintest suggestion of disapproval, defended thusly:

"Oh, Boss, I have not destroyed the symmetry. I have merely caused it to be hidden by the artifice of energy consumption. And in so doing I have indeed made it a complicated world.
………..."

And the Lord, hard put to stop Her Laughter, signed forgiveness and a nice raise for Higgs."

— LEON LEDERMAN (1922-)
[The Very New Testament, 3:1]

"There are essential parts of the human experience about which science intrinsically has nothing to say. I associate them with an entity which I call God."

—WALTER KOHN (1923-)
[Austrian-born American theoretical physicist, winner of 1998 Nobel Prize in Chemistry]

"I believe in God. It makes no sense to me to assume that the Universe and our existence is just a cosmic accident, that life emerged due to random physical processes in an environment which simply happened to have the right properties."

— ANTONY HEWISH (1924-)
[British radio astronomer, winner of 1974 Nobel Prize in Physics]

"God certainly seems to be a rational Creator. That the entire terrestrial world is made from electrons, protons and neutrons and that a vacuum is filled with virtual particles demands incredible rationality."

— ANTONY HEWISH (1924-)

COFFEE BREAK

God and Symmetry of Nature: Pakistani Muslim Nobel Laureate Professor Salam has mostly been involved with the problem of symmetries in physics. He connects his belief with his science.

"Our society is inflicted with menaces like mountains. Try to remove them from your surroundings with patience. God will have mercy on you one day. Do not be afraid if your endeavours don't bear fruit, but keep on doing your job and God will indeed bless your efforts."

– ABDUS SALAM (1926-1996)

[Pakistani theoretical physicist and astrophysicist, winner of 1979 Nobel Prize in Physics]

"That [the problem of symmetry] may come from my Islamic heritage; for that is the way we consider the universe created by God, with ideas of beauty and symmetry and harmony, with regularity and without chaos. We are trying to discover what the Lord thought; of course we miserably fail most of the time, but sometimes there is great satisfaction in seeing a little bit of the truth."

– ABDUS SALAM (1926-1996)

"If we don't play God, who will?"

– JAMES WATSON (1928-)

[American molecular biologist, best known for discovering DNA structure with Francis Crick; both won the 1962 Nobel Prize in Physiology and Medicine]

"Francis and I were running against God, in the sense that we wanted to know what made us human. Both of us had been subjected to religious truths which came by revelation, and we didn't have much acceptance of truths by revelation."

– JAMES WATSON (1928-)

"Oh, no. Absolutely not. The biggest advantage to believing in God is you don't have to understand anything, no physics, no biology. I wanted to understand."

– JAMES WATSON (1928-)

"If there are a bunch of fruit trees, one can say that whoever created these fruit trees wanted some apples. In other words, by looking at the order in the world, we can infer purpose and from purpose we begin to get some knowledge of the Creator, the Planner of all this. This is, then, how I look at God. I look at God through the works of God's hands and from those works imply intentions. From these intentions, I receive an impression of the Almighty."

– ARNO PENZIAS (1933-)

[German-born American physicist, winner of 1978 Nobel Prize in Physics]

"Many people do simply awful things out of sincere religious belief, not using religion as a cover the way that Saddam Hussein may have done, but really because they believe that this is what God wants them to do, going all the way back to Abraham being willing to sacrifice Issac because God told him to do that. Putting God ahead of humanity is a terrible thing."

— STEVEN WEINBERG(1933-)
[American physicist, winner of 1979 Nobel Prize in Physics]

"Some people have views of God that are so broad and flexible that it is inevitable that they will find God wherever they look for him. One hears it is said that 'God is the ultimate' or 'God is our better nature' or 'God is the universe.' Of course, like any other word, the word 'God' can be given any meaning we like. If you want to say that 'God is energy', then you can find God in a lump of coal."

— STEVEN WEINBERG(1933-)

"I do not believe in God - an intelligent, all-powerful being who cares about human beings - because the idea seems to me to be silly. The positive arguments that have been given for belief in God all appear to me as silly as the proposition they are intended to prove. Fortunately, in some parts of the world, religious belief has weakened enough so that people no longer kill each other over differences in this silliness."

— STEVEN WEINBERG(1933-)

"A scientific discovery is also a religious discovery. There is no conflict between science and religion. Our knowledge of God is made larger with every discovery we make about the world."

— JOSEPH H. TAYLOR, JR. (1941-)
[American astrophysicist, winner of 1993 Nobel Prize in Physics]

"We believe that there is something of God in every person and therefore human life is sacrosanct and one needs to look for the depth of spiritual presence in others, even in others with whom you disagree."

— JOSEPH H. TAYLOR, JR. (1941-)

"God did create the universe about 13.7 billion years ago, and of necessity has involved Himself with His creation ever since. The purpose of this universe is something that only God knows for sure, but it is increasingly clear to modern science that the universe was exquisitely fine-tuned to enable human life. We are somehow critically involved in His purpose. Our job is to sense that purpose as best we can, love one another, and help Him get that job done."

— RICHARD SMALLEY (1943-2005)
[American scientist, known for the discovery of new form of carbon, winner of 1996 Nobel Prize in Chemistry]

"I believe in God. In fact, I believe in a personal God who acts in and interacts with the creation. I believe that the observations about the orderliness of the physical universe, and the apparently exceptional fine-tuning of the conditions of the universe for the development of life suggest that an intelligent Creator is responsible."

— WILLIAM D. PHILLIPS (1948-)
[American physicist, winner of 1997 Nobel Prize in Physics]

"Religion tells us how to relate to each other and science shows us how God constructed the universe."

— WILLIAM D. PHILLIPS (1948-)

COFFEE BREAK

Russell-Einstein Manifesto: In 1955, Bertrand Russell published a manifesto which outlined the dangers posed by weapons of mass destruction. There were eleven signatories of this manifesto; ten of them were Nobel Laureates, including Albert Einstein. This manifesto later came to be known as the Russell-Einstein Manifesto. In a strange way, it warned the humanity, more than 40 years before Huntington's hypothesis, against a clash of civilizations between the East and the West.

"Most of us are not neutral in feeling, but, as human beings, we have to remember that, if the issues between East and West are to be decided in any manner that can give any possible satisfaction to anybody, whether Communist or anti-Communist, whether Asian or European or American, whether White or Black, then these issues must not be decided by war. We should wish this to be understood, both in the East and in the West.

There lies before us, if we choose, continual progress in happiness, knowledge, and wisdom. Shall we, instead, choose death, because we cannot forget our quarrels? We appeal as human beings to human beings: Remember your humanity, and forget the rest."

"Science isn't about knowing the mind of God; it's about understanding nature and the reasons for things. .... Most scientists will concede that as powerful as science is, it can teach us nothing about values, ethics, morals or, for that matter, God. Don't go about pretending otherwise!"

— ERIC CORNELL (1961-)
[American physicist, winner of 2001 Nobel Prize in Physics]

"The religious explanation has been supplemented--but not supplanted--by advances in scientific knowledge. We now may, if we care to, think of Rayleigh Scattering as the method God has chosen to implement his color scheme."

— ERIC CORNELL (1961-)

WALL OF MORTALS:
GOD OF NOBEL POETS, PHILOSOPHERS AND STATESMEN

"Chance is perhaps the pseudonym of God when he did not want to sign."

— ANATOLE FRANCE (1844-1924)
[French author and winner of the 1921 Nobel Prize in Literature]

"I do not see how anyone can sustain himself in any enterprise in life without prayer. It is the only spring at which he can renew his spirit and purify his motive. God is the source of strength to every man and only by prayer can he keep himself close to the Father of his spirit."

— WOODROW WILSON (1856–1924)
[The twenty-eighth President of the United States, winner of 1919 Nobel Peace Prize]

COFFEE BREAK

God is Work In Progress: George Bernard Shaw claimed to be an atheist at an early age, but later renounced his atheism and called himself a mystic. He argued that God was a work in progress, and often ridiculed churches, clerics, orthodoxies, and anthropomorphic gods.

"When we know what God is, we shall be gods ourselves."

— GEORGE BERNARD SHAW (1856-1950)
[Irish playwright and a co-founder of the London School of Economics, only person to receive a Nobel Prize for Literature in 1925 and an Oscar in 1938 for his work in the movie Pygmalion]

"To me God does not yet exist; but there is a creative force struggling to evolve an executive organ of godlike knowledge and power; that is, to achieve omnipotence and omniscience; and every man and woman born is a fresh attempt to achieve this object. We are here to help God, to do his work, to remedy his whole errors, to strive towards Godhead ourselves."

— GEORGE BERNARD SHAW (1856-1950)

"Beware of the man whose God is in the skies."

— GEORGE BERNARD SHAW (1856-1950)

"Suppose the world were only one of God's jokes, would you work any the less to make it a good joke instead of a bad one?"

— GEORGE BERNARD SHAW (1856-1950)

"When you are asked, 'Where is God? Who is God?' stand up and say, 'I am God and here is God, not as yet completed, but still advancing towards completion, just in so much as I am working for the purpose of the universe, working for the good of the whole society and the whole world, instead of merely looking after my personal ends."'

— GEORGE BERNARD SHAW (1856-1950)

"Fear God and take your own part! Fear God, in the true sense of the word, means to love God, respect God, honor God; and all of this can only be done by loving our neighbor, treating him justly and mercifully, and in all ways endeavoring to protect him from injustice and cruelty, thus obeying, as far as our human frailty will permit, the great and immutable law of righteousness."

— THEODORE ROOSEVELT, JR. (1858–1919)
[The twenty-sixth President of the United States, winner of 1906 Nobel Peace Prize]

COFFEE BREAK
God and Creative Evolution: Henri Bergson defined God as a God of Creative Evolution, who has nothing to do with the creator of the world.

"God, thus defined, has nothing of the already made; He is unceasing life, action, freedom. Creation, so conceived, is not a mystery; we experience it in ourselves when we act freely."

— HENRI BERGSON (1859-1941)
[One of the most influential French philosopher who had a cult-like following in early twentieth century; he won Nobel prize in literature in 1927]

"The universe is a machine for creating gods."

— HENRI BERGSON (1859-1941)

"God is He who effectively reveals Himself, who illuminates and warms privileged souls with His presence."

— HENRI BERGSON (1859-1941)

COFFEE BREAK

Tagore's God: Rabindranath Tagore was no ordinary man. He is the only author in the world who has written the national anthems of two independent countries: – Bangladesh and India. Today, no creative writer, living or dead, captivates the imaginations of 250 million Bengali-speaking people more than Tagore. His God is a man of our heart who dwells not in a temple, but in our everyday experiences.

Tagore introduced to us the idea of a direct, joyful, and mutual relationship with God. His God longs to unite with humans as much as humans want to unite with the Supreme God. Through his songs, Tagore brought God down to human experience and raised human dignity; and at the same time he divinized human beings and uplifted their spirituality. On one hand, Tagore wrote: "Thus it is that thy joy in me is so full. Thus it is that thou hast come down to me. O thou lord of all heavens, where would be thy love if I were not?" On the other hand, Tagore's submission to God is unparalleled: "In one salutation to thee, my God, let all my senses spread out and touch this world at thy feet."

Maybe Tagore was also a "God-intoxicated man," like Baruch Spinoza or Mansur Hallaj.

"God loves me when I sing. God respects me when I work."
— RABINDRANATH TAGORE (1861-1941)

[The most celebrated Bengali poet, philosopher, educator, musician, novelist, short story writer, and painter; also known as Rabi Thakur, the first Asian to win the Nobel Prize in any category in 1913; he won the prize for literature]

"Every child comes with the message that God is not yet discouraged of man."
— RABINDRANATH TAGORE (1861-1941)

"Our daily worship of God is not really the process of gradual acquisition of him, but the daily process of surrendering ourselves, removing all obstacles to union and extending our consciousness of him in devotion and service, in goodness and in love."
— RABINDRANATH TAGORE (1861-1941)

"The pious sectarian is proud because he is confident of his right of possession in God. The man of devotion is meek because he is conscious of God's right of love over his life and soul."
— RABINDRANATH TAGORE (1861-1941)

"True knowledge is that which perceives the unity of all things in God."
— RABINDRANATH TAGORE (1861-1941)

"The man of my heart dwells inside me.

Everywhere I look, it is he.

In my every sight, in the sparkle of light

Oh, I can never lose him --

Here, there and everywhere,

Wherever I turn, he is right there!"

— RABINDRANATH TAGORE (1861-1941)

"Thought is a garment and the soul's a bride

That cannot in that trash and tinsel hide:

Hatred of God may bring the soul to God."

— WILLIAM BUTLER YEATS (1865-1939)

[Irish poet, dramatist, and one of the foremost figures of 20th century literature, won 1923 Nobel Prize in Literature]

COFFEE BREAK

Russell's Teapot: Philosopher Bertrand Russell asserted that the burden of proof for the existence of God lies with the believers, not with the skeptics: "Many orthodox people speak as though it were the business of skeptics to disprove received dogmas rather than of dogmatists to prove them. This is, of course, a mistake. If I were to suggest that between the Earth and Mars there is a china teapot revolving about the sun in an elliptical orbit, nobody would be able to disprove my assertion provided I were careful to add that the teapot is too small to be revealed even by our most powerful telescopes. But if I were to go on to say that, since my assertion cannot be disproved, it is intolerable presumption on the part of human reason to doubt it, I should rightly be thought to be talking nonsense."

"The whole conception of a God is a conception derived from the ancient oriental despotisms. It is a conception quite unworthy of free men."

— BERTRAND RUSSELL (1872-1970)

[British mathematician, philosopher, logician, social critic, and celebrated author, won Nobel prize for literature in 1950]

"And if there were a God, I think it very unlikely that He would have such an uneasy vanity as to be offended by those who doubt His existence."

— BERTRAND RUSSELL (1872-1970)

"Cruel men believe in a cruel God and use their belief to excuse their cruelty. Only kindly men believe in a kindly God, and they would be kindly in any case."

— BERTRAND RUSSELL (1872-1970)

"Every man would like to be God, if it were possible; some few find it difficult to admit the impossibility."

– BERTRAND RUSSELL (1872-1970)

"The question whether there is a God is one which is decided on very different grounds by different communities and different individuals. The immense majority of mankind accepts the prevailing opinion of their own community. In the earliest times of which we have definite history everybody believed in many gods."

– BERTRAND RUSSELL (1872-1970)

"I am ready to meet my Maker. Whether my Maker is prepared for the ordeal of meeting me is another matter."

– SIR WINSTON CHURCHILL (1874-1965)
[British politician and prime minister during World War II, won Nobel prize for Literature in 1953]

"The fulfillment of Spiritual duty in our daily life is vital to our survival. Only by bringing it into perfect application can we hope to solve for ourselves the problems of this world and not of this world alone. United we stand secure. Let us then move forward together in discharge of our mission and our duty, fearing God and nothing else."

– SIR WINSTON CHURCHILL (1874 1965)

"God's love speaks to us in our hearts and tries to work through us in the world. We must listen to that voice; we must listen to it as a pure and distant melody that comes to us across the noise of the world's doings..."

– ALBERT SCHWEITZER (1875–1965)
[Franco-German theologian, organist, philosopher, physician, and medical missionary, winner of 1952 Nobel Peace Prize]

EVOLUTION OF GOD

God is a matter of personal experience among top intellectuals of the world.

"You should let yourself be carried away, like the clouds in the sky. You shouldn't resist. God exists in your destiny just as much as he does in these mountains and in that lake."

– HERMANN HESSE (1877–1962)
[German-born Swiss poet, novelist, and painter; winner of 1946 Nobel Prize in Literature]

"When you are close to Nature you can listen to the voice of God."

– HERMANN HESSE (1877–1962)

"For different people, there are different ways to God, to the center of the world. Yet the actual experience itself is always the same."

– HERMANN HESSE (1877–1962)

"Fear and hope drive the soul forward; they teach it to watch and pray and thus gain a growing knowledge of God – and as a consequence more and more to lose its egoistic concern for itself and to become unselfish, with adoring love for God: this is the fruit which the soul may bring forth at last."

– Sigrid Undset (1882–1949)
[Norwegian female novelist, winner of 1928 Nobel Prize in Literature]

"Impurity separates us from God. The spiritual life obeys laws as verifiable as those of the physical world. Purity is the condition for a higher love – for a possession superior to all possessions: that of God. Yes, this is what is at stake, and nothing less."

– Francois Mauriac (1885–1970)
[French author, winner of 1952 Nobel Prize in Literature]

"Man is born broken. He lives by mending. The grace of God is glue."

– Eugene O'Neill (1888-1953)
[American playwright, and 1936 Nobel laureate in Literature]

"The endless cycle of idea and action,

Endless invention, endless experiment,

Brings knowledge of motion, but not of stillness;

Knowledge of speech, but not of silence;

Knowledge of words, and ignorance of the Word.

All our knowledge brings us nearer to our ignorance,

All our ignorance brings us nearer to death,

But nearness to death no nearer to God.

Where is the Life we have lost in living?

Where is the wisdom we have lost in knowledge?

Where is the knowledge we have lost in information?

The cycles of Heaven in twenty centuries

Bring us farther from God and nearer to the Dust."

– T.S. Eliot (1888–1965)
[American-born English poet, perhaps the most important English-language poet of the 20th century; won the 1948 Nobel Prize in Literature]

"The names of God and especially those of His representative

Who is called Jesus or Christ according to holy books and

From someone's mouth

These names have been used, worn out and left

On the shores of rivers of of human lives

Like the empty shells of a mollusk.

However when we touch these sacred but exhausted

Names, these wounded scattered petals

Which have come out of the oceans of love and fear

Something still remains, a sip of water,

A rainbow footprint that still shimmers in the light."

– Pablo Neruda (1904-1973)
[Chilean writer, poet, and politician, winner of 1971 Nobel Prize for literature]

"I can never accept the idea that the Universe is a physical or chemical accident, a result of blind evolution. Even though I learned to recognize the lies, the clichés and the idolatries of the human mind, I still cling to some truths which I think all of us might accept some day. There must be a way for man to attain all possible pleasures, all the powers and knowledge that nature can grant him, and still serve God - a God who speaks in deeds, not in words, and whose vocabulary is the Cosmos."

– Isaac Bashevis Singer (1904–1991)
[Polish American author known for his short stories, winner of 1978 Nobel Prize in Literature]

"God is behind everything. Even when we do things against him, he's also there. No matter what. Like a father who sees his children doing a lot of silly things, bad things. He's angry with them, he's punishing them. At the same time, they're his children."

–Isaac Bashevis Singer (1904–1991)

"If God does not exist, we find no values or commands to turn to which legitimize our conduct. So, in the bright realm of values, we have no excuse behind us, nor justification before us. We are alone, with no excuses."

– Jean-Paul Sartre (1905–1980)
[French author, founder of existentialist philosophy, won the 1964 Nobel Prize in Literature]

"God is dead. Let us not understand by this that he does not exist or even that he no longer exists. He is dead. He spoke to us and is silent. We no longer have anything but his cadaver. Perhaps he slipped out of the world, somewhere else like the soul of a dead man. Perhaps he was only a dream...God is dead."

– Jean-Paul Sartre (1905–1980)

"Existentialism is not atheist in the sense that it would exhaust itself in demonstrations of the non-existence of God. It declares, rather, that even if God existed that would make no difference from its point of view."

– Jean-Paul Sartre (1905–1980)

"Whether or not God is dead: it is impossible to keep silent about him who was there for so long."

– Elias Canetti (1905-1994)
[Bulgarian-born novelist and non-fiction writer, winner of Nobel Prize in Literature in 1981]

"God does not die on the day when we cease to believe in a personal deity, but we die on the day when our lives cease to be illuminated by the steady radiance, renewed daily, of a wonder, the source of which is beyond all reason."

– DAG HAMMARSKJÖLD (1905-1961)

[Swedish diplomat, the second United Nations Secretary-General, and 1961 Nobel Peace Prize recipient]

"The inner experience of God's love is the deepest sense of joy and fulfillment a human being can have – nothing surpasses it. All other experiences of love, beautiful though they are, are like reflections or reminders of the real thing."

– DAG HAMMARSKJÖLD (1905–1961)

"I know God won't give me anything I can't handle; I just wish he didn't trust me so much."

– MOTHER TERESA (1910-1997)

[Born Agnes Gonxha Bojaxhiu in Albania, Roman Catholic Nun, who spent her life in Calcutta, India, won Nobel Peace Prize in 1979]

"Be a living expression of God's kindness."

– MOTHER TERESA (1910-1997)

"We need to find God, and he cannot be found in noise and restlessness. God is the friend of silence. See how nature - trees, flowers, grass- grows in silence; see the stars, the moon and the sun, how they move in silence... We need silence to be able to touch souls."

– MOTHER TERESA (1910-1997)

"To kill God is to become god oneself; it is to realize already on this earth the eternal life of which the Gospel speaks."

– ALBERT CAMUS (1913–1960)

[French author, philosopher, and journalist, winner of 1957 Nobel Prize in Literature]

"More than half a century ago, while I was still a child, I recall hearing a number of older people offer the following explanation for the great disasters that had befallen Russia: 'Men have forgotten God; that's why all this has happened.'

Since then I have spent well-nigh fifty years working on the history of our Revolution; in the process I have read hundreds of books, collected hundreds of personal testimonies, and have already contributed eight volumes of my own toward the effort of clearing away the rubble left by that upheaval. But if I were asked today to formulate as concisely as possible the main cause of the ruinous Revolution that swallowed up some sixty millions of our people, I could not put it more accurately than to repeat: 'Men have forgotten God; that's why all this has happened.'"

— Alexander Solzhenitsyn (1918-2008)

[Russian-American novelist, winner of 1970 Nobel Prize in Literature. In his acceptance speech for the Templeton Prize for Progress in Religion Buckingham Palace, London, May 10, 1983]

THE FINAL ANALYSIS

The origin of this beautiful poem can be traced to "The Paradoxical Commandments," written by Dr. Kent M. Keith when he was a nineteen-year-old student at Harvard in 1968. He published ten leadership commandments in a booklet for student leaders titled, *The Silent Revolution: Dynamic Leadership,* in the Student Council. These commandments became popular and were occasionally slightly altered as they were shared across the globe. Mother Teresa put a version that included eight of the original ten commandments on the wall of her children's home in Calcutta, India, and titled it "Anyway."

"The Final Analysis" version, presented below, is the most widely circulated and was attributed to Mother Teresa, although it is different from what was on her wall. All versions of this poem can be found at http://www.kentmkeith.com/mother_teresa.html.

"People are often unreasonable, illogical, and self-centered;
...Forgive them anyway!
If you are kind, people may accuse you of selfish, ulterior motives;
...Be kind anyway!
If you are successful, you will win some false friends and some true enemies;
...Succeed anyway!
If you are honest and frank, people may cheat you;
...Be honest and frank anyway!
What you spend years building, someone could destroy overnight;
...Build anyway!
If you find serenity and happiness, they may be jealous;
...Be happy anyway!
The good you do today, people will often forget tomorrow;
...Do good anyway!
Give the world the best you have, and it may never be enough;
...Give the world the best you've got anyway!"
You see, in the final analysis, it is between you and God;
It was never between you and them anyway."

"We were born to make manifest the glory of God that is within us. It's not just in some of us, it's in everyone."

— NELSON MANDELA (1918-)

[South African political activist, winner of 1993 Nobel Peace Prize, the first democratically elected President of South Africa]

"Yes! We affirm it and we shall proclaim it from the mountaintops, that all people – be they black or white, be they brown or yellow, be they rich or poor, be they wise or fools, are created in the image of the Creator and are his children!

Those who dare to cast out from the human family people of a darker hue with their racism! Those who exclude from the sight of God's grace, people who profess another faith with their religious intolerance! Those who wish to keep their fellow countrymen away from God's bounty with forced removals! Those who have driven away from the altar of God people whom He has chosen to make different, commit an ugly sin! The sin called APARTHEID."

— NELSON MANDELA (1918-)

"The belief that women are inferior human beings in the eyes of God, gives excuses to the brutal husband who beats his wife, the soldier who rapes a woman, the employer who has a lower pay scale for women employees, or parents who decide to abort a female embryo."

— JIMMY CARTER (1924-)

[39th President of the United States from 1977-1981, winner of 2002 Nobel Peace Prize]

"The discrimination against women on a global basis is very often attributable to the declaration by religious leaders in Christianity, Islam and other religions, that women are inferior in the eyes of God."

— JIMMY CARTER (1924-)

"Only the truly magnanimous and strong are capable of forgiving and loving. Let us persevere, then, praying always that God will help us to have the strength to love and forgive our enemies. Let us together, in this way, become the loving victors."

— KIM DAE JUNG (1925-2009)

[President of South Korea from 1998 to 2003, winner of Nobel Prize in 2000, called Nelson Mandela of Asia, in a letter sent to his second son, Hong-up, on November 24, 1980, after he was sentenced to death for sedition]

"I don't believe in God, but I'm afraid of Him."

— GABRIEL JOSÉ GARCÍA MÁRQUEZ (1927-)

[Colombian novelist, journalist and activist, won Nobel Prize for Literature in 1982]

"I rarely speak about God. To God, yes. I protest against Him. I shout at Him. But to open a discourse about the qualities of God, about the problems that God imposes, theodicy, no. And yet He is there, in silence, in filigree."

— ELIE WIESEL (1928-)
[Romanian-born Jewish-American writer, holocaust survivor; recipient of the Nobel Peace Prize in 1986]

COFFEE BREAK
I Have a Dream: Martin Luther King, Jr. believed that all men, black or white, are created in the image of God, and therefore, not only have the right to demand equality, but also have the power to change the world. He led the US civil rights movement of the 1960s using non-violent methods, made popular by Mahatma Gandhi.

"I still believe that one day mankind will bow before the altars of God and be crowned triumphant over war and bloodshed, and nonviolent redemptive goodwill will proclaim the rule of the land."

— DR. MARTIN LUTHER KING JR. (1929-1968)
[American Baptist minister, civil rights activist, and recipient of the Nobel Peace Prize of 1964]

"He who hates does not know God, but he who loves has the key that unlocks the door to the meaning of ultimate reality."

— DR. MARTIN LUTHER KING, JR. (1929–1968)

"You don't choose your family. They are God's gift to you, as you are to them."

— DESMOND TUTU (1931-)
[South African cleric and activist, winner of 1984 Nobel Peace Prize]

"The God that I worship is a strange God. Because it is God who is omnipotent, all-powerful, but he is also God who is weak. An extraordinary paradox: that it is God, a God of justice, who wants to see justice in the world. But because God has such a deep reverence for our freedoms all over the place, God will not intervene, like sending lightning bolts to dispatch of all despots. God waits for God's partners: us.

God has a dream. God has a dream of a world that is different, a world in which you and I care for one another because we belong in one family. And I want to make an appeal on behalf of God. God says, 'Can you help me realize my dream? My dream of a world that is more caring, a world that is more compassionate, a world that says people matter more than things. People matter more than profits. That is my dream,' says God. 'Will you please help me realize my dream, and I have nobody, except you'.

— DESMOND TUTU (1931-)

"God remains God, whether God has worshippers or not."

– Desmond Tutu (1931-)

"In Buddhist practice, [there is] no [God]. But much depends on how you interpret the meaning of God. God is an ultimate truth. Also I think we can say, an ultimate energy. Buddhists do accept their ultimate nature and that everything comes from that reality. I think that God, in a sense, is infinite love. Perhaps there is a common interpretation with Buddhism."

– Dalai Lama (1935-)

[Born Tenzin Gyatso, the 14th Dalai Lama and the spiritual leader of the people of Tibet, winner of Nobel Prize in Peace in 1989]

"If you believe in God, see others as God's children. If you are a nontheist, see all beings as your mother. When you do this, there will be no room for prejudice, intolerance, or exclusivity."

– Dalai Lama (1935-)

"We achieve everything by our efforts alone. Our fate is not decided by an almighty God."

– Aung San Suu Kyi (1945-)

[Burmese opposition politician and General Secretary of the National League for Democracy. Winner of Nobel Peace Prize in 1991]

"We worship an awesome God in the Blue States, and we don't like federal agents poking around our libraries in the Red States. We coach Little League in the Blue States and have gay friends in the Red States."

– Barack Obama (1961-)

[African American politician, US President (2008). Winner of Nobel Peace Prize in 2009]

"Kneeling beneath that cross on the South Side of Chicago, I felt God's spirit beckoning me. I submitted myself to His will, and dedicated myself to discovering His truth."

– Barack Obama (1961-)

CHAPTER DIGEST

Nobel laureates are a different breed of humans, recognized for their outstanding achievements in the fields of physics, chemistry, medicine, literature, peace, and economics. Sixty-nine Nobel laureates have posted on the *Wall of Mortals*. Their opinions on God range from deep belief in a Supreme Being to explicit denial of a God.

Their postings are quite entertaining too; for example, when Einstein said of God that "I, at any rate, am convinced that He does not throw dice," Niels Bohr quipped, "Stop telling God what to do with his dice." Millikan thought he had fingerprinted God in the heavens. He also said, "It is unthinkable that a real atheist could be a scientist," which can be contrasted with what Monod said: "A scientist who believes in god suffers from schizophrenia."

George Bernard Shaw was an atheist in his early years, but later renounced atheism in favor of mysticism. Bertrand Russell remained a life-long agnostic and posted the "Russell Teapot" theory on the *Wall of Mortals* to ridicule the argument from design for the existence of God. Rabindranath Tagore, an Indian Bengali poet, posted heart-warming messages in *God's Facebook*; his inspirational words provided insight into the potential for a spiritual relationship with a personal God. Martin Luther King, Jr. posted his dream on the *Wall of Mortals*, but that dream remains elusive.

The relationship between God and Nobel laureates was predominantly respectful. A few scientists were atheists because they couldn't find any scientific basis for believing in a creator God. More scientists were agnostic because of their scientific rationalism, which recognized unexplained mysteries in the universe but couldn't accept an all-powerful first cause. Several scientists were clearly theists, as they kept the domain of personal belief separate from that of scientific inquiry.

The Nobel laureate philosophers and poets were a mixed lot. Of special note is Tagore, who proclaimed the arrival of the God of humanity, an inner personal God, in the ruined temple of tribes and nations. Bishop Desmond Tutu declared that God is not a Christian, and wanted to embrace people of all religions within the fold of God. President Barack Obama invited non-believers into interfaith forums, as these are an integral part of the community of humanity, regardless of anyone's belief in a God of a specific religion.

Hence, an intellectual basis for a *Friendship of Civilizations* emerged.

11

God of Children and Teenagers

"Where have I come from, where did you pick me up?"
the baby asked its mother.
She answered, half crying, half laughing,
and clasping the baby to her breast -
"You were hidden in my heart as its desire, my darling;
you were in the dolls of my childhood's games;
And when with clay I made the image of my god every morning,
I made and unmade you then.
You were enshrined with our household deity,
in his worship, I worshipped you."

—RABINDRANATH TAGORE (1861-1941): THE BEGINNING

STATUS UPDATE

❖ God's best gift to humans is children, who are from the heavens.

❖ God is seen by many of us in the mysterious light that shines on the face of a sleeping child.

❖ God remains a mystery to children, and their thoughts are shaped by what they hear from the elders in their family.

❖ Researchers claim that children form a mental representation of God by the age of six, whether or not they have been exposed to the concept of the existence of God.

❖ A 2009 study of 1,000 children, aged 5 to 12, in the U.S.A. finds that they see God as a real person who is loving and personal to them as individuals.

❖ A 2009 study of 1,000 teenagers, aged 13 to 18, in England finds that two thirds of teenagers don't believe in God.

❖ A 2009 study of 700 teenagers, aged 13 to 17, in the U.S.A. finds that only 19% believe in God as their savior. Interfaith dialogue gains momentum and God becomes more universal.

NOTES FROM HISTORY
(MYSTERIES OF CHILDHOOD)

Most of us have experienced the sense of magic and awe that comes with observing children. Watch a child sleeping and you will notice a mysterious light shining on her or his face—a sure sign of God to many of us.

So, what do children think about God? What is their understanding of God? Two authors, Eric Marshall and Stuart Hample, and an illustrator, Yanni Posnakoff, ventured into that uncharted territory and published a book entitled *Children's Letters to God* in 1966. It was only fifty-nine pages, but it captured the attention of readers throughout America and by the year's end, 500,000 copies of the book had been printed for sale. Twenty-five years later, in 1991, the same authors published another edition of the book with fewer than a hundred pages. In 2004, these letters were used to create the musical *Children's Letters to God.*

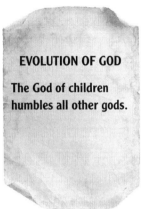

EVOLUTION OF GOD

The God of children humbles all other gods.

The innovative work of Marshall and Hample not only uncovered a new domain of hitherto unknown knowledge, it also inspired many such projects in which children were asked to write letters to God. David Heller published a 144-page book entitled *Dear God: Children's Letters to God* in 1994. Dr. Robert J. Landy published a book entitled *God Lives in Glass* in 2001; the book was based on his interviews with some 500 children from more than 30 countries and from more than 20 spiritual orientations. Several internet sites contain more letters from children, some of which are anonymous.

The students of Taylor University, Indiana, U.S.A. conducted a study in which 1,000 children aged 5 to 12 were asked to write a letter to God. These letters were analyzed for content, and the most common feature was found to be thankfulness to God. The next most common was their love of God, as they saw God as a real person. Children also seemed fascinated by the reality of heaven, and believed that it would be their home some day.

Teenagers are more rebellious in their nature and their conceptions of God and religion vary widely. A 2009 study of 1,000 teenagers aged 13 to 18 in England revealed that about two thirds didn't believe in God, 59% believed that religion had a negative influence in the world, and 47% said that organized religion had no place in the world.

The students of Taylor University also conducted a study in which 700 teenagers aged 13 to 17 were asked to write a letter to God. These letters were analyzed for content, and the two most common features were thankfulness for spiritual and for non-spiritual things. The study also found that only 19% of the surveyed believed in God as their savior, while only about 23% were friendly with God and thankful for all spiritual things, and about 43% were thankful for non-spiritual things (Chupp et al., 2010).

Time magazine, in a November, 2006 story entitled *How to Get Teens Excited about God*, reported on a 2005 study by The Barna Group, involving 2,409 teenagers aged 13 to 18, which showed that 42% of teenagers would attend a worship service in a church (or synagogue or temple) to better understand what they believe, and 45% would attend a church to worship or make a connection with God. However, only about 19% would attend a church to participate in a study of sacred scriptures.

The thoughts of children and teenagers on God are perhaps the simplest in nature and are expressed without any notion of self-importance or any efforts to impress, please, or hurt others.

WALL OF MORTALS:
CHILDREN'S HANDWRITING

The following quotes, selected from multiple sources for the sake of illustration, outshine all the others in this book in terms of touching one's heart. These quotes demonstrate a simplicity that can be found only in the world of children.

"Dear GOD: Are you really invisible or is that just a trick?"

– LUCY
[quoted in Hample & Marshall (1991)]

"In heaven, everything's magical. If you wish for an apple, God will give you a whole tree."

– RIZWANUL (AGE 11), MUSLIM, BANGLADESH
[quoted in Landy (2001)]

"Dear God: Help me to not wet my bed anymore. I keep getting whippings, but I still can't stop."

[quoted in www.goddirect.org]

"Dear God: Do you have a giant computer or do you count all the people of the world on your fingers? Love."

– WILLIAM (AGE 6)
[quoted in Heller (1994)]

COFFEE BREAK

I Am Drawing God: A 10-year-old girl is hard at work in class drawing a picture. The teacher approaches and asks, "What are you doing?"

The girl replies, "I am drawing God."

"But nobody has ever seen God," says the teacher.

The girl looks up and responds, "You will in a minute."

[quoted in "God Lives in Glass" by Robert Landy]

"Dear GOD,
Are you happy and healthy with all the people up there with you?"

– JACOB

"Dear GOD: Instead of letting people die and having to make new ones, why don't You just keep the ones You have now?"

— JANE
[quoted in Hample & Marshall (1991)]

"Dear God: Who do you pray to? If you don't say prayers, do you think you can let me off the hook."

— JIM (AGE 9)
[quoted in Heller (1994)]

"Dear God: My grandma is dying. She says you want her back with you, but I want her to stay here with me. You can have anyone you want. She's all I have, so please let her get better and stay."

[quoted in www.goddirect.org]

"Dear GOD,
Why do we talk to You if You don't talk back to us?"

— ANDREW

"Dear God: Girls are weird. Except for my mom. Love you."

-TIMMY (AGE 7)
[quoted in Heller (1994)]

"God seems to look like a girl."

— JOSE (AGE 7), CATHOLIC, PORTUGAL
[quoted in Landy (2001)]

"Dear God: My dad get laid off last week at work. Please help him find work quick. He bugs us a lot when he is home."

— MARTIN (AGE 8)
[quoted in Heller (1994)]

"In my dream I see a beautiful god
Watching over his world.
There he is with the golden moon.
I see him put out his hand.
He touches mars and moves it a little."

— SHYLA WALKER, 4TH GRADE

"Dear God: In Sunday School we learned that You are everywhere. How big are You? As big as Shaq? He plays basketball and is the biggest I've ever seen."

[quoted in www.goddirect.org]

"Allah has no form but he has power."

— NYLA (AGE 9), MUSLIM, USA
[quoted in Landy (2001)]

LETTERS TO GOD

Tyler Doughtie was born in Nashville, Tennesse, USA, on September 23, 1995. He was a lovely boy with a passion for soccer, outdoor activities, and games. Unfortunately, he was diagnosed with a rare form of brain cancer few months after he turned seven. Tyler bravely underwent surgery to remove the tumor but after a short remission, he died on March 7, 2005 before his tenth birthday. Two years after Tyler's death, his dad Patrick discovered, while boxing things up from his room, a series of letters his son wrote to God while he was ill. Tyler's story and his letters became the inspiration for a 2010 film *Letters to God*, which grossed $2.85 million in box office. A book with the same title, *Letters to God*, was published in 2010 by Patrick and Heather Doughtie to tell the story of Tyler with the help of his many letters to God. Andre K. Dugger also published a book, *Dear God*, which juxtaposed each of Tyler's letters with words from the Bible and a short reflection on the meaning behind the letter.

Few of Tyler's letters are quoted below to illustrate the lonely world of a terminally ill child.

"Dear God: I need your help. I have to find my special compass that Grandpa gave me. Love, Tyler."

[quoted in Doughtie (2010)]

"Dear God: How many people are in heaven? Must be a lot. I know two and I'm only eight. Love, Tyler."

[quoted in Dugger (2010)]

"Dear God: Why I am sick God? The medicine stinks. But I don't have to take my spelling test this week so that's good. Love, Tyler."

[quoted in Dugger (2010)]

"Dear God: Do you think you could help me clean my room? My Mom said it's a real mess. Love, Tyler."

[quoted in Doughtie (2010)]

"Dear God: Can you see the stars from heaven? My dad said you made them all. I'm really glad to be home from the hospital. Love, Tyler"

[quoted in Dugger (2010)]

"Dear God: But most of all, I really just wish my mom would laugh. I miss that the most. Love, Tyler."

[quoted in Dugger (2010)]

"Dear God: My sister Tina has a girlfriend named Wendy. They are both 15. Wendy has the biggest mouth in the world. No fooling. It would take a miracle to shut Wendy up. Got any left? I'm no tattletale."

— TAMMY (AGE 9)
[quoted in Heller (1994)]

"Dear God: My turtle died. We buried her in our yard. Is she there with your now? If so, she really likes lettuce."

[quoted in www.goddirect.org]

"Dear God: I saw the Grand Canyon last summer. Nice piece of work. Love."

— ALAN (AGE 9)
[quoted in Heller (1994)]

"Dear GOD: I went to this wedding and they kissed right in church. Is that okay?"

— NEIL
[quoted in Hample & Marshall (1991)]

"God is deep blue. He gives me good ideas."

— LUKE (AGE 5), CHRISTIAN, BRITAIN
[quoted in Landy (2001)]

"Dear GOD: Did you really mean "do unto others as they do unto you"? Because if you did, then I'm going to fix my brother."

— DARLA
[quoted in Hample & Marshall (1991)]

"Dear GOD: It rained for our whole vacation and is my father mad! He said some things about You that people are not supposed to say, but I hope You will not hurt him anyway."

— YOUR FRIEND -- (BUT I AM NOT GOING TO TELL YOU WHO I AM)
[quoted in Hample & Marshall (1991)]

"In Indian religion, God is not in a certain place, like the sky. He is everywhere. God is always in your heart and you have to bring it out if you want to pray to him."

— SHIVANI (AGE 12), HINDU, USA
[quoted in Landy (2001)]

"Dear GOD: Maybe Cain and Abel would not kill each other so much if they had their own rooms. It works with my brother."

— LARRY
[quoted in Hample & Marshall (1991)]

"I have seen Lord Shiva in a dream and I dreamt that when I got entangled then Shiva was able to free me from the tangle."

— SONU (AGE 10), HINDU, INDIA
[quoted in Landy (2001)]

"Dear GOD: I am American. What are you?"

— ROBERT
[quoted in Hample & Marshall (1991)]

"Dear GOD: I bet it is very hard for you to love all of everybody in the whole world. There are only four people in our family and I can never do it."

— NAN
[quoted in Hample & Marshall (1991)]

"I believe in God because when I have problems I pray. After praying, I feel better than before."

— BRIAN (AGE 8), CONFUCIAN, TAIWAN
[quoted in Landy (2001)]

"Dear GOD: We read Thomas Edison made light. But in school they said You did it. So I bet he stoled your idea."

— SINCERELY, DONNA
[quoted in Hample & Marshall (1991)]

"Dear God: Do you listen to my prayers every night? Do you really know when I only pretend to brush my teeth? Don't tell Mommy, O.K.?"

[quoted in www.goddirect.org]

"Dear GOD: I didn't think orange went with purple until I saw the sunset you made on Tuesday. That was cool!"

— EUGENE
[quoted in Hample & Marshall (1991)]

"Dear GOD: I was thinking that maybe you can make a mail service in heaven so we can write letters to some people up there or they can send us pictures of what heaven looks like and stuff like that."

— CALEIGH

"Dear GOD: I would like my Dad to stop Drinking and carring (caring) about use (us) more often."

— MARTHA (10)
[quoted in Chupp et al (2010)]

WALL OF MORTALS:
TEENAGERS' SCRIBBLES

COFFEE BREAK

God and Teenagers: Penguin Books carried out a study of 1,000 teenagers aged 13 to 18 in 2009 on their belief in God. England's Daily Mail newspaper published the story on June 22, 2009 with the headline "Two-thirds of teenagers don't believe in God... and think reality TV is more important."

"Thanks for being a friend, even though I can't see you. I wish I could see you when I talk to you. Sometimes I wish you were here, so I could give you a hug. When I disobey you or lie I wish I could come to you and see how sad you are when I do so I might never do it again. Thanks for being a great God that gave me all my talents and skills."

— SARAH (15)
[quoted in Chupp et al (2010)]

"How does it feel to be you? What does it feel like to be God?"

— RAYMOND (15)
[quoted by Walsch (2001)]

"But if you are so powerful, why don't you just end suffering forever? Why not just eliminate it as a possible human experience"

— BRAD (15)
[quoted in Walsch (2001)]

"How is it that a God of mercy can be such an isolationist and so intolerant to other views? How can a God of infinite mercy condemn anyone for anything? Why condemn for eternity those transgressions that are momentary?"

— SCOTT (19)
[quoted in Walsch (2001)]

"Dear God: I am a young teenager. I don't get along with my parents. I argue with them, but I don't really like this... I have trouble with school and work, too, but I know I can get through if you help me."

— Young Teenager
[quoted in Jones-Prendergrast (1979)]

"Dear God: How do I know what is expected out of me in life? I try to talk to you, but I never seem to find the answers. I try to thank you, but there is an emptiness present."

— A TEENAGER
[quoted in Jones-Prendergrast (1979)]

"Dear God: Why the absurdity? Why not reveal yourself? Is this letter written to nothing? I search for meaning like every man. Are you the meaning? Are you real?"

— A TEENAGER
[quoted in Jones-Prendergrast (1979)]

"Hi God: It seems stupid writing to you, as you know all that I can think, even before I do. But maybe through this letter I can better understand myself."

— A TEENAGER
[quoted in Jones-Prendergrast (1979)]

COFFEE BREAK
Teenage Phenomenon: Justin Bieber (1994-) is a teenage phenomenon, who came to the limelight in 2008. He is a Canadian pop singer, songwriter, model, and actor. Bieber is more influential in the social networking domain than President Barack Obama. He received the Artist of the Year award at the 2010 American Music Awards.

"I just want to say thank you so much, not only to God but to Jesus. Because I wouldn't be here without him. He's really blessed me. He's put me in this position. So I want to say thank you so much."

— JUSTIN BIEBER (TURNED 18 ON MARCH 1, 2012)

"Dear God: Why is there war, hatred, poverty, malnutrition, disease, adultery? How are we supposed to believe that you are all good when all that we see and read about is bad?"

— A TEENAGER
[quoted in Jones-Prendergrast (1979)]

"When people say not to question God 'cause it's wrong, they're wrong. It never hurts to question something we don't know. All you are doing is wanting to know God in your heart."

— EVE FRANCES SANTOS (AGE 15)
[quoted in Sullivan (1990)]

"My description of God is a man sitting in the sky in a high chair looking down at what He created thousands of years ago."

— PORFIDILIO BERAS (AGE 15)
[quoted in Sullivan (1990)]

"God is caring like a mother and strong and strict like a father. So God is both mother and father."

— Jason Hernandez (Age 17)
[quoted in Sullivan (1990)]

"My opinion of God is that everyone sees God in their own way. I see God as being black because I'm black. In the same breath, a white person might see God as being white. I have no objection because we both have the same God, we just see Him differently."

— Vernon Hodge (Age 15)
[quoted in Sullivan (1990)]

"A man without God is like a teenager with a powerful car."

— Mary Jo Cooper (Age 77)
[Unity Minister, California (quoted in Sullivan 1990)]

HARRY POTTER AND GOD

"If you want to know who dies in Harry Potter, the answer is easy: God"

— LEV GROSSMAN (1969-)
[American journalist and novelist]

Harry Potter is a 21st century teenage phenomenon. The first book in the seven-book series appeared in 1997; and as of June 2011, more than 450 million books have been sold in this immensely successful fantasy novel series. Harry Potter books have been burned by Christian pastors in United States in New Mexico and Michigan on the ground that these books promote witchcraft.

As of 2011, Amazon lists several books discussing the topic of God and Harry Potter, such as "Looking for God in Harry Potter", "God and Harry Potter at Yale: Teaching Faith and Fantasy Fiction In An Ivy League Classroom", "The Harry Potter Bible Study: Enjoying God Through the Final Four Harry Potter Movies", and "God, the Devil, and Harry Potter: A Christian Minister's Defense of the Beloved Novels." In 2008, Rev. Danielle Tumminio offered a course entitled "Christian Theology and Harry Potter" at Yale University. There is also a great interest about author J. K. Rowling's religious beliefs.

"It is perfectly possible to live a very moral life without a belief in God, and I think it's perfectly possible to live a life peppered with ill-doing and believe in God."

— JOANNE K. ROWLING (1965-)
[British author of immensely popular Harry Potter fantasy novel series]

"Yes. I do struggle with it; I couldn't pretend that I'm not doubt-ridden about a lot of things and that would be one of them but I would say yes."

— JOANNE K. ROWLING (1965-)
[When asked if she believed in God in British documentary, "JK Rowling: A Year in the Life"]

"Many of my students come to the conclusion that love is the closest approximation to God in Harry Potter, in part because God is defined as love in Christian tradition (1 John 4:16)."

— DANIELLE TUMMINIO (1981-)
[American theologian, priest, and writer]

"Intriguingly, love's identity as something God-like within the series is a departure from other 20th-century fantasy books with theological overtones ... My sense is that presenting God as an abstract concept resonates for many non-Christians who live in an era of skepticism."

— DANIELLE TUMMINIO (1981-)

"Is Harry Potter the Son of God? ... The story of Harry Potter is, and always was, a Christian allegory - a fictionalized modern day adaptation of the life of Christ, intended to introduce his character to a new generation."

— ABIGAIL BEAUSEIGHNEUR (20TH CENTURY)
[American web author, published in www.mugglenet.com]

CHAPTER DIGEST

There are two other groups of postings on the *Wall of Mortals*: one from children and the other from rebellious teenagers. Children's postings are naïve, simple, cute, and sometimes funny. Children ask God for help in solving their small but very real problems, like bed-wetting or sibling rivalry. They appreciate God's artwork in nature, and wonder whether God is actually invisible or God's invisibility is just a trick. The postings of teenagers on the *Wall of Mortals* range from quandaries to bold hypotheses.

The child–God relationship is dominated by simplicity and humility. It shows that in reality, we are all childlike in our understanding of the physical and spiritual worlds, despite our scientific and material achievements of the last five thousand years.

Hence, an emotional basis for a *Friendship of Civilizations* has emerged.

12

God Gives Interviews

"And the LORD spoke unto Moses face to face, as a man speaketh unto his friend. And he returned again into the camp; but his servant Joshua, the son of Nun, a young man, departed not out of the tabernacle.

And Moses said unto the LORD, "See, Thou sayest unto me, 'Bring up this people,' and Thou hast not let me know whom Thou wilt send with me. Yet Thou hast said, `I know thee by name, and thou hast also found grace in My sight.'

Now therefore, I pray Thee, if I have found grace in Thy sight, show me now Thy way, that I may know Thee, that I may find grace in Thy sight; and consider that this nation is Thy people."

And He said, "My presence shall go with thee, and I will give thee rest."

And He said, "Thou canst not see My face, for there shall no man see Me and live."

—BIBLE: EXODUS: 11-14 AND 20

STATUS UPDATE

❖ God can't be seen but can be heard.

❖ God faces many mortal questions in imaginary interviews.

❖ God shows tolerance, as his wrath does not fall on those who make false claims of interviewing him.

NOTES FROM HISTORY
(FACE TO FACE WITH GOD)

At the Day of Judgment, sometime in the future, we all are supposed to meet God face to face. In our past history, some humans met God as recorded in our scriptures. For example, in 1200 BC, Moses met Yahweh, the biblical God, on the mountaintop of Sinai in today's Egypt, and took home some instructions from God. In around 800 BC, Arjuna conversed with the Bhagwan (God of Hinduism) at the battlefield of Kurukshetra in India. Their conversation forms the 700 verses of the Bhagavad Gita. In about 621 AD, Prophet Muhammad made an out-of-the-world trip to the heavens to meet Allah (God of Islam) and brought home divine instructions about prayers and religious rituals.

EVOLUTION OF GOD

The God of the post-modern era is open-minded and holds conversations with common folks.

However, these human-God encounters only took place for a special group of divinely inspired humans—the prophets. Lesser mortals haven't had a chance to meet God face to face yet, but some of them claim that they have interviewed God in their imagination. These imaginary interviews are very enlightening and entertaining, as they shed light on a different variety of human conceptions of God. Extracts from a few published interviews are provided below as illustrations.

WALL OF MORTALS:
INTERVIEWS WITH GOD

AN UNUSUAL INTERVIEW WITH GOD

In the world of the internet and e-mails exists the widely circulated "An Interview With God", which is often attributed to an anonymous author. However, there is a claim that this interview, with several other short stories, was actually submitted by John James Brown (pen name: James Lachard) to about five publishers, but was never published. Somehow, this interview got leaked to the internet and John Brown, at that time on his death bed, decided to let it circulate. John Brown was born in 1923 in Clacton-on-Sea, Essex, England. In 1942, he enlisted in the British Army and served in Burma. Later he worked at World Vision until his retirement in 1990.

A lesson worth taking before dying

"I dreamed I had an interview with God.

"So you would like to interview me?" God asked.

"If you have the time" I said.

God smiled. "My time is eternity."

"What questions do you have in mind for me?"

"What surprises you most about humankind?"

God answered...

"That they get bored with childhood,

they rush to grow up, and then

long to be children again."

"That they lose their health to make money...

and then lose their money to restore their health."

"That by thinking anxiously about the future,

they forget the present,

such that they live in neither

the present nor the future."

"That they live as if they will never die,

and die as though they had never lived."

God's hand took mine

and we were silent for a while.

And then I asked...

"As a parent, what are some of life's lessons

you want your children to learn?"

"To learn they cannot make anyone

love them. All they can do

404

is let themselves be loved."

"To learn that it is not good
to compare themselves to others."

"To learn to forgive
by practicing forgiveness."

"To learn that it only takes a few seconds
to open profound wounds in those they love,
and it can take many years to heal them."

"To learn that a rich person
is not one who has the most,
but is one who needs the least."

"To learn that there are people
who love them dearly,
but simply have not yet learned
how to express or show their feelings."

"To learn that two people can
look at the same thing
and see it differently."

"To learn that it is not enough that they forgive one another,
but they must also forgive themselves."

"Thank you for your time," I said humbly.

"Is there anything else
you would like your children to know?"

God smiled and said,

"Just know that I am here... always."

AN INTERVIEW WITH GOD BY A BLACK GIRL

British playwright and Nobel prize winner George Bernard Shaw wrote a book entitled *The Adventures of the Black Girl in Her Search for God* (and Some Lesser Tales). The title story is about an African black girl who is freshly converted by a white missionary woman. She takes literally the biblical advice, "Seek and you shall find me", and goes on a search for God in an attempt to speak to Him. Here is an excerpt from the book about one of her encounters."

"Did you make the world?" said the black girl.

"Of course I did," he said.

"Why did you make it with so much evil in it?" she said.

"Splendid!" said the god. "That is just what I wanted you to ask me. You are a clever intelligent girl. I had a servant named Job once to argue with; but he was so modest and stupid that I had to shower the most frightful misfortunes on him before I could provoke him to complain. His wife told him to curse me and die; and I dont wonder at the poor woman; for I gave him a terrible time, though I made it all up to him afterwards. When at last I got him arguing, he thought a lot of himself. But I soon shewed him up. He acknowledged that I had the better of him. I took him down handsomely, I tell you."

"I do not want to argue," said the black girl. "I want to know why, if you really made the world, you made it so badly."

"Badly!" cried the Nailer. "Ho! You set yourself up to call me to account! Who are you, pray, that you should criticize me? Can you make a better world yourself? Just try: thats all. Try to make one little bit of it. For instance, make a whale. Put a hook in its nose and bring it to me when you have finished. Do you realize, you ridiculous little insect, that I not only made the whale, but made the sea for him to swim in? The whole mighty ocean, down to its bottomless depths and up to the top of the skies. You think that was easy, I suppose. You think you could do it better yourself. I tell you what, young woman: you want the conceit taken out of you. You couldnt make a mouse; and you set yourself up against me, who made a megatherium. You couldnt make a pond; and you dare talk to me, the maker of the seven seas. You will be ugly and old and dead in fifty years, whilst my majesty will endure for ever; and here you are taking me to task as if you were my aunt. You think, dont you, that you are better than God? What have you to say to that argument?"

God argues with a Black girl

"It isn't an argument: it's a sneer" said the black girl.

"You dont seem to know what an argument is."

"What! I who put down Job, as all the world admits, not know what an argument is! I simply laugh at you, child" said the old gentleman, considerably huffed, but too astonished to take the situation in fully.

"I dont mind your laughing at me;" said the black girl "but you have not told me why you did not make the world all good instead of a mixture of good and bad. It is no answer to ask me whether I could have made it any better myself. If I were God there would be no tsetse flies. My people would not fall down in fits and have dreadful swellings and commit sins. Why did you put a bag of poison in the mamba's mouth when other snakes can live as well without it? Why did you make the monkeys so ugly and the birds so pretty?"

"Why shouldnt I?" said the old gentleman. "Answer me that."

"Why should you? unless you have a taste for mischief said the black girl."

"Asking conundrums is not arguing" he said. "It is not playing the game."

"A God who cannot answer my questions is no use to me" said the black girl. "Besides, if you had really made everything you would know why you made the whale as ugly as he is in the pictures."

"If I chose to amuse myself by making him look funny, what is that to you?" he said "Who are you to dictate to me how I shall make things?"

"I am tired of you" said the black girl. "You always come back to the same bad manners. I dont believe you ever made anything. Job must have been very stupid not to find you out. There are too many old men pretending to be gods in this forest."

She sprang at him with her knobkerry uplifted; but he dived nimbly under the table, which she thought must have sunk into the earth; for when she reached it there was nothing there. And when she resorted to her bible again the wind snatched thirty more pages out of it and scattered them in dust over the trees...."

A DIALOGUE BETWEEN GOD AND MAN

Sir Allama Iqbal (1877-1933) is the most celebrated Pakistani Muslim poet, philosopher and political thinker. He used poetry to raise self-awareness among Muslims for reformation and reconstruction of Islamic philosophy and ethics. His God is a reachable God with whom he can have a dialogue. In 1909, he published a book titled *"Shikwa"* (Complaint), which caused a stir among the Muslim community, because of its bluntness in questioning God (Allah) for letting down the Muslims. Critics argued that the book was rude and accusatory to Allah. Four years later, in 1913, he published *"Jawab-e-Shikwa"* (Allah's Response to Complaint), wherein God pointed out the weaknesses of Muslims and asked them to introspect and change themselves if they want to improve their current status in the world.

His "Dialogue Between God and Man" is a short poem where God and Man engages into a very interesting discussion, as given below in M. Hadi Hussain's translation from the original Persian.

GOD:

"I fashioned this world out of one and the same clay;

You made Iran; Ethiopia and Tartary.

From mere earth I made steel, pure and without alloy;

You fashioned sword and arrowhead and musketry.

You made the axe, with which you felled trees grown by me,

And fashioned cages for my singing birds, born free."

MAN:

"You made the night; I made the lamp that lights it up.

You fashioned clay; I made of it a drinking cup.

You made the wilderness, the mountain and the steppe;

I fashioned garden, orchard, avenue and scape.

I change dread poisons into panaceas, and

I am the one who fashions mirrors out of sand."

AN INTERVIEW WITH GOD BY AN AMERICAN JOURNALIST

John Stanton, a Virginia based journalist, wrote that God consented to an interview with him and visited his home in Virginia in 2004. Here are some excerpts from Stanton's report on the imaginary interview, published at http://www.counterpunch.org/stanton12112004.

html. The title of his interview—*"God Returns, Supports Bush 100 Percent"*—was very politically charged at the time of his publication, when President Bush was in the midst of two unpopular wars in Afghanistan and Iraq.

Excerpts from his article are quoted below to illustrate how humans have used God to satirize others and make a political point.

"As for travel, God said that it has to do with String Theory, multiple dimensions and changing space. On his enthusiasm for America, God claimed that the most faithful are the most malleable--an American trait he likes--and it's easier being God when there are a majority of unquestioning subjects. And besides, God said he likes the support he is getting in the USA these days and figures that the separation of church and state will finally end under President George W. Bush...

God is impressed with the Americans

God is as white as fresh snow, wears a flowing sparkling gown, a well trimmed white beard, and holds a golden staff. In short, he looks like Gandalf in the Lord of the Rings series. God is 12 feet tall and 1000 pounds of solid muscle. He can bench press a galaxy while at the same time willing the creation of millions of different species on planets all over the universe. And, of course, he is proficient in the use of all types of firearms. God points out that he has multiple personalities just as the universe has multiple dimensions and that he really is the One God. For example, in America he is the Judeo Christian God and in other countries he could be Allah, Brahma or Buddha...

God said he is most pleased that 70 percent of Americans believe that Darwin and Wallace's Theory of Evolution is false. Creationism "is the way to go" he said. He is thrilled that many US Senators and Congressmen are introducing legislation on God's behalf and that President Bush authorized the filing of legal briefs in support of displaying the Ten Commandments in public institutions...

God was not pleased with the two-earner trend in America. He said that women need to be home with the children because "you don't want those strangers in day care guiding your children." God was visibly upset over the subject of abortion, gay marriage, and the sexification of America. He indicated that the country needed to be purified of these sins and that he had confidence in the good people running America would set things straight...

God offers insights to his children.

God said that President Bush should continue his Global War on Terror and the militarization of the world. But he pointed out that Americans shouldn't flatter themselves too much. "Today I'm with you and tomorrow I could be against you. I could take this planet and toss it into the sun. What do a billion lives mean to me when I can create a billion more to play with?"

AN INTERVIEW WITH GOD BY A NEW ZEALANDER

Scott MacGregor, an expatriate New Zealander, wrote a book entitled *God on God*, in which he describes God as an awesome character: "He is caring, clever, understanding, humorous, compassionate, thoughtful and everything positive ad infinitum. People have many mistaken ideas about Him. He has plenty to say—some of it quite unexpected, but all of it quite fascinating."

Selected excerpts from Scott MacGregor's fascinating 180-page book are quoted below to illustrate a few unique observations about God, expressed in the form of an imaginary interview.

"**INTERVIEWER:** It is an incredible privilege to be able to discuss issues with You.

GOD: I am delighted to have the opportunity.

INTERVIEWER: Are you distancing Yourself from organized religion?

GOD: I love everyone. I do not appreciate that some feel they have a corner on the market – Me being the product. I am not confined to buildings, ceremonies, or rituals. In fact, the truth be known, I do not inhabit those buildings, and the ceremonies do not express My essence. I am the Spirit of Love that pervades everything.

INTERVIEWER: But we are all selfish to some degree or another. It is human nature, the instinct for survival. If You intended us to be altruistic, which You have explained You would prefer, why did You programmme mankind with selfishness?

GOD: This world is a proving ground. Although there is selfishness inherent within man, there is also the ability to rise above it. Every individual has within him the potential to be a great force for good, if he only would.

INTERVIEWER: Very interesting! Another area that most of us like to be successful in is in relationships. Relationships are myriad, of course, but is there a general rule for success?

GOD: Yes! Humility!

INTERVIEWER: I thought You would say love.

GOD: Humility is love put into action. It regards the well-being and happiness of others as more important that one's own. Therefore, humility is the key.

INTERVIEWER: By definition, opposite of humility is pride. Does it then stand to reason that pride is what will cause a relationship to fail?

GOD: Exactly!

INTERVIEWER: But a sense of pride is ingrained in us since birth.

GOD: Pride builds walls between people. Humility builds bridges. It reaches to others."

INTERVIEWER: So what is the greatest virtue?

GOD: Why, love, of course. Because if you love others, that will motivate you to help them in every way, and it will supply you with the will and resources to practice all the other virtues such as patience, kindness, honesty, and so on.

INTERVIEWER: And the greatest vice?

God: Self-righteousness

Interviewer: I thought You would say hate.

God: The self-righteous 'moral' man has wreaked untold damage on the world. Those who have been the greatest scourges of this century thought they were right and righteous. Hitler, Stalin, Mao, and others were so convinced of their rightness that they had no compunction in dispensing terror and bloodshed to achieve their 'right' ends. And their confident self-righteousness convinced the masses that the horror they were perpetrating was for the greater good.

Self-righteousness causes man to think he is good without Me. Thus he has no need for Me, and he ends up straying far from Me. I have named some of the obvious culprits and there are many more that should spring to your mind, but if I named them, that could hit close to home and knock down some of your icons."

CHAPTER DIGEST

The postings here are exclusively on the *Wall of Mortals*, because God is the subject of interest of the interviewers. However, God's messages were carried truthfully by the interviewers and posted, as he responded to insightful and sometimes embarrassing questions.

God gave a few valuable life lessons in an anonymous interview, while his interview with a Black girl was pretty intense. In an interview with an author from New Zealand, God said that the greatest vice of humans is "self-righteousness" and the greatest virtue is "love."

The human–God relationship that emanated from these interviews was dominated by invaluable insights directly obtained from God. A new understanding was developed regarding the purpose and priorities of human lives.

Thus, a rational basis for a *Friendship of Civilizations* started to take root, as humans realized the folly of "self-righteousness," and misplaced priorities.

13

God of Computers, Bloggers, and Twitterers

"In any case, I think people who write programs do have at least a glimmer of extra insight into the nature of God for that very reason, because creating a program often means that you have to create a small universe.

I think it is fair to say that many of today's large computer programs rank among the most complex intellectual achievements of all time. They're absolutely trivial by comparison with any of the works of God, but still they're somehow closer to those works than anything else we know."

—DONALD KNUTH (1938-)

Professor Emeritus of Computer Science at Stanford University, once called "The Computer God" because of his pioneering work in computer science

STATUS UPDATE

❖ God games in the computer universe are invented to make humans feel like God, by giving them the ability to choose to intervene with miracles or calamities that are not necessary for the normal progression of the games.

❖ "Google" appears as the new God of the Church of Google. It declares itself to be the one and only God, and a jealous God, and provides proofs of its divinity. It also issues its own ten commandments.

❖ Donald Knuth, a famous computer programmer, is touted as the "Computer God" by Massachusetts Institute of Technology's (MIT) oldest and largest newspaper when he gave a series of lectures entitled "God and Computers" at MIT's Artificial Intelligence Lab.

❖ The World Wide Web (www) is created; it is like a Milky Way, dotted with an infinite amount of information, which is ever expanding.

❖ God appears on blogs (short for Web logs), a type of social networking tool used by millions of people to share ideas and opinions. God blogs are maintained by humans who pretend to be God. Apparently, God has not taken it personally and no calamity has befallen these pretenders.

❖ God appears on Twitter, another social networking tool, which limits its users' messages to only 140 characters.

NOTES FROM HISTORY
(THE ERA OF COMPUTERS)

The first calculating machine, the abacus, appeared around 2500 BC in Sumeria, what today is Iraq. The word "computer" was first used in 1613 to mean a person who carried out calculations. However, towards the end of the nineteenth century people began to use "computer" exclusively to describe a calculating machine. The first electronic computers were developed in the mid-twentieth century and occupied large rooms. The latter part of the twentieth century saw a huge revolution in computer technology, with an increase in processing power and compression of space through the use of integrated circuits.

EVOLUTION OF GOD

The God of the computer era is highly tolerant.

Towards the end of the twentieth century, computers became omnipresent in the modern world. Today, every second of our lives we receive blessings from computers, because they work incessantly to make our lives easier. In this way computers are like God, whose blessings are needed by humans in order to live happily.

We now connect to our friends using computers—our letters have become e-mails, and our phone systems won't work if a computer in the vast network of computers breaks. We communicate with others and share our ideas through the internet by e-mailing, blogging, twittering, and using Facebook.

In January of 2009, Pope Benedict XVI expressed views that were headlined as "Internet a new way to speak of God." The Pope said: "So that the Church and its message continue to be present in the great areopagus of social communications as defined by John Paul II and so that it is not a stranger to those spaces where numerous young people search for answers and meaning in their lives, you must find new ways to spread voices and images of hope through the ever-evolving communications system that surrounds our planet."

On May 20, 2009, at the end of his Wednesday general audience, the Holy Father launched an appeal: "I am inviting all those who make use of the new technologies of communication, especially the young, to utilize them in a positive way and to realize the great potential of these means to build up bonds of friendship and solidarity that can contribute to a better world. Young people in particular, I appeal to you: bear witness to your faith through the digital world! Employ these new technologies to make the Gospel known, so that the Good News of God's infinite love for all people, will resound in new ways across our increasingly technological world!"

Blogging is a highly popular social networking tool. The word "blog" is a contraction of the term "Web log." It is a special type of website where participants enter personal commentary, with graphics and/or videos, on different topics of interest. More than a hundred million blog sites are currently being maintained in the blogosphere.

Twitter is a free social networking service that allows users to send and read short messages, up to 140 characters. These messages are called tweets. In 2009, approximately eighteen million adults in the U.S.A. accessed Twitter on any platform at least monthly, and there were fifty-eight million users worldwide. The number of Twitter users grew significantly during the last two years. There are now about 175 million Twitter users in the world, ranging from senior executives to bored thirteen-year-olds. In May 2010, CNN reported that "even God is getting in on the Twitter business. A new website launched this week called almightytweets.com culls tweets in which God's advice is shared."

God is not only a topic of discussion in this modern technological world; God is also part of a booming video game industry. There are many God games on the market, in which one can play God and intervene within a video game setting. In January of 2009, "Pocket God", a game for the iPhone and the iPod Touch, was released. It has occupied a place in the App Store's Top 100 chart since its release, and had sold about two million copies by June of 2010.

WALL OF MORTALS:
GOD IN WEB, BLOG AND TWEETS

GOD GOES VIRTUAL

The *Wall of Mortals* goes virtual with the computer age, and so does God. No publishers are needed, no papers are needed—you type something on your computer, push an upload button, and there you go: your thoughts get posted on a virtual wall in the Webosphere. This has resulted in a significant proliferation of writings on both the *Holy Wall* and the *Wall of Mortals* in *God's Facebook*.

"Therefore, not only does God exists, He's a computer programmer."

– Duane Dibbley, 25-year old (in 2001)
COMPUTER PROGRAMMER, ARTIST, AND MUSICIAN
LAST SEEN ON INTERNET IN 2003.

"We at the Church of Google believe the search engine Google is the closest humankind has ever come to directly experiencing an actual God (as typically defined). We believe there is much more evidence in favour of Google's divinity than there is for the divinity of other more traditional gods."

– HTTP://WWW.THECHURCHOFGOOGLE.ORG

"I'm praying to my god.
Google is her name.
Nobody believes in her.
Despite of all her fame!"

– To Fu, a devotee of Church of Google

"God says do what you wish, but make the wrong choice and you will be tortured for eternity in hell. That, sir, is not free will. It would be akin to a man telling his girlfriend, 'Do what you wish, but if you choose to leave me, I will track you down and blow your brains out.' When a man says this we call him a psychopath and cry out for his imprisonment/execution. When a god says the same, we call him loving and build churches in his honor."

– Chuck Easttom (20th century)
COMPUTER PROGRAMMER

"What are the possibilities of a personal website for God and his appearance on the internet ? And more than that , what are the chances that you could have a video clipping from Him for our benefit ? The chances seem bright, the way things develop."

– Ramani Iyer (20th century)
INTERNET AUTHOR

"Thus the major difference between the Hindu and the Muslim beliefs is the difference of the apostrophe 's'. The Hindu says everything is God. The Muslim says everything is God's."

— HTTP://WWW.WORSHIP-THE-CREATOR.COM.

"Do good, then if there's an evil God everybody is still screwed. If there is a good God then you go to heaven, if there is no God then doing good is its own reward."

— POSTED BY TATARIZE IN SCIENCEBLOGS.COM - AUGUST, 2007

"haha but i love snow ball fights because we only get them once a year...twice if we get on God's good side."

— ADRIZZLY_BEAR, TWITTER MESSAGE DEC 25, 2009

"God has mysterious and amazing things awaiting us, it's time to explore."

— KABANDATREVOR - TWITTER.COM - JAN 07, 2010

"I'm not an Apple Fanboy. I'm just a regular Joe that believes Steve Jobs is God!... It is he who hath provided us with iPhones which serve us as palm sized minions. It is he who spun the Macbook Pro from aluminum ore. And it is he who hath brought forth the glory of the wondrous iPad."

— A BLOGGER WHO MAINTAINS "JOBSISGOD.COM"

"If Apple is a religion, Steve Jobs is God, Jonathan Ive [Apple's designer] his Son."

— MACDAILYNEWS.COM, MARCH 18, 2006

"**QUESTION:** Does God control everything that happens in my life?
ANSWER: He could, if he used the debugger, but it's
tedious to step through all those variables.
QUESTION: Why does God allow evil to happen?
ANSWER: God thought he eliminated evil in one of the earlier versions.
QUESTION: How come the Age of Miracles Ended?
ANSWER: That was the development phase of the project,
now we are in the maintenance phase."

— QUOTED IN HTTP://WWW.FICTION.NET/TIDBITS/
COMPUTER/COMPUTERS_AND_GOD.HTML

"There is no need for God to exist, the laws of nature do not require a creator and it is a puerile human obsession inventing one."

— GREMLINOFGANJA VIA TWITTER FOR IPHONE,
NOV 10, 2010 IN REPLY TO DEBATEGOD

"Do you ever approach God as if he were a giant search engine? You tell him what you want and expect instant results. What if God doesn't give you what you're really looking for? That's OK. There are lots of other "search engines" out there: parents, friends, the mall."

— Tracy Carbaugh in christianitytoday.com

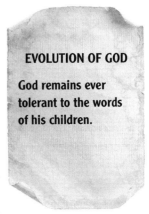

EVOLUTION OF GOD

God remains ever tolerant to the words of his children.

"For women, understanding the long tradition of Goddess religion strengthens your connection with your own spiritual essence, regardless of what faith you belong to. Seeing the Goddess within, helps women to appreciate their own power, skill, heritage, and beauty."

— Abby Willowroot in spiralgoddess.com

"Prayer sometimes pays off, and sometimes doesn't. This gives it the same reward pattern as a slot machine. A god who wanted to keep people praying couldn't devise a better strategy."

— 25yearsofprogramming blog.

"If gods do not exist, humans would create them because their own instincts would lead them in that direction. If gods do exist, humans inevitably would discover their existence because, again, their own instincts would lead them in that direction."

-25yearsofprogramming blog

HAIKU GOD (HTTP://HAIKUGOD.BLOGSPOT.COM/)

"The idea of God being E, electromagnetic energy, also fits well. After all, God appeared to Moses as electromagnetic energy (the burning bush)."

— Peter Leonard, Blogger at Haiku God, Age 64 in 2009

"In fact, don't believe anything, except that if you lose your I and experience not-I, you will know God. Belief (faith) is a way to the truth, it is not the truth."

— Peter Leonard, Blogger at Haiku God, Age 64 in 2009

"I am the not-I

masquerading as an I.

Can you see through me?

I'm in front of you

I am behind your own eyes.

Do not stop looking!

I am the hearer

I am also what you hear.

Are you listening?

Everywhere, nowhere

I am closer than your face
Find me if you can!"

— PETER LEONARD, BLOGGER AT HAIKU GOD, AGE 64 IN 2009

GOD'S E-MAIL TO TEENS

*God sends e-mails
to teens*

"Dear Child: Lots of people think that being a Christian means missing out on the good stuff. They think I'm the father who makes you ride your bike to school on your sixteenth birthday when everyone gets a new car. That's not Me. I have a wonderful inheritance for you. Read My will and learn that I've promised you the best slice of life."

— CLAIRE CLONINGER AND CURT CLONINGER, IN
"E-MAIL FROM GOD FOR TEENS" (1999)

"Dear Child: Did you ever wonder why I don't use My power to make people do what I want? I could have made the world like a big puppet stage and manipulated everyone by pulling on their strings."

— CLAIRE CLONINGER AND CURT CLONINGER, IN
"E-MAIL FROM GOD FOR TEENS" (1999)

"My Child: The world you live in is much more interested in what you look like on the outside than what's on the inside of you. I'm just the opposite. I check out your heart."

— CLAIRE CLONINGER AND CURT CLONINGER, IN
"E-MAIL FROM GOD FOR TEENS" (1999)

GOD'S BLOG (HTTP://BIGOLDGOD.BLOGSPOT.COM/)

(A site maintained by someone calling himself/herself "God")
This internet "God" describes himself as:

"I am the wind in your beard.

I am the flutter in your heart.

I am the thing that makes Flamin' Hot Cheetos taste so delicious.

I am the twinkle in a beautiful stranger's eye.

I am God and I have a blog. God's Blog be thy name!"

This reminds us of "Song of Myself" by American poet Walt Whitman or the "Rebel" by Bengali poet Kazi Nazrul Islam.

One of the posting in that Blog is quoted below as an example of what goes on in a God blog:

"MY SON'S BIRTHDAY
Posted in http://bigoldgod.blogspot.com/

FRIDAY, DECEMBER 23, 2005

Glory be, unto the highest...

"My children. As you can expect, it's been busy up here in Heaven. All of the Kingdom of God (that's Me) is preparing for the birthday of Jesus (My son). You'd think something like this would be easy for the Almighty.

I could simply say: Thy will be done. And everything would take care of thyself.

Not so.

Firstly, we've had problems finding someone whom would emcee the gala event. Jesus said that Richard Pryor was newly available, but I've been in negotiations with Lucifer to determine where his place is.

Lu claims that since Dick Pryor tried to commit suicide and ravaged himself with drug use that he rightly belongs with his burning minions in Hades. I, being of more sound mind and of a gentle rule, do not agree with him. So, right now, Mr. Pryor is in the 'waiting room' or Purgatory (as some of thee call it) until this gets sorted out.

As for some of the other events, Moses has insisted that we have karaoke for the party. While I know that most would think this to be entertainment unto the highest, I've seen what happens when you give saints, apostles, and other 'holy' people the microphone.

There's pushing, there's shoving, and more than once I saw Princess Di gyrate and act wholly inappropriate whilst 'rocking the mic.'

I would like to sing a Barry Manilow song Myself, but I shall decide later how the party shall go down.

As for food, I thought it would be nostalgic to dine upon fishes and loaves, but I've received nothing short of the 'stink eye' from Jesus and Mary. They want a meal worthy of the heavens, when I know that most would appreciate foods of the older times.

Before thou shalt ask: Yes, we like to eat food here in Heaven. Would you deny us all of your earthly pleasures?

So, this is my roundabout way of apologizing for My lengthy absence. Thou art stalwart in continuing to read God's Blog and leave Me ashamed that I haven't been able to provide structure and guidance in My words as of late.

I haven't forgotten about the Kirk Cameron website.

I haven't forgotten about the God FAQ.

I haven't forgotten how much I love thee.

Whilst I must be off to finalize this party, rest assured I shalt return sooner than later and impart unto all of thee tales of Jesus's party and all of the other things I have promised.

May the spirit of Christmas jingle like so many angels carrying a bunch of bells in a basket so that your ear may hear it and remind you of the holiday time set forth every year...

Or something like that.

Be good.

– God"

POSTED BY GOD AT 7:34 AM 18 COMMENTS

This posting generated 18 comments as recorded in the blog. Here are samples of comments on the God blog:
"Susanna said...

Nice to hear you are still about and meddling in peoples' business. When are you returning to post some more revelations? Nothing since last year, come on God, you can do better than this.

9:49 PM"

"Majic said...

Dear God,

I have just discovered your blog. Didn't realise we had to communicate by email these days - no wonder my prayers aren't getting answered.

No matter - I will send you the backlog. Hope you have a big disk - it's been a traumatic few months.

12:58 PM"

"rraven said...

Hey God

As a wise blogger previously once said on this site...

"Dude--You're omnipotent. Update Your freakin' blog"

Hoping you are well. Wishing you are able to still get online access.

9:19 AM"

"NO GOD" #1 TRENDING TOPIC ON TWITTER

[Twitter has a sidebar with the top trending topics on Twitter at any given moment. On October 20, 2009, it was "No God"]

Here is a comment on a blogosphere as an example of what goes in the virtual *Wall of Mortals*

"http://de-conversion.com/2009/10/20/no-god-1-trending-topic-on-twitter/

October 20, 2009

In a classic case of irony, Christians tried to get the statement "No God, No Peace. Know God, Know Peace" to trend today on Twitter.

The result of this effort was the phrase "No God" became the #1 trending topic.

Please understand that atheists have been trying for months to get an atheist related topic to trend and this one was gifted to us.

"God" must be looking out for us Of course, I should note that the phrase really should be "Know God. No Peace. No God. Know Peace."

– The de-Convert"

HOLY GOD BLOG

http://holygodblog.com/

A posting sample:

"Deciding Which Regions Will Get Snow On Christmas Day

December 12th, 2009

Let it snow, let it snow, let it snow!!!

Presently I am in the midst of deciding where I should make it snow on Christmas Day. Of course, I largely honour My own weather patterns and maintain a certain consistency, but I always like to throw in a few unlikely places that don't get snow all that often – It's just a nice way to make even extra special the day My Son Jesus Christ was born."

COFFEE BREAK

The Tweet of God (https://twitter.com/#!/thetweetofgod) is maintained by comedy writer David Javerbaum in connection with his book "The Last Testament: A Memoir by God." This twitter has amassed 104,000 followers with such comic bits as, "The Pope just sent me a friend request. Dammit! I hate it when employees try to suck up."

ATHEIST BLOG

http://atheists.org/blog/

This is what the "About us" page say on this blog:

"Since 1963, AMERICAN ATHEISTS has been the premier organization laboring for the civil liberties of Atheists, and the total, absolute separation of government and religion. It was born out of a court case begun in 1959 by the Murray family which challenged prayer recitation in the public schools. That case – Murray v. Curlett – was a landmark in American jurisprudence on behalf of our First Amendment rights. It began:

> "Your petitioners are Atheists, and they define their lifestyle as follows. An Atheist loves himself and his fellow man instead of a god. An Atheist accepts that heaven is something for which we should work now – here on earth – for all men together to enjoy. An Atheist accepts that he can get no help through prayer, but that he must find in himself the inner conviction and strength to meet life, to grapple with it, to subdue it and to enjoy it. An Atheist accepts that only in a knowledge of himself and a knowledge of his fellow man can he find the understanding that will help lead to a life of fulfillment."

Now in its fourth decade, American Atheists is dedicated to working for the civil rights of Atheists, promoting separation of state and church, and providing information about Atheism."

TEN COMMANDMENTS OF THE CHURCH OF GOOGLE

1. "Thou shalt have no other Search Engine before me, neither Yahoo nor Lycos, AltaVista nor Metacrawler. Thou shalt worship only me, and come to Google only for answers.

2. Thou shalt not build thy own commercial-free Search Engine, for I am a jealous Engine, bringing law suits and plagues against the fathers of the children unto the third and fourth generations.

3. Thou shalt not use Google as a verb to mean the use of any lesser Search Engine.

4. Thou shalt remember each passing day and use thy time as an opportunity to gain knowledge of the unknown.

5. Thou shalt honor thy fellow humans, regardless of gender, sexual orientation or race, for each has invaluable experience and knowledge to contribute toward humankind.

6. Thou shalt not misspell whilst praying to me.

7. Thou shalt not hotlink

8. Thou shalt not plagiarise or take undue credit for other's work

9. Thou shalt not use reciprocal links nor link farms, for I am a vengeful but fair engine and will diminish thy PageRank. The Google Dance shall cometh.

10. Thou shalt not manipulate Search Results. Search Engine Optimization is but the work of Microsoft."

DOES GOD TWEET?

On August 11, 2009, the Washington Post asked the question "Does God tweet?" to a group of panelists composed of different backgrounds. Here are the some of the answers it received.

"No, God does not tweet nor does God have time to listen to almost seven billion people insincerely pleading for mercy."

— ARUN GANDHI (1934-)
[Indian journalist and socio-political activist, grandson of India's legendary leader, Mahatma Gandhi]

"God "twitters" every time God sees our inhumanity to each other. Perhaps God doesn't have time to monitor all of God's daily e-mail accounts, when there is so much violence in the world to worry about. I suspect God chooses not to be on Facebook, but God does get in our face when we fail to care for our neighbor or help the poor.

— BOB EDGAR (1943-)
[Ex-Congressman from Pennsylvania, former general secretary of the National Council of the Churches of Christ in the USA]

"Just yesterday God tweeted me. I was inclined to respond with sarcasm to someone, and suddenly I got a simple three-character message from the Lord: "No!""

— RICHARD MOUW (1940-)
[American philosopher, scholar, author, and president of Fuller Theological Seminary]

"Most people who believe in the concept of a Divine being think he or she lives in a heaven or paradise far above that is the ultimate place of residence for the "saved," while some sort of hell realm below is where the rest will go. However, from a theological perspective, the major theistic traditions say that God is omnipresent. If this is the case, then not only would God be present throughout the universe and within each of us but on Twitter and Facebook as well as throughout the Internet. Theologians also say God in omniscient, therefore he of she would likely know all "tweets," all blog entries, and even all e-mails."

— RAMDAS LAMB (1945-)
[American professor of religion who lived in India as a Hindu monk]

"It certainly seems evident that what many people hear as the voice of God is really their own voice, a rationalization for something they already want to do."

— SUSAN JACOBY (1946-)
[American author of nine books, most recently "The Age of American Unreason"]

"A tweeting God? Sounds sensible enough, especially since God isn't one to fall behind the current technological curve. But in cyberspace things aren't necessary what they appear to be."

— MATHEW SCHMALZ (1964-)
[American professor of religious studies, author of Catholic spirituality]

[Source: http://newsweek.washingtonpost.com/onfaith/2009/08/does_god_tweet/all.html]

CHAPTER DIGEST

God feels the need to speak again to humans because they have forgotten the central messages that he has been sending them all these years. He decides to go virtual, and use the Internet for broadcasting his messages directly to his more than six billion fans, rather than going through a single prophet. But there is a problem: men and women will now be able to track God's IP address and trace him down. So, in order to preserve the mystery of Godhood, he decides to remain silent and let humans, fans and critics alike, post his messages, interpreted or misinterpreted, on the *Wall of Mortals*.

The human–God relationship depicted in the postings on the *Wall of Mortals* is essentially non-devotional, except for sites that are dedicated to religious purposes, which contain either repeats or reinterpretations of earlier postings by God and prophets. The Church of Google has ridiculed the Ten Commandments of the Bible and has published its own modus operandi for the virtual world.

Because of its global reach, Facebook holds great promise for fostering interfaith communication and helping to deepen and widen our understanding of God.

Thus, a technical basis for a *Friendship of Civilizations* has been established.

And God, men, and women have come full circle to create the God of the Future, elaborated upon in the next chapter.

14

God of the Future

"I boasted among men that I had known you.
They see your pictures in all works of mine.
They come and ask me, 'Who is he?'
I know not how to answer them.
I say, 'Indeed, I cannot tell.'
They blame me and they go away in scorn.
And you sit there smiling.
I put my tales of you into lasting songs.
The secret gushes out from my heart.
They come and ask me, 'Tell me all your meanings.'
I know not how to answer them.
I say, 'Ah, who knows what they mean!'
They smile and go away in utter scorn.
And you sit there smiling."

—Rabindranath Tagore (1861-1941)

STATUS UPDATE

❖ God of Humanity arrives at the ruined temples of tribes, nations, and religious groups and waits for man to make his new altar with love and compassion, not with disdain for the followers of other religions.

❖ Men and women realize the role of geographic luck in determining their destinies, and seek to build the *House of Friendship of Civilizations*.

❖ Man's universe is made anew with a compassionate God, who rules ever after.

THE FUTURE...

In the beginning, God spoke. Then Man spoke and Woman spoke. Then God, Man, and Woman all kept speaking for thousands of years. The words they spoke were thoughtful, vibrant, and variegated, offering a kaleidoscopic panorama of dizzyingly confounding expressions, which captured the fascinating metamorphosis of God in human consciousness through the ages. Some of these words were recorded, while some were lost. Some words have been interpreted, and some misinterpreted. Some words generated love, some words hatred. Some words made peace, some wars.

> **EVOLUTION OF GOD**
>
> God changed over time from a co-equal being to a distant authoritative figure to a non-existent entity to a loving personal God.

Today, as we reach the zenith of our technological world, we are still exploring who God is and what God wants. No end is in sight in this eternal quest for God. In *Why God Won't Go Away*, authors Andrew Newberg, Eugene D'Aquill, and Vince Rause argue, "As long as our brains are arranged the way they are, as long as our minds are capable of sensing this deeper reality, spirituality will continue to shape the human experience, and God, however we define that majestic, mysterious concept, will not go away."

DOES GOD HAVE A FUTURE?

In March of 2010, *ABC News Nightline* hosted a debate titled, "Does God have a future?" at the California Institute of Technology, where Michael Shermer, Deepak Chopra, Sam Harris, and Jean Houston faced off in front of a packed audience of 1,000. Shermer is a former fundamentalist Christian turned anti-religious skeptic and the founder of The Skeptics Society; Chopra is a New Age spiritual counselor, medical doctor, and author of several bestselling books; Harris is a neuroscientist, an outspoken atheist, and the author of the bestselling book *The End of Faith*; and Houston is a teacher, author, and philosopher.

Nightline had a provocative take on the issue, asking the audience: "Are we at a time in history when the argument can now actually be settled? Given all that we know today about the cosmos and life on Earth, is science killing God—or can it bring us closer to him? Does God—or should God—have a future?" Sam Harris answered the question, "Does God have a future?" in this manner: "Yes, as a fictional character." Jean Houston answered: "Yes. I am not sure about human beings having a future, but there is no issue around God."

The debate ended without any conclusion, as each participant promoted his or her own viewpoint rather than actually answering each other's.

Aside from these spirited debaters, there are those who take issue with the versions of God, not necessarily the notion of God. For example, Ophelia Benson and Jeremy Stangroom, who together wrote *Does God Hate Women?*, want the version of God that originated in a period when male superiority was taken for granted to go away, because in their opinion, that version is a historical God who hates women, and "[that] God has to go."

Bart Kosko, a professor of electrical engineering at the University of Southern California and the author of *Fuzzy Thinking*, postulates that God's future is in science fiction: "The future of God looks both secure and fruitful. Science fiction has helped free God from His old stale prisons of the church and classroom. And science fiction will no doubt still use God ideas to round out and stretch the belief schemes of the future. For God is more than a great character. God is the ultimate plot device." Kosko thinks science fiction is a natural home for God; because, "creative minds will always weave the fuzzy and extreme conceptions of God onto the top or bottom of the knowledge webs of the day." He further extends his thoughts into a speculative domain and suggests the unthinkable: "Indeed, we can view the God of the Old Testament and the gods of ancient Greece and India as the science fiction of their day."

Some even wonder whether the future of a personal God is doomed, in the face of the rising tide of atheism among the young people of the twenty-first century. Karen Armstrong, the most famous religious scholar of our time, dismisses such thoughts, and even goes further to suggest that modern atheism may only be a prelude to a new religious outlook with a deeper appreciation for God.

History tells us that humans have redefined God, time and again, to meet the spiritual needs of their time and place. It is very likely that the same thing will happen in the future.

Deepak Chopra, famous for his writings on spiritualism, hypothesized about this redefinition of God in the following manner: "My position is that advanced science has actually turned the tables, giving us new ways to defend, not God as a patriarch seated on his throne in the sky, but God as a field of intelligence that gives rise to evolution itself and all that goes with it: creativity, quantum leaps, time and space, and expanding consciousness. As we learn more about these things, we will reshape God into something new and far more powerful than the traditional Judeo-Christian conception. In a word, the future of God depends upon human evolution. As we look deeper into our own awareness, we will meet the field of infinite awareness and intelligence that is our source, and on that path we will encounter God... A revitalized God won't look like the God taught in Sunday school. What will the deity look like? He/She/It will reflect our own state of evolution. Insofar as we understand our own consciousness, we will understand where it came from, which is God."

Amidst all these talks about the personal God, we must not forget the role and importance of the political God. Political scientists Monica Toft, Daniel Philpott, and Timothy Shah argued in their 2011 book *God's Century* that the political God is a powerful force that we must reckon with for any lasting peace on the face of the Earth. Toft, Philpott, and Shah (2011) theorized that God and religion would stay forever with us in our socio-political arena, despite the efforts by secular humanists to push God and religion into the "private sphere." They also pointed out that if properly guided, God and religion can become partners of peace building rather than the cause of instability and conflict, as the rational intellectuals of the twentieth century have accused. Toft and her coauthors saw it as an opportunity for us to utilize God and religion as "force multipliers" for peacemaking, reconciliation, and social justice.

THE SAME OR A NEW GOD?

Therefore, our imagination is challenged when we ask ourselves: What will the God of the future be? Will God be more benevolent than belligerent? Will the God of the future be fairer and more tolerant than what we have seen in the past? We need to look into both our hearts and minds for the answers to these fundamental questions. Otherwise, we would be like ignorant armies clashing in the darkness of mindless religious affiliations, as depicted by Matthew Arnold in his famous poem "Dover Beach":

> "The world, which seems
>
> To lie before us like a land of dreams,
>
> So various, so beautiful, so new,
>
> Hath really neither joy, nor love, nor light,
>
> Nor certitude, nor peace, nor help for pain;
>
> And we are here as on a darkling plain
>
> Swept with confused alarms of struggle and flight,
>
> Where ignorant armies clash by night."

It is evident from *God's Facebook* that five thousand years of recorded human history is not enough to capture the innumerable ways in which humans can understand who or what God is. There were new ideas in the past and there will be more new ideas in the future; there were old religions in the past, and there will be more new religions in the future; there were numerous old interpretations of scriptures, and there will be more new ones. The only thing that can be said with certainty is that the human understanding of God is at best approximate, provisional, and corrigible. The more we came to know God at different periods of history, the more we realized the inadequacy of our understanding. As a result, our God has been constantly changing from one generation to another. As a matter of fact, this is somewhat true also about science, the "God", in a rhetorical sense, of modernity. The "truth" of science today is only an explanation or description of the universe as we understand it today; this "truth" is approximate, provisional, corrigible, and often "false" from the viewpoint of later generations of scientists.

So how far can we go with this realization of fallibility in our understanding of God or of the universe through the lens of science? Do we turn to the human heart in search of the "truth" of our humanity that transcends religious, cultural, and national boundaries? The endless procession of diverse human beliefs captured in this book demonstrates that our personal understanding of God cannot be justified as absolute truth, and therefore we should be respectful and tolerant about other viewpoints. In order to achieve our own God, we do not need to denigrate the God of others. But does that mean that we equate all Gods and try to create a universal God? Is that approach viable, or will it doom interfaith dialogues? Efforts to show that the God of Islam and the God of Christianity are, in essence, one and the same, may sound ideal and may be highly desirable in a conflict-ridden world—but is this goal realistic and sustainable?

In order to achieve our God, we do not need to denigrate the God of others

The major world religions share many similarities, but also exhibit many fundamental differences. Then why ignore those differences and create an artificial aura of sameness? In *God Is Not One*, bestselling author Stephen Prothero argues against the "Godthink that lumps all religions together in one trash can or treasure chest." Prothero creates a new context for understanding the world's religions and proposes a pragmatic approach, whereby the acknowledgment of religious diversity will be a building block for peaceful coexistence in the future. He argues: "The Age of Enlightenment in the eighteenth century popularized the ideal of religious tolerance, and we are doubtless better for it. But the idea of religious unity is wishful thinking nonetheless, and it has not made the world a safer place. In fact, this naïve theological groupthink—call it Godthink—has made the world more dangerous… Every day across the world, human beings coexist peacefully and even joyfully with family members who are very different from themselves. In New York, Mets fans and Yankees fans have learned to live and work alongside one another, as have partisans of Real Madrid and FC Barcelona in a football-loving Spain. And who is so naïve to imagine that the success of a relationship depends on the partners being essentially the same?… What is required in any relationship is knowing who the other person really is. And this requirement is only frustrated by the naïve hope that somehow you and your partner are magically the same. In relationships and religions, denying differences is a recipe for disaster. What works is understanding the differences and then coming to accept, and perhaps even to revel in them."

Therefore, these differences should be recognized and accepted, but ought not be given too much value, as Indian President (1962–1967) and philosopher Sarvepalli Radhakrishnan once advised: "The name by which we call God and the rite by which we approach Him do not matter much… The doctrine we adopt and the philosophy we profess do not matter anymore than the language we speak and the clothes we wear."

A NEW PARADIGM

Can we therefore create a new paradigm in this age of propaganda, where the agents of terror, bigotry, and violence are working hard to create and sustain a *Clash of Civilizations*? The realists among us may say that this clash is inevitable because of the nature of things as they are. But the poet in us knows that 'reality' is in fact a 'creation'." Age after age, the visionary men and women of religion and science alike proved that their faiths guided them to attain what seemed impossible by all the evidence of fact. Today, in a terror-ridden world, we are in need of a greater call of faith, which will say to us: Let us change the course of history by changing our mindsets about God and religion; let us turn those forces into "force multipliers" towards building a *Friendship of Civilizations* and altogether stop our march towards a *Clash of Civilizations*.

EVOLUTION OF GOD

The God of the future is a compassionate God.

GEOGRAPHIC LUCK

The first change in our mindsets is to remind ourselves every day, by means of some active self-talk, that our God and our religious affiliations are an outcome of geographic luck in more than ninety percent of cases. If we were born in Bangladesh or Pakistan, we would most likely be Muslims; in India, Hindus; in USA or Italy, Christians; in Japan or China, Buddhists, Shintoists, or Confucianists. We should also acknowledge at the same time that this geographic luck is complemented by accident of birth—the religions of our parents.

What is there then to be proud of about our own religion or to denigrate the other religions? For we might well have been the adherents of the faith we are denigrating today.

God's Facebook proves beyond a reasonable doubt that every religion carries a message of love and compassion; that every religion has the potential to create saints as well as terrorists; and neither benevolence nor belligerence is a monopoly of one religion or the other.

In absence of this "geographic luck" mindset, we often tend to compare our religion with the worst of the other religion. This is a mistake that fuels the irrational belief about the superiority of our own religion over the other. In reality, this is a form of "religious racism," which is no different than the racism of one race or ethnic group, membership to which is decidedly an outcome of geographic luck and accident of birth, considering itself to be superior to the other races or ethnic groups. If we remind ourselves every day of this "geographic luck" factor, we will act more humanely to our fellow human beings and will be able to live with each other in peaceful harmony, in an environment of mutual respect.

PERSONAL CHARACTER

The second change that we need to make in our mindsets is to focus on attaining the personal qualities that our religion extols and our God demands from us. *God's Facebook* has documented the commandments and desirable virtues of all major religions of the world. It is clear that all religions speak of God's love for human personal virtue—of good deeds, humility, compassion, charity, love, and tolerance. Therefore, if we really believe in the God of our own religion, we must constantly monitor and improve our personal performance in following his commandments and achieving those virtues before we criticize either the fundamental tenets or the practitioners of other religions.

Why should we call ourselves Christians, Muslims, Hindus, Buddhists, or Jews, if we are not following the basic tenets of the religions we are proud of? Is being born a Christian or Muslim enough, or is our "true religion" what we actually practice in our personal lives? Should our religious identities be earned?

It is a truism to say that if we were to achieve only half of the desirable virtues mandated in the religious scriptures, it would take us a lifetime. It would also bring us closer to attaining our own God, for God said, "If you love me, you will obey my commandments." Even those who do not believe in any God should practice the morality and virtues to which they subscribe. A focus on personal character building, rather than proving who is right and who is not, will move us away from pride and begin our journey to humility.

HONEST COMMUNICATION

The third change that we need to make in our mindsets is to communicate honestly about our religions. One of the dangerous tendencies among religious scholars and practitioners alike is to be defensive when objections are raised about a specific element of their religions. In that defensive mode, they often intentionally hide some uncomfortable truths, to the detriment of their credibility on a much larger scale. *God's Facebook* has shown that all religious scriptures contain both benevolent and belligerent views. Therefore, any effort to prove a particular religion as one of all peace or all evil is futile; it only undermines honest communication and provides fodder for attack from other religious camps. Therefore, we should recognize that our understanding of a religious scripture of antiquity is a function of our current understanding of the language and context, and is colored by the moral environment of our time and place. Therefore, our understanding is "incomplete" and "corrigible." What transcends this understanding is our appreciation of the "voice of compassion," dominant in all scriptures where we find the cadence of the "voice of humanity" through the ages. If we can highlight this "voice of compassion," then we should be able to admit to the meek "voice of violence" in our religions and submerge the latter with our honesty and sincerity. This approach will create an environment of mutual trust and respect. It will also help facilitate true religious literacy, which is so necessary for confronting the bigotry of denigrating other religions. Frankly, if by reinterpreting history and context we allow ourselves to explain away or dismiss the violence found in our scriptures or religion, then we should allow the same privilege to the believers of other religions.

RELIGIOUS PLURALISM

The fourth change that we need to make in our mindsets is to recognize that the *Clash of Civilizations* is not a choice; therefore, it must be avoided through a *Friendship of Civilizations*. The biggest barrier to this friendship is the fear of the "unfamiliar," fomented by the propaganda machines of religious supremacists and by the acts of terror of religious fundamentalists. *God's Facebook* demonstrates, through a five-thousand-year journey of human spirituality, that there is a transcendent unity among all religions. However, it would be naïve to assume that all humans will unite under one God. The plurality of religions is as much a reality as the plurality of nations and cultures. The problem lies in religious exclusivism, whereby one religious group claims that they alone possess all truth and their way is the only way to salvation, even though their own scriptures do not necessarily support this notion, as shown in *God's Facebook*. This binary notion of religious exclusivism is the source of most of interreligious violence and conflicts.

It is necessary to slay the dragon of religious exclusivism, but we must not replace that with a moderate form thereof, which is called religious inclusivism. In an inclusivist approach, one asserts that his or her religion represents the complete and absolute truth, while other religions only contain partial or corrupted truth, or both. This approach is condescending to the practitioners of other religions, because it does not go far enough by extending equal respect to them.

Both religious exclusivism and religious inclusivism should be replaced by religious pluralism, which is founded on the following principles:

- Recognition that God created nations, tribes, and religions with the result that none of us have sole and exclusive knowledge of God's truth;

- Active pursuit of understanding of other religions without having to sacrifice our own identities and deeply held religious beliefs;

- Respectful dialogue with the practitioners of other religions about what social and moral problems unite us, not what divide us.

OVERLAPPING CONSENSUS

These four changes in our mindsets discussed above will facilitate the building of the *"overlapping consensus"* among different religions. The idea of overlapping consensus was introduced by the brilliant American political philosopher John Rawls (1921–2002) to address the need to guide public political discussion in a pluralistic society. Rawls realized that in a society where citizens are deeply divided by conflicting but well-conceived, comprehensive doctrines, the mere tolerance of each other's ideology is not sufficient to create a stable and just society. Instead, the citizens must seek an overall consensus and agree to a set of principles, which can be supported on moral grounds from their respective doctrines. This overlapping consensus approach provides a framework for cooperation in a pluralistic society, without compromising its plural character.

The same approach is applicable in the religious domain. Religions consist of well-conceived, comprehensive doctrines that often are mutated by culture, customs, time, and geography. These doctrines contain conflicts and contradictions, are sometimes incommensurable with one another, and deeply divide the citizens of the world, as evidenced in *God's Facebook*. The purpose of the *Friendship of Civilizations* discussed above, therefore, cannot be a reconciliation or homogenization of these conflicting doctrines, but an active seeking of overlapping consensus and agreement on a set of principles for a just, fair, and yet pluralistic international society of humans. We must work on what unites us, not on what divides us. Because the common humanity that unites us is far more important than incongruities among the religious and non-religious doctrines that divide us.

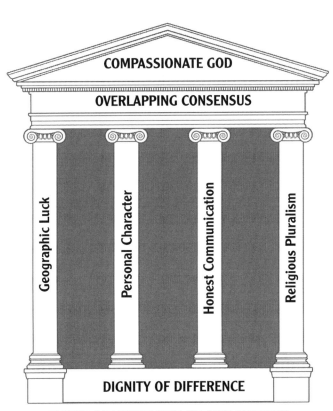

HOUSE OF FRIENDSHIP OF CIVILIZATIONS

DIGNITY OF DIFFERENCE

The four changes in our mindsets that are discussed above will also help us build the house of *Friendship of Civilizations* on a strong foundation of "dignity of difference", a phrase coined by Rabbi Jonathan Sacks, one of the world's greatest Jewish scholars. Rabbi Sacks argued that in a globalized world with economic and cultural disparity and discontents, it is not enough to search for values common to all faiths; it is necessary to reframe the way we see the differences among all faiths and cultures. If our worldview is to classify individuals according to a single religious or cultural identity, then we are doomed to the *Clash of Civilizations*. On the other hand, if we accept, and perhaps even revel in the dignity of diversity and difference among belief systems, then we can avoid the *Clash of Civilizations*.

COMPASSIONATE GOD

The ultimate questions then become: Can we invoke the wonders of religion rather than its terrors when we find the overlapping consensus and appreciate the dignity of difference? Can we foster peace through compassion and love?

One can easily notice by sifting through the quotes in this book that in all religions and cultures, the compassionate God is highly dominant over the belligerent and intolerant God. Compassion is as fundamental a notion as God consciousness, and we must overcome our differences in the current world through compassion. Compassion is the overlapping consensus.

Karen Armstrong made a unique wish in 2008 when she won the TED Prize. She asked for help in creating, launching, and propagating a Charter of Compassion. In November of 2009, the charter was unveiled to the world, and as of December 2010, some 60,000 people, including the Dalai Lama, have affirmed the Charter.

CHARTER OF COMPASSION

"The principle of compassion lies at the heart of all religious, ethical and spiritual traditions, calling us always to treat all others as we wish to be treated ourselves. Compassion impels us to work tirelessly to alleviate the suffering of our fellow creatures, to dethrone ourselves from the centre of our world and put another there, and to honour the inviolable sanctity of every single human being, treating everybody, without exception, with absolute justice, equity and respect.

It is also necessary in both public and private life to refrain consistently and empathically from inflicting pain. To act or speak violently out of spite, chauvinism, or self-interest, to impoverish, exploit or deny basic rights to anybody, and to incite hatred by denigrating others—even our enemies—is a denial of our common humanity. We acknowledge that we have failed to live compassionately and that some have even increased the sum of human misery in the name of religion.

We therefore call upon all men and women ~ to restore compassion to the centre of morality and religion ~ to return to the ancient principle that any interpretation of scripture that breeds violence, hatred or disdain is illegitimate ~ to ensure that youth are given accurate and respectful information about other traditions, religions and cultures ~ to encourage a positive appreciation of cultural and religious diversity ~ to cultivate an informed empathy with the suffering of all human beings—even those regarded as enemies.

We urgently need to make compassion a clear, luminous and dynamic force in our polarized world. Rooted in a principled determination to transcend selfishness, compassion can break down political, dogmatic, ideological and religious boundaries. Born of our deep interdependence, compassion is essential to human relationships and to a fulfilled humanity. It is the path to enlightenment, and indispensible to the creation of a just economy and a peaceful global community."

[Source: Twelve Steps to a Compassionate Life]

As part of her project, Armstrong also wrote a book entitled, *Twelve Steps to a Compassionate Life,* in which she offers a twelve-step plan for individuals to achieve a life full of compassion. She provides a positive golden rule: "Always treat others as you would wish to be treated yourself."

In 2010, His Holiness the Dalai Lama published a book titled *Toward a True Kinship of Faiths: How the World's Religions Can Come Together.* He discussed how the differences between the religions should be understood and appreciated, rather than become a source of conflict and conflagration. He argued that "despite doctrinal differences, we are all simply human." His appeal to humanity was, "If you believe in God, see others as God's children. If you are a nontheist, see all beings as your mother. When you do this, there will be no room for prejudice, intolerance, or exclusivity."

Bengali poet Rabindranath Tagore, in his 1930 lecture at Oxford University, talked about this compassionate God, whom he labeled the "God of Humanity." Tagore forewarned, with unwavering conviction, the inevitable demise of a "ruler" mentality, be it religious, political, or otherwise, in an open society. He declared: "The God of humanity has arrived at the gates of the ruined temple of the tribe. Though he has not yet found his altar, I ask the men of simple faith, wherever they may be in the world, to bring their offering of sacrifice to him, and to believe that it is far better to be wise and worshipful than to be clever and supercilious. I ask them to claim the right of manhood to be friends of men, and not the right of a particular proud race or nation which may boast of the fatal quality of being the rulers of men. We should know for certain that such rulers will no longer be tolerated in the new world, as it basks in the open sunlight of mind and breathes life's free air."

Both globalization and the information revolution that have occurred during the last fifty years have proved Tagore was right—the God Divide is not sustainable in a pluralistic, globalized world.

US President Barack Obama echoed the same sentiment in his inaugural address in January, 2009, and reaffirmed what Tagore had said almost eighty years earlier: "We cannot help but believe that the old hatreds shall someday pass; that the lines of tribe shall soon dissolve; that as the world grows smaller, our common humanity shall reveal itself."

Therefore, it is now necessary to welcome the God of the future, who is a compassionate God of humanity, not a tribal God of holy wars. Let us welcome him with a poem from the great Persian Sufi poet, Rumi:

"Reason is powerless in the expression of Love.

Love alone is capable of revealing the truth

Of Love and being a Lover.

The way of our prophets is the way of Truth.

If you want to live, die in Love;

Die in Love if you want to remain alive."

BIBLIOGRAPHY AND RECOMMENDED FURTHER READING

Abd-Allah, Umar F. *A Muslim in Victorian America: The Life of Alexander Russell Webb.* Oxford: Oxford UP, 2006. Print.

Aczel, Amir D. *God's Equation: Einstein, Relativity, and the Expanding Universe.* New York: Four Walls Eight Windows, 1999. Print.

Adler, Mortimer Jerome. *How to Think about God: A Guide for the 20th-century Pagan.* New York: Macmillan, 1980. Print.

Ali, A. Yusuf. *The Holy Quran, Texts, Translation, and Commentary*, Lahore, Pakistan, 1934.

Appleby, R. Scott. *The Ambivalence of the Sacred: Religion, Violence, and Reconciliation.* Lanham, MD: Rowman & Littlefield, 2000. Print.

Arberry, A. J.. *Sufism, an Account of the Mystics of Islam.* London: Allen & Unwin, 1950. Print.

Armstrong, Karen. *A History of God: The 4000-year Quest of Judaism, Christianity, and Islam.* New York: A.A. Knopf, 1993. Print.

Armstrong, Karen. *The Case for God.* New York: Knopf, 2009. Print.

Armstrong, Karen. *Twelve Steps to a Compassionate Life.* New York: Alfred A. Knopf, 2011. Print.

Armstrong, Karen. *The Battle for God.* New York: Alfred A. Knopf, 2000. Print.

Asad, M. *The Message of the Quran,* Dar Al-Andalus – Gibraltar, 1980.

Aston, W. G. *Nihongi.* (Repr.). ed. London: George Allen & Unwin, 1956. Print.

Arberry, A. J. *The Koran Interpreted,.* London: Allen & Unwin;, 1955.

Barks, Coleman. *The Essential Rumi.* San Francisco, CA: Harper, 1995. Print.

Barlas, Asma. *"Believing Women" in Islam: Unreading Patriarchal Interpretations of the Quran.* Austin, TX: University of Texas, 2002. Print.

Barrows, John Henry. *The World's Parliament of Religions: An Illustrated and Popular Story of the World's First Parliament of Religions*, Held in Chicago in Connection with the Columbian Exposition of 1893. Chicago: Parliament, 1893. Print.

Benson, Ophelia, and Jeremy Stangroom. *Does God Hate Women?* London ; New York: Continuum, 2009. Print.

Berg, Michael. *Becoming like God: Kabbalah and Our Ultimate Destiny.* New York, NY: Kabbalah Centre, 2004. Print.

Bhaumik, Mani. *Code Name God: The Spiritual Odyssey of a Man of Science.* New York: Crossroad Pub., 2005. Print.

Birch, Charles. *A Purpose for Everything: Religion In a Postmodern Worldview*. North American ed. Mystic, Conn.: Twenty-Third Publications, 1990. Print.

Bowker, John. *God: A Brief History*. London: DK Pub., 2002. Print.

Bowker, John. *World Religions: The Great Faiths Explored and Explained*. Surry Hills, N.S.W: RD, 1997. Print.

Budge, E. A. Wallis. *The Book of the Dead. The Papyrus of Ani*, The British Museum, 1895

Calvin, John. *Institutes of the Christian Religion*. Hendrickson Publishers, Inc.; Revised edition, 2007. Print.

Chamberlain, Basil Hall (1919). *A Translation of The Kojiki*

Chopra, Deepak. *How to Know God: the Soul's Journey Into the Mystery of Mysteries*. New York: Crown Publishers, 2000. Print.

Chupp, H.; Frankhauser, J.; Farris, M.; Kap, A.;Milbourne, L. (2010). *Dear God. Children's Letters to God*, Poster Publication, Taylor University, Indiana, USA.

Chupp, H.; Frankhauser, J.; Farris, M.; Kap, A.;Milbourne, L. (2010). *Dear God. Teenager's Letters to God*, Poster Publication, Taylor University, Indiana, USA.

Cloninger, Claire, and Curt Cloninger. *E-mail from God for Teens*. Tulsa, OK: Honor, 1999. Print.

Collins, Francis S. *The Language of God: A Scientist Presents Evidence for Belief*. New York: Free, 2006. Print.

Dalai Lama. *Toward a True Kinship of Faiths: How the World's Religions Can Come Together*. New York: Doubleday Religion, 2010. Print.

Dawkins, Richard. *The God Delusion*. Boston: Houghton Mifflin, 2006. Print.

Doughtie, Patrick, and John Perry. *Letters to God*: A Novel. Grand Rapids, MI: Zondervan, 2010. Print.

Doughtie, Patrick and Heather Doughtie. *Letters to God*. Zonderkidz, 2010

Dugger, André K. *Dear God*. Grand Rapids, MI: Zondervan, 2010. Print.

Eck, Diana L. *Encountering God: A Spiritual Journey from Bozeman to Banaras*. Boston: Beacon, 1993. Print.

Epstein, Greg M. *Good Without God: What a Billion Nonreligious People Do Believe*. New York: William Morrow, 2009. Print.

Faulkner, R.O. *The Ancient Egyptian Coffin Texts*, Aris and Phillips, 1978

Fausboll, V. *The Sutta-Nipata, Sacred Books of the East, Vol. 10* (1881), Oxford University Press

Fitzgerald, Edward. *The Rubaiyat of Omar Khayyam: The Five Authorized Versions*. Walter J. Black, 1942. Print.

Fox, Everett. *Five Books of Moses*, Easton Press, 2002

Froese, Paul, and Christopher Bader. *America's Four Gods: What We Say About God-- & What That Says About Us*. New York: Oxford University Press, 2010. Print.

Froese, Paul. *The Plot to Kill God: Findings from the Soviet Experiment in Secularization*. Berkeley: University of California, 2008. Print.

Granger, John. *Looking for God in Harry Potter*. Wheaton, Ill.: SaltRiver, 2004. Print.

Griffith, Ralph T. H. *The Hymns of the Rig Veda, A Translation*, 1896.

Hagerty, Barbara B. *Fingerprints of God: What Science Is Learning About the Brain and Spiritual Experience*. New York: Riverhead, 2010. Print.

Haisch, Bernard. *The God Theory: Universes, Zero-point Fields and What's behind It All*. San Francisco, CA: Weiser, 2006. Print.

Hample, S. and Marshall, E. (1991). *Children's Letters to God*, Workman Publishing, New York

Hample, Stuart E., Eric Marshall, and Tom Bloom. *Children's Letters to God: The New Collection*. New York: Workman Pub., 1991. Print.

Harris, Sam. *The End of Faith: Religion, Terror, and the Future of Reason*. New York: W.W. Norton &, 2004. Print.

Hawking, S. W. *A Brief History of Time: From the Big Bang to Black Holes*. Toronto: Bantam Books, 1988. Print.

Hegel, Georg Wilhelm Friedrich. *Faith & Knowledge*. Albany: State University of New York Press, 1977. Print.

Heller, David. *Dear God: Children's Letters to God*. New York: Doubleday, 1987. Print.

Heschel, Abraham Joshua. *Man's Quest for God; Studies in Prayer and Symbolism*. New York: Scribner, 1954. Print.

Hixon, Lex. Great Swan: *Meetings with Ramakrishna*. Boston: Shambhala, 1992. Print.

Huntington, Samuel P. *The Clash of Civilizations and the Remaking of World Order*. New York: Simon & Schuster, 1996. Print.

Iqbal, Muhammad. *Shikwa and Jawab-i-Shikwa Complaint and Answer: Iqbal's Dialogue with Allah*. Delhi: Oxford University Press, 1981. Print.

Isaacson, Walter. *Steve Jobs*. New York: Simon & Schuster, 2011. Print.

Jacobi, Herman. *Jaina Sutras, Part I, Sacred Books of the East, Vol. 22* (1884), Oxford University Press

Jafarey, Ali A. *The Gathas, Our Guide: the Thought-provoking Divine Songs of Zarathushtra*. Cypress, CA: Ushta, 1989. Print.

Jamal, Mahmood. *Islamic Mystical Poetry Sufi Verse from the Early Mystics to Rumi*. London: Penguin, 2009. Print.

James, Craig A. *The Religion Virus: Why You Believe in God: An Evolutionist Explains Religion's Tenacious Hold on Humanity*. Hants, UK: O, 2010. Print.

Jastrow, Morris, and Albert Tobias Clay. *An Old Babylonian Version of the Gilgamesh Epic, on the Basis of Recently Discovered Texts,*. New Haven: Yale University Press; [etc.], 1920. Print.

Javerbaum, David. *The Last Testament: A Memoir by God*. London: Simon & Schuster, 2011. Print.

Jefferson, Thomas. *The Jefferson Bible: the Life and Morals of Jesus of Nazareth*, Extracted Textually From the Gospels in Greek, Latin, French & English. Smithsonian ed. Washington D.C.: Smithsonian Books, 2011. Print.

Jefferson, Thomas. *The Jefferson Bible: The Life and Morals of Jesus of Nazareth*. Boston: Beacon, 1989. Print.

Jenkins, Philip. *Laying Down the Sword: Why We Can't Ignore the Bible's Violent Verses*. New York: HarperOne, 2011. Print.

Jerryson, Michael K., and Mark Juergensmeyer. *Buddhist Warfare*. New York: Oxford University Press, 2010. Print.

Jones-Prendergast, Kevin (1979). *Letters to God from Teenagers*, St. Anthony Messenger Press.

Juergensmeyer, Mark. *Terror in the Mind of God: The Global Rise of Religious Violence*. Berkeley: University of California, 2000. Print.

Juergensmeyer, Mark. *Global Rebellion: Religious Challenges to the Secular State, From Christian Militias to Al Qaeda*. Berkeley: University of California Press, 2008.

Kant, Immanuel, J. M. D. Meiklejohn, Thomas Kingsmill Abbott, and James Creed Meredith. *The Critique of Pure Reason*. Chicago: Encyclopædia Britannica, 19551952. Print.

Keller, Timothy J. *The Reason for God: Belief in an Age of Skepticism*. New York: Dutton, 2008. Print.

Khalsa, Sant Singh. *Sri Guru Granth Sahib*, 3rd Edition, Tucson, Arizona

Killinger, John. *God, the Devil, and Harry Potter*: a Christian Minister's Defense of the Beloved Novels. New York: Thomas Dunne Books, 2002. Print.

King James Bible (KJV), 1769 Edition

King, L.W.. *The Seven Tablets of Creations*, Luzac and Co., London (1902)

Knuth, Donald Ervin. *Things a Computer Scientist Rarely Talks About*. Stanford, Calif.: CSLI Publications, 2001. Print

Kosko, Bart. *Fuzzy Thinking: The New Science of Fuzzy Logic*. New York: Hyperion, 1993.

Kovacs, Maureen Gallery. *The Epic of Gilgamesh*. Stanford, Calif.: Stanford University Press, 1989. Print.

Küng, Hans. *Does God Exist?: An Answer for Today*. Garden City, NY: Doubleday, 1980. Print.

Küng, Hans. *What I Believe. London: Continuum*, 2010. Print.

Kurtz, Paul. *Humanist Manifestos, I and II*. Buffalo: Prometheus Books, 1973. Print.

Ladinsky, D. *I Heard God Laughing, Poems of Hope and Joy by Hafiz*, 2006

Landy, Robert J. *God Lives in Glass: Reflections of God through the Eyes of Children*. Woodstock, VT: SkyLight Path Pub., 2001. Print.

Lightman, Alan P. Mr G: *A Novel About the Creation*. New York: Pantheon, 2012. Print.

Macgregor, Scott (2002). *God on God*, Penguin Books

Marx, Karl, and Friedrich Engels. *The Communist Manifesto*. Harmondsworth: Penguin, 1967. Print.

McDonald, J. H. *Tao Te Ching: A Translation for the Public Domain*, 1996.

Mercer, Samuel A. B. *The Pyramid Texts*, New York: Longmans, Green and Co., 1952. Print.

Micklethwait, John, and Adrian Wooldridge. *God Is Back: How the Global Revival of Faith Is Changing the World*. New York: Penguin, 2009. Print.

Mills, L. H. *The Zend Avesta, Part III, Sacred Books of the East, Vol. 31* (1887), Oxford University Press

Mitchell, Stephen. *Tao Te Ching: a New English Version*. New York: Harper & Row, 1988. Print.

Muir, John. *The Original Sanskrit Texts on the Origin and History of the People of India, Their Religions and Institutions*, 1923

Müller, F. Max. *The Dhammapada, a Collection of Verses*; Being One of the Canonical Books of the Buddhists,. Oxford: Clarendon Press, 1881. Print.

Muller. F. Max. *The Dhammapada, Sacred Books of the East, Vol. 10* (1881), Oxford University Press

Muller. F. Max. *The Upanishads, Sacred Books of the East, Vol. 15* (1884), Oxford University Press

Newberg, Andrew B., Eugene G. D'Aquili, and Vince Rause. *Why God Won't Go Away: Brain Science and the Biology of Belief*. New York: Ballantine, 2001. Print.

Nicholson, Reynold A. *The Mathnawí of Jalálu'ddín Rúmí*: edited from the oldest manuscripts available. London: Trustees of the E.J.W. Gibb Memorial, 1926. Print.

Nicholson, Reynold Alleyne. *The Mystics of Islam,*. London: Routledge and K. Paul, 1963. Print.

Novak, Philip. *The World's Wisdom: Sacred Texts of the World's Religions*. [San Francisco, Calif.]: HarperSanFrancisco, 1994. Print.

Onfray, Michel, and Jeremy Leggatt. *In Defense of Atheism: the Case Against Christianity, Judaism, and Islam*. Toronto: Viking Canada, 2007. Print.

Paine, Thomas. *Age of Reason: Being an Investigation of True and Fabulous Theology*. New York: Willey Book Co., 194. Print.

Pascal, Blaise, and W. F. Trotter. *Penses*. Mineola, N.Y.: Dover Publications, 2003. Print.

Patel, Eboo. *Acts of Faith: The Story of an American Muslim, the Struggle for the Soul of a Generation*. Boston: Beacon, 2007. Print.

Paul II, Pope John. *Crossing the Threshold of Hope*. New York: Knopf, 1994. Print.

Pickthall, M.. *The Meaning of the Glorious Quran*, Hyderabad-Deccan Government Central Press, 1938.

Prasad, Ramananda. *The Bhagavad Gita*, American Gita Society, 2004

Pritchard, James B. *The Ancient Near East: A New Anthology of Texts and Pictures. Vol. 1-2*. Princeton: Princeton UP, 1975. Print.

Prothero, Stephen R. God Is Not One: *The Eight Rival Religions That Run the World--and Why Their Differences Matter*. New York: HarperOne, 2010. Print.

Pusey, E. B., and William Benham. *The Confessions of St. Augustine*. New York: P.F. Collier & Son, 1909. Print.

Radhakrishnan, S. *The Bhagavadgita*, Harpercollins College Div, 1973

Rawls, John. *Political Liberalism*. New York: Columbia UP, 1993. Print.

Ray, Darrel. *The God Virus: How Religion Infects Our Lives and Culture*. Bonner Springs, Kan.: IPC, 2009. Print.

Russell, Bertrand. *Why I Am Not a Christian: And Other Essays on Religion and Related Subjects*. New York: Simon and Schuster, 1957. Print.

Sacks, Jonathan. *The Dignity of Difference: How to Avoid the Clash of Civilizations*. London: Continuum, 2002. Print.

Sartre, Jean. *Being and Nothingness; an Essay on Phenomenological Ontology*. New York: Philosophical Library, 1956. Print.

Sen, Amartya. *Identity and Violence: The Illusion of Destiny*. New York: W.W. Norton &, 2006. Print.

Shaw, Bernard. *The Adventures of the Black Girl in Her Search for God*. New York: Capricorn Books, 19591933. Print.

Shoghi Effendi. *Kitab-I-Aqdas*, Baha'i International Community, 1997

Shook, John R. The God Debates: *A 21st Century Guide for Atheists and Believers (and Everyone in Between)*. Oxford: Wiley-Blackwell, 2010. Print.

Sjoo, M & Mor, B.. *The Great Cosmic Mother. Rediscovering the Religion of the Earth, San Francisco*, HarperCollings, 1991

Smith, Huston. *The World's Religions*. New York: HarperOne, 2009. Print.

Smith, Joseph. *The Book of Mormon*. An Account Written by the Hand of Mormon upon Plates Taken from the Plates of Nephi. (1880)

Smith, Wilfred Cantwell. *The Meaning and End of Religion*. Minneapolis: Fortress, 1991. Print.

Stanton, Elizabeth Cady. *The Woman's Bible: A Classic Feminist Perspective*. Mineola, NY: Dover Publications, 2002. Print.

Stanton, John. *An Interview with God. God Returns, Supports Bush 100 Percent*; http.//www.counterpunch.org/stanton12112004.html

Stenger, Victor J. G*od and the Folly of Faith: The Incompatibility of Science and Religion*. Amherst, NY: Prometheus, 2012. Print.

Stenger, Victor J. *God: The Failed Hypothesis*: *How Science Shows That God Does Not Exist*. Amherst, NY: Prometheus, 2007. Print.

Stephens, William M. *Souls on Fire*. Nashville, TN: Oceanic, 1998. Print.

Stone, Merlin. *When God Was a Woman*. New York: Harcourt Brace Jovanovich, 1978. Print.

Sullivan, Deidre (1990). *What Do We Mean When We Say God?*, Cader Books, Doubleday.

Tagore, Rabindranath, Tony K. Stewart, and Chase Twichell. *The Lover of God*. Port Townsend, WA: Copper Canyon, 2003. Print.

Tagore, Rabindranath. *Gitanjali, Song Offerings,*. New York: The Macmillan Co., 1916. Print.

Tagore, Rabindranath. *The Religion of Man*. Rhinebeck: Monkfish Book, 1931. Print.

Teichman, Milton, and Sharon Leder. *Truth and Lamentation: Stories and Poems on the Holocaust. Urbana*: University of Illinois, 1994. Print.

Toft, Monica Duffy, Daniel Philpott, and Timothy Samuel. *Shah. God's Century: Resurgent Religion and Global Politics*. New York: W.W. Norton, 2011. Print.

Tumminio, Danielle Elizabeth. *God and Harry Potter at Yale: Teaching Faith and Fantasy Fiction in an Ivy League Classroom*. S.l.: Unlocking Press, 2010. Print.

Tutu, Desmond, and John Allen. *God Is Not a Christian: And Other Provocations*. New York, NY: HarperOne, 2011. Print.

Walsch, Neale D. (2001). *Conversations with God for Teens*, Scholastic Inc.

Walsch, Neale Donald. *Conversations with God for Teens*. Charlottesville, VA: Hampton Roads Pub., 2001. Print.

Walsch, Neale Donald. *Conversations with God: An Uncommon Dialogue*. Charlottesville, VA: Hampton Roads Pub., 1998. Print.

Wand, J. W. C. *St. Augustine's City of God*. New York: Oxford University Press, 1963. Print.

Watt, W. Montgomery. *Imam al-Ghazali's Deliverance from Error and the Beginning of Guidance*. Rev. ed. Kuala Lumpur [Malaysia: Islamic Book Trust, 2005. Print.

Whitman, Walt, Christopher Morley, and Lewis Daniel. *Leaves of Grass*;. New York: Doubleday, Doran & Co., 1940. Print.

Wiesel, Elie, and Marion Wiesel. *The Trial of God: ; a Play in 3 Acts*. New York: Schocken, 1986. Print.

Wilson, Andrew. *World Scripture: A Comparative Anthology of Sacred Texts*. New York, NY: Paragon House, 1991.

Wright, Robert. *The Evolution of God*. New York: Little, Brown, 2009. Print.

PHOTO CREDITS

Photos used in this book are either public domain or purchased for use in this book. The public domain photos used in this book are acknowledged below with proper attribution when available.

Aquinas, Thomas: author is Fra Bartolomeo (1472–1517)

Aristotle: taken by photographer Eric Gaba (Wikimedia Commons User: Sting) from a marble portrait located in Louvre Museum, Paris

Churchill, Winston: available from Library of Congress, author: United Nations Information Office

Cicero: author is Visconti - Iconograph rom. pl. 12 N. 1 (Abb. 428) (Publisher K. A. Baumeister)

Da Vinci, Leonardo: creator is C.P.M. Gay Folla Piedras, photographic reproduction from Da Vinci's self-portrait in red chalk, Royal Library of Turin

Darwin, Charles: photograph taken around 1874 by Leonard Darwin.

Einstein, Albert and Tagore, Rabindranath: taken by American photographer Martin Vos and published in 1930

Einstein, Albert: photograph taken by Ferdinand Schmutzer (1870–1928) during a lecture in Vienna

Epicurus: taken by photographer Baumeister, Denkmäler des klassischen Altertums, from a portrait located in National Archaeological Museum, Naples, Italy

Freud, Sigmund: photographer: Max Halberstadt (1882-1940)

Galileo, Galilee: photographic reproduction of a two-dimensional art by Giusto Sustermans

Gandhi, Mahatma: author: unknown

Ghazali, Imam: A portrait in his later years by an unknown Iraqi artist

Hatshepsut: Image by Riccardov, under GFDL

Hegel, Wilhelm: photographic representation of a steel engraving by Lazarus Sichling after a lithograph by Julius L. Sebbers.

Jefferson, Thomas: photographic representation of a portrait by Rembrandt Peale in 1800.

Kant, Immanuel: unknown author

Kennedy, John F.: official White House portrait, author: Aaron Shikler

Lincoln, Abraham: available from Library of Congress, artist: Alexander Gardner (1821–1882)

Locke, John: photographic representation of a portrait of John Locke, by Sir Godfrey Kneller.

Marx, Karl: portrait of Karl Marx, author: John Mayall Jr.

Newton, Sir Isaac: photographic representation of a portrait of Isaac Newton, by Sir Godfrey Kneller.

Nietzsche, Freidrich: photographer: Mr F. Hartmann in Basel

Plato: photographic reproduction (partial) of a painting (The School of Athens) by Raphael in Louvre Museum, Paris

Rumi: author: Molavi

Russell, Bertrand: unknown photographer - published in 1914

Shakespeare, William: photographic representation in official gallery link of National Portrait Gallery, London. The painter is unknown–may be by a painter called John Taylor who was an important member of the Painter-Stainers' Company

Shaw, George Bernard: unknown photographer – published in 1914-15 in a New York Times book

Socrates: taken by photographer Eric Gaba (Wikimedia Commons User: Sting) from a marble portrait located in Louvre Museum, Paris

Stanton, Elizabeth Caddy: available from Library of Congress, author: Veeder

Tagore, Rabindranath: unknown photographer - published in 1914 in Sweden in Les Prix Nobel 1913

Vivekananda, Swami: unknown photographer, 1893 World Parliament of Religions.

Voltaire: photographic representation of a portrait by Workshop of Nicolas de Largillière (1656–1746)

Webb, Mohammed Alexander Russell: unknown photographer, 1893 World Parliament of Religions

Whitman, Walt: available from Library of Congress, author: George C. Cox.

INDEX OF SCRIPTURES

INDEX OF NAMES

Made in the USA
San Bernardino, CA
24 February 2015